History of
The British Army

Edited by

BRIGADIER PETER YOUNG
and
LT-COL. J.P.LAWFORD

ARTHUR BARKER LIMITED
5 Winsley Street London W1

KEY TO MAPS:
CONVENTIONAL SIGNS

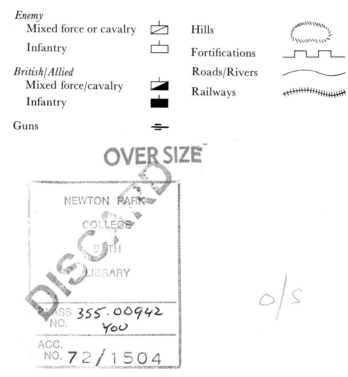

Enemy
Mixed force or cavalry   Hills

Infantry   Fortifications

British/Allied
Mixed force/cavalry   Roads/Rivers

Infantry   Railways

Guns

SBN 213 00050 4

Photoset by BAS Printers Limited, Wallop, Hants
and printed in Great Britain by Ebenezer Baylis & Son Ltd

CONTENTS

6

INTRODUCTION

This symposium on the history of the British Army has been planned, and in part written, by Military Historians of the Royal Military Academy Sandhurst, ably assisted by the librarian, Lt-Col. Alan Shepperd.

The Editors are deeply grateful to the distinguished contributors from outside Sandhurst, in particular to: the late Sir Basil Liddell Hart, perhaps the leading military thinker of his age, to General Sir Reginald Savory, the last British Adjutant-General in India, to Major-General Hubert Essame, the well-known authority on military affairs, to Brigadier A.H.Farrar-Hockley, recently commander of the 16th Parachute Brigade, to W.Y.Carman, Deputy Director of the National Army Museum, to Brian Bond of the Military History Department of the University of London and to Brigadier J.H.S. Lacey, Secretary of the Institution of Royal Engineers.

The aim of the symposium has been to tell the story both of the British Army, and the men who composed it. So long a history could scarcely be condensed into a single volume without much being left out. Contributors generally have described one or two actions in a campaign or war in some detail and then for reasons of space have had to dismiss others, possibly equally celebrated, in a few words, or a chronological table.

The symposium has been fully illustrated, and here we must pay tribute to the National Army Museum. During an existence of less than ten years, it has collected a magnificent library of military pictures, engravings and drawings. Without the unstinting help of the officials of the museum this book could not have been produced in its present form. Our thanks are also due to the Imperial War Museum which provided the photographs for the period from 1914 onwards from its unrivalled collection.

Our policy as to illustrations has been to use those by contemporary artists where appropriate, but not to exclude those painted at a later date. Our criterion has been how accurately the artist has reconstructed the scene and in this the date of the picture is by no means a sure guide.

Finally we hope that this book, despite its brevity, may yet do some justice to the British soldier whose exploits during the last three centuries have done much to shape the world as we know it today, and whose task is by no means concluded.

Opposite: The Duke of Wellington. From the painting by Thomas Heaphy. The artist spent some time with Wellington's army in the Peninsula

CHAPTER 1

The Origins and 1660–97

PETER YOUNG

The birth of the British regular army is generally, though not strictly accurately, held to have occurred in 1660 when, to the joy of a nation that had found the dictatorial methods of Cromwell little to its liking, Charles II was restored to the English throne. For the first time in English history Charles, anxious to avoid once more 'going on his travels', constituted a small professional army to guard his crown against the whims of a turbulent and inconstant people. He appointed as his Commander-in-Chief George Monck, Duke of Albemarle, the Cromwellian general to whom he owed his kingdom. Old Cavalier and Roundhead units still existed from the Civil War days, and from their ranks Monck made up his army whose strength in 1661 is shown in the appendix at the end of the book. Prior to Charles II's reign English sovereigns had only raised armies in time of war. The 1660 army itself did not become a standing army, properly speaking, until the reign of William III.

England, 'set in the silver sea', had lagged behind the masters of the continent in this matter of establishing permanent regiments of professional soldiers, depending for home defence on the militia, and for expeditions to Ireland or the continent on hastily levied units of dubious military merit. The old corps of the French Army, Picardie, Navarre and the rest, could boast a lineage dating back to 1569. Spain established the *tercios* early in the sixteenth century. The imprudent Charles I had not provided himself with a single regiment when in 1638 he thought it right that his Northern subjects should enjoy the Anglican Prayer Book. But that is not to say that there were not, in every generation, Britons who saw military service of one sort or another. Queen Elizabeth was not the person to brave the might of Spain without soldiers at her command, and if her military arrangements were defective it was rather for lack of money than of men.

In Tudor and Stuart times the Royal Household included two small bodies which still exist, namely the Gentlemen Pensioners and the Yeomen of the

Opposite: The Duke of Monmouth when he was serving under Turenne. He was an illegitimate son of Charles II, or so his mother averred; he raised an abortive rebellion against James II and was executed on Tower Hill at the behest of his aggrieved uncle. A painting by Netcher and Wyke

George Monck, created Duke of Albemarle by Charles II

Guard. The former had fought as a troop at the battle of the Spurs (1513) and at Pinkie (1547) and were to do so again at Edgehill. They were capable of producing commanders or staff officers when occasion demanded. When in 1548 the French invaded the Isle of Wight King Henry VIII sent one of their number, Sir Edward Bellingham, to command the local levies. Under his leadership they won the 'battle' of Bonchurch and successfully ejected the invaders. In the Civil Wars Pensioners obtained commands in the Royalist Army. Sir Nicholas Selwyn commanded the City of Oxford Regiment (Foot), and Major Bunnington fell at Leicester (1645) leading Prince Rupert's firelocks.

The castles and forts, many of them built by King Henry VIII, had static garrisons of gunners and infantry of which the Yeomen Warders of the Tower alone survive.

The Board of Ordnance, established at least as early as 1483, had charge of all the ordnance stores and ammunition of the kingdom and more particularly of the cannon. The officers had their houses and offices in the Tower of London.

Strangely enough Windsor Castle, which had a garrison of three companies in 1661 seems to have had no proper garrison in 1642, which suggests that Charles II had a sounder grasp of elementary strategy than had his father. In 1642 Windsor was seized by the trained bands of Berkshire and of London, which brings us to a discussion of the military merits of those bodies. Modern authors have often made merry at the expense of these 'territorials', and, of course, they had their shortcomings. Some were not diligent in their musterings, and the best of them were reluctant to stir from their own counties. But the myth that only the London trained bands had any military value has been permitted to flourish unchallenged too long. It was the *Posse Com-*

itatus led by the local gentry and Sir Ralph Hopton that drove the Roundheads out of Cornwall at the end of 1642. It was only when they reached the Tamar that the Cornishmen thought they had done enough. Then their leaders, Sir Bevile Grenvile, Sir Nicholas Slanning, and their friends fell to raising the five famous 'voluntary' regiments that were to carry the Royalist colours to Lansdown and Bristol. In Devon Hopton was to be disappointed. He described the meeting of the trained bands at Modbury 'as more like a great faire than a posse'.

In Yorkshire the regiments of Sir William Pennyman and Sir William Savile appear to have been built up on existing trained band units, while officers who had their first experience of soldiering in the militia saw a good deal of fighting in the Civil War. An example is Captain Richard Horsfall, of Sir William Savile's Regiment of Horse. A musketeer in the trained bands as early as 1626, he had risen to the rank of lieutenant by 1638 in the regiment then commanded by Savile. In the war he evidently fought at Winceby (1643), was twice taken prisoner, and later took part in the defence of Pontefract Castle.

Had the Spaniards invaded in 1588 it may be that they would have met with better soldiers than the men of 1642. One may be permitted to doubt it, but on the other hand Queen Elizabeth's Privy Council took a great deal of trouble to bring the militia to a state of efficiency. In 1584 it was laid down that there should be compulsory military exercises every Sunday afternoon. Muster masters and able captains were provided. Rachel Lloyd in her *Dorset Elizabethans*[1] has a splendid account of how the war with Spain affected the inhabitants.

> The yeomen and husbandmen of the county, grumbling but obedient, shouldered their pieces; in the Wimborne countryside they worked for that martinet Sir Henry Ashly, Sir Richard Rogers barked at them at Blandford, at Sherborne Sir John Hersey with the Grecian profile must have known how to handle men, near Dorchester that spiteful person Thomas Howard made the musters a misery for all concerned, while on the high downs above Cerne Abbas men manoeuvred under the bland but skilful handling of George Trenchard. (p. 170).

When the Armada came in 1588 the last named paid more than £100 of his own, for the repair of forts and on journeys into Somerset and Devon to muster the lieutenants. When the Armada was sighted the deputy-lieutenants and captains of several shires had made his home at Wolfeton their

[1] Bibliog. Murray – 1967.

headquarters for several days, and earlier the Queen's General, Sir John Norris (1548–97), on a tour of inspection, had descended upon him with all his retinue and it had cost him £20 to entertain them. National defence was still a matter of local, indeed private, enterprise, as much as the business of the state.

The early years of the Stuarts were, in comparison to those of Elizabeth, relatively tranquil. Nevertheless there was no lack of Englishmen – and of Scots too – to follow the career of arms. Some went very far afield. The Royalist general Sir Arthur Aston had served in Muscovy; the Roundhead Sydenham Poyntz had been in the Imperialist service, had fallen into the hands of the Sultan's soldiery, had suffered the bastinado and, in the best traditions of romantic fiction, owed his freedom to a Turkish maiden. Even before the Thirty Years War there were numbers of Englishmen serving in the Dutch Army, including the distinguished general Sir Francis Vere, whose *Commentaries* (1657) relate his experiences in the Low Countries from 1589–1601. His victory at Nieuport (1602) and the Siege of Ostend are still remembered by the Dutch.

The Buffs who came into the English service in 1665 as the Holland Regiment were the descendants of the four English regiments that fought for the States at Bois-le-Duc, Maastricht and Breda. Their history could be traced back to 1572, and they were the nurseries of such famous soldiers as Sir Jacob Astley, Philip Skippon and George Goring. In general it was difficult for English or Scots soldiers to rise beyond field rank in the Dutch Army. The Swedes were more accommodating and their generals included Alexander Leslie, (First Earl of Leven); Patrick Ruthven (Earl of Forth and Brentford) and James King (Earl of Eythin). An incomplete list of Scots officers fighting under Gustavus Adolphus at Lutzen (1642) includes at least five who saw service in the First Civil War.[2] Daniel Goodrich, a captain in the Swedish service in 1634, came home and was chosen major for the Irish

Captain Daniel Goodrich. Note his medal from King Gustavus Adolphus

expedition (1642). Others like Colonel Jacob Scott (d. 1635) made their whole career in the Swedish service. Whereas Goodrich served under the English colonel, George Fleetwood, all Scott's service from 1622 when he was a captain seems to have been in Finnish and Swedish units.

In the French army there are said to have been three English regiments, besides the famous Scots troop of the Maison du Roi – commanded at one time by no less a personage than the Marquis of Huntley, whose sons were to distinguish themselves under Montrose.

In the Spanish Army in the Netherlands there was one regiment under the Sussex catholic, Sir Henry Gage, a very able soldier, who relieved Basing House (1644), became Governor of Oxford, and lost his life in an abortive attack on Abingdon (1645).

In the Imperial service there were certainly many individuals who came from these islands. The Scot, Sir John Henderson, Governor of Newark in 1643, is only one example.

These were the men who with the help of the landed gentry or 'plain russet coated captains' led the armies at Edgehill and Marston Moor.

George Monck himself was far from inexperienced. He had been a soldier since 1625, when he had volunteered for the Cadiz expedition. Monck had fought in the Dutch Army at Breda (1637), against the Scots and the Irish; had been captured by Fairfax's army at Nantwich (1644) and from 1647 onwards had served the Parliament and

2

Lutzen	Civil Wars	Army
Lt.-Col. Ludovick Leslie	Quartermaster-General	Solemn League & Covenant.
Captain John Hamilton	Lt.-Col. Fifeshire, F.	Solemn League & Covenant.
Captain Alexander Bruce	Lt.-Col. Stirlingshire, F.	Solemn League & Covenant.
Lt. Gilbert Blair	Major, Adjutant-General, H.	Essex
Lt. William Cockburn	Routmaster, Balcarres, H.	Solemn League & Covenant.

ORIGINS

Cromwell in Ireland and in Scotland, distinguishing himself at Dunbar (1650) before turning admiral (1652). He was a notably successful Commander-in-Chief in Scotland. Monck had the backing of scores of men whose hard-won experience went back to Rhé and Rochelle and Cadiz, to Lutzen, Lemgo and Breda.

But there is another aspect to the origins of the British Army, the intellectual side. As early as 1489 the first military book had been printed in England. But if Caxton's edition of Christine de Pisan's *Art of Chivalry* can scarcely be regarded as a modern work, others of a more practical sort followed as the years went by.

In 1544, for example, Thomas Barthelet of Fleet Street, 'printer to the Kinges highnes' printed the *Statutes and ordynances for the warre*, which Henry VIII had drawn up before invading France in 1513. They were 53 in number and connoisseurs of uniform may be pleased to know that every man was to wear a cross of St George, 'sufficient and large, upon pain of imprisonment and punishment'.

The Arte of Warre by Nicholas Machiavell, ran to three English editions (1560, 1573 and 1588) in the days when the Spanish menace was building to its climax. The book was later to be a favourite with Frederick the Great.

In 1563 Thomas Gale, the first Englishman to write on the subject, published *An excellent Treatise of wounds made with Gonneshot ...* in which he set out 'a perfect and trew methode of curyng these woundes'.

One of the best military books of the time was Thomas Digges' *An Arithmeticall Militaire Treatise, named Stratioticos*, published in 1579 and dedicated to Queen Elizabeth's favourite, Robert, Earl of Leicester, who commanded the 'BEF' in the Low Countries. Shakespeare's Iago would no doubt have stigmatised Digges as ... 'one that never set a squadron in the field', but in fact Digges describes the duties of officers of every rank, foreshadows the use of dragoons or mounted infantry, lays down the preparations necessary in forming a camp as well as summarising military law by listing the 35 offences punishable by death in any army. He also offers his readers brief treatises on Arithmetic and Algebra. His book was reprinted as late as 1594, and evidently served as a manual throughout the last years of Elizabeth's reign.

The year 1586 saw the publication – originally at Leyden – of the *Laws and Ordinances* by which Leicester governed his army in the Low Countries.

The first English book on gunnery was William Bourne's *The Art of shooting in great Ordnaunce*, 1587.

Colonel Sir Henry Gage

Bourne's assertion that Englishmen know nothing of gunnery save what they had learned of the Dutch or of the Flemings is of interest, and though his work was to some extent compiled from those of foreign writers he did his countrymen a timely service in the year before the Armada.

As the years went by a number of manuals appeared, which though unofficial, gave valuable information as to the arming and training both of horse and foot. One such was Gervase Markham's *The Souldiers Ascidence. Or An Introduction Into Military Discipline*, (1625) which was reprinted during the Civil Wars in 1643. Another which proved useful was John Cruso's *Militaire Instructions for the Cavallerie* (1632), the foremost early English work on cavalry. Its author was a Fellow of Caius College, Cambridge, from 1639 to 1644 when he was ejected by the Parliamentarians. His book, printed at Cambridge, was republished during the Civil Wars and most probably proved useful to the Army of the Eastern Association, which can hardly have been the author's intention. Another valuable manual of the Civil War period was William Barriffe's *Military Discipline: Or, The Yong Artillery*

Man. Wherein is discoursed and showne the Postures both of Musket and Pike: (1635).

Barriffe belonged to the Honourable Artillery Company and, despite his somewhat misleading title, concerns himself only with infantry work.

Barriffe, a lieutenant in 1639, was major to John Hampden's Regiment of Foot in 1642, but though a Parliamentarian he was able to publish a sixth edition in 1661, by which time he was a colonel. In his first edition Barriffe foreshadows the introduction of the bayonet. Officers in several parts of Christendom were seeking to make muskets defensive as well as offensive 'by unscrewing the heads of their rests, and then screwing the staffs of their rests into the muzzle of the musket, with the arming of the pike at the lower end'. Weapons' development moved but slowly in the seventeenth century and it was not until 1706 that the pikemen vanished from the ranks of the British infantryman.

King Charles II's army though small was officered by men of very considerable military experience. The castles and forts were sufficiently garrisoned, which had never been the case in King Charles I's day. War with the Dutch led to considerable, if temporary, augmentations of the establishment. At this period, only 20 years after the end of the first Civil War, there was no lack of old Cavaliers to officer these levies, and a casual glance through the commission registers reveals the names of many who had fought for Charles I. The old Earl of Cleveland, hero of Cropredy Bridge and Second Newbury was a colonel of horse in 1666; his major, John March, had been a lieutenant-colonel in the first civil war. His troop commanders included a colonel, Sir Adrian Scrope, whose military career had begun on the field of Edgehill.

The Earl of Chesterfield had an old Royalist lieutenant-colonel, Sir Theophilus Gilby, as his major, while Lt-Col. Guy Molesworth of Prince Maurice's Regiment of Horse was content to be major of Lord Alington's Regiment of Foot. But despite occasional bursts of activity, as when in 1673 King Charles sent a contingent to serve in Louis XIV's army, there was no serious, permanent augmentation of the military establishment until the reign of King James II. That monarch came to the throne in 1685, and in the next three years, largely owing to the abortive rebellion led by the Duke of Monmouth, he managed to build up the Army to a strength of 30,000, an achievement which did little to endear him to his deeply suspicious subjects. When in 1688 William of Orange, the Stadtholder of Holland, at the invitation of many leading Englishmen invaded England, James' army, under the questionable guidance of Churchill (later Duke of Marlborough), abandoned him and dec-

The Dutch burning Chatham 1685. Proof that a standing army was needed

The Battle of Steenkirk 1692. Sir Robert Douglas, Colonel of the 7th Regiment, seeing a French officer making off with a British colour, leapt a hedge, ran the officer through and hurled the colour back to his men. He himself was shot down before he could return

lared for King William. James had to flee abroad without a fight.

To King William, his country engaged in a deadly war against Louis XIV of France, the English throne was the more attractive since it enabled him to bring aid to his own hard-pressed countrymen. Almost immediately after he had been jointly crowned with his wife, Queen Mary, he started sending British regiments to Flanders, and, as early as 1689, the 16th Foot, Hodges regiment as it was then called, distinguished itself in the action at Walcourt in the province of Namur. However King William's rule in Britain was not to go unchallenged. In Scotland John Graham of Claverhouse, 'Bonnie Dundee', led a brief revolt that died when a silver bullet slew its leader at the moment of victory at Killiecrankie. In Ireland James organised an Irish army that nearly captured the whole island. King William crossed St George's Channel, and, in 1690, trounced the Irish at the Battle of the Boyne. James made good his escape to France.

Having secured his new realm, King William in 1692 led a British army to the Low Countries, and there indulged in the long drawn out and indecisive campaigns of manoeuvre so popular at that time. He was a dogged rather than a skilful commander and was frequently outgeneralled by the French under the astute and experienced leadership of the Duke of Luxemburg. Nevertheless at Steenkirk, Landen and Namur the British soldier gave un-

mistakable evidence of his prowess. In 1697 the Treaty of Ryswick brought a short-lived peace.

If England no longer depended for her defence upon what Lord Macaulay described as 'occasional soldiers', she owed it to Charles II, James II and the men who fought for their father during the Great Rebellion. Yet something of British military tradition must be attributed to Cromwellian ideas. Noll would 'rather have a plain russet-coated captain *that knows what he fights for, and loves what he knows,* than that which you call a gentleman and is nothing else'. But it is sometimes forgotten that he added: 'I honour a gentleman that is so indeed.' For his troopers he chose men 'of greater understanding than common soldiers' who were 'more apprehensive of the importance and consequence of war and making not money but that which they took for the public felicity to be their end, they were the more engaged to be valiant ...' Thus [the chaplain] Richard Baxter, described the Ironsides.

Puritan fanaticism was no longer in season when Marlborough led his men to Blenheim, but his cavalry were not less effective than the men who rode with Cromwell – or for that matter Rupert.

The Stuarts left William an army and England a general, John, Duke of Marlborough (1650–1722), ensign (1667) in the King's Company of the Regiment that is now the Grenadier Guards, veteran of Tangier (1668–70); Solebay (1672); Maastricht (1673), Entzheim (1674) and Sedgemoor (1685).

16

Hodges Regiment, later the 16th Foot, at Walcourt 1689. The regiment, newly raised (1688), was covering a foraging expedition in the province of Namur, when it was assailed by French horse and dragoons in greatly superior strength. The colonel, a veteran of Tangier and Sedgemoor, fought a skilful rearguard action winning the praise of the Allied Commander, the Prince of Waldeck, for the *joie de combattre* of the English troops. A painting by C. C. P. Lawson

CHAPTER 2

The Technique of Sieges and Fortification

PHILIP A. WARNER

The campaigns in Flanders had largely been concerned with the besieging and protecting of the great 'barrier fortresses' that guarded the frontier between France and the Netherlands. Through the next two centuries the twin techniques of fortification and siege warfare were to influence profoundly the conduct of all military operations.

Being architectural and mathematical and therefore very difficult, siege warfare became the domain of the expert, the engineer officer. In consequence it developed a mystique, replete with incomprehensible technical terms, all its own. By the mid-seventeenth century, however, its techniques had been largely perfected and were to change little until, in the latter half of the nineteenth century, breach loading artillery and high explosive shells outmoded the masonry and ramparts of earlier days.

Hence a note on the way places were fortified and sieges carried out may help to make plans of campaign and the sieges themselves more intelligible. Although others made significant contributions, it was a Frenchman, called Vauban, who produced the most comprehensive doctrine for this type of warfare.

Vauban was born in 1633, was famous by the time he was 33, but made many enemies and fell out of royal favour some years before his death in 1707. His most famous achievements were Lille (1668), Maubeuge (1685) and Neuf-Brisach (1697).

His designs were of course highly complicated, but the principles on which they were constructed were not. The aims of military architects do not change from century to century although materials, weapons, and requirements do. A fortification, whether a medieval castle or a concrete bunker, is designed to ensure that the defence's weapons work to full advantage while the attacker's are hampered as much as possible. It should conserve manpower, and this characteristic was much more important when forces were smaller than today. Above all, it should be adapted to the strength and type of the proposed attack. Unfortunately, military architects can easily become so involved in their own ideas that they forget that fortification is only a means to an end and see it as an end in itself.

In medieval times the main features of a fortress or castle were a high position on a natural or artificial mound, or a site which could be surrounded by a broad area of water. Mound fortresses usually had thick masonry walls, and a dry or wet ditch below.

The first adaptation of these fortifications to the age of gunpowder was to build up a slope of earth from the ditch to the masonry. This was known as the scarp (see diagram A). Its opposite across the ditch became the counterscarp. Building up these two slopes of course deepened, and often widened the ditch, which was also known as a moat or a fosse. Ditches became a sort of sacred anachronism and were often used in situations where they gave more help to the attacker than to the defence. On the inside of the masonry wall would be another bank of earth, of which the slope would be called the talus. At the top of it would be the ramp or walk with a banquette or fire-step from which soldiers could fire muskets over the parapet. There might be a position half-way down the scarp from which musketeers could operate behind a low wall, known as a cordon.

On the far side of the ditch the earth would rise, as already noted, in the counterscarp at the top of which could be another rampart walk, firestep, and

Opposite above: The city of Limerick. The ramparts and towers illustrate the pre-Vauban type of fortification. From an old plan. *Below:* A sophisticated type of breaching battery engaging a town fortified after the principles of Vauban. From an old French artillery manual

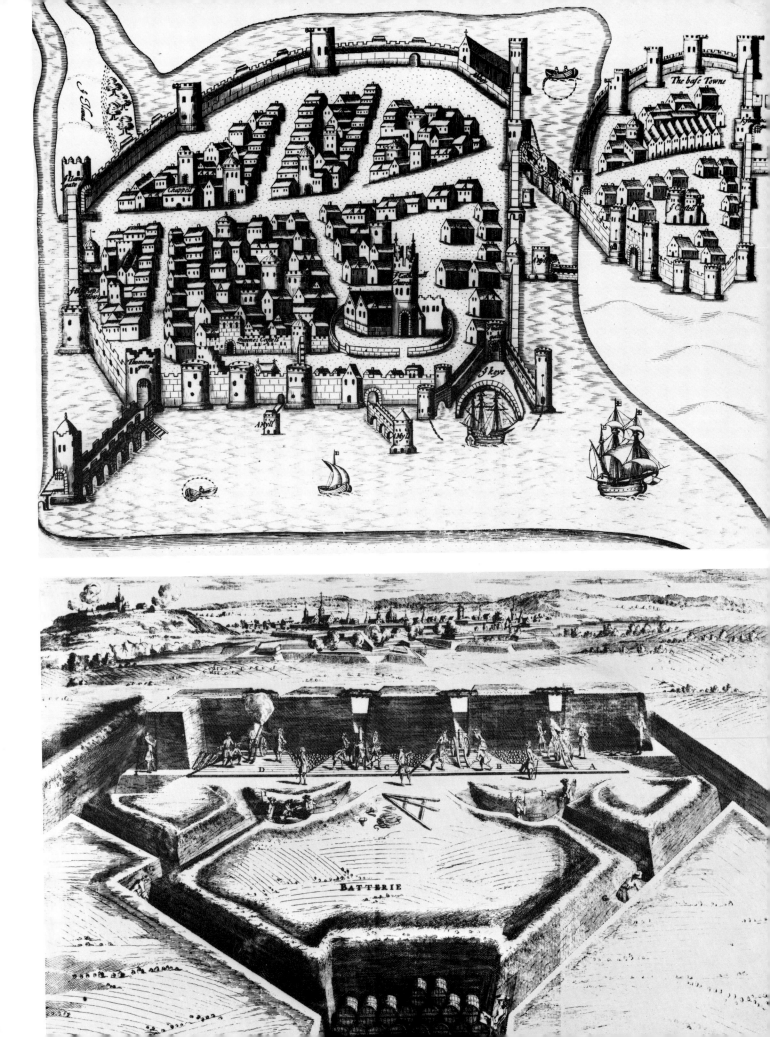

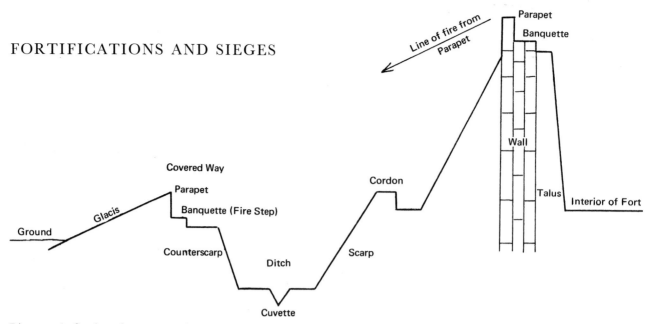

Diagram A. Section of a seventeenth century style fortification

parapet. This was known as the 'covered way' although it was merely covered by fire. From this parapet towards the enemy would be a gentle slope known as the glacis. Fire from the inner parapet was directed to graze the slope of the glacis. (See diagram A).

The importance of the ditch was such a hallowed concept that no one ever thought of discarding it, although it was soon clear that once the attackers were established in it, however uncomfortably, they were extremely difficult to dislodge. An attempt to retain the advantages of ditches while eliminating liabilities was the *indented trace*. This was an arrangement by which the faces and flanks of the walls were at right angles in regular order. It was not entirely satisfactory for there were still places which the defenders could not effectively rake with fire and they were themselves liable to be fired at by attackers entrenched on the glacis.

The solution to the problem was the *bastioned trace* which was first used by Italian engineers in the sixteenth century but was soon widespread in Europe, and particularly favoured in France. Vauban added a number of refinements to it and used it in 160 fortifications in France during the seventeenth century. It was a development of the flanking towers which are such a familiar feature of medieval castles. At first bastions signified towers, called cavaliers, which were raised on the rampart, but later were fortifications built on the salient angles of ramparts. (See diagram B) Vauban gave them two storeys.

At the bottom of the ditch, which was usually dry, was a further excavation, known as a cuvette. This was to intercept mining, and was usually about eight feet deep. The ditch was normally about 90 feet broad, and in Vauban's fortresses the total distance from the interior of the fort to the bottom of the glacis slope was about 700 feet.

In front and around the main fort would be a series of outworks which could be reached from the main building by bridges or *caponiers*. *Caponiers* were originally communication trenches, linking outworks with the main defensive wall known as the courtine or curtain. These works did not necessarily follow a standard pattern, particularly with Vauban who is credited with saying 'one does not fortify by systems but by good sense and experience'. Even so, Vauban was not without his contemporary critics who claimed, probably rightly, that his later works were over-elaborate and virtually useless. Certainly the complexity of some of the latter designs made co-ordination of defence impossible. Among those who criticised and amended Vauban's ideas were Cormontaigne, Montalembert, and Carnot. Carnot's ideas, which emphasised the need for swift counterattack, and therefore included the abolition of the counterscarp were very popular in Holland and Germany but less so in France. He was a keen advocate of high-angle fire, believing that it would destroy enemy attacks at extreme range. Unfortunately for his prestige, this theory was based on the parabolic hypothesis which is the theory of projectile flight in a non-resistant medium; in the event most of his cannon balls were spent before they reached the target.

By the early seventeenth century fortification had arrived at the stage depicted in diagram B. This is a very simple basic design but shows how ground ahead of the main fortification could be covered by

Opposite: Fort William, Calcutta. A photograph of a model showing the characteristics of bastions, ravelins, etc.

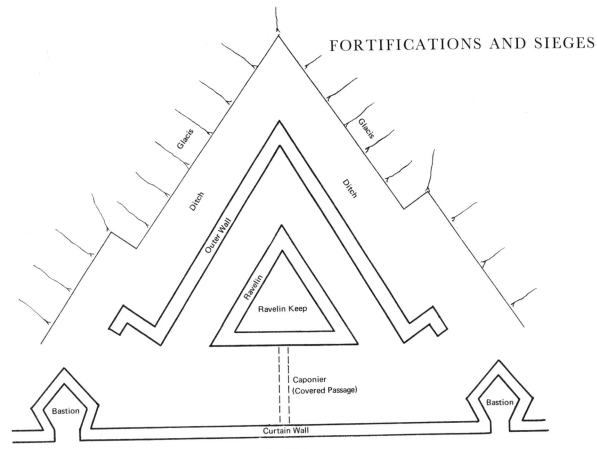

Diagram B. The bastioned trace

Labels within the diagram:

Glacis

Glacis

Ditch

Ditch

Outer Wall

Ravelin

Ravelin Keep

Caponier (Covered Passage)

Bastion

Bastion

Curtain Wall

Interior of Fortress

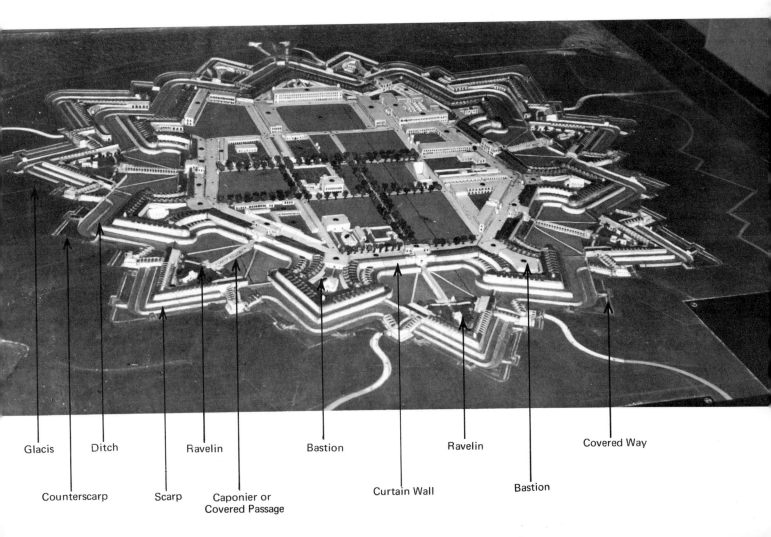

Glacis

Counterscarp

Ditch

Scarp

Ravelin

Caponier or Covered Passage

Bastion

Curtain Wall

Ravelin

Bastion

Covered Way

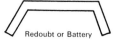

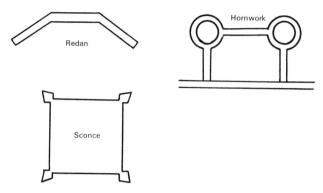

gunfire from the bastions and musketry fire from the curtains. The maximum size of a defensive pattern such as shown in diagram B was determined by the range of the cannon. In the early sixteenth century bastions would be about 500 yards (i.e. two cannon shot) apart. By Vauban's time cannon range was about 600 yards and musket range about 200. The warmest spot would be along the glacis which would have the benefit of musketry fire from the parapets while being swept by gunfire from the flanks of the bastions.

Later a more complicated form of defence was developed using the principle of the *bastioned trace*. It is illustrated in the photographed model of Fort William, Calcutta (p. 21). The curtain walls between bastions are protected by outworks known as *ravelins*.

Outworks came to play an important part in most systems of fortification. Besides *ravelins* there might be *hornworks* which were short curtains with a demi-bastion at either end; they took their name from the fact that the ends sometimes curved outwards like an animal's horns; at La Rochelle the *hornwork* was 280 metres by 200. *Sconces* were detached forts with bastions, while *demi-lunes*, or *halfmoons*, were occasionally crescent shaped, but usually had two faces forming a salient angle. In addition there were field-works which were less elaborate and could be constructed by an army in the field to strengthen a defensive position, or could be used, as at Sebastopol during the Crimean war, to supplement existing fortifications. The most important among these were *redoubts*, or *batteries*, normally small detached strongholds without flank protection, and *redans* built much like *redoubts* but with three sides, so that fire could be directed towards the flanks as well as frontally. An *abattis* was an obstacle made with logs. The shapes of all of these were far from standard, and were modified to suit the ground, or a particular task. (See diagram C.) Two more technical terms may be of interest: *gabions* were baskets filled with earth which were used to build up parapets, and *fascines* were bundles of sticks which were thrown into the ditch to make a form of bridge.

It will be noted that these complex fortresses provided a number of problems. A huge quantity of materials was required, and large numbers of men to move it; the eventual construction was so complicated and diverse that it required a near genius to command it. It is interesting to recall that Vauban's fortifications at Longwy, scarcely altered, were able to hold up the Germans for two weeks in 1914.

But Vauban was not merely a defender. His attacking strategy was probably his best contribu-

Diagram C
Outworks and field works. Basic shapes which might be modified almost out of recognition to suit the ground

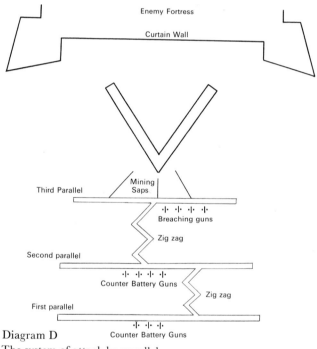

Diagram D
The system of attack by parallels

tion to the military art. The technique as may be expected was extremely methodical. He advanced towards his quarry by a series of trenches known as 'parallels' or 'approaches'. After an initial long range exchange of fire with the hostile fortress, combined perhaps with an assault on various outworks, the first 'parallel' would be established as close to the fortress as the enemy's fire permitted. Guns would be emplaced here, and an endeavour made to subdue the fire of the defenders.

Aided by this fire from the first 'parallel', and often under cover of darkness, a second 'parallel' would be constructed still nearer to the enemy fortress. For ease of movement it would be connected

FORTIFICATIONS AND SIEGES

to the first by a staggered trench called 'the zigzag'. Guns would be mounted in the second 'parallel' to bombard the ramparts; but if their fire proved ineffectual yet another 'parallel' would be dug, and so on, until the heavy siege guns began to make an impression on the enemy masonry.

While this was going on, sappers would be digging underground galleries, so they could lay mines under the ramparts and blow part of them down.

The defenders, meanwhile, would seek to hinder their adversaries by sudden attacks on the batteries to spike the guns and by countermining to destroy their underground galleries.

If the attackers prospered, either from the battering from their guns or the exploding of their mines, or from both, a portion of the enemy's ramparts would collapse, the debris often filling up the ditch in a highly convenient manner. The stage would now be set for the final act, the storm. At a given moment the besiegers would charge through the gap they had made, known as a breach, mount the ramparts and slaughter the garrison.

In the eighteenth century, with its eminently sane approach to the 'horrors of war', a convention grew up that when the besiegers had made a practicable breach, the garrison would negotiate a truce and be allowed to march out with 'the honours of war', that is to abandon their fortress and march away with their bands playing, colours flying and carrying their personal arms. If, however, the garrison forced their assailants to undergo the ordeal of a storm, if they failed to repel it they could expect scant mercy.

Napoleon, characteristically, ignored this convention and directed that all French garrisons should withstand one attempt at a storm before surrendering, an order that had much to do with the excesses committed after the storms of such places as Ciudad Roderigo and Badajoz during the Peninsular War.

This technique of besieging a fortified place by a series of parallel trenches linked by zigzag communication trenches foreshadowed the trench warfare of the twentieth century; and indeed as late as 1945 General Rees commanding the 19th Indian Division in Burma found that the thick ramparts of Fort Dufferin in the centre of Mandalay posed no ordinary military problem.

A plan by Vauban of the siege and capture of Menin after Marlborough's victory at Ramillies. The 'a's mark trenches; 'b', 'c', 'd', 'e' batteries; 'm' breaching batteries and 'k' infantry positions in the *covered way*; 'f' and 'g' breaches

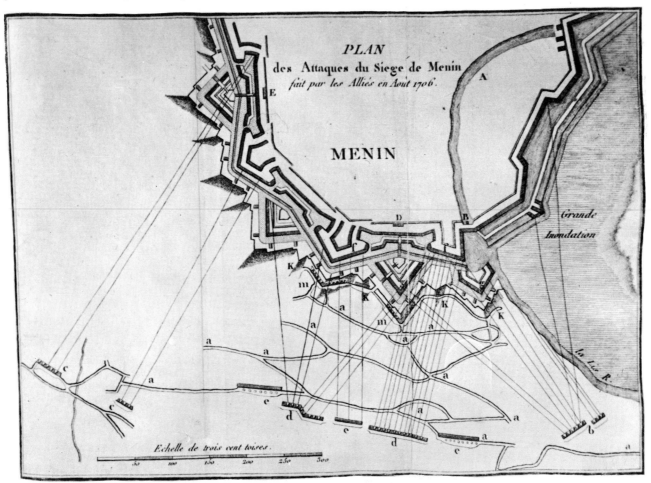

CHAPTER 3

The Army in Marlborough's Day

DAVID G. CHANDLER

After the Treaty of Ryswick, 1697, a suspicious and ungrateful Parliament forced King William to reduce his peacetime army to a mere 7,000 'Guards and Garrisons' at home and perhaps twice as many more in Ireland and overseas. At that time it would have been impossible to guess that in under a decade a greatly expanded army would be fast earning the reputation of being the finest in Europe, or that John Churchill, currently Earl of Marlborough and regarded by many as a courtier-soldier of somewhat unsavoury reputation for all his diplomatic and military gifts, would have emerged as the scourge of the proud armies of Louis XIV and one of England's greatest native-born commanders.

Much of the success earned by the army between 1702 and 1712 was due to the modernisation carried through by William. Despite the setbacks of 1697, which were more apparent than real, 'Dutch William' had laid sound tactical and administrative foundations. Above all, he had trained up a cadre of promising officers. Marlborough himself, for all his debt to his father, Sir Winston Churchill and to the great French Marshal Turenne who had conditioned his thought, and for all his varied military experience ashore and afloat since 1667, had learnt a great deal from William in both Flanders and Ireland, and despite a period in disgrace from 1692 he had been chosen and schooled for future pre-eminence by a monarch who was far from being a fool. If Marlborough was ready-groomed for greatness by 1700, he was also destined to be ably seconded. Soldiers of the calibre of 'Salamander' Lord Cutts, the Earl of Orkney, and William Cadogan (the Duke's invaluable Quartermaster-General) might be inspired by their leader's example, but they were already men of experience and repute. At

more subordinate levels stood men like John Armstrong, Holcroft Blood and the three remarkable Richards brothers, all members of the Board of Ordnance, gunners and engineers. The regiments also held a leavening of loyal and promising officers – the Kanes, Parkers, even the handful of dour Blackadders – from whose writings we can gain some conception of life in the army under the great Duke. Their expert testimony is supported from the ranks by the no less interesting recollections of such soldiers as Sergeant Millner, Corporal Bishop and Private Deane, not to overlook such scoundrels as Peter Drake and the slightly suspect testimony of the famous *vivandière*, 'Mother' Ross. If the majority of Marlborough's formations were made up of the most depressed classes of society, there was much gold amongst the dross.

In the early eighteenth century, every army was recruited from a variety of sources. A substantial part of the British army was composed of mercenaries – Danes, Hanoverians and Hessians for example – hired out by their rulers on contracted terms, one campaign at a time. Another group of foreign troops in the Queen's pay was formed by regiments of exiles, most particularly French Huguenots. Such forces were occasionally unreliable and frequently ill-equipped, but by 1709 they accounted for 81,000 out of 150,000 in the field. This, incidentally, represented the largest military establishment of Queen Anne's reign.

The balance was made up of native troops. As there was no form of compulsory service (save in the Militia, which could not, however, be made to serve outside the shire boundaries), the individual colonels of regiments were responsible for finding their own recruits. Every winter, recruiting parties, typified

Opposite: The Duke of Marlborough

by Captain Plume and Sergeant Kite of Farquhar's contemporary play, *The Recruiting Officer*, (1706) would tour the villages, drumming up volunteers. In prosperous days these were hard to find, so low was the popular estimation of the military life, but in hard times 'the poor starve, thieve or turn soldier' (Defoe). Even so recruits became increasingly hard to find as the war progressed. Recourse was made to the proceeds of the biannual jail-deliveries, which conveniently unloaded the criminal classes into the forces to the advantage of the local ratepayers, but even the offer of ever larger bounties (£4 a head was the rate in 1708) failed to bring in the requisite numbers of men. Whereupon Parliament empowered justices to enlist forcibly all vagrants and vagabonds (terms capable of liberal interpretation), and the authorities frequently turned a blind eye on the most flagrant misdemeanours committed by recruiters, desperate to fill their quotas, although there was never a legalised press-gang system such as operated for the navy.

Thus, although there was in every formation a leavening of genuine volunteers and adventurers, true professional soldiers, the great majority were very unwilling warriors indeed, and the ancient adage, 'the army passed over into Flanders and swore horribly' must have often provided an apt description.

Such unpromising military material could only be controlled by ferocious discipline and terror – or so many contemporaries believed. Doubtless the lash, noose and firing-squad had to be very much in evidence if the criminal minorities were to be contained, but inevitably the innocent suffered with the guilty, and much unnecessary brutalisation was the result. Nevertheless, these men could fortunately be inspired as well as terrorised, and few generals have been more adept at man-management than Marlborough. Many men frankly worshipped him, aware of the care he bestowed on their well-being and confident in his record of success cheaply bought. 'The known world could not produce a man capable of more humanity' recalled Corporal Bishop, and Captain Robert Parker was even more enthusiastic about the confidence inspired by Marlborough's presence at times of danger:

... while I was musing, the Duke of Marlborough, (ever watchful, ever right) rode up quite unattended and alone ... It is quite impossible for me to express the joy which the sight of this man gave me at this very critical moment. I was now well satisfied, that he would not push the thing, unless he saw a strong probability of success; nor was this my notion alone; it was the sense of the whole army, both officer and soldier, British and foreigner. And indeed we had all the reason in the world for it; for he never led us on to any one action, that we did not succeed in.

England was fortunate to possess a leader capable of inspiring such devotion and loyalty amongst the rank and file, for the conditions of service, disciplinary aspects included, were generally appalling. Enlistments were usually for the duration of the war, or until death or serious disablement intervened. Ex-soldiers, wounded included, were left to shift for themselves; a few of the latter might find a place at Chelsea or one of the other military hospitals, but the majority had only recourse to charity, the Poor Law or a life of crime when their services were no longer required. Their comrades retained to man the skeletons of the reduced peacetime regiments would be left to rot in the sheds of ale-houses, for regular barracks had not yet become customary. Governmental neglect and popular scorn was all too often the lot of the common soldier.

Thanks to administrative inefficiency, the soldier on active service was not often very much better off, although Marlborough did a great deal to improve conditions in the forces directly under his command. A private soldier's pay was 8d. a day, divided into sixpence subsistence (for food) and twopence 'offreckonings' (for everything else, less a number of standard deductions for clothing, Chelsea Hospital, the Paymaster-General, etc.), but all too often the Treasury was months in arrears with its issues. Conscientious officers would pledge their credit to the point of bankruptcy to provide funds for the purchase of food for the troops; bad officers simply left their men to starve. Small wonder that desertion and marauding were rife, or that officers condoned many irregularities. Peter Drake claimed that he drifted from regiment to regiment, and even from army to army, with both impunity and personal profit. Certainly a whole class of 'bounty-jumpers' appeared, professional war profiteers who, despite ferocious paper regulations against deserters, enlisted to gain the bounty-money and then promptly deserted to re-enlist in another regiment and repeat the process. Questions were seldom asked although occasional examples were made at the triangles or hanging-tree.

The standard of officer varied greatly. Many were conscientious and able, but in an age when most appointments and promotions went by purchase or favour rather than merit, a number were unscrupulous entrepreneurs with an eye to the main chance. It was not unknown for children to have commis-

Left: Lord Cutts who led the British attack on Blenheim village. He was nicknamed *Salamander* Cutts for his reckless courage
Right: The First Earl of Cadogan. From a portrait attributed to Louis Laguerre

sions bought for them, and many a deserving officer had the bitter experience of seeing coveted promotions awarded to less worthy but wealthier socialites. A commission was often regarded as a financial speculation, little more, and an 'indolent spark' could hardly be expected to care much for the welfare of his men. Professional incompetence was also encountered:

I was once at a review, when the commanding General of the troops was reviewing a Regiment of Foot, where were present the Colonel, Lt. Colonel, Major and most of all the Captains, and yet not one of them capable of going thro' the discipline [*drill*] of the Regiment, of which the General very justly took publick notice. (Kane)

Another bane was officer absenteeism. At times even the Captain-General himself had to intervene – almost intercede – with wayward or home-loving officers to induce them to make an appearance in their units, 'for want of which the Queen's service and the regimental duty doth suffer daily'. On the other hand, almost all officers could be relied upon to display bravery to the point of folly on days of battle; unfortunately at less exciting times this energy and gallantry could often be diverted into the less commendable activity of duelling at the least provocation. Under Marlborough, however, standards of all sorts tended to improve, although life in the regimental mess could still be lively. 'Involved all night in a multitude of promiscuous company', lugubriously recorded the dour Lowland Scot, John Blackadder. 'But they put the conversation on such a footing, either by swearing, profane talking, bantering, or some impiety or other, that I can take little part'. (1709).

There were no formal training establishments for officers of horse or foot. The vast majority learnt the rudiments of their profession 'at the cannon's

mouth'; a few of the most favoured might spend a period on the staff of a famous continental soldier, serving a type of military apprenticeship. Some gunners and engineers attended rudimentary courses at the Tower or the Moorfields Gun Foundry (destroyed by an explosion in 1716), a few more were sent abroad to study fortification, but there was hardly a regular training programme for the Ordnance's personnel.

Such, then, was the human material that went to make up the British Army in the time of Marlborough. Despite many deficiencies and disadvantages, it proved possible to weld the components into a devastating weapon of war.

The Army was organised into a number of branches, of which Whitehall controlled the Horse and Foot, the Board of Ordnance organised the Train (comprising the guns, engineers, bridging, munitions and pioneer services), whilst numerous Boards and contractors supervised most matters pertaining to transport and supply with varying degrees of efficiency.

Under the sovereign, authority was exercised through the Secretaries of State, the Secretary at War, and the Paymaster-General, not to forget the quasi-independent Master-General of the Ordnance. In the field, armies were normally commanded by a captain-general, seconded by varying numbers of lieutenant-generals and major-generals commanding wings or sectors of the double battle-line, taking post according to strict seniority. There were no corps or divisions, and even brigades were essentially temporary formations. As a result, commands were directly communicated to the regiments, the captain-general having a staff to assist him. This was not a properly-trained Staff Corps, but rather a group of officers selected by the general from the regiments. Marlborough chose a small group of key men with unerring skill, in which Cadogan was Quartermaster-General (and unofficial Chief of Staff), Adam Cardonnel served as the Duke's Secretary (and diplomatic adviser), and Henry Davenant was financial agent. These three were aided by a number of assistants and specialists (such as Armstrong of the engineers and Blood of the gunners), whilst a group of aides de camp and special running footmen carried messages and made situation reports. At times of great crisis it was customary to hold councils of war, to which all the generals and specialists would be summoned, but Marlborough used these sparingly and never let them dictate his courses of action.

Whether at peace or war, the regiment was the

fundamental formation. Colonels were very much the proprietors of their units, and when a new regiment was raised the government would issue a contract to a well-to-do officer. He in turn would sell companies to aspiring captains. There was a thriving market in commissions and appointments, but most bargains required official approval at both army and regimental level. The government would provide most equipment, and a uniform grant.

The mounted arm was the social élite of the army, and it included several categories. The Horse, properly so-called, comprised the Troops of Life Guards and Horse Grenadiers, the Royal Regiment of Horse Guards (the Blues), and six regiments of cavalry. Next there were the Dragoons, expected to fight on foot or horseback. Apart from the Queen's Dragoons (or Tangier Horse), which ranked next after the Blues, this type of cavalry was regarded as inferior to the Horse, and the pay scales reflected the distinction. A Colonel of Horse received 41/– a day to a Colonel of Dragoons' 35/–; a simple trooper was paid 2/6 to the Dragoon's 1/6. Finally, there were numbers of 'hostilities-only' regiments, both of Horse and Dragoons, which were disbanded at the peace.

Cavalry establishments varied considerably in detail, but a broad idea can be given. The regimental headquarters would comprise a colonel, lieutenant-colonel, a major, adjutant, chaplain, surgeon and kettle-drummer. The basic unit was the troop, of

British cavalry going into action at Ramillies. Even well trained troopers had difficulty in preserving their order. Painted by Henri Dupray. The French artist Henri Dupray painted a series of pictures commemorating great events in the history of the British Army.

which there were often nine (which would be grouped by threes into temporary squadrons for action). A troop was commanded by a captain, assisted by a lieutenant, cornet and quartermaster. There would be two or three corporals of horse, a trumpeter and up to 60 troopers, but many averaged about 40. Dragoon units broadly followed the same establishment as the Horse, save that there were normally only between 38 and 54 ordinary dragoons in a troop, and they commonly had a sergeant or two as well as corporals, and hautbois players instead of trumpeters. The Life Guards were a law unto themselves, with extra officers and different ranks, whilst the troops (of which there were three or four) held 156 'gentlemen' apiece (or 145 in the Horse Grenadiers). They also enjoyed privileges of pay and conditions of service.

The Foot comprised four battalions of Guards (two of Foot Guards and one each of Coldstream and Scots), a large number of line regiments (called after their colonels' names, and consisting of a single battalion apiece except the Royal Scots who boasted two) and a group of foreign formations and independent companies, most of them of temporary status. A typical regiment consisted of a head-quarters and twelve companies, making a paper strength of 44 officers and staff and 780 NCOs and men. Besides the usual officers to be found in a mounted regimental headquarters, an infantry formation included a surgeon's mate, quarter-master, solicitor, drum-major and deputy-marshal. Of the companies, eleven were line, each with a captain, lieutenant and ensign, two or more sergeants and as many corporals, a drummer, and between 50 and 60 rank and file. The remaining company was made up of grenadiers, with a second full lieutenant instead of the ensign. At least three, and sometimes four, of the line companies would be commanded by the Colonel and the other senior officers, who drew a company commander's emolu-ments (basically 10/– a day before allowances) in addition to their regimental pay. The Guards and Royal Scots enjoyed rather larger establishments.

Many regiments were commanded in the field by the second-in-command or even the major, for colonels often held higher army appointments which made it impossible for them to serve with their units. The use of numbers to determine regimental seniority was becoming commonplace by the Peace of Utrecht; the higher the number, the less the likeli-hood of complete disbandment in the peacetime reductions. Even those regiments that survived were severely cut back. In 1697, for instance, the

Royal Regiment of Foot of Ireland (or 18th Foot) was reduced to merely three companies of 39 NCOs and men apiece. In peace or war, one or two places per company would be left vacant for 'widow's men' – in other words pay would be drawn for non-existent soldiers and used for charitable purposes. Occasionally officers' servants were included in the total number of privates, though this was discouraged.

The scarlet coat and tricorne hat were universally worn in both Horse and Foot, with varying facings, linings and lacings to distinguish regiments and rank (see illustrations). Including his weapons, equipment, haversack, cloak and cooking-pot, a private soldier carried about 50 lbs. weight on campaign. Quality of material and equipment varied as the colonels were allowed much latitude, but under Marlborough many regulations enforcing minimum standards were introduced. Clothing was issued on a two-year cycle, and part of a soldier's 'off-reckonings' were stopped to reimburse the cost.

As for weapons, mounted officers carried swords and pistols; those on foot often carried a spontoon as well. Cavalry troopers were armed like mounted officers, but dragoons additionally carried a carbine. In the Foot, owing to the introduction of flintlock muskets and socket bayonets in place of matchlocks and pikes (a process largely completed by 1703), every NCO and man now carried a firearm except the sergeants, who bore half-pikes or halberds. The standard weapon was a variation of the 'William III land-musket', (the immediate predecessor of the famous 'Brown Bess'), a weapon of ·85 inch calibre, five feet in length (without bayonet) weighing about 11 lbs., and firing about two one-ounce balls in a minute. Maximum range was in the order of 250 yards, but most firefights were engaged at about 60 paces or even less. Pre-packaged paper cartridges, holding both powder and ball, were soon in widespread use, and a soldier carried about two dozen into battle in his pouch. This weapon was considerably more reliable than its predecessors, but flints needed frequent replacement, and the employment of ramrods made of wood (which tended to snap) was a continuing hazard.

The use of body armour had completely gone out for the infantry, and although the breastplate was reintroduced for some cavalry regiments in 1707, it was worn *under* the coat. Some senior officers continued to sport ceremonial armour on days of battle, but this was becoming less customary.

Turning to describe the artillery, we find a branch of the services practically independent of the rest of the army. The powerful Board of Ordnance was virtually a department of state, with full authority over all matters pertaining to gunnery, weapons, munitions, fortification, military engineering and pioneers, and certain aspects of transport and general supply in addition. Its blue-coated servants owed absolute obedience to the Master-General and his principal officers, and even in the field were only subject to the Captain-General's orders. This jealously-guarded status and the Ordnance's slightly better rates of pay were often sources of friction, and it was only gradually that artillery and engineer officers were granted truly equivalent ranks with their cavalry and infantry comrades. Nevertheless there was a considerable degree of officer interchangeability, both within the various branches of the Ordnance and between it and the line regiments. The happy chance that made Marlborough Master-General of the Ordnance as well as Captain-General paved the way for the real integration of the artillery into the rest of the army, and it was the Duke who pressed for the creation of the Royal Regiment of Artillery in 1716. In earlier years he took great pains to iron out difficulties, and he was continually encouraging the development of improved weapons and equipment, including a light two-wheel cart which for many years bore his name on the continent.

His work notwithstanding, the guns presented many practical problems in the field. They were very cumbersome, the nine-pounder demi-culverins, for example, weighing three tons, and this made their movement over the inadequate roads of the day both slow and hazardous. Most cannon needed at least eight or ten horses to drag them, harnessed in tandem, and both the beasts and their drivers were hired from civilian contractors. The team-drivers had a particularly unenviable reputation for abandoning their charges and fleeing at the first sound of shot and shell.

In size, field guns ranged from 24-pounders to minute 1½-pound pieces which fired 'partridge-shot' (canister). Siege guns went as large as 48-pounders, but these travelled independently from the army's base to specific sieges, whenever possible by water. Few field-guns had ranges of much over 600 yards, and for siege-work batteries were often planted close by the enemy's ditch to batter the final breach. Cannon firing solid shot were supplemented by howitzers and mortars throwing shells and bombs. In battle or siege, the guns were often grouped in temporary batteries of six or eight pieces.

The support and maintenance of these monsters

The action at Wynendael. The sergeant (with Halberd) and escort belong to the 1st Regiment of Foot, The Royal Scots

of brass or iron and their crews of gunners and matrosses (an inferior grade of gunner) required large numbers of specialist craftsmen and vast quantities of stores and munitions. An army's trains would comprise many hundreds of waggons and pontoons and they inevitably imposed a major drag on the speed of movement. On some occasions Marlborough was constrained to leave his larger guns behind (as in 1704). Nevertheless, officers of the calibre of Blood, Armstrong or the Richards brothers performed miracles of improvisation and devotion to bring the guns into action when and where required, and all in all the Ordnance performed indispensable services throughout the wars in Flanders and Spain.

Although the Ordnance trains carried the ammunition for the whole army, both powder and shot, the bulk of the food and forage was supplied and transported by arrangement with civil contractors in association with special commissioners appointed by the government. In times of peace or winter quarters the troops were usually left to fend for themselves, buying food with their subsistence money (when forthcoming) or living by their wits.

On campaign, however, although 'grand forages' were organised whenever possible to eke out supplies, the bulk of an army's requirements had to be drawn from pre-stocked arsenals and further huge convoys. Although hostile areas were put under 'contribution', it was deemed that to turn the troops out to live off the countryside would encourage large-scale desertions. Hence the almost total reliance on contractors for both supplies and transport.

In Marlborough's day the most important bread contracts went in the main to Dutch or Spanish Jews, such as Solomon and Moses Medina, Mynheer Hecop and the less satisfactory Machado and Vanderkaa. By tradition, the Captain-General had the right to a percentage on the bread contract, but it was on this count that the Duke's political foes were able to bring him down with charges of malversation in 1712 when he forfeited the Queen's favour. This was paradoxical, for no commander ever did more to improve the workings of the inadequate supply machinery, and to extirpate or at least control the worst abuses. Above all he ensured, through his close relationship with Godolphin, the Lord Treasurer, a ready supply of gold for local purchases, and this was one factor underlying the success of his march to the Danube in 1704, of which Captain Parker observed, '... surely never was such a march carried on with more order and regularity, and with less fatigue both to man and horse'. As Marlborough himself was moved to observe of the main theatre of war:

... Everything has been so organised, and there has been so little cause for complaint, that all know our army in Flanders has been regularly supplied with bread during the war, and has received it with an exactness that will hardly be thought consistent with the secrecy and suddenness of some of the moves.

Of course the comparative prosperity of the Flanders region greatly eased the contractor's problem. In Spain and North America on the other hand, where both supplies and beasts of burden were in very short supply, the situation was often almost impossible, and much suffering was the result. In any case it was something of a miracle that the contractors were willing to undertake their work at all, as the government was often extremely dilatory in settling their accounts, and huge debts were amassed.

Even when the contractors had fulfilled their bargains, and provided both supplies and transport (sub-contracted from local hauliers on a 48-hour or weekly basis in the vicinity of the army's anticipated line of march), much depended on good staff

On the march – French troops. A painting by C. C. P. Lawson

work to bring the convoys to the rendezvous on time. In William Cadogan, however, Marlborough possessed a Quartermaster-General of rare administrative excellence.

For the comforts of life, such as they were, the troops on campaign were largely dependent on the multitude of sutlers and *vivandières* who followed the army. Every regiment appointed its own 'grand' and 'petty' sutlers, but stringent regulations ensured that their carts and tents did not impede the movement of the troops or fighting trains. Mother Ross and her ilk made a pretty, if hazardous, profit from their trade, selling liquor and other wares at a high price, and buying loot and booty at a low. In the course of the war she survived several husbands, and

… never lost an opportunity for marauding; to this end I was furnished with a grappling iron and a sword, for I must acquaint my reader that on the approach of an army the boors throw their plate, copper etc. into wells … With my grapple I searched all the wells I met with and got good booty.

Such camp-followers also performed many humane acts, often at 'the hazard of being killed or stripped'. Although doubtless many a wounded man, particularly a foe, received a quick quietus for the

sake of his possessions, others owed their lives in no small part to the ministrations of women like Mother Ross. At Tournai, for instance, she helped the surgeon amputate the shattered leg of a Captain Brown: 'His servants and nurses not having the courage to hold the candle, I performed that office and was very intent on the operation, which no way shocked me, as it was absolutely necessary.' They were hard times, but clearly she was equal to them. On another occasion, a slightly-grazed lieutenant, exaggerating his head wound, begged her to summon a surgeon, 'but his panic was so great that I believe, had he been examined at both ends, he stood in more need of having his breeches shifted than his wound dressed …'

Medical services were very rudimentary; each regiment had its surgeon and his mate but they were rarely the cream of the profession; each unit also had a special cart set aside for the wounded, and hospitals of sorts were set up in big towns behind the front. The less said about these the better; suffice it to record that a soldier's chance of surviving a major wound was only one in three. Small wonder contemporaries made little distinction between killed and wounded in assessing casualties.

CHAPTER 4

The War of the
Spanish Succession
1702-12

DAVID G. CHANDLER

Such was the army that Marlborough led to victory during the long War of the Spanish Succession. The war itself was a struggle waged to contain the ambitions of France which, for over fifty years had been the bully of Europe, and thereby to safeguard the European balance of power together with

Opposite above: Marlborough watching the opening stages of the Battle of Blenheim. Cutts is attacking the village of Blenheim (left of picture). In the background is the village of Sonderneim (Sonderen) and centre background Unterglau (Unterklaw). Oberglau is still further to the right, and obscured by the smoke of battle. *Below:* Malplacquet. The chequered captured colour in the centre is Bavarian, the other is French. The French had fortified their position with redoubts and abattis

On the march – British troops. A painting by C. C. P. Lawson

various politico–religious and commercial questions associated with it. To these Allied war aims was later added (unwisely as it proved) a further objective, namely the replacement of King Charles II of Spain's designated successor, Philip of Anjou, by an Austrian claimant. Ranged against France and Spain stood the forces of the Second Grand Alliance, England, the United Provinces and Austria, with the myriad states of the Holy Roman Empire more or less behind them. In 1703 Savoy and Portugal joined the cause.

For the historian of the British army the war presents interesting contrasts in performance and leadership. The troops serving under Marlborough's personal command in Flanders and Germany were destined to take part in some of the army's most glorious hours, as the battle-honours commemorating the Duke's quartet of victories, together with such names as Wynendael, Lille and Bouchain, amply testify. Such was Marlborough's personal success in the field through ten successive campaigns that his first major biographer, Thomas Lediard, could justly claim that

… he passed all the rivers and lines he attempted, took all the towns he invested, won all the battles he fought, (this often with inferior, rarely with superior force), was never surprised by his enemy … was ever beloved by his own soldiers and dreaded by those of the enemy.

There was, however, a reverse to the medal. From 1707, despite occasional successes, there was often news of disasters in Spain to balance the latest tidings of triumph from Flanders. For all their not inconsiderable talents and the valour of their men,

such leaders as the mercurial Peterborough, the gallant Galway or the impetuous Stanhope were not equal to the challenges presented by daunting climate and terrain, querulous Allies, long communications over land and sea, and a bitterly hostile Spanish population. Indeed the Iberian front proved as detrimental to the Allied war effort in the early 1700s as it was to prove to Napoleon a century later, despite unquestioned Anglo-Dutch naval command of the Mediterranean from 1704.

Nor, of course, did the war run consistently smoothly in 'the Cockpit of Europe'. Even Marlborough had occasionally to accept second best in the interests of the Alliance; for all his grasp of administrative problems and his ability to keep together the many discordant Allies, he was from first to last severely hampered by political and military restrictions, such as the Dutch field deputies attached to his headquarters with the power of veto over operations involving their men.

In the end his jealous foes secured his fall, and for England the war ended on a jarring and unworthy note as a treacherous Tory government hastened to conclude a private peace with France, deserting the Allies of a decade in return for commercial and colonial advantages. For this the soldiers happily bear no responsibility.

Thus the rich tapestry of England's part in this long war possesses its darker as well as its brighter areas, but it was a dynamic period in the history of British arms, brightly refurbishing this island's martial reputation.

Before describing some of the actions, a brief description of the conventions of warfare and basic tactics of the early eighteenth century is necessary to serve as an introduction. The conduct of war as a whole was considerably circumscribed by restrictions. In the first place purely physical problems – the inadequate system of road and water communications, the primitive means of food conservation, and the critical shortage of fodder in the winter months – limited most campaigns to the period between the recession of the spring floods and the onset of the autumnal rains. Occasional sieges went on into November, but as a rule active campaigning ceased each October, when the troops entered winter quarters. Secondly, Western European campaigns almost invariably centred around two regions, namely the Low Countries (the 'Cockpit of Europe') and the North Italian plain. The reasons were the comparative wealth and fertility of these areas, reflected in the large numbers of towns and fortresses they contained, their respective strategical location in guarding important approaches towards the heartlands of France, the United Provinces, North Germany and Austria (via the Alpine passes), and the relatively high degree of development of their regional communications, river, road and canal. In the third place, the effectiveness of warfare was to varying extents limited by humanitarian considerations which discouraged military excesses and long casualty lists – the furore in England after Malplaquet being a case in point. The sum result of these restrictions was to make warfare episodic, regional and limited in impact. Preference was often expressed for wars of siege and manoeuvre rather than ones of battle and decision, and even the bright genius of a Marlborough, who was aware that wars could only be won by hard and direct methods, had all too often to comply with the prevalent attitudes of Allied governments which favoured limited warfare and hence encouraged mediocre generalship and ineffectual campaigning.

Tactical operations can be divided here under four main headings as, the time-consuming and convention-bound siege warfare has already been treated in Chapter 2. These four comprise marches, encampments, foragings and field engagements ranging from skirmishes to set-piece battles.

Armies often marched in five columns, placing the guns and baggage in the centre. Varying in size between 50,000 and 100,000 men, with an average of one cannon per thousand troops, armies habitually used only one line of march, moving as a single entity. Encumbered by the heavy guns and trains, it was rare for a force to cover more than ten miles in a day although there were exceptions. Marlborough specialised in movement by night or early morning, thus reducing the strain on his men, and enabling him to 'steal a march' over his adversaries, particularly when he wished to surprise an opponent and force an engagement. 'If they are there, the devil must have carried them! Such marching is impossible!' was Marshal Vendôme's reaction to Marlborough's sudden appearance on the Scheldt on 11 July 1708. Similar unconventional moves preceded a number of other famous feats of arms in 1704, 1705 and 1711. The troops marched in carefully-regulated order to enable them to form the elaborate battle formations as quickly as possible. March discipline was rigidly enforced, the most heinous offence being the obstruction of the ponderous Ordnance trains.

After completing the day's stage, armies camped on sites pre-selected by the staff. Camp lines were

An infantry battalion advancing in line at the Battle of Ramillies. In the foreground is probably the Duke of Marlborough looking at the unfortunate Colonel Bringfield who has just been killed by a roundshot while holding the Duke's horse.

carefully laid out in advance to reproduce the order of battle, but the artillery normally encamped some little way apart to reduce the fire danger. Elaborate chains of sentinels, picquets and main guards protected security. Marlborough was noted for having supplies, spare saddlery etc., ready waiting for the marching columns, so that 'the soldiers had nothing to do, but to pitch their tents, boil their kettles, and lie down to rest' (Parker). Permanent camps were frequently entrenched and fortified.

When conditions permitted, part of the army would be sent out to conduct a 'grand forage'. Within a carefully delimited area, the troops would be set to cutting hay for the animals of the army, and often a little marauding to supplement their rations was tacitly encouraged. Strong security measures would be in force, however, both to guard against the possibility of enemy surprise and to discourage would-be deserters from slinking away. Some invariably succeeded, nevertheless.

On days of action, much time was needed to complete the elaborate battle arrays. The army would be drawn up in two lines of units, each with two wings (usually cavalry) and a centre, although Marlborough occasionally varied the formation, as at Blenheim. He also habitually took unusual care to check the siting of his artillery. In this war the British army and its Allies invariably advanced to the attack, marching forward in line of battalions and squadrons to within 100 yards of the enemy supported by artillery fire, before beginning the main engagement. This would take the form of a whole series of attacks designed to distract the enemy's reserves from the sector selected for the main break-through attack. Duke John almost always chose the centre for his battle-winning strokes. The pursuit operation launched after Ramillies in 1706 was unique in its scale and effectiveness for the period.

Marlborough believed that cavalry should be used for shock-action, in twin-squadron charges, four ranks deep, wielding cold-steel, sword or sabre. The Duke '... would allow the Horse but three charges of powder and ball to each man for a campaign, and that only for guarding their horses at grass, and not to be made use of in action.' (Kane). Massed cavalry attacks clinched all four of his great battles.

The Foot fought by battalions, drawn up in line, three ranks deep. The line was subdivided into up to 24 platoons, organised into three 'firings' (groups of eight staggered platoons which discharged all at once or in a predetermined order). This type of fire proved greatly superior to the French line or company volleys, enabling the British to maintain incessant, well-directed fire, one third of a battalion always being reloaded. The English practice of attaching two light guns to each battalion paid further dividends, and Marlborough encouraged his colonels to make far more aggressive use of their

men than the French. The system in action is well illustrated by Parker's account of an incident at Malplaquet:

Colonel Kane, who was then at the head of the Regiment, having drawn us up, and formed our platoons, advanced gently towards them (the enemy) with the six platoons of our first fire made ready. When we had advanced within a hundred paces of them, they gave us a fire of one of their ranks: whereupon we halted, and returned them the fire of our six platoons at once; and immediately made ready the six platoons of our second fire, and advanced upon them again. They then gave us the fire of another rank, and we returned them a second fire, which made them shrink; however they gave us the fire of a third rank after a scattering manner, and then retired into the wood in great disorder: on which we sent our third fire after them, and saw them no more ... We had but four men killed and six wounded: and found near forty of them on the spot killed and wounded ... This is undoubtedly the best method that has yet been discovered for fighting a battalion.

Such remorseless pressure, backed up with the bayonet, was one secret of victory.

The artillery fought in *ad hoc* batteries, and became adept at resiting their cannon in mid-battle (as at Blenheim and Ramillies) which was most unusual at that period. Blood and others were capable of performing wonders with the unwieldy guns.

Without inspired direction from the top, however,

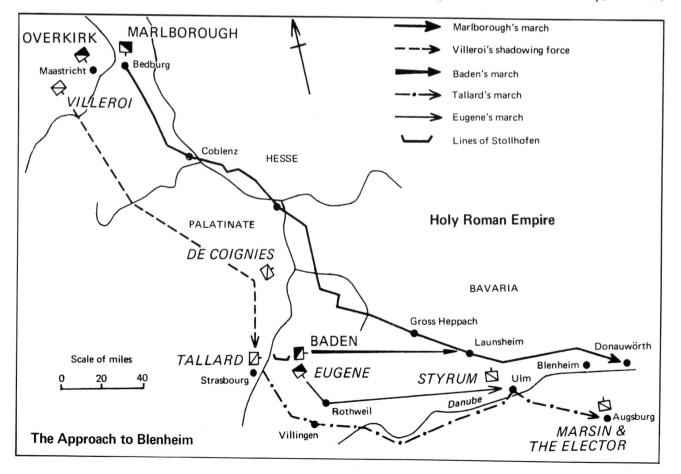

The Approach to Blenheim

Marlborough's march
Villeroi's shadowing force
Baden's march
Tallard's march
Eugene's march
Lines of Stollhofen

OVERKIRK   MARLBOROUGH
Maastricht   Bedburg
VILLEROI
Coblenz   HESSE
PALATINATE
DE COIGNIES
Holy Roman Empire
BAVARIA
Gross Heppach
Launsheim   Donauwörth
Scale of miles
TALLARD   BADEN   STYRUM   Ulm   Blenheim
0   20   40   Strasbourg   EUGENE
Danube
Rothweil
Augsburg
Villingen   MARSIN &
THE ELECTOR

all this would have been to little avail. 'Corporal John' was famed for his coolness in action and his complete grasp of complex situations despite the dense clouds of powder-smoke which soon obliterated the scene. Guided by his intuition and the reports of his invaluable aides, he had a knack of making an appearance at all the critical moments to rally the men and inspire them with his presence. Few commanders have been more adept at leadership, or at divining a foe's intention; but his men were also worthy of him.

The campaigns of 1704 and 1711 will amply serve to demonstrate the generalship of the Duke of Marlborough and the martial qualities of the army he led. These two years contain examples of every major type of operation – strategic marches, a resolute storming and a major battle (1704); the forcing of strong lines, the fooling of a famous opponent and the successful conduct of a rule-defying siege (1711). Here is to be found the whole spectrum of early eighteenth-century warfare, and with it the emergence of the British Army to European primacy.

In early 1704, the French were threatening to mount a major drive on Vienna; if they succeeded, the Grand Alliance could hardly survive the blow. To avert this peril, Marlborough secretly determined to transfer part of the Allied army from the Netherlands to the Danube, there to reinforce the weak Imperial forces, and with them attempt to drive France's ally, Bavaria, out of the war before Marshal Tallard's strong army could move to its aid.

Such a bold concept was beset with difficulties. The Dutch, fearful for their own security, could veto the enterprise if they got wind of it, whilst the German princes and the Danes were already behind-hand in sending forward their contingents. Should the foe fathom the Duke's intention too soon, they could easily intercept the march or sever the army's vulnerable communications. In any case such a long march would inevitably place a great strain on all participants, and the administrative problems appeared insuperable. But Marlborough knew that the risk had to be taken, 'Should I act otherwise,' he wrote, 'the Empire would be undone, and consequently the confederacy.' As reinforcements were already reaching Bavaria in April, no time could be lost.

Every problem was imaginatively tackled. Both French and Dutch were misled by ostensible preparations for a Moselle campaign. The tardy allies were persuaded to send their men to rendez-vous on the line of march, causing Marlborough's force to snowball from 21,000 (including 16,000 English) troops on 19 May to 40,000 by the 20 June, the date the army finally joined the Margrave of Baden's Imperialists. Successive bluffs against the Moselle and then the Strasbourg sectors kept the French off-balance, causing them to comply with the Duke's moves rather than take the initiative. Highly effective administrative measures – hidden marches in the cool of the early morning, pre-arranged depots of supplies, alternative communications running down the river Main, and liberal rest-days – reduced the wear and tear to a minimum, and refuted Blackadder's gloomy prophecy of 'great fatigue and trouble'. Above all, the strictest secrecy was maintained over the critical period, and the main section of the march – some 250 miles – was successfully completed in five weeks. The troops demonstrated their fine fettle and high morale by the successful though very costly storming of the Schellenberg Heights overlooking Donauworth on 2 July to gain a bridge-head over the Danube.

Some time earlier the Duke had met Baden and Prince Eugene of Savoy to determine their strategy (Gross Heppach, 12 June). Whilst the brilliant Eugene undertook the task of observing the movements of Tallard's and Villeroi's stunned forces, who were still awaiting new orders from Versailles, Marlborough took the cantankerous Baden and a joint 100,000 men to force the Elector of Bavaria to fight or negotiate under the threat of military execution for his country.

The Elector proved unexpectedly stubborn, however, and refused to adopt either course. Whilst the Allies cruelly ravaged his countryside – 'We spared nothing,' recalled Mother Ross, 'killing, burning, or otherwise destroying whatever we could not carry off' – he remained with his army secure within his fortresses, aware that they were impregnable owing to the Allied shortage of cannon, and that French aid could not be long delayed. In both calculations the Elector proved correct. On 5 August, after a ponderous and expensive march from the Rhine, Tallard reached Augsburg. Marching north, the united Franco-Bavarian army crossed the Danube, and proceeded to advance slowly towards Donauworth, threatening to trap the main Allied army south of the mighty river. With only 15,000 men, Eugene could only fall back before the foe.

For the Allies the crisis had come – but Marlborough was on his mettle. Ridding himself of the obstructive Baden, sent off with 15,000 men to besiege the town of Ingolstadt, the Duke forced-

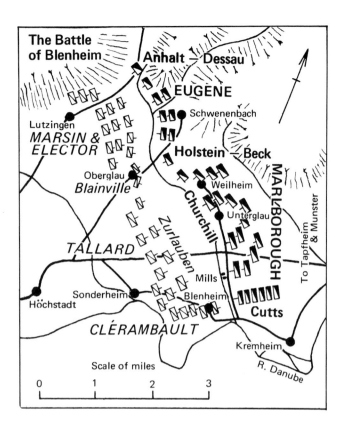

The Battle of Blenheim

marched his men to join up with Eugene on the north bank (completed on 11 August) and together they determined to force a major battle on the supine Tallard despite their inferiority of force (52,000 Allies against 56,000 enemies, and 60 cannon against 90). It was a case of win or lose all.

Advancing in nine columns before dawn on 13 August, the Allies came up to Tallard's outposts concealed by a dense mist. To his immense surprise, the French commander found a major battle on his hands – the last thing he had anticipated. However, as Eugene on the Allied right was badly delayed by difficult country, the French were given ample time to prepare for action whilst Marlborough patiently awaited the arrival of his ally. Only at 12.30 p.m. could the first attack go in.

Tallard's position was strong. His flanks were protected by hills and the Danube; his front was covered by the Nebel stream and its marshes, with three villages well sited for use as strongpoints; a low ridge overlooked the stream at half a mile's distance. Hoping to lure Marlborough into a premature attack over the central reaches of the Nebel, Tallard packed infantry around Blenheim and Oberglau ready to take the obstructed Allied advance in flank, and massed his cavalry (70 squadrons) and a few battalions on the ridge, ready to give the *coup de grâce*. His left he entrusted to the

The Battle of Blenheim. The captive Marshal Tallard with Marlborough. Detail from the Blenheim Tapestry

Elector and Marshal Marsin, with orders to contain Eugene.

Marlborough's questing spyglass had revealed this danger – and also the opportunity of splitting the enemy asunder *if* the villages could first be neutralised before the crossing of the Nebel in the centre was attempted in force. About 1.00 p.m., Lord Cutts' wing advanced against Blenheim, English battalions to the fore. The French garrison held their fire until the Foot were within 30 paces; the English, until their commander, Brigadier Rowe, could strike the palisades with his sword. The town proved too strong to storm, but the French sector commander, Clérambault, lost his head and eventually packed 27 battalions within its defences. Seeing this, the Duke ordered Cutts to call off a third assault, and contain the milling and useless garrison instead. Thus a mere 16 battalions had sealed Blenheim off.

Against Oberglau, the initial attack also failed, and for a time disaster seemed imminent as Marsin charged down on the exposed right wing of Marlborough's centre as it tried to deploy over the Nebel's marshes. With great coolness, the Duke supervised Colonel Blood's heroic re-siting of nine cannon to retrieve the situation, and then requested the use of a brigade of cavalry from Eugene to regain the initiative. This the hard-pressed Prince of Savoy unquestioningly and instantly released. By 3.30 p.m. the crisis was over, and Oberglau in its turn had been contained.

Soon all was ready for the advance in the centre. The first attempt was checked as Tallard flung all his cavalry forward in a desperate charge. But aid was at hand.

I marched with my battalions to sustain the Horse, and found them repulsed, crying out for Foot . . . I went to the head of several squadrons and got 'em to rally on my right and left, and brought up four pieces of cannon and then charged. (Brigadier-General Lord Orkney).

Tallard's last fling foundered before this combined counter-attack. Time was now running out for the French. A tide of Allied horsemen returned to the charge, and by six o'clock Tallard's tired squadrons were fleeing the field, many to drown in the Danube, whilst his nine battalions died to a man where they stood. The battle was won, and Tallard himself a prisoner. Whilst the Elector and Marsin beat a hasty retreat, the garrison of Blenheim were bluffed into surrender by 9.00 p.m. The result was 14,000 prisoners, the élite of the French infantry; hardly any had fired a shot all day.

For a cost of 12,000 casualties, Marlborough and Eugene had achieved 'the greatest and completest victory that has been gained these many ages' (Orkney). The French had lost up to 40,000 men (deserters included), and with them their long-established reputation for invincibility. As a result of the battle, Bavaria was overrun by the Allies and before the close of the campaign they had also captured Landau on the French side of the Rhine. The whole face of the war had been transformed in six short months; Duke John and his army had made their reputation. All Europe marvelled.

Six campaigns separate Blenheim from Marlborough's final campaign – years of fluctuating fortune for the Grand Alliance although the Duke's military record remained unsullied. But by 1711 political enemies had gained the ear of Queen Anne, and her great general found himself with far less freedom of action than heretofore. Nevertheless, Marlborough's last campaign was to prove in some ways his best; in it he showed himself to be a consummate master of typical 'restricted' eighteenth-century warfare.

Following their loss of Douai (1710), the French had constructed imposing lines from the Channel coast to the Ardennes to secure what was left of their frontier region. To hold them Marshal Villars had an army of 110,000 men, and so confident was he in the lines' strength that he called them '*Ne Plus Ultra*' ('nothing further is possible') and boasted that in him the Allies had at last met their match.

It was true that Marlborough had only some 90,000 soldiers after detaching Prince Eugene with a strong corps for the Rhine front (April); it was also true that his health was bad, and that his popularity at Court was rapidly declining. Several vain months were spent trying to lure Villars out of his positions, but in July Marlborough devised a plan that demonstrated all his skill as a commander in the field.

To force lines without great loss of life entailed fooling the foe as to the point of crossing, and then suddenly passing them before he recovered his balance. The only sector Marlborough favoured for such an attempt was near Cambrai, but the sole practicable crossing place was dominated by the fortified town of Arleux, set a short way in front of the main lines; to take this post would inevitably alert Villars of what was afoot, and give him time to mass in the vicinity. To avert this, the Duke resorted to superb duplicity: he would induce the French to

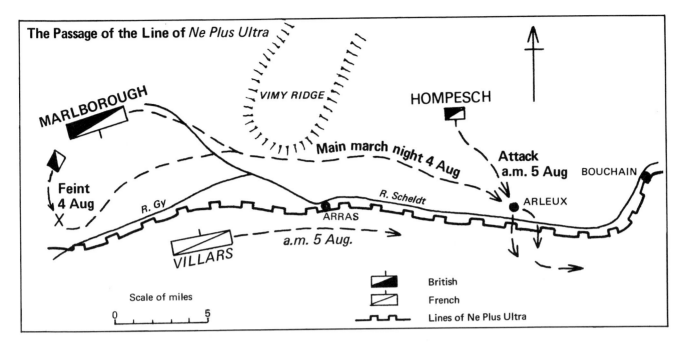

The Passage of the Line of *Ne Plus Ultra*

MARLBOROUGH

VIMY RIDGE

HOMPESCH

Main march night 4 Aug

Attack a.m. 5 Aug

BOUCHAIN

Feint 4 Aug

R. Gy

R. Scheldt

ARLEUX

ARRAS

a.m. 5 Aug.

VILLARS

Scale of miles

0   5

British

French

Lines of Ne Plus Ultra

destroy Arleux themselves prior to the major Allied crossing operation.

On 6 July an Allied force surprised Arleux's garrison and occupied the town; Villars reacted as anticipated, but Marlborough then moved away, leaving a weak garrison with orders to strengthen the defences. Villars deduced that his enemy wanted to draw him away from Arleux and refused to budge, and on the 19th he moved in force to retake the post. Feigning alarm, Marlborough detached the trusted Cadogan with a picked force to 'rush' to the garrison's aid. But Cadogan had secret instructions that he was to *'festina lente'*, and arrived too late. So Arleux passed back into French hands (22nd), and to rub in his success, the flamboyant Villars instantly razed the town and its defences. On news of this, Marlborough threw a fit of rage for the benefit of the spies he knew were at his elbow, but secretly was well pleased.

The Allies next marched on Avesnes-le-Comte as if to reconnoitre a crossing there, whilst the guns and baggage slipped off to join General Hompesch at Douai, using the cover afforded by Vimy Ridge to hide their move from the preoccupied French who shadowed the main movement. On 4 August the Duke conducted a full reconnaissance, and everybody, the Allies apprehensively and the French jubilantly, was sure that a full assault would follow. None noticed Cadogan slip away quietly towards Douai.

Then, shortly after dusk, aides ordered the Allies to assemble in silence. Leaving blazing camp-fires,

the whole army then began to march with all speed for Arleux, the dragoons in rear of the column picking up the stragglers. Meantime, Cadogan and Hompesch issued out from Douai, and, bypassing the deserted ruins of Arleux, secured an uncontested bridgehead through the vaunted French lines beyond, in the early hours.

Not until 2.00 a.m. did Villars realise what was afoot. By that time the Allies had gained too good a start, and although the Marshal galloped ahead of his men (almost getting captured in the process) it was too late to block the breach. All morning of the 5th the tired Allies poured through the Lines – most of them had covered the amazing distance of 39 miles in 18 hours – and, deprived of his position, Villars did not dare to give battle when his columns made their belated appearance.

So Marlborough fooled the cocksure Villars with consummate artistry, and achieved a bloodless victory which once more became the talk of Europe. But Marlborough had not yet completed his plan; he was now determined to capture the inaccessible fortress of Bouchain from under the very nose of a superior but humiliated Villars, daring him to intervene. By 9 August the Allied army was under the walls.

The Duke's staff were of the opinion that this project was impossible. Not only was Bouchain strongly fortified, placed amidst treacherous marshes, and garrisoned by Comte de Ravignan with 5,000 men, but the close proximity of Villars with 100,000 more troops made the whole under-

The Siege of Bouchain. Detail from an engraving by the Dutch artist C. Decker

taking seem hazardous in the extreme. Indeed, the main French army had already established contact with the garrison through the marshes along the 'cow path', protecting this tenuous link with a strong position at Wavrechin. Only Colonel Armstrong of the Engineers thought 'that it might be done' (Kane), but Marlborough backed his subordinate, confident that he had the measure of the blustering Villars.

The first task was to protect the numerically-inferior Allied army from their more powerful adversary. By dint of hard digging, lines of circumvallation were constructed from the Allied camps to the River Scarpe, whilst lines of contravallation were dug facing Bouchain. In all 30 miles of positions were extemporised. But still the French held Wavrechin and the 'cow path', and until the latter

was cut the town was not truly besieged. A plan to assault the former was given up as too difficult, but in a single night the indefatigable Armstrong constructed a 24-gun battery which completely neutralised the French position.

Next the garrison's lifeline amidst the marshes had to be severed. Marlborough wrote on the 17th:

We have not yet quite overcome our difficulties, though we have forced them from several posts; they have none left but a path called the Cow Path through a great bog, at which they can only pass one in front (i.e. in single file).

Later that same day, however, a force of 400 grenadiers waded up to their necks to surprise the garrison, and take the path at a cost of six casualties. Bouchain was at last truly invested.

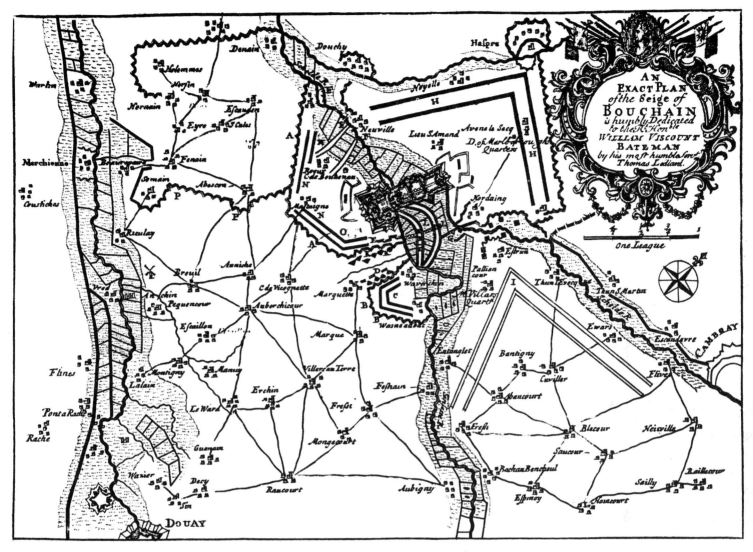

The Siege of Bouchain. A plan given by Thomas Lediard in his life of Marlborough 1736

The siege now followed a more normal course. On 18 August some 80 siege guns arrived from Tournai, and on the 21st three sets of attack trenches were opened. By the 30th the breaching batteries were in position, and a remorseless bombardment was soon battering Bouchain's defences. All the while Villars remained in camp, a hypnotised spectator, trying to devise futile diversions but not daring to call Marlborough's bluff and force a major battle – so high stood the Duke's martial reputation. The siege went relentlessly from stage to stage. On 4 September the Allies stormed the covered way of the great hornwork, and by the 7th they held the counterscarp as well. In desperation, Villars mounted a raid against Douai, but his intention was betrayed. Despairing of receiving effective help, de Ravignan beat a parley on 11 September, and three days later, after tortuous negotiations which gained him not a jot, the Governor and his 3,000 survivors marched out to become prisoners of war. For a cost of 5,000 casualties, Marlborough had achieved the seemingly impossible: he had become master of Bouchain in spite of the most unfavourable and discouraging circumstances imaginable. It proved 'his last conquest and command' (Churchill), for the success earned him scant credit with Queen Anne, who was determined to replace him. Nevertheless, it is fitting that Marlborough's active military career should end on such a glorious note. Duke John had led the British army to imperishable fame which even the disgraceful conduct of his immediate political and military successors could not obliterate.

CHAPTER 5

The Army of the Georges and the War of the Austrian Succession 1713–47

PETER YOUNG

After the recall of Marlborough England soon withdrew from the War of the Spanish Succession. In 1713 a general European peace was negotiated at Utrecht. A Bourbon succeeded to the Spanish throne, but the Spanish Netherlands and the Spanish possessions in Italy went to Austria.

In 1714 Queen Anne died and the Elector of Hanover ascended the British throne as George I. That monarch and his immediate successors in their anxiety to preserve their Hanoverian possessions, an anxiety which their British subjects by no means always shared, brought Britain into all the dynastic quarrels of western Europe.

Almost immediately after his accession, George I faced a Stuart challenge. A half-hearted Jacobite revolt in Scotland petered out after the battles of Sheriffmuir and Preston. Britain now settled down to nearly 30 years of peace. After the unvarying British fashion the Army was starved of all financial resources and the military machine allowed to decay. No British politican has yet learned the wisdom of the old Roman adage, 'If you wish for peace prepare for war.'

When George II, himself a veteran of Oudenarde, came to the throne in 1727, he was by no means indifferent to military problems, and as Elector of Hanover he was anxious to support his German subjects in times of danger with British regiments. The Royal collection affords ample evidence of the interest which he and his second son, the Duke of Cumberland, took in the life and especially the dress of the British Army. If we know fairly well what our soldiers of 1742 and 1751 looked like it is largely thanks to paintings which our Hanoverian rulers commissioned.

The British Army had enjoyed no mean reputation in the period of Marlborough's triumphs. After the 1715 uprising this situation gradually changed for the worse. In 1725 an officer was actually tried for his life when in the course of the murderous Glasgow riot known as 'Shawfield's Mob' he was ordered by a magistrate to open fire and his company succeeded in killing 19 of its assailants. This incident does not seem to argue that the army was held in very high esteem. The work on the roads in Scotland on which large numbers of soldiers were employed, though it added sixpence a day to their meagre pay, did not exactly enhance the military reputation of the British redcoat. 'Wade's Highwaymen' were probably better navvies than soldiers.

The death of the Emperor Charles VI (20 October

Opposite: George II at the Battle of Dettingen before he found it easier to conduct the battle on his own feet. This was the last time that an English monarch commanded an army in the field. A painting by John Wootton

44

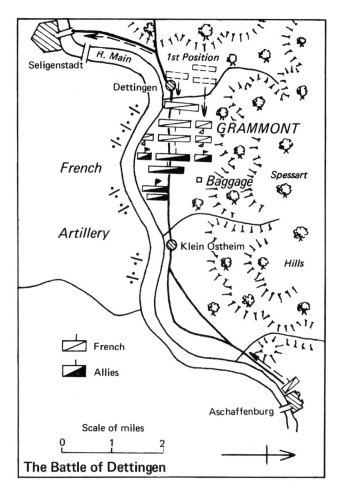

The Battle of Dettingen

1740), the Hapsburg ruler of Austria, left his youthful and inexperienced successor, Maria Theresa, practically alone amidst a sea of enemies. King Frederick of Prussia, not yet surnamed the Great, lost no time in overrunning the province of Silesia. In England there was much sympathy for the Empress, and for once King George II found himself in tune with his subjects. In May 1741, despite the opposition of his Prime Minister, Walpole, he set off for Hanover to put himself at the head of a force of British, Hanoverians, Dutch, Danes and Hessians, which he was collecting there. His threatening attitude at least compelled Frederick to divert reinforcements intended for Silesia in order to observe Hanover and Saxony.

Frederick's army had won him a victory at Mollwitz (10 April 1741), but Maria Theresa remained resolved not to yield one jot of her just claim to Silesia. Frederick therefore entered into alliance with France, Germany's greatest foe during the last 100 years.

By the middle of the summer of 1742 16,000 British troops had been concentrated in Belgium under a Marlburian veteran, Lord Stair. It was not much of a force, but, thanks to Walpole's short-sighted economy and persistent neglect of the army, it was all that could be scraped together.[1]

The 'Pragmatic Army', as George II's host was called saw no fighting until 1743. In the summer of that year it was campaigning on the River Main, where a French army, of very mixed quality but 60,000 strong, under the Duc de Noailles (1678–1766) held them in check. King George, who was no great strategist, and preferred the advice of his Hanoverians to the experienced Stair, succeeded in getting himself and his 44,000 men into a mouse-trap.

Shortage of supplies had compelled the King to retreat up the Main from Aschaffenburg, only to find his path barred by Noailles' nephew, de Grammont, just east of Dettingen. To the north impenetrable wooded slopes barred all organised movement; across the river French batteries played unchecked on the marching British, while a French army was in the process of crossing the Main at Aschaffenburg to march on the British rear. The trap had been sprung. Fortunately Stair now 'thought it time to meddle' and succeeded in sorting things out. The French were beaten by sheer hard fighting. The cavalry of the *Maison du Roi* were repulsed by the British infantry, and then driven back by the 4th, 6th, and 7th Dragoons and two Austrian regiments. Encouraged by this success the Allied infantry pushed forward, the British infantry, in traditional style, laying the French low with murderous volleys of musketry. The Austrian marshal, Neipperg, said afterwards that he 'never saw such a firing'. The French broke and fled for the bridges and Stair naturally meant to give de Grammont's corps the *coup de grâce*. It was not to be. King George forbade it and pushed on to his base at Hanau leaving his wounded on the field. To the credit of de Noailles it must be said that he did his best for them.

The casualties were heavy on both sides. The Allies lost 750 killed and 1,600 wounded, 826 being British, 550 Hanoverian and 1,000 Austrians. The French losses were not less than 8,000.

This was the last occasion upon which a British monarch led his army in the field. Early in the action the King's fine big white charger ran away with him, after which he fought on foot remarking that he could trust his own legs not to run away with him. He is said to have donned the coat he wore at

[1] Four troops of Household Cavalry, 8 regiments of horse and dragoons, 3 battalions of the Guards, and 12 of the Line.

Oudenarde for the occasion. In the evening he knighted Lord Stair and Trooper Thomas Brown of the Third Dragoons who had rescued a standard at the cost of seven wounds. This was the last instance of British soldiers being made Knights Banneret in the field.

George II's Army had done well enough, but it had its weaknesses. Lt-Col. Russell (1st Guards) thought that with three or four exceptions the generals 'were of little service'.

The men and their regimental officers gained the day; not in the manner of Hide Park discipline, but our Foot almost kneeled down by whole ranks, and fired upon 'em a constant running fire, making almost every ball take place, but for ten or twelve minutes 'twas doubtful which should succeed, as they overpowered us so much, and the bravery of their *mason du roy* [sic] coming upon us eight or nine ranks deep; yet our troops were not seen to retreat, but to bend back only, ... and that only when they fresh loaded; then of their own accord [they] marched boldly up to 'em, gave 'em such a smash with loud huzzas every time they saw them retire, that then they were at once put to flight; ...

Ensign and Adjutant James Wolfe (12th Foot), aged 16, describes in a letter how he and the commanding officer, Major John Cosseley, begged and ordered the men 'not to fire at too great a distance'. But the redcoats knew better and the 'whole of them fired when they thought they could reach them which had like to have ruined us. We did very little execution with it. As soon as the French saw we presented [took aim], they all fell down, and when we had fired, they all got up and marched close to us in tolerable good order and gave us a brisk fire, which put us into some disorder and made us give way a little, particularly ours and two or three more Regiments, who were in the hottest of it. However we soon rallied again and attacked them with great fury, which gained us a complete victory ...' It seems these old battles were not quite such drill parades as we are sometimes asked to believe.

The campaign of 1744 was a peaceful one for George II's forces, partly because he proved more active as King of England than as Elector of Hanover. Instead of using the English subsidies to pay his Hanoverian troops, as he did, 'one's right hand paying one's left' Robert Trevor, the minister at The Hague called it, he might have hired Hessians and other German mercenaries and built up a more formidable army. Nothing, in Trevor's view 'would so much contribute to save Europe, encourage the Empire and strengthen the Ministry's hands ... as our Royal Master's drawing his Electoral sword and his Electoral purse-strings gallantly and unreservedly in support of our common cause'.

It was not until May 1745 that the British Army was to see serious fighting once more. By this time the Duke of Cumberland was Commander-in-Chief of the Allied forces, some 53,000 strong. Marching to the relief of Tournai he fell upon Marshal de Saxe, who had 70,000, though 27 battalions of infantry and 17 squadrons were before Tournai.

Saxe's prestige as a leader of military thought was only equalled by his prowess as a rake. Though stricken with dropsy and commanding his army from a horse-drawn wicker carriage, he was more than a match for Cumberland. Saxe had selected a strong defensive position five miles south-east of Tournai, and had fortified it with redoubts and batteries, somewhat as Villars had done at Malplaquet, but yet more skilfully.

The Allies reconnoitred this position on 10 May and came to the conclusion that the ground between Fontenoy and the Wood of Barry was clear, whereas in fact it was protected by the Redoubt d'Eu. Their plan was for the Austrians and the Dutch to assault the French right on the Antoing-Fontenoy front, while the British were to break through between Fontenoy and the Wood of Barry. The Austrians and Dutch were repulsed with heavy loss, while Brigadier Ingoldsby, detached with a force of British and Hanoverians to take the Redoubt d'Eu, proved worse than useless, and failed utterly.

From about 6.00 a.m. until 10.30 the British deployed under a heavy fire before beginning their

Dettingen. The 'Black Horse' (7th Dragoon Guards) capture the French kettle drums. The drums are now in the National Army Museum

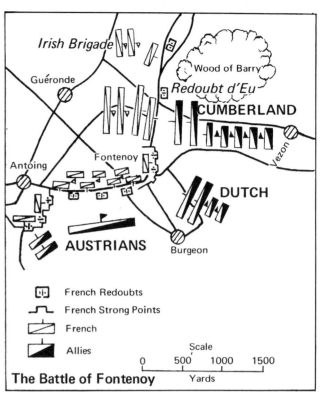

The Battle of Fontenoy. *Tirez les premiers, Messieurs les Anglais.*
The *Garde Français* await the onslaught of the British
Guards. A painting by C. C. P. Lawson

majestic advance against the plateau. Their drill and
discipline had improved since Dettingen: three
years overseas had made veterans of them. There was
no question of their opening fire when they were out
of range. The strange episode of Lord John Hay
raising his flask, and toasting the *Gardes Françaises*
with 'Tirez les premiers, Messieurs les Français', is
explained not by the medieval courtesies of Amadis
de Gaule, so much as by the tactical advantage to be
gained by inducing the enemy to open fire beyond
effective range – then about 60 yards. Marching up
close to the French the British delivered a devastating volley right in their teeth which is said to have
laid low 700 men – though how one compiles a
statistic of that sort in the heat of battle is not
explained. The British pressed on into the French
camp, their two lines compressed by this time into
a massive column, not perhaps unlike those which
the French themselves were to form under the
Empire.[2] It was not the best formation for developing one's fire-power, and it was to their musketry
that the British owed their superiority. Nevertheless

[2] Macdonald's corps at Wagram or d'Erlon's at Waterloo.

the infantry of the French Household and Dillon's
Irish hurled themselves in vain against this phalanx.

Once more the Dutch assaulted Fontenoy. Once
more they failed. The British withdrew to the crest
of the ridge, reformed, and then advanced again.
The French gunners had long since exhausted their
grapeshot, and were loading their cannon with stones
and broken glass! The crisis had come: Saxe, like a
hardened gambler, flung in his last reserve. The
Irish Brigade, five regiments of the 'Wild Geese',
charged the British right, while the French and
Swiss Guards supported by regiments of the line
assailed Cumberland's left. It was enough: the
Duke was compelled to order a retreat. Slowly and
majestically as they had come the redcoats fell back,
facing about ever and anon, to discourage pursuit
with a blast of musketry. The hard-fought battle
cost both sides about 7,000 casualties.

The Dutch failure at Fontenoy probably permitted
de Saxe to draw off forces to the front, where the
British and Hanoverian infantry were pressing so
strongly. Had the Dutch even succeeded in pinning
the troops opposite them it seems unlikely that the
French could have held Cumberland's column.

Ten days after the battle the Dutch surrendered
Tournai, after a defence which added nothing to
their laurels. Cumberland, unable to protect both
Ghent and Brussels, saw the former fall on 11 July.

His operations were further hampered when, in consequence of the landing of Prince Charles Edward in Scotland (25 July), he was ordered to send home 10 battalions of infantry, and later his whole army except 5 regiments of horse and one of foot. The 1745 uprising enabled the French to overrun West Flanders with comparative ease.

The campaign against Prince Charles Edward is not especially instructive. The successes of the Highland Army at Falkirk and Prestonpans were won against weak and demoralised forces under inept commanders. Had the Scots pushed on from Derby it may be that the capital would have been in real danger. Once he went over to the defensive the Prince could look for little success, especially since he seldom attempted to imitate the 'Commando' tactics of Montrose, but employed his Highlanders as if they were infantry of the line, a rôle for which they were ill-fitted. To the man who had given the great Saxe a rough day at Fontenoy, Culloden was a picnic, if only because Charles Edward, besides being no general, was outnumbered by nearly two to one, and considerably out-gunned.

The British had two more sharply-contested actions before the War of the Austrian Succession came to an end: Roucoux (11 October 1746) and Lauffeldt (2 July 1747). On both occasions Saxe added to his laurels. Lauffeldt has been described as 'a repetition of Fontenoy' and indeed there are similarities between the two battles. For one thing the two commanders were the same: Saxe and Cumberland. For another the Austrians, notoriously immobile and poor at manoeuvring, permitted Saxe to neglect them and concentrate against the British and their Hanoverian and Hessian auxiliaries.

Once more the brunt of the fighting fell on the British and German troops who conducted themselves nobly, but in vain.

Taken all in all the War of the Austrian Succession was not a period of great success for British arms. Stair and brave old Ligonier were respectable generals. Cumberland, though diligent and not incapable, cannot be regarded as outstanding. George II for all his valour had neither the skill nor the experience to fit him as a Commander-in-Chief. The rank and file, somewhat erratic at Dettingen, their chief victory, behaved splendidly at Fontenoy and Lauffeldt only to meet with defeat. It seems ironical, but nobody who has been in a war will be surprised to learn that military virtue is not always rewarded.

The shortcomings of the British Army in this war illustrate the obvious fact that without a strong cadre of regular troops, especially officers and NCOs, it is impossible to expand the army in wartime, and to build up a large and efficient expeditionary force to make headway against the leading continental power of the day. The wonder is that the Army, neglected alike by Whig and Tory should have acquitted itself as nobly as it did.

The spirit which pervaded the armies of the Austrian Succession War was very much akin to that of Marlborough's era. Frederick had not yet reached the height of his powers. Only de Saxe can be considered in the first class, a man who might rival Villars or cope with a Marlborough or a Eugène. It was a war fought by the veterans of the War of the Spanish Succession on the ideas of that period. Between 1748 and the outbreak of the Seven Years War in 1756 we seem to step from one era to another. When we read of the operations of the latter war, we seem at last to be dealing with modern times, to be reading about officers, who, despite their occasional oddities, the duels, the purchase system and so on, are living in a world where the ideas which still affect us are beginning to germinate. The Industrial Revolution and *les droits de l'homme* are only just around the corner. The Age of Methodicism is passing. The Age of Reason is in its high summer.

The Battle of Culloden from a sketch by Thomas Sandby who, as private secretary to the Duke of Cumberland, accompanied him to Scotland. The sketch shows the opening phase of the battle. The Scots on the right of the picture, 'greatly surprised and disordered' by the hail of shot from the ten British 3-pounders are beginning their attack. In the distance the men of Lord George Murray's wing are attacking Barrel's and Munro's regiments

CHAPTER 6

The Seven Years' War –
The Conquest of Canada
1754–63

G. ALAN SHEPPERD

THE ORIGINS OF THE WAR
By the Editors

The statesmen who in 1748 brought an end to the War of the Austrian Succession by the Treaty of Aix-la-Chapelle would have been rash indeed had they proclaimed it a lasting peace, for by it Frederick kept Silesia and, with Maria Theresa burning for revenge, it could scarcely endure. Nevertheless war when it came started not in Europe but on the continent of North America. Here the French sought by a chain of forts to link their colony of Canada with that of Louisiana on the gulf of Mexico. Had they been allowed to carry out their project unchecked, the British Thirteen Colonies would have been confined between the Appalachian mountains and the Atlantic sea-board.

Clashes in America flared up into a full scale Anglo-French war, one that soon spread to Europe. Maria Theresa, eager to regain Silesia, obtained an alliance with France. Frederick the Great, anticipating her intentions, attacked Austria. Since this brought Prussia into collision with France, Britain threw in her weight on Frederick's side. Soon the whole of Europe was embroiled and the conflict spread over half the globe.

For the British the main fighting on land took place in North America, Western Germany and India. The British fleet swept the seas and sea-power laid the foundations for victory in America and India. In Europe British armies helped to safeguard Hanover and protect Frederick from the west. Both in Germany and America the war opened disastrously for British arms.

THE CONQUEST OF CANADA

In 1754 the French, forcibly driving away some Virginian militia under George Washington, established Fort Duquesne at the forks of the River Ohio. As the route up the Mohawk River to Oswego on Lake Ontario was commanded by Fort Frontenac, and that up the River Hudson to Lake Champlain by the French-held fort at Crown Point, all the three routes to the west were now effectively blocked.

After much hesitation and delay troops were despatched from England (the 44th and 48th Foot) 'with arms for two Provincial regiments raised into British pay. The command was given to General Braddock, 'an officer of forty five years service, rough, brutal and insolent, a martinet of the narrowest type, but wanting neither spirit nor ability and brave as a lion'. In April 1755 Braddock and several of the Governors held a council of war, arriving at the grandiose plan that Braddock

Opposite : The action on the Monongahela River. The death of General Braddock, as portrayed by a contemporary artist. In fact the French and their Indian allies fought behind the trees, while Braddock, a martinet of the old school, tried to employ the tactics of continental Europe

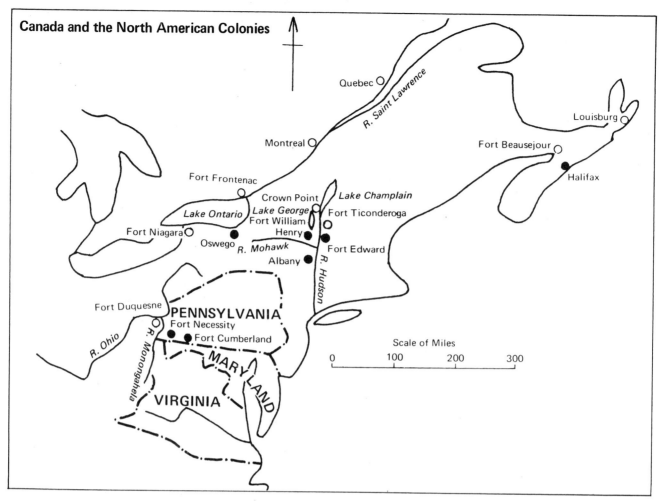

Canada and the North American Colonies

should attack Fort Duquesne, while Provincial troops advanced on Fort Niagara and Crown Point and Lieutenant Colonel Monckton with New England volunteers sailed against Fort Beauséjour.

By mid May, after much difficulty over collecting supplies and transport, Braddock's force was assembled at Fort Cumberland, 'an oasis in a desert of leaves'. Here the drilling of four hundred Provincial recruits continued for a month while Braddock waited with growing impatience and irascibility for the arrival of his guns. The two regiments still only mustered 700 men each, but a Royal Artillery detachment and nine companies of Virginian Militia brought the force to 2,200 men, plus a waggon train and 600 baggage horses. The column finally moved off on 10 June, but only covered 30 miles in the first eight days. Many men fell sick with fever and the horses, without proper fodder, were near exhaustion. Fearing the arrival of French reinforcements, Braddock decided to push on with 1,300 men and ten field guns, leaving the sick to guard the heavy baggage. By 7 July Braddock was within nine miles of his objective. To avoid a dangerous defile he decided to ford the Monongahela and recross at a second ford. 'Three hundred axe men led the way,

to cut and clear the road, and the long train of pack-horses, waggons, and cannon toiled on behind, over the stumps, roots, and stones of the narrow track, the Regulars and Provincials marching in the forest close on either side. Squads of men were thrown out on the flanks, and scouts ranged the woods to guard against surprise.'

The garrison at Fort Duquesne consisted of only a few companies but the commander Contrecœur had assembled a number of Canadians and Indians, whose scouts now had the column under close observation. One of his captains, Beaujeu, now proposed laying an ambush at the second ford and the following morning a company of Regulars, some Canadians and well over 600 Indians moved off towards the ford. Half the Indians unexpectedly swung off on a separate path and this delayed Beaujeu from reaching the ford ahead of Braddock's column, which arrived there unmolested. Covered by a strong advance party under Lt-Col. Gage, the main body crossed under Braddock's eagle eye 'with perfect regularity and order'. In a cloudless sky, the sun, hardly seen during the weeks of marching through the forest, struck down on the accoutrements of the mounted officers and troop of light cavalry and on the scarlet of the Regulars and the blue coats of the Militia, while the guns and waggons and trains of pack horses and cattle slowly crossed the shallows and re-entered the forest. After a short halt the advance was resumed along a narrow path.

Ahead lay a wide and bushy ravine the far side of which was overlooked by a hill. Gage's advance guard had just crossed the ravine when a man in Indian dress but wearing an officer's gorget suddenly appeared in the path. In a moment a war cry was echoing through the forest which suddenly was alive with men. Gage's column deliberately formed line to the front and firing volley after volley slowly advanced against the now invisible enemy. Beaujeu himself fell and many of the Canadians turned back. Gage's guns were now in action but without any visible targets, nevertheless the Indians began to give way. The French Regular troops, however, held their ground and thus encouraged the Indians rallied, many making for the nearby hill. Gage's close-packed and bewildered force was now under an accurate and deadly fire from all directions.

At the sound of the first volley Braddock, leaving the waggons and 400 men as a rear guard, pushed forward with the remainder of the main body, only to find Gage falling back, having been forced to abandon his guns. The situation quickly became chaotic. Units from the rear crowded in on the remnants of the advance guard and quickly became split up, forming a confused mass, some facing one way and some another but all exposed to a withering fire. Only the Virginians were equal to the emergency and adopting the tactics of their Indian opponents fought back from behind trees and fallen trunks. Many who attempted to make use of cover were beaten back into line by Braddock with the flat of his sword.

The murderous fire tore into the close-packed ranks of men, who were shot down before they even caught a sight of the enemy. As the panic increased Braddock ordered an attack against the hill from where the heaviest fire now came but this was beaten back. Braddock, 'storming like a madman', and having had four horses shot from under him, at last ordered a withdrawal. Minutes afterwards he again fell, shot through the lung. After three hours under fire the confused mass of soldiers, heedless now of their officers, broke and poured back over the Monongahela, where Gage only succeeded in rallying sufficient men to cover what had now become a complete rout.

Braddock died two days later during the withdrawal back to Fort Cumberland. The defeat had been crushing. Sixty-three out of 86 officers had been killed or disabled and of the 1,373 men involved in the engagement only 459 escaped unharmed. The wounded left on the field were murdered by the Indians in their customary barbarous manner. The French lost seven officers and nine men and the Indians suffered less than 50 casualties. Of the other expeditions Monckton's was the only one to succeed, Fort Beauséjour being taken after a fortnight's siege.

The Indians now swarmed into Virginia, Maryland and Pennsylvania to murder and pillage, while Washington, who miraculously had survived the Battle of Monongahela, vainly attempted to protect 300 miles of frontier with 1,500 Militia and no help from the neighbouring provinces.

In England the effete administration now made feeble and belated attempts to counter the growing power of France. Two regiments were despatched to New York and four battalions of 'Royal Americans' (numbered the 60th) were raised locally. Over the next 18 months, however, Braddock's successor, Lord Loudon, conspicuously failed to counter the aggressive tactics of the Marquis of Montcalm. Oswego and Fort William Henry were both sacked by the French and Montcalm held Ticonderoga with 5,000 troops.

At this critical stage William Pitt came to power in Britain. Pitt was a man not only of strategic vision but a meticulous administrator of tireless energy. Turning as far as possible from continental involvement, he concentrated on blocking the French home ports and attacking their overseas possessions both in India and the New World. No fewer than eight regiments were dispatched to North America. Loudon was replaced by General Abercromby who took with him General Amherst and three new brigade commanders Lawrence, Whitmore and Wolfe. Working with feverish energy Pitt now prepared plans for three main operations for 1758, the Siege of Louisburg, an overland attack on Montreal and an advance to the Ohio. Nearly 26,000 Regular and 25,000 Provincial troops, five times as many as in any previous year, were to be employed in North America. Amherst himself was put in charge of the assault of Louisburg, for which 14,000 Regular troops were allocated.

The passage of the Regular troops from England, in a convoy commanded by Admiral Boscawen, took eleven weeks and it was the end of May, 1758, before a force of 157 ships with over 11,000 Regulars and about 500 Rangers sailed from Halifax to reach Gabarus Bay on 2 June. Amherst

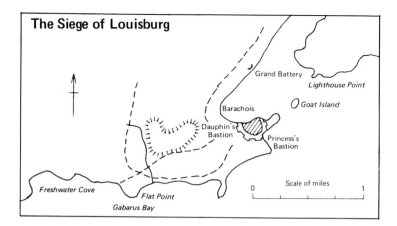

The Siege of Louisburg

immediately reconnoitred for landing places and decided there were three west of the town and one beyond the harbour's mouth. The most westerly point was Freshwater Cove about two miles from the landward defences of the fortress.

The fortress itself, triangular in shape, stood on the near point of the landlocked harbour, the entrance to which was covered by Goat Island battery. The French commander Ducour, a gallant and experienced officer, had 4,000 Regular troops, several companies of Canadians together with 236 cannon and mortars available for the defence of the fortress. Anchored in the harbour were twelve fully manned ships of the line and frigates mounting a considerable armament.

For five days fog and high seas prevented any disembarkation or further reconnaissance. The plan was to threaten all four landing places simultaneously, while the main effort was made by Wolfe at Freshwater Cove with a handpicked force of 13 companies of grenadiers, 550 marksmen picked from the different regiments, Frasers Highlanders and a body of Rangers. Finally, at dawn on 8 June, frigates followed by transports moved in and opened fire on the entrenchments. Fifteen minutes later on the extreme flank the boats carrying Wolfe's troops started pulling for the shore.

The cove extended for about 400 yards and the approaches were in fact covered by eight carefully concealed cannon and swivel guns and entrenchments manned by 1,000 men. The invaders were met at close range by a storm of grape and musket fire. Wolfe, judging the landing could but fail, had in fact signalled the boat to pull away when he saw that three boat loads of light infantry had succeeded in landing behind some rocks on the extreme right. The whole force now made for this point and the nearest

battery was taken with the bayonet. Lawrence's brigade and further reinforcements under Amherst now landed at the far end of the cove with little resistance. The French, fearing they would be cut off, poured back into Louisburg, abandoning 33 guns. The British losses totalled about 100. After much difficulty from the pounding surf and the loss of over a hundred boats, the siege guns and stores were now brought ashore at Flat Point, north of which Amherst established his camp.

The land approaches to the fortress were covered by extremely marshy ground except near the head of the harbour, at which point Amherst opened his siege operations. But first a road through deep mud and morasse, up which the guns and siege material could be moved, had to be built and screened by earthworks from the fire of a frigate anchored in the Barachois. These preparations took three weeks, and in this interval Wolfe marched round the harbour past the abandoned Grand Battery to reach Lighthouse Point where he set up his guns. With the help of the guns of the fleet the French battery on Goat Island was quickly silenced. Fearing a direct attack by the British fleet the French blocked the harbour mouth by scuttling six large ships. Meanwhile Wolfe had marched back to open siege works opposite the Princess's Bastion and on the evening of 16 July he personally led an assault on a small hill near the Dauphin's Bastion. All French efforts to dislodge his party failed and within five days a second parallel had been opened within two hundred yards of the ramparts. The same afternoon a lucky shell set fire to one of the French battleships. Blazing furiously she drifted from her mooring and fouled two other ships. Overnight the three ships completely burned out. A few nights later 600 British sailors quietly rowed into the harbour and boarded the two remaining ships of the line. 'One, being aground, was burned, and the other was towed off, in contempt of the fire from the fortress.'

Louisburg as a fortress proved to be a complete white elephant. The fortifications had cost the French a fortune but were never really completed. The masonry split each winter from the intense frost and could never be properly repaired during the short summer weeks, as fog and rain prevented the mortar from setting. By now a British battery had been established north of the Barachois Lagoon and the western face of the fortress was being steadily pounded in enfilade. The main barracks had long before been burned down and there was not a house in the town that had not been hit. One eyewitness recorded that in 36 hours 'a thousand or twelve hundred bombs, great and small, have been thrown into the town, accompanied all the time by the fire of forty pieces of cannon … the surgeon trembles as he amputates a limb amid cries of *Gare la bombe!* and leaves his patient in the midst of the operation, lest he should share his fate.'

By 26 July a breach had been opened and the last gun on the western face silenced. With the lives of 4,000 civilians and 1,200 wounded at stake, Ducour had no option but to capitulate. The next day Amherst's troops marched in. The French prisoners numbered 5,600 men and over 200 cannon and a large quantity of arms and stores were surrendered with the fortress. French casualties had been heavy particularly from sickness. The British losses in the whole siege were 500 all ranks killed and wounded. Much credit for the whole operation is due to Amherst, who left nothing to chance.

Abercromby's force of 7,000 Regular and 9,000 Provincial troops for the attack on Crown Point was assembled at the head of Lake George. This took some time as the river passage from Albany to Fort Edward involved three portages and the convoys had to be protected from attack by the Indians. Several of the British commanders had taken pains to learn something at first hand of Indian tactics. Brigadier Howe 'made officers and men, alike of Regular and of Provincial troops, throw off all use-less encumbrances; he cut the skirts off their coats and the hair off their heads, browned the barrels of their muskets, clad their lower limbs in leggings to protect them from briars, and filled the empty space in their knapsacks with thirty pounds of meal.' A Regiment formed for scouting and skirmishing was issued with 'dark brown skirtless coats without lace of any description' while 'officers were dismayed to find they were expected to wash their own clothes without the help of the regimental women and to carry their own knives and forks with them according to Howe's example.'

On 5 July Abercromby's force embarked in 1,200 canoes and whaleboats while *bateaux* carried the stores and baggage. At daybreak on 6 July, having driven back a French outpost the force landed on the western side of the narrows and rapids that joined with Lake Champlain, the approach to which was guarded by the French fort of Ticonderoga. On the opposite side of the narrows the French had cut a carrying place leading to a sawmill and a bridge, now destroyed. Ignoring this route Abercromby's force advanced into the virgin forest where one of the columns and the retreating French advance party, both having lost their directions, blundered into

each other. In the sharp engagement that ensued Lord Howe was killed and the whole of the British force thrown into confusion.

Montcalm was content to withdraw his outposts into the fort overnight and allow Abercromby to cross to the carrying place and rebuild the bridge unmolested. Abercromby was now within two miles of Ticonderoga. Montcalm, however, had set his garrison of 3,600 men to work and within 24 hours a massive breastworks of logs had been piled nine feet high on a ridge that crossed the peninsula about half a mile from the fort. In front of the breastworks the forest was felled, with the tops of the trees point-ing outwards, and the whole area covered with heavy boughs with sharpened points and branches interlaced to form an almost impenetrable obstacle. At dawn on 8 July Abercromby sent engineers to reconnoitre from the nearby hill Mount Defiance. Unfortunately he received a completely misleading report that the unfinished breastworks could be taken by direct assault. No attempt was made to recon-noitre the flanks or even bring up the guns that from Mount Defiance could have raked the breastworks from end to end. The assault was to be made with the bayonet.

Skirmishers drove in the French piquets but behind the breastworks eight battalions of Regulars and 450 Canadians were standing to arms, com-pletely concealed from the advancing columns that outnumbered them four to one. Coming out at last into the open, seven British regiments advanced into the maze of fallen trees, 'whose leaves hung wither-ing in the July sun', still only able to catch glimpses of the tops of the breastworks. With increasing difficulties the columns struggled forward and at the moment that those in the van suddenly found them-

Montcalm at Ticonderoga receiving the plaudits of the garrison after the repulse of the British

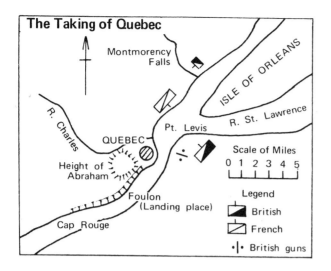

The Taking of Quebec

Montmorency Falls

ISLE OF ORLEANS

R. Charles

R. St. Lawrence

Pt. Levis

QUEBEC

Height of Abraham

Scale of Miles

0 1 2 3 4 5

Foulon (Landing place)

Cap Rouge

Legend

British

French

British guns

eight officers and 300 men killed and 17 officers and 316 men wounded. The French losses were less than 350. While Abercromby brooded over his misfortunes and did nothing, John Bradstreet, an energetic New Englander, succeeded in capturing Fort Frontenac and the entire French naval force of nine vessels on Lake Ontario. Fort Duquesne was now cut off and in the face of a determined advance by a small force, led by Brigadier Forbes in appalling weather, was blown up and abandoned by the French.

Abercromby was recalled and Amherst given overall command. His orders from Pitt were to send detachments to reoccupy Oswego and capture Fort Niagara while personally directing operations to open up the Lake Champlain route. At the same time Wolfe would sail up the St Lawrence and make the main effort against Quebec. The preliminary operations were completely successful and by early August 1759 the French had withdrawn to the northern end of Lake Champlain. The loss of Niagara and the obvious threat of Abercromby's advance considerably alarmed and depressed the Marquis de Vaudreuil, Governor of Quebec, and Montcalm now engaged in its defence.

Wolfe with 8,500 Regular troops and six companies of Rangers embarked in 21 ships left Louisburg on 6 June and after 'a superb feat of pilotage up the St Lawrence' landed on the Isle of Orleans three weeks later. An unsuccessful attempt to fire the fleet while at anchor was foiled by the British sailors who coolly rowed out and towed the fire ships clear, a useless enterprise that cost the French a million *livres* worth of shipping. Wolfe had meanwhile reconnoitred the city from across the river and sent Monckton's brigade to build batteries near Point Levis, which opened up on the night 12/13 July. In the first twelve hours of the bombardment over 3,000 bombs fell on the upper and lower town, causing much damage. By the end of August 29 guns were pounding Quebec and a number of serious fires had destroyed more than half the buildings. Believing that no foreign ship would attempt the intricate navigation of the river above the town, Montcalm had drawn up his forces of five Regular battalions supplemented by Canadians (totalling some 14,000 men) to cover the north bank of the river between the cataracts of the Montmorency and the St Charles River. On the walls of Quebec itself over a hundred cannon were mounted

selves right against the high defences, where the piled logs afforded innumerable loopholes, the whole 'breastwork broke into a sheet of flame and a storm of grape and musketry swept the ranks from end to end.' After an hour of desperate attempts to scale or even reach the breastworks the attack fell back, the commanders considering the position impregnable. Abercromby, who had never left the sawmills, promptly ordered a renewal of the assault. The main action had started about 2.00 p.m. and throughout five separate attacks the slaughter continued. The 42nd Highlanders, held back in reserve, were unable to stand by and watch the agony of their comrades trapped in the maze of fallen trees. Drawing their claymores the men rushed forward to cut their way through and climbed on each other's shoulders in an attempt to scale the defences, but to no avail. One such rush, made to a flank, had a fleeting chance of success when an officer and a few men scaled the breastworks. But Montcalm personally led forward his reserves and the gallant Highlanders were bayoneted to a man. After five hours fruitless effort the 'Retreat' was sounded. The Highlanders, who had fought throughout with a cold fury and a complete disregard for casualties, at first refused to abandon their wounded. The withdrawal, marred by many instances of panic and ill-discipline, did not stop until Abercromby's humiliated force, having suffered nearly 2,000 casualties in killed and wounded, reached the original embarkation point at the head of Lake George. The casualties to the 42nd were appalling –

Opposite: The Battle of Blenheim, 13 August 1704. The British under Lord Cutts attack the village of Blenheim. A water-colour by R. W. Simkin

Overleaf left, above: The Battle of Ramillies, 23 May 1706. Marlborough and his staff under fire

Below: The Marquis of Granby with a sick soldier. He was famous for the consideration he showed to his men. Painted by Edward Penney (1714–91)

Overleaf right: The First Viscount Southwell in the uniform of the Coldstream Regiment of Foot Guards, c. 1738. From a portrait attributed to Charles Gervas (1675–1739)

and a floating battery of twelve heavy guns and several gunboats guarded the approaches to the St Charles.

Wolfe now concentrated his two remaining brigades on the eastern side of the Montmorency Gorge. Meanwhile on the night of 18 July HMS *Sutherland* slipped past the French batteries and anchored above the city and a detachment of Rangers was sent to ravage the countryside to the west of Quebec; but Montcalm could not be drawn from his main entrenchment. With no other plan and the weeks slipping by, Wolfe accepted the challenge and decided to attempt a landing with 5,000 men across the strand west of the Montmorency, hoping to draw Montcalm into a general action. HMS *Centurion* and two armed transports covered the troops from Point Levis who rowed out to make a demonstration opposite the French camp. The landing was led by a body of Grenadiers and the 60th who carried a redoubt on the edge of the mud-flats. The assault however failed and drenching rain halted the action, but Wolfe lost 500 of his best troops.

Wolfe now set about strengthening his hold on the only supply route left to the French, the St Lawrence itself. More and more British ships slipped past the town batteries and a force under Murray carried out raids to destroy any magazines of stores that could be found. The French garrison was now on short rations and their only hope was that winter conditions would drive the British shipping out of the river before Quebec was starved out. Exhausted by hard work and anxiety, Wolfe fell seriously ill. Still all his plans aimed at attacking the main French entrenchment. The Brigadiers, however, had their own ideas 'to direct the operations above the town', arguing that Montcalm would then be compelled to 'fight us on our own terms'. Somewhat recovered, but still in great pain, Wolfe now lost no time. The evacuation of the Montmorency camp was skilfully carried out and the main body reassembled close to Point Levis, leaving two battalions to guard the Isle of Orleans and Point Levis itself.

By 7 July a force of about 3,600 men had embarked in Admiral Holmes's squadron and sailed up to Cap Rouge. Here a French force of 3,000 men under Bougainville were occupied in keeping an eye on the movement of the British shipping up and down the river, while nearer the town three fortified posts were built to cover paths up the cliff face. The next three days were spent on reconnoitring down the river. One of the posts closely examined from across the river by Wolfe and his commanders was the small

Left: General Wolfe, the captor of Quebec. An engraving by J. Chapman. *Right:* Field Marshal Lord Amherst. He captured Louisburg, Fort Duquesne, Ticonderoga, Crown Point and Montreal

cove at Anse du Foulon. The chief engineer Major Mackellar later wrote, 'the bank which runs along the shore is very steep and woody, and was thought so impracticable by the French themselves, that they had then only a single picket (of about 100 men) to defend it.' A narrow path running up from the shore was 'barricaded with an abattis, but about 200 yards to the right there appeared to be a slope in the bank, which was thought might answer the purpose'.

Montcalm was convinced that Wolfe's departure upstream was a ruse to draw him away from the Beaufort positions. The food situation was worse than ever and he had had to send away 3,000 Canadians to help save the harvest. Wolfe now completed his plans. Orders were given for the two guard battalions to move up opposite Foulon, and Admiral Saunders assembled the main part of the fleet opposite Beaufort so as to simulate landing preparations. On the evening of 12 September Holmes's squadron with the transports and armed sloops once more moved upstream in the hopes of drawing off Bougainville's mobile column. At 1.35 a.m. on 13 September the tide began to ebb and the ships' boats, with the first flight of 1,800 men, dropped off down stream, followed three-quarters of an hour later by the whole assembly of shipping. Only HMS *Sutherland* remained off Cap Rouge. The well-known incident of the approaching boats being

Opposite: British troops landing on Dominica, 6 June 1761. After the capture of Canada, Pitt, exploiting sea-power, sent troops from North America to attack the French West Indian possessions. The picture shows Lord Rollo's men landing at Roseau; they captured the island by the next day. Painted on the spot by Lt Campbell

The attack on Quebec. The picture shows three phases of the operation: the ship to shore movement, the scaling of the heights, and the battle that followed

challenged by French sentries was noted by Townshend, 'Captn Frazer who had been in ye Dutch Service & spoke french – answered – la France & vive le Roy, on which ye French Centinels ran along ye Shore in ye dark crying laisser les passer ils sont nos Gens avec les provisions. ...'

Wolfe probably intended to land upstream of the Foulon cove but the first boats struck the gravelly beach just below the path shortly before first light. Having landed without being fired on and keeping clear of the path, Colonel Howe led his light infantry straight up the face of the cliff, pulling 'themselves by the stumps and boughs of trees that cover'd the declivity.' The French pickets were taken in the flank and quickly dealt with. According to Mackellar's account the follow-up battalions 'were formed upon the beach as they landed and now began to get up the bank and form above. ...' It was now about 'clear daylight', the landing having started at about 4.00 a.m., and the boats were moving back to bring in the next flight. The whole force, including the two battalions from the south bank was assembled in battle order at the top of the cliff by 8.00 a.m. – a truly remarkable and successful combined operation. Wolfe himself had mean-

while completed a personal reconnaissance of the ground towards the town.

Vaudreuil was first told that the landing was on the lower town but at 6.45 a.m. he sent word to Bougainville that the landing was at Foulon. It is uncertain when Montcalm learned the news. Most of his men had been kept up all night by Saunders' diversionary moves. By 7.00 a.m., however, the regiments were on the march streaming across the floating bridge to the heights beyond Quebec where Wolfe waited. At last Montcalm was out in the open.

By about 9.30 a.m. Montcalm reached the Heights of Abraham with 4,500 men and halted some 600 paces from the British. His five Regular regiments, flanked by Canadian Militia battalions, were formed in line with skirmishers spread right and left. Astride the road to Sillery six British regiments supported by only two guns were drawn up in line, a scarlet thread of men standing three deep. The 48th was in reserve and a battalion of Royal Americans guarded each flank, while the 15th blocked the road along which Bougainville might soon appear. Under the fire of about five guns and the large number of skirmishers the British were already suffering casualties and on Wolfe's orders lay down on their

62

arms. They did not have to wait long. At Montcalm's order the drums rolled and with a loud cheer the French advanced at a run. Before them now stood a thin wall of men immobile and silent. The French opened fire at about 130 yards, the Canadians kneeling and then throwing themselves down to reload, and their line soon lost cohesion. Still there was no movement by the British and it was not until the uneven ranks of the French Regulars were considerably closer that the order was given for fire by platoons in succession. Then with the British ranks advancing with perfect discipline to clear the smoke and with the range now less than 30 paces a general volley crashed into Montcalm's men. As the smoke cleared the ranks of the French regiments were seen to waver and turn and then pour back towards the city.

The whole action had only lasted a few minutes and the British were now advancing with the bayonet and claymore, checked only by fire from some Canadian skirmishers who for a time stood their ground. On the battlefield Wolfe lay dying, wounded for a third time as he led the 28th forward in pursuit. But the British victory was complete. The casualties

on both sides were heavy. The British losses were 58 killed and about 600 wounded and were mostly incurred during the pursuit. Montcalm's army was shattered and he himself lay mortally wounded in the city where there were barely enough men to man the walls. Bougainville had turned back and Vaudreuil was already hurrying west toward Jacques Cartier with the survivors of his army. Brigadier Townshend took the surrender of Quebec five days later.

The following spring the French made a determined effort in the action at St Foy to retake Quebec but this was their last counter attack. By the autumn of 1760 Amherst, 'with great patience' and displaying a remarkable talent for organisation, had assembled 17,000 men outside Montreal and on 8 September took the surrender of the garrison of 3,000 men, all that remained of the French Army in Canada.

French power in North America was now spent. In India Britain was gaining the upper hand, and a bitter struggle still raged in Europe. But when the war was ended by the Treaty of Paris, 1763, France relinquished to Britain all her Canadian territories.

Carved contemporary powder horn. It shows New York and the country traversed by troops from that city during the conquest of Canada. Photographed by Francis of Camberley

63

CHAPTER 7

The Seven Years' War –
The Campaigns in
Western Germany
1757–63

SIR REGINALD SAVORY

CHRONOLOGICAL TABLE

1757	26 March	Opening of hostilities
	26 July	Battle of Hastenbeck
	8 September	Convention of Kloster Zeven
	23 November	Ferdinand of Brunswick takes command
1758	12 June	Action at Rheinberg
	23 June	Battle of Krefeld
	5 August	Action at Mehr
	23 July	Action at Sandershausen
	17 August	First British contingent arrives at Coesfeld
	10 October	Action at Lutterberg
1759	13 April	Battle of Bergen
	1 August	Battle of Minden
1760	7 January	Operations round Dillenberg
	17 June	Second British contingent arrives
	10 July	Action at Korbach
	16 July	Action at Emsdorf
	31 July	Battle of Warburg
	1 September	Action at Löwenhagen
	15 October	Battle of Kloster Kamp
1761	21 March	Action at Grunberg
	15-16 July	Battle of Vellinghausen
1762	19 April	Capture of Arnsberg
	24 June	Battle of Wilhelmsthal
	23 July	Battle of Lutterberg
	30 August	Battle of Nauheim
	22 September	Action at Brücke Mühle
	1 November	Capitulation of Kassel
1763		
	16 February	Treaty of Paris

As in North America the war opened with a disaster. In July 1757, 'His Britannic Majesty's Army in Germany', composed mainly of Hanoverians, was defeated at Hastenbeck, near Hameln on the Weser, and withdrew to the mouth of the Elbe. On the 8 September its commander the Duke of Cumberland signed a Convention by which his army was to be dispersed. This Convention was not ratified by either of the two contestants. The Duke of Cumberland was recalled and relieved by Prince Ferdinand of Brunswick fresh from the Prussian victory at Rossbach. No sooner had he assumed command than he surprised the French, drove them out of Germany and in June 1758 crossed the Rhine and defeated them at Krefeld.

This victory aroused such enthusiasm in England that six regiments of infantry and six of cavalry were sent to Germany.

They disembarked at Emden on 3 August 1758 and marched to join Ferdinand's veterans just back from their successful operations across the Rhine.

It was nearly a year before they had any fighting, though three of the cavalry regiments were at Bergen, near Frankfurt, where Ferdinand was defeated in April 1759 and forced to withdraw northwards. He was followed by the French under the Marquis de Contades. On his way north, he was joined by the rest of the British contingent and together they all marched on Osnabrück. But Contades did not follow him directly. Instead he made for Minden, one of Ferdinand's fortified supply-bases situated on the bank of the Weser; it was of great strategic importance. On 9 July 1759, Contades captured it. He was now astride Ferdinand's communications, blocking his way down the Weser to his base at Bremen and threatening the road to Hanover.

Ferdinand, now in grave danger, marched at once to the Weser. Near Kutenhausen, he prepared

Opposite above: The Battle of Minden. Kingsley's brigade repulses the French. A water-colour by Harry Payne. *Below:* The action at Emsdorf. In this brilliant affair the 15th Light Dragoons captured sixteen French colours, nine guns and 1,655 prisoners. A painting by Gilbert Halliday.

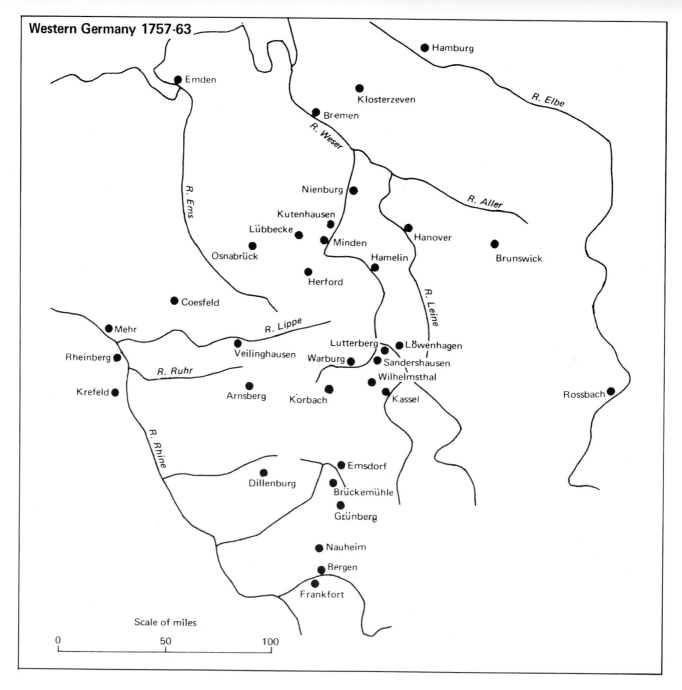

Western Germany 1757-63

Hamburg

Emden

Klosterzeven

R. Elbe

Bremen

R. Weser

R. Aller

R. Ems

Nienburg

Kutenhausen

Lübbecke

Hanover

Minden

Brunswick

Osnabrück

Hamelin

Herford

R. Leine

Coesfeld

Mehr

R. Lippe

Rheinberg

Lutterberg

Löwenhagen

R. Ruhr

Veilinghausen

Warburg

Sandershausen

Krefeld

Wilhelmsthal

Arnsberg

Korbach

Kassel

Rossbach

R. Rhine

Emsdorf

Dillenburg

Brückemühle

Grünberg

Nauheim

Bergen

Frankfort

Scale of miles

0   50   100

an entrenched position covering his advance base at Nienburg; and there he decided to stand and fight.

It took Contades six days to draw in the tail of his long marching column and concentrate his army in an almost impregnable camp south of Minden, with 'his back covered by the Weser; his front by the marsh and the Bastau stream; his left on the hills; and his right on Minden. ... It is impossible' wrote Ferdinand, 'to have a stronger one. On the other hand, the enemy cannot leave his camp except at a disadvantage. ...'

The two armies then faced each other across a no-mans-land some four miles wide, with Ferdinand trying to tempt Contades to come out and fight and Contades refusing. Otherwise all was pretty quiet.

Mounted patrols were out in front passing each other sometimes so close that the officers exchanged bows. There were occasional clashes. In one of these a mortally wounded British dragoon was taken prisoner. He was well looked after; but when a kindly French officer enquired if he had any dying wish, the dragoon replied 'God damn the French' and promptly expired. This little story went the rounds of both armies, confirming the reputation of the British soldier of those days as a tough if godless warrior.

Ferdinand, having failed so far to bring Contades to battle, decided to shift him by threatening his communications. So, on 27 July, he sent his nephew the Erbprinz with some 9,000 men across the hills near Lübbecke to march on Gohfeld and seize the bridge there. Then, leaving General Wangenheim to hold the Kutenhausen position with 15 battalions, 7 cavalry regiments and 24 guns, he moved his main army from its camp, four miles north of Kutenhausen, to another between Hille and Friedewalde. There he was so placed as to be able either to help the Erbprinz should Contades turn against him or engage Contades should he come north into the Minden plain. There was no secrecy about this move. It was made with bands playing and colours flying just as it was getting light on the morning of the 29th.

While his troops were marching and settling into camp, Ferdinand rode ahead to reconnoitre a position on which his army was to form-up should the French come into the plain. He chose a line between the villages of Hahlen and Stemmer, about three miles in front of the new camp, and ordered his staff to ensure that the troops could occupy it, whether by day or night, without confusion.

The move forward was to be made in eight columns, each moving by its special route. Each route was to be carefully prepared. Gaps were to be made in walls and hedges where necessary, particularly in Nord Hemmern; foot bridges constructed over the marshy-banked Lander stream; local guides engaged and instructed; nothing was to be left to chance.

The right column was to consist of six British and five Hanoverian cavalry regiments all under the command of Lt-Gen. Lord George Sackville, with the Marquis of Granby as his second-in-command. Then came a column of guns followed by the British infantry, consisting of two brigades; the first-line under Maj-Gen. Lord Waldegrave contained three British and two Hanoverian battalions: the second-line under Colonel Kingsley contained three British battalions. There was also a 'brigade' of British light artillery (nine guns) under a Captain Macbean. The whole was commanded by a Hanoverian General Spörcken.

To their left came three more infantry columns and one of cavalry, in that order. In the centre of the whole was a strong column of artillery.

By about midday, then, on 29 July, Ferdinand had perfected his plan. His patrols were out; and he, at his headquarters at Hille, was sifting their information as it came in. Two days passed. All reports indicated an enemy concentration on Minden. The question was whether the French would then turn south towards Gohfeld or north into the plain. On the 31st, Ferdinand himself climbed the Wiehen Gebirge, had a look, and concluded that it was to be the plain. He returned to camp; summoned his generals at 5.00 p.m.; ordered them to have their troops ready by 1.00 a.m. (as usual) with the men dressed and accoutred, the horses saddled, and the gun-teams harnessed, but not to stand to arms until further orders. He also pressed them to make themselves familiar with the positions they would have to occupy and the routes leading to them.

Thus, while the generals and their staffs bustled about, the men got ready, and stood around; and probably grumbled, for they had often done this before and there had been so many false alarms. Only this morning, shots had been fired near Hartum, but it had merely been some locals having a pot at the plovers. …

The outposts watched and listened and, although Ferdinand had told them to be specially alert that night, reported nothing. Not even a negative report came in. The hours of darkness passed peacefully enough, disturbed only by a violent storm, until at about 3.30 a.m., two French deserters were escorted into Hille. They had come from Hartum where the Prinz von Anhalt, commander of the outposts, had kept them waiting for five valuable hours: and the information which they brought was of the most pressing importance. … The French army had begun crossing the Bastau at midnight!

There was no time to lose. The army must stand to arms at once and go forward. 'In less than eight minutes' the 20th Foot, who with the 12th Foot were guarding Ferdinand's headquarters, had turned out and were on their way (two miles) to join Kingsley's brigade. A few minutes more, and the whole army was hurrying forward in column of route. All, that is, except Sackville's cavalry, which, not having saddled-up as ordered, was late.

Ferdinand had been taken unawares. His outposts had failed him. And when those two deserters had arrived at Hartum, Prinz Anhalt had not realised the significance of what they said and had delayed in sending them on; it is even possible that he resented being disturbed at that hour of the night and kept them waiting. We shall never know. …

Ferdinand's first action after getting his army on the move was to gallop over to Anhalt and order him to collect his men (some 1,600 infantry, 200 cavalry and 9 British guns under Captain Foy) and occupy Hahlen before the French could get there. It was then about 5.00 a.m. and broad daylight. He went on, accompanied only by his orderly and discovered that the French were already in the village. This was a shock. If the enemy were in Hahlen, what was happening on the rest of the front? Still accompanied only by his orderly, he rode along to the left. A strong French force was advancing on Kutenhausen. Todtenhausen was in flames: the west wind was blowing almost a gale and no sound of battle was audible. Then Ferdinand galloped back along the heads of his advancing columns, meeting their generals on the way and telling them to hurry. It was going to be a near thing. If the French deployed first, they could catch his army on the move when it would be very vulnerable. Then he returned to Hahlen. Anhalt's men were halted outside. Ferdinand brusquely ordered them to attack. The heterogeneous collection of picquets stormed forward. The houses caught fire. The wind fanned the flames. The French, unable to stand the heat, withdrew to the eastern outskirts. Foy's guns helped them on their way and Anhalt occupied the rest of the village.

Meanwhile, Waldegrave's brigade had appeared on the scene. Hurrying forward in columns of fours, they were ahead of the rest. As they approached the windmill near Hahlen, Spörcken deployed them into half-battalions (i.e. each battalion in two lines) and sent Macbean's guns to join Foy's and cover them while doing so.

It was then that Ferdinand gave an order which

The Battle of Minden from a contemporary print.
Ferdinand of Brunswick watches the British
infantry shatter the first line of the French cavalry

was destined to upset not only his whole plan but that of the French too. This order was that 'when the troops advance, they will do so with drums beating'. But the ADC who took it to Spörcken and Waldegrave (a certain Count Taube) gave it as 'Your regiments will advance with drums beating and attack whatever lies in front'. ... Up rose Waldegrave's infantry and off they dashed. Giving no time for Kingsley's men to deploy, they raced ahead so fast that they left their own battalion-guns behind and were soon in front of all the other columns. If they went on like this, they would be dangerously isolated. So Ferdinand sent Taube again telling Waldegrave to halt and adding that if he allowed his men to double, they would be out of breath when they reached the enemy. Then, to quote Ferdinand's own words, 'they made a little halt, near a little copse, which gave some protection, and then broke out again and, with proud and defiant bearing, marched on the enemy with such spirit that the second line and the artillery of the centre could scarcely keep up. ...!' Nothing could stop them; not even their own Commander-in-Chief! Nor could the French artillery, which was pounding Waldegrave and Kingsley (hurrying along behind) and inflicting cruel casualties. 'I saw', wrote Lt. Thomas of the 20th Foot, 'heads, legs and arms taken off. My right-hand file of men ... were by one ball dashed to pieces and their blood flying over. ...'

Waldegrave's battalions, very naturally and probably unwittingly, veered away from those guns and inclined to their left; and in so doing, moved across the front of the next column and crowded them out, leaving room for only one battalion to squeeze in. So Waldegrave now had six battalions, three British and three Hanoverian. On they went, marching diagonally to their left and going straight at the French cavalry which, instead of being on the flanks as was their custom, were in the middle. ... Those proud and glittering horsemen could not believe their eyes. That mere 'foot' should attack unshaken 'horse' was unheard of. Such impudence deserved to be taught a lesson. ... Eleven squadrons of the French front line drew their sabres and galloped down on Waldegrave's battalions, who halted and prepared to receive them. Each battalion was arrayed in two lines (half-battalions) each of three ranks, the front two kneeling and the third standing. ... What a test this was going to be. ... Each man could fire one round and then, while reloading would be very vulnerable. Every shot would have to tell. ...

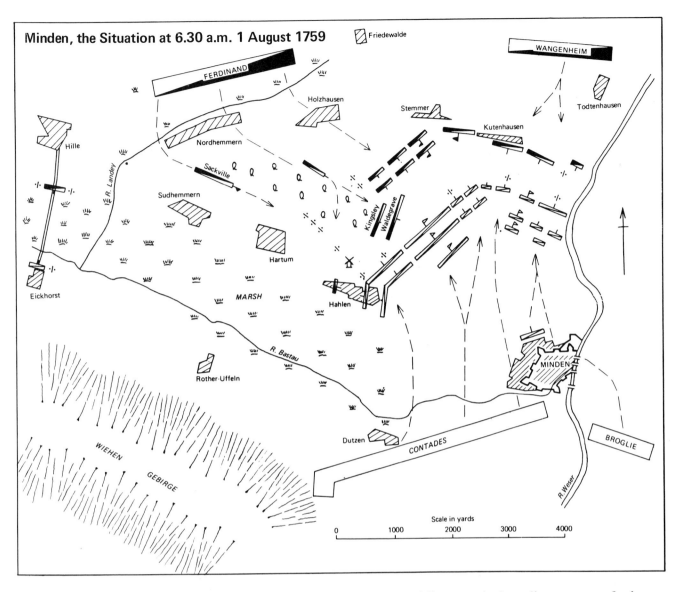

Minden, the Situation at 6.30 a.m. 1 August 1759

A French eye-witness describes what then happened ... '... the enemy', he wrote, 'were unmoved. They waited until our cavalry were ten paces off; met them with a brisk and well-sustained fire; and finished off with the bayonet those who reached the front rank. ...'

The infantry closed the ranks, distributed the ammunition from the wounded and dead, passed the wounded to the rear, pulled the dead out of the way and were preparing to advance again, when in came another charge.[1]

This was no unsupported onslaught. It was led by Lt-Gen. du Mesnil and backed by the fire of 30 guns and had it not been for the British and Hanoverian artillery, now reinforced, the result of this great battle might have been very different. Twenty-two

[1] When the fighting was at its height, Ferdinand received a message from Wangenheim. Written at 3.00 a.m. it said that he had no news of the enemy and that their camps had not changed. At that very moment Wangenheim was about to be attacked!

squadrons fell upon six battalions, some of whom gave ground, but in the end all stood firm, holding their fire and then letting the French have it. A few brave cavaliers got in among the infantry but only to be shot down and bayoneted as they lay. Once more the ranks were closed; once more the ammunition was distributed; and then these gallants waited no longer to be attacked, but went into the attack themselves. With tattered colours, with drums beating, with furious bravery, faster than ever, on they stormed.

But they exposed their right flank even more than before; and Count Guerchy, commanding the infantry on the French left, decided on his own initiative to drive them back. Eight fresh battalions assaulted Waldegrave's battered six. Kingsley, who had come up, having suffered heavily on the way, formed his men half-right to meet them; and Ferdinand, seeing the danger, sent round to their support those five battalions which had been

E

The action at Warburg. The Marquis of Granby, losing hat and wig, goes 'bald-headed' for the enemy. A painting by Gilbert Halliday

crowded out by Waldegrave's impetuous advance.

Scarcely had they got on the move than another charge came thundering down. This was by two of France's crack cavalry regiments, the Gendarmerie de France and the Carabiniers, 18 squadrons led by Lt-Gen. de Poyanne.

Both attacks arrived almost simultaneously. Guerchy's infantry suffered so heavily from the British and Hanoverian guns that they wavered and withdrew.

Poyanne's attack really was dangerous. It fell chiefly on Waldegrave's flanks and rear. His rear ranks turned about and stood back to back with their comrades: so did Kingsley's. ... The officers steadied their men ... and then the charging Frenchmen were on them. Once again, with superb discipline, that fire was held; once again that controlled salvo rang out, but probably not quite so imperturbably as before. Some of the attackers hacked through Waldegrave's lines, only to be met by the murderous fire of Kingsley's in support and of the German column on their left which had drawn level. Then followed hand-to-hand fighting; bayonet versus sabre; and no mercy. Shoulder to shoulder the infantry stood against the weight and momentum of those galloping cavalry, and, to quote Ferdinand's

own words 'Not a man flinched'. Seldom can the strict discipline of the barrack-square have been better vindicated. ... It was all the work of a few minutes; and in a few more minutes all was over. The Gendarmerie and Carabiniers between them lost no fewer than 76 officers killed and wounded; and the survivors made their way back as best they could, leaving the ground littered with men and horses.

There followed a lull. Some of the infantry broke ranks and searched the dead for souvenirs. The Hanoverian Guards picked up 20 (some say 80) gold watches; and their officers discarding their pikes (spontoons) armed themselves with cavalry sabres. But order was restored and they went on, picking their way past dead and wounded and all the strewn débris of a battlefield.

By then it was only about 8.00 a.m. and fighting had spread all along the line, where it raged intense and bitter, with horse, foot and even guns mixed in mêlée and local commanders acting on their own.

Spörcken's men, battered but unyielding, pushed grimly on. They were isolated no longer, for those five battalions had come up on their right and 29 extra guns had joined those near the windmill. When, therefore, 13 battalions of Saxons sallied out from behind Hahlen, Spörcken was able to deal with them. Their attack was bravely pressed, but broke down under the fire of the guns; and they withdrew, forming square as they went, for Sackville's cavalry were nearby and uncommitted.

One final charge was attempted, under Lt-Gen. de Vogué, but it had to negotiate such a labyrinth of dead and wounded men and horses, dismounted troopers trying to get clear and loose horses galloping frenzied about that it lost cohesion and was not pressed.

But where all this while was Lt-Gen. the Lord George Sackville? ... Where indeed? ... 'Has no one seen the cavalry of the right wing?' Ferdinand was heard to exclaim. And then, exasperated, 'My God! Is there no way of getting these cavalry to advance?'

Not one of the aides-de-camp sent to Sackville, ordering and almost imploring him to advance, had met with more than mere evasion; and when Lord Granby, his second-in-command, (during Sackville's temporary absence to receive Ferdinand's personal orders) led them forward on his own responsibility, they were halted by Sackville on his return. And so those fine regiments were kept safely out of cannon shot while their countrymen were fighting for and losing their lives. When at length they did move, they went to the edge of the marsh and dismounted. By then the fighting was finished and the French were streaming back, sped by the British and Hanoverian light artillery, which had gone forward to the Bastau.

As for Spörcken's infantry, they stopped (without orders; and who can blame them?) near the heavy guns which had supported them so nobly, and began to lick their wounds. But not for long, for the adjutant-general galloped up and ordered the heavy guns to join the light and the infantry to accompany them. A few more parting shots were fired. Then, about midday, all was over.

What a day it had been for Spörcken's column! Having received a distorted order, they had advanced too soon and too fast and then had gone in the wrong direction! But their dash was so great, their fire-discipline so strict and their bravery so sublime that they carried all before them and won everlasting fame. Even Contades paid them tribute. In his despatch, written on 11 August, he wrote … 'Eight or ten battalions on an open heath have defeated sixty-one French squadrons; if I had not seen it, I would not have believed it'.

There was no immediate pursuit. Ferdinand's army paraded next day to fire a *feu-de-joie* and sing a *Te Deum*. The British infantry appeared wearing in their caps roses plucked from the cottage gardens. The British cavalry 'full of ardour and spirit' appeared 'in mournful silence, as if covered in shame … sending Mylord George to the devil'. Thus wrote Ferdinand's secretary and added 'Minden resembles Rossbach; but had it not been for Mylord George, it could have been a Blenheim'.

A fortnight later Ferdinand wrote to King George II, saying that unless Sackville was recalled, he himself would serve no more. On 23 August, Sackville departed. He was replaced by the Marquis of Granby, with strict instructions to obey 'all military orders which His Serene Highness the Duke Ferdinand should see fit to give you'.

Granby was a generous, genial character, much loved by his men, but regarded by many of his officers as very easy-going. According to them, he dealt too leniently with deserters. Perhaps the officers were right: it is always difficult to draw the line. But the men were '… haris'd almost out of their lives with duty and the want of the common necessaries of life, that cannot be procured with no regularity, as our bread waggons come very uncertain … we dress and accoutre every morning at two o'clock and the Rolls is called at five o'clock and several other times in the day. …' Thus wrote Corporal Todd of the 12th Foot; and it is difficult not to feel considerable sympathy with him. But Captain Bell of the 5th Foot had different ideas. '… our men desert fast', he wrote, 'owing to the shameful timidity of Lord Granby who will never execute any that are caught …' Be that as it may, Granby was a 'soldier's general' and certainly not lacking in courage. It was under him that the British cavalry re-established its reputation.

At Warburg on the river Diemel on 31 July 1760, a year after Minden, a strong French force was drawn up facing east with the river at its back. Its left flank had been attacked at dawn, but the frontal attack by 16 British battalions was so delayed by bogs and standing corn that they could not get up in time, strive as they might. Ferdinand ordered Granby to pass through the struggling and exhausted infantry and charge. Granby rose nobly to the occasion. His 22 squadrons had some five miles to cover and, trotting and cantering most of the way, they at last bore down upon the French. Granby in the excitement of the moment lost his hat, but his bald head shining in the sun (it was a sweltering day) acted as a beacon for his men to follow and, catching the French cavalry in the act of preparing to withdraw, he burst 'bald-headed' among them. Two brigades of French cavalry counter-attacked, but they were counter-charged by Granby's own regiment, The Blues, and routed. On swept the British cavalry among the fleeing French. Up swept the British artillery who had followed close behind, and completed the rout by shooting at the fugitives as they floundered across the shallow river. Minden was avenged; and the cavalry who were present that day now bear the battle-honour 'Warburg' with as much pride as the infantry do 'Minden'.

The war went on. The British troops fought with their usual bravery at Kloster Kamp, Vellinghausen, Wilhelmsthal and the Brücke Mühle, where, on 15 November 1762, hostilities ceased. They had upheld their reputation for 'unshakable courage, great tenacity in defence, and often reckless dash in attack', but were said to be 'difficult to discipline, quarrelsome in quarters and haughty in their attitude to other troops'. As for their generals; they 'knew little about war', but learnt as they went along! Nevertheless, the British contingent was the backbone of that army whose exploits caused Pitt to declare in the House of Commons on 13 November 1761: 'America has been conquered in Germany, where Prince Ferdinand's victories have shattered the whole military power of that great Military monarchy, France.'

CHAPTER 8

The Establishment
of British Power in India
1615–1761

JAMES P. LAWFORD

The bitter feud between the French and British in India reached its climax during the Seven Years' War, but the feud itself had started long before.

Early in the seventeenth century a joint stock company, the East India Company, solicited and received a royal charter which authorised it to be the sole British trader with the East Indies. In 1615 James I despatched Sir Thomas Roe as his ambassador to the court of Jehangir, the Mogul Emperor of India. In 1618 the company received authority from the Emperor to establish 'factories'. In 1639 Fort St George was built at Madras. In 1662 Catherine of Braganza brought Bombay under the British Crown as part of her dowry, and in 1690 Job Charnocke founded Calcutta.

During the seventeenth century the Honourable East India Company, as it became, depended on the sanction of the Mogul Emperor and the favour of the local princes for its existence. With the coming of the eighteenth century, however, the rule of the Moguls began to collapse. In central India the great Mahratta confederacy broke away, and in the south the Mogul viceroy, the Nizam, ruler of the Deccan, declared his independence. Princes, known as rajahs or nawabs, who had ruled provinces and states in the name of the Emperor discarded their allegiance. Now that the Emperor lacked the power to nominate a successor, the death of a ruler almost invariably provoked dispute, assassination and strife.

It was no easy time for traders. To add to the difficulties of the company whose shareholders, in common with most, preferred dividends to explanations, a new, energetic and thrusting rival had appeared on the Indian scene. In 1673, at Pondicherry on the east coast of India some 150 miles

Opposite: Robert Clive

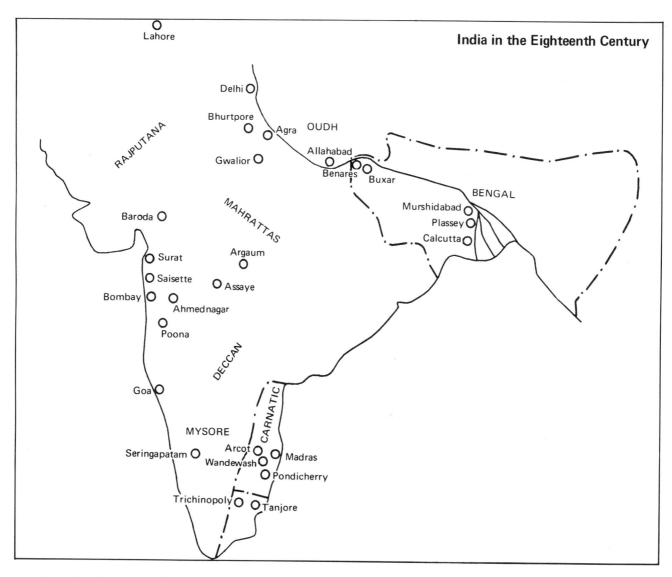

south of Madras, the French founded one great trading centre, and at Chandernagore, uncomfortably close to Calcutta, another.

The French at Pondicherry at first under Dumas, and then under their great governor, Dupleix, began to meddle in the Indian civil wars. Then in 1744 the war of the Austrian Succession brought Britain and France into conflict. Both Madras and Pondicherry lay within the Carnatic, a province ruled by a Nawab called Anwar-ud-din who had ousted the old dynasty and owed his position to the Mogul viceroy, the Nizam. Dupleix, threatened by a British fleet off Pondicherry, appealed to Anwar-ud-din to prevent the European war spreading to Indian soil. Anwar-ud-din duly issued a prohibition and the British fleet sailed away. Two years later, however, on the appearance of a French fleet, Dupleix promptly besieged Madras. Fort St George fell after a week, two British and four 'others' were killed; the defence was less than spirited.

His action had far-reaching consequences. In London the directors of the company realised that while trained soldiers might eat up dividends they might also be a horrid necessity to avoid a heavy capital loss. In India the results were of even greater significance. Anwar-ud-din, incensed by the French action, sent an army of 10,000 men to recapture Madras. In November 1746 near the village of St Thomé a few miles from Madras, a French force amounting to 230 European soldiers and 750 sepoys (European-trained Indian soldiers), under the command of a Swiss officer named Paradis, encountered Anwar-ud-din's army. Paradis recognised that if he retreated he was lost. He boldly led his little force against his enemy and after a brief combat routed them. Suddenly it was revealed that the great technical skills, particularly in musketry and artillery fire, that a century of almost constant warfare had taught the very professional armies of Europe, gave European trained soldiers a tactical advantage over the ill-organised hosts of the Indian princes comparable to that enjoyed by the Roman legionaries over their barbarian foes in the days when the power of Imperial Rome was at its height. A new era had begun.

At the Treaty of Aix-la-Chapelle in 1748 the French handed back Madras to the East India Company. But although peace had been declared the next few years, thanks to the genius of Dupleix, were to bring perils that nearly proved fatal to British interests in India.

Two men saved the company, John Stringer Lawrence and Robert Clive. Lawrence, a regular captain aged 49 recently retired after service during the rebellion of 1745, was hired by the company at a salary of £250 a year. He was a quiet unassuming man with the valuable if rare military habit of winning battles. Clive, originally his subordinate, was the founding hero of the British Empire in India.

Lawrence on arrival in India at once set about organising a proper military force. He constituted seven European companies each of a captain, a lieutenant, an ensign, four sergeants, four corporals, three drummers and 70 rank and file. These companies eventually formed the Madras European battalion. They served with great distinction, their descendants as 'Neill's blue caps' won fame during the Indian Mutiny and, as the Royal Dublin Fusiliers, equal renown at Gallipoli. Lawrence organised Indian sepoy companies in the same way each under command of an Indian officer known as a 'subedar'. British officers commanded a sepoy company or a number of them as the occasion required.

It was well that Lawrence had turned the ragtag and bob-tail of store guards and policemen that had hitherto been the company's soldiers into a regular force, as Dupleix had planned and carried out a master stroke.

The old Nizam died in 1748. Dupleix at once supported one of the claimants, and, in addition, produced Chunda Sahib of the old ruling house of the Carnatic as a rival to Anwar-ud-din. Under the command of his brilliant subordinate Bussy, despite an apparently disastrous mutiny, the French troops carried all before them. They triumphantly installed a puppet Nizam, Anwar-ud-din was killed in battle, and the French protégé, Chunda Sahib, seized the Carnatic.

The company's council at Madras seems to have been paralysed by the speed and success of Dupleix's statecraft. It was, however, obvious that unless Chunda Sahib could be unseated the company was ruined.

Mohammed Ali, Anwar-ud-din's son, had taken refuge in Trichinopoly about 260 miles south-west of Madras, and the company resolved to support his claims to the Nawabship.

Now a war more typical of the twentieth century was fought. Britain and France were officially at peace. No French troops might fight on the British soil near Madras, nor British on French soil near Pondicherry, although both might incite an Indian prince to attack the other. Each side therefore had an inviolate base where reinforcements might be accumulated and armies refit.

The initial British intervention was disastrous. In the absence of Lawrence in England, Captain Gingen led a British force to the relief of Trichinopoly. The able Chunda Sahib trounced it, chased the survivors into Trichinopoly and besieged them there.

Now the company's cause looked hopeless, but out of the shadows stepped Robert Clive whose genius and unswerving courage were to transform the situation and set the British on the road to a new empire.

Madras had been denuded of troops. However a force of 200 European and 300 sepoys was scraped together and put under Clive. Such a contemptible army had no hope of relieving Trichinopoly; but Clive reasoned that Chunda Sahib must have most of his troops investing that town; by a lightning stroke he might seize Arcot, the capital of Chunda Sahib's Carnatic about 60 miles from Madras, and compel him to loosen his grip on Trichinopoly. It was a brilliant but desperately risky scheme.

After an epic march Clive arrived out of a thunderstorm to capture Arcot before the amazed defenders knew an enemy was near. Chunda Sahib hastily despatched his son, Reza Sahib, with 4,000 men to recapture his capital. For 50 days and nights Clive and his devoted band defeated every effort of his adversary and broke up every assault. At last on

A view of Trichinopoly from the Northwest by Elisha Trapand c. 1785. Trichinopoly was the scene of the first great clashes between the British and French in India. From 1751 it was alternately besieged or blockaded by the French and their allies until 1754 when the recall of Dupleix brought an end to hostilities

An engraving of Fort William, Calcutta. A newly arrived East Indiaman is firing a salute

21 November 1751 Reza Shah in despair abandoned the siege. Out of his 500 men Clive had only some 240 fit for duty, but his triumph resounded throughout India.

A roving Mahratta chieftain, Morarji Rao, now allied himself with Clive. The Mahrattas were uncertain allies. They fought only for gain. They were reluctant to attack unless sure that their enemies' treasure chest would recompense them adequately for their labours. Nevertheless with the assistance of Morarji Rao and his 3,000 Mahratta horsemen, Clive at the Arni river and at Covrepauk defeated two armies Chunda Sahib sent to retake Arcot.

The great peril was now over. In March Lawrence arrived back from England. Under his guidance the company's troops inflicted defeat after defeat on the French forces blockading Trichinopoly. Once he captured the complete French army, twice he captured their commanders. The gallant Chunda Sahib perished. But the iron Dupleix would not accept defeat. As one army was destroyed he formed another, as one Indian alliance dissolved he negotiated its replacement. Fortunately the French government of Louis XV was cast in less stern a mould. Dupleix undoubtedly had won honour and influence for the French, equally undoubtedly he had emptied the coffers of his company. Britain perpetually complained to Versailles about his 'lawless' acts. In 1754 while the British sent out the 39th Foot to Madras, the regiment that subsequently adopted the proud motto of 'Primus in Indis', the French government recalled Dupleix. The Honourable East India Company had survived the greatest peril it had to face until 1857.

PLASSEY

But in 1756 this was by no means obvious. On 9 April of that year Surajah Dowla succeeded to the viceroyalty of Bengal. The young prince, perhaps eager to show his prowess, perhaps, after seeing the example of Bussy in the Deccan, genuinely fearful of European domination, marched on Calcutta. After a brief siege he stormed Fort William. The garrison was composed of the usual riff-raff of adventurers and foreign mercenaries typical of Madras before the days of Stringer Lawrence. Its defence was a strange mixture of cowardice, treachery and heroism.

In Madras, despite the dangers in the Carnatic, no one doubted that Calcutta had to be recovered at once. A squadron comprising the *Kent* (64 guns), *Cumberland* (70), *Tyger* (60) and *Salisbury* (50) together with some transports, all under the command of Admiral Watson, a brave, bluff, not over-intelligent sea-dog, sailed for Calcutta on 17 October. It carried Clive as land forces commander, three companies of the 39th Foot, five companies of the Madras European regiment, and 1,200 sepoys, the cream of the Madras army. Eyre Coote who was to play a not insignificant part on the Indian scene commanded a company of the 39th.

Winds were adverse and progress slow. However on 1 January 1757, after the British fleet by superb navigation had sailed up the Hoogly river to Calcutta, Fort William, after a feeble resistance, surrendered to the guns of Admiral Watson. The reappearance of the British roused Surajah Dowla to action, and he marched with an army to the outskirts of Calcutta. Clive tried to surprise him by a night approach followed by a dawn attack. He was partially foiled by an unexpected and heavy morning fog. In a confused action Clive inflicted casualties on the Prince's army, but suffered severely himself.

However it was enough for Surajah Dowla. He at once concluded a treaty restoring all its old privileges to Calcutta and returned to his capital, Murshidabad, some 120 miles up the river.

While these events were taking place it was rumoured that war had broken out in Europe. Clive was anxious to return to the Carnatic, but felt Calcutta was not safe while the French held Chandernagore less than 30 miles up the Hoogly river.

Admiral Watson, until he received his personal copy of Britain's declaration of war on France, was not prepared to move. Then Clive needed sanction from Surajah Dowla before he began a war in the Prince's territory. The vacillating and unhappy Prince kept changing his mind. Afghans came raiding down towards his north-western border and frightened him into a conciliatory gesture. He gave Clive a qualified assent. He countermanded it within 24 hours, but it was too late. Directly he received permission Clive acted, the counter-order he simply ignored.

The French at Chandernagore fort resisted valiantly. Clive, attacking from the landward side, made slow progress. Then the fleet displaying magnificent seamanship anchored opposite the riverine ramparts of the fort. A mud battery on the river bank was destroyed and the fleet closed into musket-shot range. *Kent* and *Tyger* now poured their broadsides into its ramparts, but the undaunted French gunners gave a ferocious reply. For three hours the ships and fort remained locked in battle. Guns were disabled, casualties mounted, at one moment *Kent* caught fire, but gradually the British gained the mastery. At last, with all his guns silenced, Renault, the French commander, surrendered. The two ships *Tyger* and *Kent* between them lost nearly 130 men in the action.

Surajah Dowla, thoroughly alarmed at the British success, started to intrigue with the Mahrattas for help. But the young Prince by his arrogance and his ungovernable temper linked to a cowardly and vacillating nature had alienated most of his principal followers. A conspiracy organised by one of his generals, Mir Jafar, and one of his ministers, Dulab Rao, was joined by Clive. Those who treat with treachery rarely escape being tainted. Clive was no exception. A great merchant, Omichand, threatened to betray the conspiracy unless he received an exorbitant amount of money on its success. To accede to his demand was impossible, to refuse it imperilled the lives of the conspirators. Clive made a spurious treaty with Omichand which met his demands; and a separate genuine treaty with Mir Jafar that ignored them. Admiral Watson to his credit refused to sign the spurious treaty and his signature was forged.

The monsoon rains were now approaching. Clive had to act quickly. He marched up the Hoogly, followed its western tributary, the Cossimbazar river, and against little opposition took Cutwa Fort, about 40 miles downstream from Murshidabad.

Hearing of Clive's advance, Surajah Dowla assembled an army of 50,000 men, and took post at an old encampment near the village of Plassey some 18 miles from Cutwa. Clive had with him 750 European soldiers, 50 sailors to man his guns, 2,500 sepoys, 8 six-pounder field guns and 2 howitzers. He had expected to meet Mir Jafar at Cutwa, but, ominously, the latter had failed to arrive. Clive for this first and only time in his life called a council of war.

On the hot humid morning of 21 June 1757, while the heavy rain-laden monsoon clouds raced overhead, Clive and a small group of junior officers debated an action which would probably decide the fate of British rule in India.

Clive said that Surajah Dowla had taken the field with 50,000 men amongst whom the men under

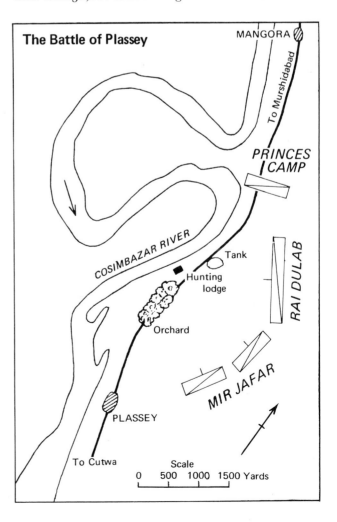

The Battle of Plassey

Clive meets Mir Jafar after the Battle of Plassey

Mir Jafar might at best remain neutral. A French force was within three days march of the Prince. He wanted his officers' views on two alternatives. Should they attack the Prince; or should they remain in their present position during the monsoon period, and seek help from the Mahrattas after the rains when campaigning again became possible? Clive then called for a vote. Ten including Clive voted for staying at Cutwa, seven, including Eyre Coote, voted for an immediate battle.

It is uncertain exactly when or for what reason, but some time on the evening of the 21st or morning of the 22nd Clive made up his mind to disregard this verdict and put everything to the test of battle.

In steady rain he and his little army forded the Cossimbazar river and marched sixteen miles to Plassey, arriving on a dark lightning-lit midnight.

Beyond Plassey a little to the north and about 50 yards east of the river bank lay a mango orchard. It was rectangular in shape; the long sides were 800 yards and ran roughly parallel to the river, while the short ones were 300 yards and fronted Surajah Dowla's encampment and Plassey village respectively; the whole was surrounded by a low mud wall. On the river bank itself and a little nearer the encampment was a hunting lodge belonging to the Prince. Clive put a garrison of 500 men into the lodge and its grounds, moved into the lodge himself, and had the rest of his army bivouac in the orchard for what remained of an unpleasant night.

When an angry dawn broke, the Prince's encampment came into view rather closer than expected. As a dense host of horse, foot and guns began to pour out of it, Clive drew up his tiny army in line just forward of the orchard. The European regiment he deployed in the centre with the sepoy companies on either flank and his guns in front. He himself remained by the lodge.

One body of Surajah Dowla's men made straight for the orchard, while a mass of men and cavalry, fetching a wide sweep round the far side of the orchard from the river, looked as though they intended to attack Clive's right flank and rear.

About 200 yards away from the British front line was a large village pond surrounded by an embankment, locally known as a 'tank'. Here the Prince's troops emplaced some guns and opened fire on the British line. The British guns replied and a heavy cannonade ensued. Clive, seeing his men exposed to no purpose, withdrew them into the shelter of the orchard.

The artillery duel continued until midday, but the remainder of the Prince's army seemed reluctant to come to close quarters. Some cavalry who made a tentative charge retired hastily after receiving a few rounds of grape. At about 12.30 p.m. the heavens opened and for half-an-hour the rain descended in torrents. The British gunners kept their powder dry and continued their fire, but the enemy gunners, apparently less successful in keeping out the rain, seemed to be in trouble. Their firing faltered, then stopped, and they started to move back. Major Kilpatrick at once rushed the front edge of the 'tank' with two companies from the European battalion. Clive dashed out of the lodge and shouted angrily at him for advancing without orders. He then ordered Kilpatrick back to the orchard and took command of the men himself.

Clive knew that any withdrawal would prove fatal. He was like a lion-tamer in a cage of angry lions; let him show the least weakness or lack of confidence and he must be torn in pieces.

He manned the front edge of the 'tank' and gradually built up his strength there, his movements being impeded by the threat of a cavalry charge from large bodies of horsemen hovering uncertainly round the right flank of the orchard. Then from the encampment a large body of infantry charged towards Clive's small party. For a time his position looked dangerous. But before the steady controlled fire of Clive's men and his guns the attackers first halted then started to give back. Clive at once ordered the charge and stormed into the encampment on the heels of the fugitives. Suddenly all resistance collapsed. Surajah Dowla had already fled the field and the remnant of the army still loyal to him followed their master.

The whole encampment, replete with stores of all kinds, fell into the hands of the British.

In the battle Clive's army suffered some 60 casualties. Clive estimated the Prince had lost perhaps 500 dead. As regards casualties the action was a trifling affair, but its consequences were immense. As Mir Jafar came into the camp to join him, and the wretched Prince fled back to Murshidabad and assassination, the East India Company became the uncrowned rulers of the vast province of Bengal. Fortescue in his *History of the British Army* perhaps best sums up Clive's achievement 'The campaign of Plassey is less a study of military skill than of the iron will and unshaken nerve that could lead three thousand men against a host of unknown strength and hold them undaunted, a single slender line, within a ring of fifty thousand enemies.'

Clive placed his nominee Mir Jafar on the throne of Bengal. He stayed on in Calcutta for two more years. He crushed a Dutch attempt to penetrate Bengal and returned to England in 1760.

While Clive was laying the foundations of British rule in Bengal, Madras, stripped of its troops, faced a new menace from the French. In 1758 Lally became governor of Pondicherry. He was a brave but arrogant man, lacking in military judgment and overbearing to his inferiors, among whom he numbered nearly all the inhabitants of Pondicherry, French or Indian. He had with him two French regular infantry regiments. He captured the British Fort St Andrew while Madras watched helplessly, but Admiral Pocock with the British Fleet arrived from Calcutta in time to save Madras from the immediate threat of a siege. Thwarted, Lally found a pretext to march against the Rajah of Tanjore. However, he failed to capture Tanjore itself, and returned to Pondicherry with his reputation diminished and his troops disheartened. But the British Fleet had gone and he saw an opportunity to take Madras. On 2 January 1759 his batteries opened on Fort St George. The aging Stringer Lawrence performed his last service to the Company, and against his vigorous leadership Lally had little chance of success. Then on 16 February Admiral Pocock reappeared and Lally hastily abandoned the siege leaving fifty guns behind him.

In 1760 Eyre Coote arrived with reinforcements and took the field. He brought Lally to battle at Wandewash and utterly routed him. He followed the French to Pondicherry and after a lengthy blockade compelled them to surrender on 16 January 1761. French power in India had been extinguished. By the Treaty of Paris, 1763, French possessions were reduced to a few unfortified factories. Both in India and America, Britain had virtually eliminated her European rivals; in India her future conflicts were to be with potentates native to that sub-continent, while in America her own colonists were shortly to take up arms against her.

Eyre Coote accepting the surrender of Pondicherry from Lally

CHAPTER 9

The American Revolution
1763–83

PETER YOUNG

CHRONOLOGICAL TABLE

1773	The Boston Tea Party
16 December	
1775 19 April	The actions at Lexington and Concord
20 April	The blockade of Boston
17 June	The Battle of Bunker Hill
30 December	Americans repulsed at Quebec
1776 17 March	The British evacuate Boston
4 July	The Declaration of Independence
27 August	Howe turns Washington out of Island
28 October	Howe turns Washington out of White Plains
8 December	Howe captures Trenton
25 December	Washington recaptures Trenton
1777 3 January	The action near Princeton
6 July	The action at Ticonderoga
16 August	Ambush near Bennington
11 September	The Battle of Brandywine Creek
19 September	Burgoyne checked at Bemis Heights
4 October	The Battle of Germantown
7 October	Burgoyne repulsed at Bemis Heights
17 October	Burgoyne surrenders at Saratoga
1778 6 February	France declares war
June	Clinton withdraws from Philadelphia
18 December	Action at Vigie Point, St. Lucia
1779 3 March	Prevost defeats the Americans at Briar Creek
16 June	Spain enters the war
21 June	Gibraltar besieged
9 October	Franco-American assault on Savannah repulsed

1780 12 May	Lincoln surrenders at Charleston
16 August	The Battle of Camden
7 October	The action at King's Mountain
20 December	Britain declares war on Holland
1781 17 January	The Battle of Cowpens
15 March	The Battle of Guilford Courthouse
25 April	The Battle of Hobkirk Hill
9 May	The fall of Pensacola
8 September	The Battle of Eutaw Springs
19 October	Cornwallis surrenders at Yorktown
1782 5 February	The surrender of Minorca
October	Gibraltar finally relieved
1783	The Peace of Paris
1784	Peace with Holland

When at the Treaty of Paris 1763 France yielded Canada to Britain, the American colonists, many of whose ancestors had left Britain to escape from persecution by Church or State, lost their most potent reason for remaining loyal to their parent country. While France loomed threateningly on their borders they were happy to rely on the strong arm of Britain. Now the French were gone, the need for the strong arm became less apparent, while the suggestion that they should pay part of its expenses appealed to the colonists not at all.

The British, on the other hand, never eager at the best of times to spend money on their armed forces, viewed with even greater distaste the prospect of paying soldiers to protect colonies which refused to contribute themselves. The quarrel, like so many family quarrels, began over money, but it soon developed into a bitter dispute over sovereignty. 'No taxation without representation,' cried fiery New

The raid on Concord. Firing has broken out on the village green at Lexington and the British
troops (right background) are delivering a volley. A painting by W. B. Wollen

George Washington

General John Burgoyne. He later became Commander-in-Chief of Ireland

Englanders whose ancestors had helped unseat Charles I over this very issue. 'No tampering with the ultimate authority of Parliament,' the British in essence replied. Britain, who had just fought a costly war caused in large part by rivalry between French and British colonists in America, felt not a little aggrieved at the attitude of these same colonists which the cynics suspected, perhaps unjustly, owed more to a desire to avoid expense than any deep attachment to philosophical principle.

The liberal policies British Governments had pursued in the past undermined Britain's ability to impose her will. For years the colonists had enjoyed a regime as democratic as any in the world at that time. Each colony had an elected legislative assembly known as the Council of Burgesses. The franchise might be limited but in practice was certainly no more so than in England. The royal governors could dissolve the assemblies and veto their resolutions, but they did so at their peril. The governor's power might stem from the British Crown, but Britain was far away, and they had little to depend on other than the prestige of their positions and the goodwill of the chief citizens. The judicature was mainly drawn from the colonists themselves and, most significant, the local militia gave their allegiance not to the governor but to the assembly. Thus when the break with Britain came, there already existed within the colonies all the apparatus for a popular

government, and the decisions taken by that government, when formed, expressed the views held by at least the politically active majority of the citizens, an unpalatable fact that the British Government was slow to realise. The quarrel began almost immediately after the Treaty of Paris and continued for ten long years with Parliament vacillating unhappily between asserting its right to tax the colonists and repealing the taxes it had imposed.

Boston was the centre of American disaffection. Its mob was unruly, and the city magistrates did little to curb its anti-British activities. British officials trying to implement their country's regulations might expect to be tarred and feathered for their pains, while the few British soldiers in the garrison were abused and maltreated. Neither could hope for much redress in the courts.

Gradually the protracted dispute came to a head. The East India Company whose activities in India had brought it close to bankruptcy was granted a monopoly for the supply of cheap tea in the American market. This move aroused intense indignation among the colonists; it became a patriotic duty to drink coffee – a habit that has persisted to the present day – and in Boston a party of citizens disguised as Indians boarded some East India Company vessels and dumped their cargo of tea in the harbour.

The British Government could scarcely ignore such an outrage and ordered the port of Boston to be closed, an order that spelled eventual ruin to that city. In reply the colonists set up a central Congress consisting of representatives from all the colonial assemblies and organised a boycott of all British goods. Governors who dissolved provincial legislatures had their orders circumvented and the local militias started arming and drilling.

But a single incident was now needed to turn economic strife into active war and again it came from Boston. General Gage, the British Commander-in-Chief and Governor of Massachusetts, heard of an illegal store of arms and ammunition at a village with the inappropriate name of Concord. He sent a column of troops by night to destroy it. As is usual in such circumstances the colonists received ample warning of the British plans, and at five o'clock in the clear light of dawn the British column passing through Lexington stumbled on some local militia drawn up on the village green. How or why firing started is uncertain, but once the first shot was fired a general engagement ensued. Eight of the militiamen were killed and the remainder fled. The British continued on to Concord, found and destroyed some weapons and then withdrew towards Boston. But the alarm had been sounded and the hunt was up. From every hedge, from every tree, from every house and wall the British were relentlessly shot at and harried. Loosing an occasional volley against their unseen foes the troops marched grimly on, but by the time they reached Boston 280 of their number were casualties. In its execution and result the raid on Concord portrayed in microcosm the shape of the war to come.

The situation that had burst upon them was never fully understood by the British Government. They mistook for an insurrection what was really a war between sovereign powers, and a war moreover entirely different from those of eighteenth century Europe. European conflicts of that period had been largely dynastic affairs, duels between rival monarchs fought by regular armies which conformed to a strict code of conduct designed to reduce the shedding of blood and inconvenience to the bystanders. The populace at large, unless unfortunate enough to be living close to the actual battlefield, were little involved, and watched the performance of their armies with scarcely as much interest as is now given to the progress of a national team in an international competition. Too many defeats were bad for international prestige, and a succession might lead men to agitate for a change of management, but meanwhile there was the serious business of living to be pursued. Laurence Sterne, for instance, during his sentimental journey through France thought nothing of travelling in that country while it was at war with Britain and suffered merely minor inconvenience from that not unusual state of affairs.

But in America Britain confronted a nation in arms with a philosophy, or in more modern terms an ideology, to unite it. Of course both in America and Britain there were many who deplored the conflict, but as the war progressed their influence steadily declined. The British Government persistently deluded itself that it enjoyed a large measure of support, but once British soldiers were shooting Americans, as George Washington insisted that they should be called, every natural instinct urged the colonists to aid their countrymen against these soldiers who had come from over the seas.

It was this that baffled the British generals even more than the difficulties of the terrain or the novel tactics adopted by the colonists. British troops had been familiar with conditions in America since the days of the Seven Years War, they lost few major engagements and they could capture the chief American cities almost at will. But this mattered little while the countryside remained hostile, a countryside populated moreover by a tough, resolute people, by pioneers, frontiersmen and hunters born to the use of arms, men who compensated for their lack of discipline by the ruggedness of their temperament and their skill with their weapons.

Just how formidable the problem was the British generals were soon to discover. While from Connecticut Benedict Arnold and Ethan Allen with a handful of men sought to conquer Canada, the New England militias which after Lexington had blockaded the landward side of Boston were transformed into the 'Continental Army', brought under the control of the Central or Continental Congress and given General George Washington as Commander-in-Chief. Reinforcements for Gage came from England; they included Generals Howe, Clinton and Burgoyne. The newcomers were exasperated by Gage's inactivity and urged him to drive his adversaries away. But before Gage acted, the Continental Army struck first. On the night of 16 June a large party, later brought up to a strength of 800 men, occupied Breed Hill, an eminence that commanded Boston harbour, and working furiously through the night, crowned it with a redoubt and entrenchments.

When early next morning Gage heard of this move, he resolved on an immediate attack. Since Breed Hill lay across the harbour from the British lines, Gage ordered Howe to take 2,500 men by

The raid on Concord. The Colonists harass the British withdrawal to Boston.

boat across the estuary and drive the rebels away. The action that followed has generally been called the Battle of Bunker Hill.

Having disembarked from their boats, the British troops carrying full equipment including three days rations moved to the attack on a bright and extremely hot summer afternoon. An attempt by light troops to turn the colonists' flank failed dismally and the outcome of the battle came to depend on the attack up Breed Hill.

The British watchers across the harbour could see a long, slow-moving, steeltipped hedge of red advancing up the hill. As the hedge neared the top, lightning seemed to flicker momentarily about it followed by rolling claps of thunder, then the summit blossomed in clouds of black smoke. As the smoke cleared away the hedge, now rent and torn, dissolved into a moving field of poppies descending the hill, but some remained behind crumpled and bent. Hoarse shouting could be heard. The leading lines of poppies stopped and the hedge reformed. Again the hedge mounted the slope and again the thunder clouds broke and dissolved it.

Gage, horrified at the sight, sent Clinton and a battalion to the help of Howe's stricken men. The hedge re-formed and again moved up the slopes now dotted with little motionless clumps of red. This time the thunder sounded weaker and uncertain; the hedge became a red wave that curled and broke over the redoubt; now on the far side of the hill blue dots appeared moving swiftly away. British valour had carried the day, but at a terrible cost; out of the small British force over a thousand were disabled.

The British victory was barren and boded ill for the future. The colonial militia had shown themselves to be not a rabble to be dispersed by a volley, but a body of steadfast, determined fighting men, ready to die for their beliefs. Gage with his army crippled could do no more. The Continental Army, elated by the stand it had made and the casualties it

had inflicted, tightened its grip on Boston.

Now Britain's weakness stood fully revealed. The Army in England amounted to fewer than 30,000 men. For nearly a year Britain remained powerless while regiments were raised at home and hired from abroad. The use of German mercenaries has been criticised but Britain's lack of preparation left her no choice if any sort of land action was to be attempted. Some indeed suggested that all British troops should be withdrawn and the American coast blockaded. But such a blockade would bear on innocent and guilty alike, and Britain still cherished the illusion that many of the colonists remained loyal – which indeed was true in some of the southern provinces – and awaited only the presence of British troops to declare for King George. Certainly later experience with economic sanctions gives little reason to suppose that such a blockade would have been successful.

So for nearly a year Britain waited mustering her forces. In Canada the colonists were repulsed. At Boston Howe replaced Gage, and as Washington closed in on the harbour, he evacuated the city and sailed away to Halifax. On 4 July 1776 the Continental Congress proclaimed the independence of the thirteen colonies. That same month Howe, having built his army up to a strength of 25,000, arrived off Staten Island to crush the Revolution.

On 27 August Howe defeated Putnam and an American army, as after the declaration of Independence it may more properly be termed, at Long Island; then in a series of skilful actions he drove Washington and his men out of New York state; by 8 December he had recaptured northern New Jersey and established an outpost at Trenton on the Delaware River less than thirty miles from the capital of the Revolution, Philadelphia. To outward appearances the British cause was prospering. Washington himself had to face stern criticism from a disconsolate Congress. But just when he seemed utterly beaten, that great man prepared an audacious counterstroke. Howe, who saw little virtue in discomfort when comfortable quarters were to hand, had retired to New York for the winter, leaving a brigade of Hessians to garrison Trenton.

The Hessians, accustomed to more formalised, or probably in their view more civilised, forms of warfare, had been celebrating Christmas Day in traditional style, when suddenly Washington and a band of desperate Americans broke into their revels. The Hessian commander Colonel Rall, perhaps the only man capable of noticing what was happening, was shot, and the remainder to the number of a

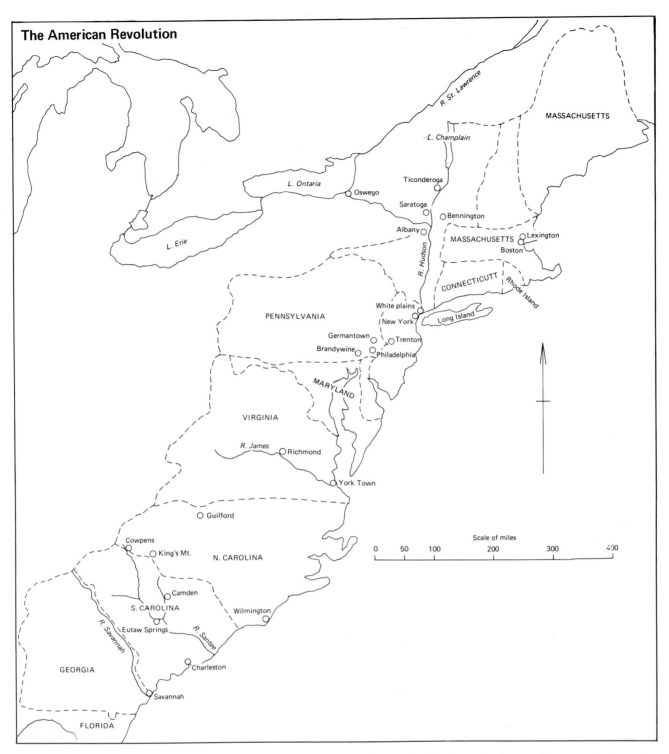

thousand surrendered. Howe came out to succour his outposts, but Washington skirted his left flank and hastened towards Princeton where there was a considerable magazine of British stores. On a foggy winter morning he fell in with a weak British brigade and cut it to pieces, although the 17th Foot who had been isolated avoided capture by a brilliant bayonet charge.

Howe saved his stores at Princeton and withdrew to New York. The inhabitants of New Jersey who

had previously thought it prudent to declare for England lost no time in proclaiming their loyalty to the Revolution. Two reverses in which the main British Army had played no part had nevertheless been sufficient to rob Howe of most of what he had gained in a brilliant campaign.

The writing on the wall was clear enough, but no one in England was prepared to read it, least of all a newly promoted Lt-Gen. John Burgoyne who, fresh home from Canada, had met Lord George

F

Princeton. The 17th Foot, under Colonel Charles Marshwood, were cut off by the Americans in great force. Abandoning their packs, they cut their way out with the bayonet. Painted by Gilbert Halliday

Germaine, the Secretary of State for Colonies, in London, and was eagerly pressing on him an ambitious plan for the campaign of 1777.

In the colonies movement inland generally was only possible along the waterways. Burgoyne proposed to take an army from Canada and penetrate down the Hudson River to the town of Albany, about 150 miles north of New York. Howe was to advance northwards up the river and meet him at that town. The armies were to crush the rebels between them, take control of the Hudson and cut off New England, the centre of disaffection, from the rest of the colonies. New England could then be subjugated at leisure. It seems almost inconceivable that a recently promoted lieutenant general and a secretary of state should design the plan of campaign without consulting General Howe, the Commander-in-Chief in America. Whether Howe was ever fully informed of the plan remains in dispute. What is certain is that his actions never properly conformed to it.

Burgoyne, his plan approved, sailed to Canada, and with some 7,000 men including some 3,000 Germans and 400 Indians embarked on his hazardous mission. On 6 July 1777 he encountered an American army of 3,000 under General St Clair encamped near Fort Ticonderoga, and drove them

away with some ease, a victory that increased his unwarranted contempt for his opponents. Full of confidence, Burgoyne pushed southwards, the Americans falling back before him. As he struggled on through forest-clad hills intersected by streams and morasses the appalling difficulties he would have to overcome if he was to feed and supply his men were gradually borne in on him. He wrote:

The great bulk of the country is undoubtedly with Congress ... wherever the King's forces point, militia to the amount of 3,000 or 4,000 assemble in 24 hours. They bring with them their subsistence, etc. and the alarm over they return to their farms. ... In all parts the industry in driving cattle and removing corn are [sic] indefatigable.

By 30 July the Americans had retired to Saratoga. Now Burgoyne had to decide whether to cross to the west bank of the Hudson and continue his advance or else abandon the whole enterprise. He knew nothing of what was happening elsewhere. No messengers seemed able to get through to Howe and no couriers from New York had managed to penetrate the American lines.

It was an agonising decision that he had to make. If he crossed the Hudson, a comparatively small party of Americans could block his line of retreat in that difficult country. If he went on, he would have to gamble on help from Howe or else fight his way through to New York. The church bells in England had rung out for his victory at Ticonderoga, there would be little applause for a general who returned to Canada defeated not by the Americans, but by problems of supply and his own fears. And what of Howe who might even now be advancing on Albany? To withdraw and release the Americans to concentrate against him might ruin the main British Army. Gentleman John Burgoyne, as he was known to his troops, was not the man to leave a friend in the lurch. He had a cheerful sanguine temperament, and was perhaps a little over-fond of champagne and good-looking women, as the wife of a brother officer somewhat acidly noted. For him only one decision was possible. He must go on with what was, after all, his plan; but the cheerful optimism of London by now was a little tempered. Meanwhile, unknown to Burgoyne, Howe was pursuing his original design to seize Philadelphia, and capture or drive away that pestilential Congress.

Burgoyne had decided to continue the advance, but he was almost destitute of provisions. Hearing that the Americans had collected a quantity of supplies at the village of Bennington, he sent some 500 Germans to take them by surprise. On 16 August the little force, wandering uncertainly along forest trails, was led by treacherous guides straight into an ambush laid by about 1,500 'Green Mountain Boys'. Surrounded and attacked from all sides, Baume, their commander, fell sword in hand leading a charge to break open the trap; all his men either died or were captured. A force Burgoyne sent to support them was compelled to retreat with the loss of two guns.

Burgoyne perforce halted and spent nearly a month gathering in supplies. He estimated that he needed thirty days' provisions before it was safe to resume his advance. The Americans watched and waited. Away to the south Washington, incredulous at the folly of the British, despatched every man he could spare to reinforce his men near Saratoga.

On 10 September Burgoyne resumed his advance. General Gates who now commanded the American Army, about 10,000 strong, fell back before him and fortified a position on some forested hills called Bemis Heights which lie some eight miles south of Saratoga. On 19 September Burgoyne, although outnumbered by two to one, attacked a hill on the American left hoping to take the rest of their position in the flank. A desperate combat developed at an American forward post at Freeman's Farm, and despite the utmost gallantry the British attack was held short of its objective.

Now Burgoyne's peril was great. He could not go forward and he dare not go back. He fortified a camp near the American position and anxiously awaited relief from New York. Even then he did not entirely despair of success. As September gave way to October his army went on to half rations, but courage and morale never wavered. Gates, although his army now numbered some 15,000, hesitated to close. Clinton at long last left New York, but with a hopelessly inadequate force stormed the fort of Montgomery commanding the Hudson and advanced towards Albany.

His provisions almost exhausted and convinced retreat was impossible, on 7 October Burgoyne resolved once again to attempt to break through his now vastly superior enemy. Leaving the balance of his men to hold his camp he led about 1,500 men to attack the American left. A furious battle developed. It was Benedict Arnold who brought disaster to the British. Arnold, a soldier of uncertain moral principles but a veritable salamander in a fight, disregarded the orders of his cautious superior and led his men into battle with the fury of an Achilles. Before his inspired leadership and the overwhelming strength of their adversaries the British were forced

back to their encampment. But Arnold was not satisfied. He pressed the retreat relentlessly and actually broke into the British camp.

Now the end was near. During the night Burgoyne left a camp he could no longer defend, abandoning all his sick, wounded and baggage to the enemy. For four more days, surrounded by an army nearly four times their strength, constantly shot at and sniped, Burgoyne and his men held on without shelter and virtually without food. Gates prudently awaited the inevitable. On 12 October the British commander planned to slip away northwards under cover of darkness, but the alert American sentries rendered the project hopeless. On the 13th he set out to treat for terms and a cease-fire was ordered for that night. On 17 October Burgoyne surrendered with fewer than 4,000 fit men. Including the sick and wounded they had captured earlier, fewer than 6,000 men fell into the hands of the Americans. Gates, whatever his merits as a general a generous adversary, subsequently wrote to Burgoyne: 'If courage, perseverance and a faithful attachment to your prince could have prevailed I might have been your prisoner.'

Near Philadelphia, away to the south, Howe thrashed Washington at Brandywine creek on 11 September and on the 25th captured that city. Again at Germantown the British were victorious, but in this type of warfare one British setback outweighed a dozen victories and the surrender of fewer than 6,000 soldiers at Saratoga, little more than Howe had captured in his successful campaign, was to reverberate through Europe.

A disaster at the beginning of a war was no novelty to Britain and generally had the useful effect of shaking the British nation out of its habitual torpor. Burgoyne's capitulation unfortunately waked more than the British sleeper. The French, who had been surreptitiously helping the Americans, now felt assured that Britain faced a major conflict in North America and hastened to take advantage of the situation. In February 1778 France formally declared war on Britain. Spain followed suit next year, while Holland organised an 'Armed Neutrality' of the northern European states to break the British blockade of the American coast. Now Britain was fighting for survival. The war in America had to take second place.

To Washington wintering in wretched huts at Valley Forge watching his half clad, underpaid and semi-mutinous army melt away, it might seem that it needed but one more push from the British for the Revolution to founder. Howe, comfortably ensconced in Philadelphia, perhaps read the omens more correctly. He was an exceedingly able general, and the indolence of which he has been accused may have been not far removed from wisdom. He might well reflect that, although he had won every battle he had fought, it had profited him little. He might chase Washington and beat him again, but what then? Little would be gained by chasing a phantom army over an icy waste. Meanwhile Philadelphia had much to offer, and in the spring he could hope to be relieved of a task which he had found from the first distasteful and now suspected might be impossible.

In May 1778 he handed over command to Clinton and sailed for home. Clinton's position was far from happy. No help could be expected from England, and now that France had entered the lists troops were urgently required to protect the West Indies from the French fleet. For the time being nothing could be done to put down the Revolution, and since Britain's naval supremacy was now very far from unquestioned his position at Philadelphia was one of some peril. In June, accompanied by an enormous baggage train and bands of unhappy loyalists, he made a skilful withdrawal to New York. Except for an ineffectual skirmish, all Washington's efforts to harry the British columns were thwarted. Once Clinton had established himself at New York Washington, perhaps the only man fully to understand the nature of the conflict, declared: 'We should on all occasions avoid a general action nor put anything to the risk unless compelled', and contented himself with a blockade. For the rest of that year the British were too weak to make any serious military effort in the North and the Continental Congress was granted another respite in which to consolidate its rule and train its armies, now equipped with the not unmixed blessing of Prussian drill sergeants. During that winter, however, both in the province of Georgia and the West Indies British arms were to secure a measure of success.

In the West Indies, the fate of the islands depended on sea rather than land battles. But one remarkable action on the Island of St Lucia is worthy of record. By a lightning stroke Admiral Barrington with a few ships and a handful of soldiers captured the French-held island. The day after its captured the Comte d'Estaing arrived with the French fleet and a considerable number of troops. After some naval skirmishing D'Estaing landed his troops in the Anse du Choc and struck towards Vigie Point which overlooked the harbour. A British force under Colonel William Medows, a veteran of the Seven Years' War,

held the Point. He had with him only 1,300 men but they were picked veterans who had seen a deal of fighting. The force included the 35th Foot and the flank companies of the 4th, 15th, 27th, 28th, 40th, 46th and 35th massed together with those of the 5th into a grenadier battalion and a light battalion.

The fight began about 8.00 a.m. on 18 December 1778 after a night of heavy rain. Two French battalions advanced towards the narrow neck of land under cover of low brushwood, and tried to surprise five light companies which Medows had posted on two low hills to his front. The General was on reconnaissance at the time from the main position and it looked as if he was going to be cut off. However he got back safely. 'The Light Infantry will take care of themselves', he said; 'as for you, stand fast.'

Fortescue's[1] description of the light infantry's work cannot be bettered;

> Then was seen the potency of the tactics learned in America. Advancing in skirmishing order and keeping themselves always under cover, the light companies maintained at close range a most destructive fire upon the heavy French columns. If the enemy attempted to extend, they threatened a charge with the bayonet; when the French closed up, they were already extended and pouring in a galling fusillade; when the French advanced with solidity and determination they fell back and disappeared, but only to renew their fire, themselves invisible, from every direction.

One of the French battalions broke and fled, pursued by the Light Infantry who had not observed the approach of the main French columns advancing against the main position. The Light Infantry escaped by dashing into the scrub. Their retreat was covered by Captain Downing, Lt Waring and Privates Rose, Duffy and Hargrove.

Medows was hit early on but the main French attack was halted by the grenadiers and the artillery. The men had gone into action with only 30 cartridges each and were running out of ammunition when a gigantic grenadier officer named Hill came up with a box of ammunition which two men could scarcely carry. It was opened and the cartridges, stored too long, immediately dissolved into dust.

Major George Harris (1746–1829) commanded the grenadiers.[2] Medows, still in control despite his wound, gave him the order to cease fire. The men must endure the fire of the French skirmishers until such time as the columns were near enough to be

---

[1] Vol III, p. 269.

[2] He had been badly wounded at Bunker Hill leading the Grenadier Company of the 5th Foot and some kind friend had rigged up a system of mirrors so that he could see his own brain.

Lord Cornwallis. He was later Governor General in India

charged with the bayonet. Drill and discipline count for something in the heat of action. The British did not fire another shot: it is said that though the order 'present' had been given they responded to the command 'recover' and instead of loosing off their pieces, brought down their muskets. The French rallied and pushed on but there was a moment of confusion when they received a salvo from the two British 12-pounders – their last two rounds as it happened. Harris saw that it was 'now or never', and gave the order to fire into the most confused parts of the French columns. This was too much for the French who turned about and began to fall back. Though to their credit they maintained some sort of order they had no intention of renewing the attack. The three hours' fight was over.

In this classic action the British sustained 171 casualties, only 13 of whom were killed. The Light Infantry lost 60 men and the Grenadiers 90. The French with odds of nearly ten to one in their favour lost the astonishing total of 1,600: 400 killed and 1,200 wounded. Medows, who visited all his casualties before he allowed the surgeon to dress his wound, recovered, became a general and had a distinguished career in India. Harris was to capture Seringapatam, and win a barony besides a fortune in prize money. Deeply mortified by this reverse, D'Estaing paused to bring off his sick and wounded

before sailing away to Martinique.

Meanwhile Clinton at New York, hearing that there were many loyalists in Georgia, boldly sent Lt-Col. Campbell with some 4,000 men, half of whom were provincial militia, to recover that province with the help of General Prevost who was operating at that time with a small force in Florida.

On 29 December 1778 Campbell defeated a weak American army near Savannah and occupied that town. By the end of February 1779 the whole of Georgia was once more under British rule. An American attempt to reconquer it met with disaster at Briar Creek, and for a period Prevost actually threatened Charleston in South Carolina. General Lincoln, the American commander, anxious lest Prevost provoke a loyalist rising, persuaded D'Estaing with the French fleet to help him capture Savannah. For a month the French fleet blockaded the port, while on land a Franco-American force endeavoured to reduce the British fortifications. Washington, encamped near New York, was enraged to see the main French fleet engaged on so unimportant a task, but was unable to intervene. To add to his fury, when the allied force did try a storm they met with a bloody repulse. D'Estaing sailed away in disgust, Lincoln was happy to regain Charleston, while Prevost remained the unchallenged master of Georgia. With the onset of the hot weather the fighting came to an end, but the success in Georgia had not gone unremarked in Whitehall.

Although in June 1779 Spain had joined France against Britain and for a brief period a Franco-Spanish fleet had controlled the Channel, and Gibraltar was besieged, by the end of the year Britain, as the result of immense exertions, had dispelled the immediate peril and felt strong enough once again to make a serious military effort to reconquer at least part of the Thirteen Colonies. After Saratoga it had been recognised that the North was lost, but the recovery of Georgia led to extravagant hopes being entertained about the number of loyalists in the South, and from London Germaine ordered Clinton to invade the Carolinas. The ensuing operations, first in South Carolina then in North, were to reveal the true issues at stake. Howe had come to learn that, whatever their feeling about the Revolution, it was difficult for Americans to stomach watching Britains shoot fellow Americans, and that the operations of the British armies, however successful militarily, excited more hostility than any victory could offset, a lesson that Cornwallis was now doomed to learn.

Clinton, taking a powerful detachment from his army at New York, landed in South Carolina, drove Lincoln into Charleston and on 12 May 1780 compelled him to surrender with 5,600 men. He then handed over command to Cornwallis and returned to New York. Cornwallis had with him the brilliant cavalry leader Tarleton and about 7,000 men, including Tarleton's Legion, a hard-riding, hard-marching unit Tarleton had raised in the North. As he marched inland on Camden, Cornwallis was everywhere welcomed and enlisted many of the local inhabitants into the provincial militia, as it was called. He reached Camden and the whole of South Carolina appeared to be in his hands. Then news came that Gates had arrived with an American army in North Carolina. Now the loyalty of some of the colonists performed some surprising somersaults, complete militia units lost their loudly proclaimed devotion to King George, and the guerrilla leader, Sumter, started attacking isolated British posts though without notable success. Cornwallis needed a victory to stiffen the resolve of the waverers. Gates, hitherto more conspicuous for caution than dash, suddenly decided to oblige him. He advanced on Camden with about 3,000 men. Cornwallis could muster only 2,000 but,

delighted to have a tangible enemy, advanced to meet him. The two armies encountered each other unexpectedly about nine miles from Camden, and in the battle that followed on 16 August 1780 the American army was destroyed. Tarleton, after a merciless pursuit of the Americans, turned on Sumter and taking him by surprise, scattered his band. But Sumter's guerrillas had only gone to ground to re-appear as soon as the immediate danger was over.

Cornwallis, flushed with success, resolved to advance on North Carolina, despite the growing guerrilla threat to his rear. Now, however, a remarkable incident occurred that completely dislocated all his plans. A detachment of provincial loyalists under Major Ferguson, reputedly the best rifle shot in the British army, had been chasing a band of guerrillas and had incautiously become widely separated from the main British Army. Suddenly the area in which they were moving spewed forth armed men. Ferguson recognised his danger and tried desperately to rejoin Cornwallis, but his assailants, local hunters and backwoodsmen, mounting their horses, galloped all round his men and compelled him to stand and fight. Ferguson took up a strong position on a hill called King's Mountain. The backwoodsmen, many armed with

Cornwallis surrenders at Yorktown. From Godefroy's history

The capture of Pensacola. Galvez, the Spanish governor of Louisiana, gained this town as the result of an explosion in a bomb-proof magazine on 9 May 1781. From Godefroy's history

rifles, crawled and shot their way up the hillside, taking advantage of every bush and rock for cover. The militiamen replied with volleys and bayonet charges. But at each charge the backwoodsmen in front ran back, while those at the side poured in a deadly fire. The struggle continued for some hours, but with Ferguson dead and some 400 of their number dead and wounded the rest surrendered. The backwoodsmen hanged nine of the militiamen to make clear their views as to loyalty to the Revolution, and then dispersed to their more normal vocations.

With his communications to South Carolina now unprotected, Cornwallis had to abandon his plan of campaign and fall back to Winnsborough near Camden. Although he had utterly defeated his adversary, he had been robbed of the fruits of victory by forces that neither he nor his opponent knew existed. This might have warned him of the futility of trying to subdue a state that was steadily growing more hostile. But Cornwallis refused to admit defeat and instead resolved at all costs to come to grips with his enemy.

In December General Greene took over command of the American Army now concentrated at Charlotteville, North Carolina. He decided to split his army and harass Cornwallis's communications. Cornwallis, reacting swiftly, sent Tarleton to destroy the Americans operating in the north. Tarleton, marching with his usual speed, brought them to action at Cowpens on 17 January 1781. His men were exhausted with their long marches and fortune favoured the Americans. Tarleton's column was virtually annihilated.

The reverse merely spurred Cornwallis on. He advanced on Guilford in North Carolina while Greene fell back before him, hardly daring to hope that the British would be mad enough to follow. After some manoeuvring Greene offered battle by Guilford Courthouse. On 15 March 1781 Cornwallis attacked and after a bitter struggle forced him from the field. But the British Army had suffered heavily. His offensive blunted, Cornwallis abandoned North Carolina to Greene and retreated to Wilmington.

The frustrations that he had suffered, his pyrrhic victories, seem now to have afflicted Cornwallis with a sudden madness. Concluding it was useless to attempt to subdue the Carolinas while Virginia was an inviolable sanctuary for the American armies, he advanced on Richmond 200 miles to the north. The garrisons he left behind him had to withdraw to Charleston or else face certain capture. As Greene tried to hasten their departure he was administered

two sharp rebuffs at the battles of Hobkirk hill and Eutaw Springs (8 September 1781) but by the end of September the Carolinas were irretrievably lost. At Pensacola near New Orleans Colonel Campbell and 900 British soldiers, after their magazine had blown up, had to capitulate to a Spanish army about 5,000 strong on 9 May 1781.

Unperturbed by the inevitable consequences of his action, Cornwallis penetrated deep into Virginia, ineffectually chasing Lafayette and a small American army. Washington was not the man to neglect the opportunity now presented to him. The French had secured temporary command of the sea; Clinton dare not stir from New York. Leaving a small force to watch him, Washington concentrated every man he could against Cornwallis. On 14 September with 16,000 men he pinned him into Yorktown, while the Comte de Grasse cruised off shore with 28 ships of the line. After a siege lasting a little over a month, Cornwallis with 4,000 men surrendered. Although Clinton maintained himself in New York until peace was signed in 1783, and Britain recognised the independence of the United States, the war in America, to all intents and purposes, was over.

Why did Britain lose, or perhaps more appropriately, could Britain have won? A fortnight after Bunker Hill Lt-Gen. Edward Harvey, Adjutant General to the forces in America, wrote:

'Taking America as it stands, it is impossible to conquer it with our British Army. ... To attempt to conquer it internally by our land force is as wild an idea as ever controverted common sense.'

When the Revolution started, many were probably apathetic and a significant minority loyal to Britain. If at the outset a powerful blow could have been struck the Revolution might have collapsed. But after Bunker Hill for a year Britain could do nothing and the delay was fatal. It is possible that without the intervention of France, some form of compromise might have been achieved; but when all is said, it was the stubborn resolution of the colonists and their leaders that led to the British defeat. It might be said that Britain, like Mark Antony, 'was a Roman by a Roman valiantly vanquisht.'

The British soldier was conscious that although he had lost the war he had not been defeated in battle. But it would be idle to deny that in the eyes both of his fellow-countrymen and Europe his reputation had been temporarily diminished. But even as the Thirteen Colonies were slipping out of British hands, far away in India British arms were building another Empire to replace the one that had been lost.

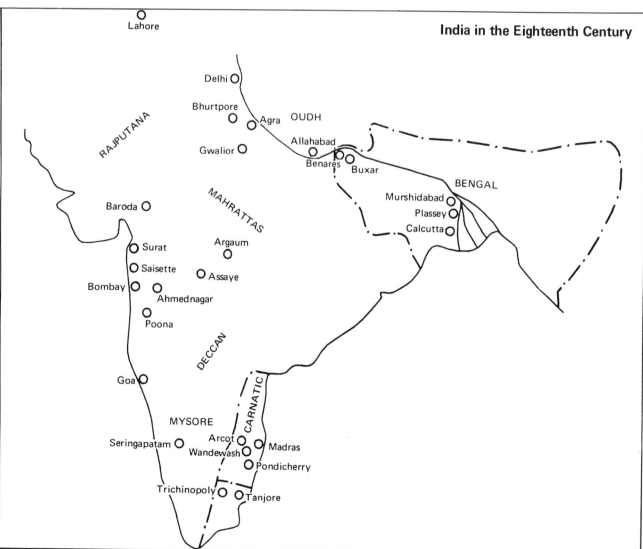

India in the Eighteenth Century

Lahore

Delhi

Bhurtpore

Agra   OUDH

RAJPUTANA

Allahabad

Gwalior

Benares   Buxar

BENGAL

Murshidabad

Baroda

MAHRATTAS

Plassey

Calcutta

Surat

Argaum

Saisette

Assaye

Bombay

Ahmednagar

Poona

DECCAN

Goa

CARNATIC

MYSORE

Arcot

Seringapatam

Madras

Wandewash

Pondicherry

Trichinopoly   Tanjore

CHAPTER 10

India: The Wars against the Mahrattas and Mysore 1763–1818

JAMES P. LAWFORD

When France signed the Treaty of Paris in 1763, The Honourable East India Company had triumphed over its last serious European rival. The following year the Nawab of Oudh and the near powerless Mogul Emperor Shah Alam conspired to drive the British out of Bengal, but at the battle of Buxar the conspirators were soundly beaten by a small British army under Major Hector Munro.

Now the Company was the unchallenged ruler of a land area and population which were both greater than those of the United Kingdom. This unprecedented situation was further complicated by problems of time and space. To sail from England to India took between six months and a year and the journey itself was not without peril. One royal commision disappeared without trace in the Indian Ocean.

In India, the Governor General from his capital, Calcutta, gradually came to wield supreme power, although the governors of the Madras and Bombay Presidencies, as the territories round these cities were called, could be both dilatory and obstructive. At first the Governor General was appointed by the Company's court of directors in London and, in theory at least, was answerable to it, but as the Company's dominion extended further and further, the British Government, the ultimate fount of sovereignty, increasingly took over control of high policy.

For the remainder of the eighteenth century, however, the Company's directors largely determined policy. They wanted trade not war. But the hopeless state of anarchy prevailing in India, and, be it said, the imperial ambitions nursed by one or two of the governor generals, compelled the Company to undertake conquest after conquest, merely to safeguard what it already held.

The armies that were to carry British rule from Calcutta in the east to the Khyber Pass in the northwest, were composed of three differing elements. There were the regular forces of the Crown serving in India to protect British territories from the machinations of the foreigner; then there were the company's European regiments, paid, recruited and organised by the company; and finally there was an ever growing army of Indian regiments, recruited locally, and officered, so far as the senior ranks were concerned, by Britons commissioned into the Company's service.

Armies composed of these three elements, gener-

Opposite: Major-General Stuart inspecting the Madras Artillery at Trichinopoly *c.* 1781. From a water-colour by an officer of the garrison. Stuart, by order of a corrupt Madras Council, in 1776 placed the Governor General, Lord Pigot, under arrest. Pigot died before orders for his release came out from England. A court-martial acquitted Stuart for his part in this extraordinary affair

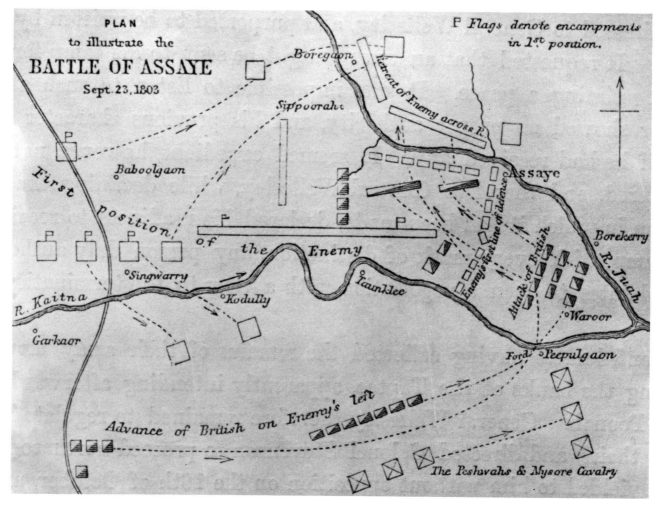

An old plan of the Battle of Assaye

ally commanded by an officer of the regular forces, operated with amazingly little friction. The Company's troops were all trained and organised on British regular lines, the men of the European regiments were largely recruited from among ex-soldiers of the Crown, and many of the British officers, having been commissioned into the British Army, had transferred to the service of the Company in search of better pay and promotion. Seldom long absent from active service, totally professional in their military outlook, these armies reached at this period a standard of technical skill probably excelled nowhere else in the world. They developed a tradition of victory that made them well-nigh invincible.

The Indian princes, mounted on their huge, gun-shy elephants, commanding vast ill-organised semi-feudal hosts could make no head against the far smaller armies of the Company. The more far-sighted among them hired European adventurers to train their infantry and artillerymen, and the armies of these Princes, although generally handicapped by commanders more notable for noble blood than

ability, could be formidable on the battlefield.

After the victory of Buxar, the Company was confronted by two great adversaries. In southern India a military adventurer named Hyder Ali had dispossessed the ruling house and reigned over the state of Mysore. With French help he had created a powerful army, and his restless ambition made a collision merely a matter of time. To the north lay the state of Hyderabad ruled by a Prince with the title of Nizam; save for a brief period, he remained a faithful ally of the British. To the north again and sprawling right across central India was the Mahratta Confederacy, the mightiest power in India.

The Confederacy, founded by Sivaji in the seventeenth century, had dissolved in all but name. Five great princes, the Peshwa, the hereditary chief minister who reigned in Poona, the rajahs of Berar and Baroda, and the heads of the great houses of Holkar of Indore and Scindia of Gwalior, had all carved out independent realms for themselves. But they were little better than brigand chiefs; they depended on hordes of fierce undisciplined cavalry for their strength and plunder for their wealth; no border was sacred to them and in the past their horsemen had pillaged up to the gates of Calcutta and Madras.

The mutual jealousies and hatreds of the five princes prevented them from combining against the Company. Nevertheless it took three wars and 50 years to subdue them. The first Mahratta war arose out of a dispute as to who was to succeed as Peshwa. The Bombay Presidency, anxious to obtain Salsette island which commanded Bombay harbour, saw an opportunity to obtain it as the price of their support for one of the candidates. In 1779 it despatched an army of 4,000 men to capture Poona. The enterprise was a perilous one and to ensure disaster command was entrusted to a committee of three. The committee and its army duly scaled the Western Ghauts and advanced gingerly on Poona. To their dismay they learned that a large Mahratta army was encamped there. The committee lost its nerve and ordered a hurried retreat. The watchful Mahratta cavalry swooped down on the marching columns and forced a disgraceful capitulation known as the Convention of Wargaon. Fortunately one of Britain's

greatest Governor Generals, Warren Hastings, was at Calcutta. He despatched troops across the breadth of India, the situation was retrieved, and eventually at the treaty of Salbai, 1782, an honourable settlement was reached.

While Nana Furnavis, the wise and statesmanlike chief minister to the Peshwa lived, the Mahrattas respected the treaty and avoided raiding into British territory, but after his death all restraint was thrown aside. During the war that followed, General Lake fought some brilliant actions in the north, but the battle of Assaye won by Arthur Wellesley, better known as the Duke of Wellington, put the final issue beyond doubt. The battle epitomises the warfare of that day.

ASSAYE

On 23 September 1803 Wellesley, advancing from Ahmednagar, at about 1.00 p.m. stumbled on the united armies of Berar and Scindia encamped by the River Kaistna. In the camp were more than 20,000 of the famous Mahratta cavalry, some 12,000 infantry and 100 guns; the two armies amounted in all to about 40,000 men. The infantry and gunners,

Assaye. Wellington leading the 78th in the last charge of the day. In this charge a Mahratta gunner 'piked' his horse. Drawn by James Godwin, engraved by Thomas Williams

MAHRATTA AND MYSORE WARS

trained and led by European adventurers (Wellesley to his intense indignation suspected the presence of some Englishmen among them), were organised in properly formed and disciplined units.

Wellesley had with him the 74th and 78th Highlanders, four sepoy infantry battalions, the 19th Light Dragoons, three native cavalry regiments and a handful of guns, a total strength of about 6,000. In addition he had contingents of irregular Mysore and 'Friendly' Mahratta horse whose fighting power was as suspect as their loyalty.

The cold blue eyes of the future victor of Waterloo surveyed the sprawling Mahratta camp. Inaccurate information had placed him in an awkward position. A retreat before that mass of cavalry invited disaster, a frontal assault across the Kaistna would be ruinous. To offset his weakness in numbers he had to confuse that vast host by the speed and audacity of his movements. East of the camp he noticed that a small steep-sided river, the Juah, ran into the Kaistna. From their junction the two rivers formed a narrow V with the open end pointing towards the Mahratta left. He resolved to cross the Kaistna well clear of the Mahrattas, swing left-handed, and then with his left flank covered by the Kaistna and his right by the Juah, attack their camp in the flank and rear. He gambled on crossing the Kaistna before the unwieldy Mahratta army could redeploy and face him.

As his tiny army marched on, a large body of Mahratta cavalry came across to the British side of the Kaistna. Wellesley opposed them with his own irregular horse; the two bodies of cavalry throughout the subsequent action sat on their horses looking at each other suspiciously awaiting the outcome of the battle to decide where their loyalties lay.

The British army crossed the Kaistna and began to form up on the narrow isthmus between the two rivers. But the Mahratta artillery, moving unexpectedly fast, took post with their 100 guns across the open end of the V making the third side of a triangle. Behind the guns columns of infantry could be seen forming line. As each gun reached its allotted position it opened fire.

With his infantry ranged in two lines and his cavalry forming a third, Wellesley ordered the advance. The drums beat out their pulse-quickening tattoo, the pipes of the Highlanders, the 74th on the right, the 78th on the left, pealed out their high challenge. Magnificent in the afternoon sun the long redcoated lines, the light flashing from white cross straps and glittering bayonets, moved steadily forward over the level brown earth.

The Mahratta guns, well served and laid, redoubled their fire. The British artillery was speedily disabled; and as the long lines of infantry breasted a slight swell, they moved full into a hurricane of shot. Black smoke and dust wreathed the Mahratta guns, the ground shook with the thunder of their discharge, and the air cracked and whined as ball and grapeshot swept by killing and maiming. The 78th never paused. Then through the smoke the Highlanders with the redcoated sepoys on their right loomed by the muzzles of the guns. Their bayonets flashed down for the charge. The Mahratta gunners never flinched and most died by their cannon, but the infantry behind, appalled by these apparently indestructible redcoats turned and ran back.

On the right, however, the battle went badly. By the River Juah on the right side of the V lay the little village of Assaye. The Mahrattas had ringed it with guns. Here the pickets of the advance-guard followed by the 74th, against Wellesley's wishes, veered towards the village. A deadly blast of fire smote them. The 74th coming up behind had their ranks dis-

Assaye. The 74th Highlanders have come under a tremendous fire from the Mahratta guns ringing Assaye. In a few minutes the Mahratta cavalry will be charging them. The cactus hedge can be seen on the right of the picture. A modern reconstruction: it is doubtful if the 74th wore the kilt in India at this time

ordered by a cactus hedge. Men fell not in ones and twos but in groups. The survivors, desperately trying to close in on their colours fluttering above the murk, refused to retreat. Then from behind the pall of dust and smoke came a tremendous drumming of hooves, and a horde of Mahratta horsemen shrilling their high-pitched battle-cry surged down on the stricken 74th. Colonel Maxwell, commanding the cavalry in the third line, saw the bright Mahratta scimitars hewing that regiment to pieces.

He ordered his trumpeter to sound the charge and the 19th Light Dragoons with the 4th Native Cavalry beside them crashed home on the lighter Mahratta horse. For a few moments there was a wild hurly burly, then the Mahrattas wheeled about and galloped pellmell for the Juah. Maxwell's cavalry careered on into the Mahratta infantry by Assaye. The Mahratta's ranks were broken by the shock and the whole confused sabring fighting mass erupted into the Juah and streamed away on the far side. Of the 74th scarcely 100 men remained standing.

The situation on the right flank had been restored, but the Mahratta centre had fallen back intact towards Assaye and had there been joined by their second line. A great body of unbroken infantry still remained with their backs to the Juah. Wellesley riding over the battlefield like a demon, although he never lost his icy composure, ordered the two battalions of his second line towards them, while the 78th wheeled across and watched a disorderly mob of Mahratta cavalry hovering uncertainly in the distance.

The battle roared on. As the redcoated sepoys with their short white drawers and brown legs closed in, they met with a tremendous reception from their undaunted adversaries. Spurts of flame flickered up and down the long lines, black musketry smoke rolled down, cleared and rolled down again, the continuous sound of firing was punctuated by the cries of the wounded, the oaths and battle cries of the contestants, the incessant thrumming of the drums. Then the sepoys slowly gave back.

But now Maxwell, having rallied his cavalry, had led them back to their original positions. Ordering him to watch the Mahratta Cavalry Wellesley formed up the 78th and the 7th Native Cavalry to break the stubborn enemy infantry by Assaye. While he marshalled them, a cannon ball killed his horse. He remounted without pause. As the 78th moved majestically forward, the sorely tried Mahratta infantry wavered before their steel-tipped lines. Then the Highlanders' muskets came up to their shoulders, and their levelled weapons belched

Tippoo Sultan. A portrait by Godefroy

flame, smoke and destruction. Men fell by the score. The Mahrattas broke, and fled across the Juah with the sepoys chasing them like terriers worrying rats; but the 78th preserved their ordered ranks, and it was well that they did so.

Mahrattas had filtered back to the guns which the 78th had taken earlier, and swinging them round had opened fire on the rear of that regiment; through the haze of dust and smoke, formed bodies of Mahratta infantry could be seen beyond the Highlanders' left. Wellesley directed Maxwell to take his cavalry and destroy the remaining Mahratta infantry while he himself led the 78th and the 7th Native Cavalry back to recapture the guns. Again the trumpets blared out the charge. Maxwell's troopers flogged their blown and weary mounts forward. The Mahratta infantry coolly stood their ground. Then they loosed off a devastating volley. The gallant Maxwell fell dead and his men recoiled; but the Mahrattas only used their brief success to make good their escape, while away on the left Scindia's splendid gunners fell before the bayonets of the unconquerable 78th and the sabres of the Indian troopers; not however before a gunner had speared Wellesley's horse and forced him to remount once again.

It was 6.00 p.m. and the battle was over. The Mahratta cavalry who but for one charge had done so little to justify their fame had ridden away; the

The storming of Seringapatam. On the right the stormers are firmly established on the ramparts. On the left a colour has been planted on the top of the breach and the stormers are about to carry it. Section of a print from the painting by R. K. Porter

Mahratta infantry were dispersed and their guns taken. Wellesley's crippled army could not pursue. A quarter of its number littered the battlefield. Suddenly Wellesley's superhuman energy drained away. The victor sat on the ground, his head between his hands, and thus remained through the night, unsleeping and silent.

On 1 November at the bitterly fought battle of Laswari, Lake was to destroy the last of Scindia's European trained infantry; the war itself was to drag on another two years, and Wellesley was to win the Battle of Argaum and Lake to fail before the grim walls of Bhurtpore; but after Assaye the final victory was never in doubt.

THE STORMING OF SERINGAPATAM

But before the Battle of Assaye, a reckoning had been taken with Mysore. In 1779 Hyder Ali had challenged the might of the Company, and although the ageing Eyre Coote had saved Madras by his successive victories at Porto Novo, Polilur and Sholinghur, Hyder Ali died while still successfully defying the armies of the Company. His son, Tippoo, made peace, but could not long keep his ambitions in check. He invaded Tanjore, an ally of the British. The Governor General, Cornwallis, unperturbed by unhappy memories of Yorktown, took the field. He drove

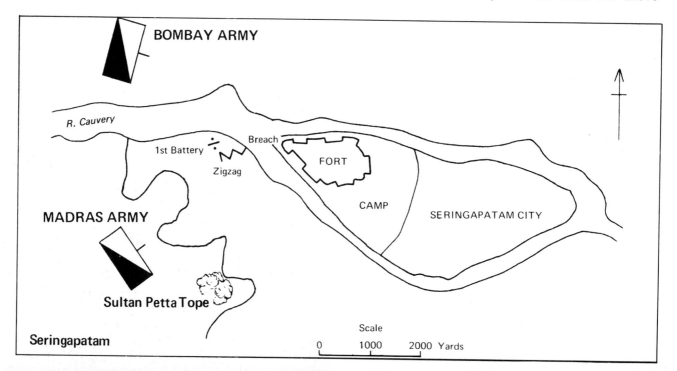

BOMBAY ARMY

R. Cauvery

1st Battery

Breach

Zigzag

FORT

CAMP

SERINGAPATAM CITY

MADRAS ARMY

Sultan Petta Tope

Seringapatam

Scale

0   1000   2000 Yards

Tippoo into his supposedly impregnable fortress of Seringapatam and surrounded him there. Tippoo came to terms, ceded half his state, and surrendered his two sons as hostages for his good behaviour.

Then in 1798 Tippoo started intriguing with the French. With that nation occupying Egypt, such contacts could not be tolerated, and in the spring of 1799 a large army under General Harris converged on Seringapatam. This time it was to be a fight to a finish.

On 5 April the siege began. It was not without its dangers. The fortress was situated on an island in the Cauvery River. When the rains came towards the end of May the Cauvery would become unfordable, Harris's lines of communication would dissolve in a sea of mud and he would have to retreat. The Mysore irregular cavalry, like the Russian cossacks, could cut a retreating army in pieces. Harris had to storm Seringapatam before the end of May, or risk a catastrophe.

The capture of Seringapatam was to earn Harris a peerage and the Governor General an Irish marquisate. (The latter was to complain bitterly that he had bargained on a dukedom, or at least advancement in the English peerage). The news of it was to send a shiver of awed wonder through the cities of India.

The main fortifications consisted of an outer rampart by the river's edge and an inner one separated from it by a ditch. On 4 May the Engineers reported that, in their opinion, a practicable breach had been blown in the north-west ramparts, just south of where the Cauvery divided. Harris resolved to storm on the 5th.

General Baird, at one time a prisoner in Seringapatam, was appointed to command the stormers, some 5,000 picked men. He divided them into two parties. One under Colonel Sherbrooke was to turn right at the top of the breach, the other under Colonel Dunlop left. The two parties were then to clear the ramparts until they met on the far side of the fortress.

Under cover of darkness the stormers filtered forward to the front trenches and sweltered there under an unusually hot sun, while the guns thundered on. Then at 1.00 p.m. General Baird gave the order to assault. Like a tidal wave bursting up a river the stormers rushed across the Cauvery and up the breach. A deadly hail of grapeshot and musket balls tore through their ranks, but nothing could stop them. They gained the top of the ramparts in six minutes. Colonel Sherbrooke's men now turned right and drove on against a faltering opposition.

On the left a sterner contest developed. As the stormers came to a corner in the ramparts they ran into a ferocious fire. Here Tippoo himself commanded. Twice they charged and twice they were beaten back. Fortunately, at the breach, Captain Goodall of the 12th Foot had led some men on to the inner rampart. They now overlooked Tippoo's men, and delivered a tremendous volley on the massed defenders. The defenders, hitherto so staunch, suddenly panicked and, losing all order, jumped down into the ditch between the two walls. Their assailants, still gripped with the berserk frenzy of the storm, granted no quarter. Some fired down into the milling mob below, others leapt into the ditch to club and bayonet the hapless fugitives like hunters slaughtering young seals. The defenders fought each other to escape from the fortress by the narrow water-gate. Here Tippoo fell unnoticed, his corpse speedily concealed under a mound of dead. At last the massacre came to an end and a great cheer announced that the two parties of stormers had met on the eastern ramparts. Seringapatam had fallen and 10,000 of the defenders with it.

When his body had been recovered, Tippoo was buried with full military honours. A truncated state of Mysore was handed back to the old ruling house. No substantial threat to British rule now remained in southern India, and for some 150 years, save for one or two minor insurrections and occasional forays against bandits, that part of the subcontinent was to know a sleepy peace that led it to be christened the 'sloth belt'. But in Europe the convulsions caused by the French Revolution, which had already affected India, were by no means abated.

A photograph of the watergate where Tippoo died

The storming of Fort Royal, Martinique, by General Sir Charles Grey and Admiral Sir John Jervis 1794. Sir Charles Grey saw action in the Seven Years' War, being ADC to Prince Ferdinand of Brunswick at Minden, and in the American Revolution. He won the sobriquet of 'No Flint Grey' for a gallant night attack which he made with cold steel. General 1795, Baron 1801, Earl 1806

CHAPTER 11

The Early Campaigns against Revolutionary France
1793–1810

ANTONY BRETT-JAMES

French intervention in the War of the American Revolution had proved fatal to British sovereignty over the Thirteen Colonies in America, but by some strange irony it was to prove equally fatal to the rule of the house of Bourbon. The quest for liberty which inspired Lafayette and his comrades spread with their return to France, and the Revolution of 1789 in that country owed much to the ideas of the American colonists. The forces now unloosed threatened every dynasty in Europe. Britain at first remained aloof but when in 1793 French armies menaced the Netherlands, she could no longer stand aside. The conflict that followed lasted virtually without intermission until 1815.

Regrettable as it may be, during the first fifteen years of this prolonged war the British Army remained about the least respected of all the armies contending with France. Because the decade which followed the American Revolution had witnessed deplorable neglect of factors which make an army capable of waging war, much had to be reformed in 1793, and this took time. Dismal shortages of almost every item of military equipment became as apparent as the weakness in manpower. It needed only the first campaign in Flanders to reveal the inadequacy of the British to influence events on land, whatever victories they might gain at sea.

'There are risks in a British warfare unknown in any other service' wrote that veteran commander of expeditionary forces, General Sir Ralph Abercromby, in 1801, shortly before he was mortally wounded in Egypt. He spoke the truth from mortifying experience.

The risks stemmed from many and various causes. A mere catalogue of the expeditions upon which British forces, large and small, were sent in this period indicates the range and degree of dispersion. 1793 saw, besides the Duke of York's army in Flanders, two battalions and a few guns trying to help a royalist revolt in Toulon. Whereas 1794 found 2,000 troops in Corsica and another 7,000 sent to the West Indies to capture St Lucia, Martinique and Guadeloupe from the French, the following year was marked by the fruitless despatch of 5,000 men to the island of Yeu off Brittany, and the arrival of a similar force at Cape Town, which belonged to the Dutch. In 1797 4,000 troops landed in the Spanish possession of Trinidad, while 12,000 were garrisoning Ireland against a threat of French invasion; this number rose to some 40,000 in the following year, when 1,400 men were sent on a raid to Ostend and 3,000 seized Minorca.

The year 1799 witnessed the largest expedition yet: to the Helder in northern Holland, where over 36,000 British troops tried to co-operate with a smaller Russian force. If 1800 saw 13,000 troops sent to north-west Spain to destroy, if possible – it turned out to be the reverse – the dockyard, arsenal and fortifications at Ferrol, then 1801 had 15,000 British

G

soldiers sailing to Egypt to defeat the French army abandoned there by Napoleon. In 1804 it was Surinam; in the following year the scene was Hanover, whither about 25,000 British and German troops were ordered; and in 1806 we have 5,000 men landed from Calabria in Sicily to win one of the Army's rare victories at this period: Maida. This and the next year are especially eventful, for 17,000 British soldiers and 8,000 Germans bombard and capture Copenhagen, 6,000 take the Cape of Good Hope again, about 1,500 set forth from there to South America and have to be reinforced, first by another 2,000 from the Cape, next by over 4,000 diverted to Buenos Aires from another destination, and finally by 1,800 troops brought by General Whitelocke, the man who became a byword for military disgrace, ineptitude, even cowardice.

Though 1808 brings the opening of British operations in Portugal and later Spain, it is also notable for one of the most absurd and frustrating of all expeditions: Sir John Moore's arrival in Sweden with 10,000 troops in response to a request for aid, only to find that his men are forbidden to land, and he himself is placed under house arrest when he travels to Stockholm to negotiate with the King.

As for 1809, though it produced Sir Arthur Wellesley's successes at the crossing of the Douro and at Talavera, it was marred by the disastrous outcome of the largest expedition to leave England – that despatched to Walcheren to destroy a French fleet being built in Antwerp. Of the 40,000 troops involved, one tenth died of fever. There was also an attack on Martinique, with Guadeloupe again and later Mauritius in 1810. British troops found themselves even further afield in the following year, this time away to the east in Java, where half the 12,000 troops were British; and in 1812 many more of them went in the opposite direction, across the North Atlantic to Canada and America. Two years' fighting there culminated in failure at New Orleans, where part of Wellington's victorious Peninsular army had to fight in vain. Nearer home sees a small force in northern Germany at the time of Leipzig, in 1813, and another in the Low Countries to aid a Dutch uprising. Even peace and Napoleon's abdication and departure to Elba brought respite to comparatively few of the long-suffering troops, since many of them served with an army of occupation or prepared to sail back from North America, only one brigade doing so in time to fight on the battlefield of Waterloo.

The list is long enough, in all conscience, denoting as it does an odyssey to destinations where the rewards of effort were too often outweighed by the cost in human life. The saga is longer still if we mention the campaigns of Wellesley and Lake in India, and the force sent from Bombay to the Red Sea under Baird's command to participate in the battle for Egypt in 1801. One must be thankful, as no doubt the troops would have been had they but known, that proposed expeditions to Venezuela, to Mexico, even round Cape Horn to Chile, with a subsequent march across the Andes into the Argentine, were never launched.

The naval and military commanders had enough problems in getting the troops to the destination and executing their orders on arrival without having to cope with certain extra burdens imposed upon them too frequently by the ignorance, indecision, and improvidence of ministers at home. Sometimes troops were sent off with little or no thought on how they were to be resupplied and reinforced. Too little account was taken of such paramount factors as time and distance, trade winds and climate. Plans were often based upon bad information, underestimates of the opposition to be encountered, even on misconceptions about the number of troops and ships available to a force commander. Ministers were prone to think wishfully and toy with over-sanguine projects, some of which were quite impossible. The worst offender was probably Henry Dundas, upon whom Sir John Fortescue unleashed a pen filled with the ink of irony and indignation. Not only was his attitude to difficulties inclined to be airy if not downright casual; his instructions were sometimes as vague as his intentions were indecisive. It was tiresome enough for generals to have to remind Dundas that he appeared to have omitted this or that vital factor or snag from his calculations, but it was intolerable that Sir Charles Stuart's expedition to Minorca should be exposed to the risks of a security leak from Dundas's own office.

Not that some of his successors were a great improvement, with their contradictory orders to men like Whitelocke. And in fairness one must say that errors and abortions were often no fault of the Government. For example, it was largely Commodore Popham's fault that an expedition ever sailed to the River Plate. Sir John Moore was sent to Sweden in all good faith. On occasion an ally was found to have been knocked out of the war before promised aid could be sent, though the Prussian statesman Haugwitz had some justification for his bitter remark to a diplomat in 1807: 'You English are always two months too late!'

For the first decade of the long war, this dispersal

The Battle of Maida, 1806. Here Sir John Stuart with 5,000 men beat a French army of nearly 6,500 under General Reynier. Except for cracking a few jokes Sir John was happy to allow the battle to take its course without any interference from him. The well-drilled fire of his infantry, drawn up in line, shattered the French columns and presented the delighted but amazed British general with a victory that led him to declare 'Begad I never saw a thing so glorious as this'. Unhappily he was quite incapable of profiting from his success

of Britain's military strength stemmed from the Government's 'blue water' policy, by which Pitt in particular, seeking to take full advantage of Britain's naval strength, planned to attack France and her Spanish ally on the water and to strip them of their sugar-island colonies. The wealth derived from this source would, it was hoped, equip coalition armies to engage France on land and provide subsidies to keep Austria and Prussia in the field.

Whereas, apart from garrisons stationed in overseas possessions, most of Britain's enemies and allies reached their theatres of war overland – Napoleon's seaborne expedition to Egypt is a notable exception – British troops had invariably to travel there by ship. And what ships! Regiments might be fortunate to go in old ships of the line from which the guns had been removed; but often they were cooped up in such 'transports' as a small schooner built for the coastal coal trade and having its hold still deep in black dust, or in a Newcastle collier loaded with more men and horses than she could well accommodate.

One soldier tells us that when part of the Brigade of Guards sailed to Flanders in 1793, 'the men were stowed in the holds in such numbers that one third of them were constantly obliged to keep on deck of nights, to afford the others space sufficient to breathe in freely.' Many of the transports were unseaworthy, or wretched sailors, and certainly unfit for the service for which they were hired. Such vessels might be tolerated for a short journey across the North Sea or

Channel, but were often unsafe as well as grotesquely uncomfortable. Add to all this the hazard produced by certain masters and mates whose incompetence was only surpassed by their intoxication, to such a degree that one Army captain found himself obliged to assume command of the transport in which he and his men were unfortunate enough to be travelling, and navigate it home from the West Indies.

Once the troops had embarked in the transports, a convoy could not necessarily set off, since contrary winds frequently prevented the ships from leaving harbour. In October 1800, for instance, the 20th Foot went on board at Spithead on its way to Minorca. After sailing twice, only to be forced back each time by unfavourable winds, the regiment left Spithead finally in mid-December, but was compelled by the weather to put into Falmouth, where the transports were delayed a further five weeks before leaving for Minorca at the end of January 1801. Even then their troubles were not over. Gales in the Bay of Biscay sent several ships on to the rocks, and those which reached Lisbon safely had to spend a week while the damage was repaired and the scattered convoy collected. March was nearly over before the 20th reached Minorca, yet the men, despite spending nearly six months on board, were reasonably healthy and contented. At least the battalion kept together, which was not the fate of the 28th who, while bound for the West Indies in 1796, had six companies driven back by a storm and sent eventually for duty in Gibraltar, while the remainder reached their proper destination, were placed under command of another regiment, and helped to suppress two revolts before rejoining their own headquarters.

Many British soldiers never reached their appointed destination. When, in 1805, the 26th Foot was sent to Hanover, part was lost on the Goodwin Sands, while part was wrecked on the French coast and taken prisoner. Later in the same year the 54th was ordered home from Gibraltar, but the vessel conveying two companies, along with half another regiment, parted company with the convoy in the Bay of Biscay and fell into the hands of a French naval squadron on its way to Mauritius. The prisoners were put aboard a frigate and this eventually sailed into Table Bay in March 1806, all unaware that Cape Colony had just been recaptured by the British, who were delighted to release their compatriots.

Wind and weather also played their part when the troops did eventually arrive at some distant shore. So also did the Royal Navy, who had escorted the convoy across the sea. Whether or not the enemy opposed the disembarkation, the problems of getting the soldiers ashore were considerable. The earlier expeditions were, in this as well as other respects, handicapped by sheer lack of experience. For one thing, there was usually no time or opportunity to rehearse the operation. For another, the Navy were seldom aware of the need to land a battalion together on the same beach at the same time, rather than have the companies scattered along several miles of coast and landed in different phases.

Although, in March 1801, the Navy lost all hope of surprise by bringing Abercromby's army straight opposite Alexandria, so that progress along the Egyptian coast to the intended landing place could be watched by the French, and despite a gale which blew for three days beforehand, the disembarkation was a success, and none too costly, thanks in part to numerous rehearsals in Marmarice Bay, Turkey. The French piquets were posted along the curve of Aboukir Bay and largely concealed by sand-hills and clumps of trees. Soon after daylight on 8 March the first wave of troops stepped into small boats from the transports, anchored six miles offshore. Lt-Gen. Sir Henry Bunbury relates what happened next:

Much time was consumed in disentangling the boats, and arranging them according to the line of battle of the army, so that when they touched the beach each brigade, battalion, and company might be in its proper place. ... It was 8 o'clock a.m. before the line of boats pulled on abreast, and in steady order, towards the shore, and till that time the enemy had lain in silence observing our movements; but as soon as our boats came within their reach, fifteen pieces of cannon opened upon them with round shot, though the enemy's fire was somewhat disturbed and confused by that of several English gunboats which had been thrown in advance of our line. So closely were our soldiers packed in the boats that they could not move, and indeed the strictest orders had been given that they should sit perfectly still. The seamen pulled steadily onward, the pace of each boat being regulated by that on the extreme right. In this calm order on they came, till they were within reach of grape shot, and then the fire became terribly severe and destructive. Some boats were sunk, and many of our men were killed or wounded as they sat motionless and helpless under the storm of shot, to which both seamen and soldiers answered occasionally by loud hurrahs!

When still nearer, the musketry of the French was poured in, quick and sharp, and our men were falling fast; but at length the boats upon the right felt the ground. Out sprang our hard-tried soldiers, each man was in his place, and with Moore and Spencer at their head, the 23rd and 28th regiments, and the four flank companies of the 40th, breasted the steep sand-hill. Without firing a shot, they rushed at one burst to the summit of the ridge, driving headlong before them two battalions of the enemy and capturing four pieces of field artillery.

Over 5,000 troops were landed that day in the face of an enemy prepared to meet them – at a cost of 641 Army and 178 Navy casualties.

Things did not always go as well, even with the Egyptian experience to build upon. In 1809, for example, when part of the army sent to take Walcheren tried to land on the south shore of the Scheldt estuary, the wind and surf prevented a landing on the first day. Next morning the wind was still blowing too hard, and the boats laden with troops were in danger of drifting under the French batteries. By this time the enemy's strength had grown to 1,000 men, whereas the naval boats could not carry more than 700 soldiers at a time. Since an hour and a half would elapse before reinforcements could be landed in a second wave, the military commander postponed the landing till the morrow, by which time the French garrison numbered some 4,000 troops, and increased still further. At this juncture the attack was put off altogether, with serious consequences for the operation as a whole.

British soldiers were always so heavily laden that if a boat was hit by artillery fire or if, as occurred near Cape Town in 1806, it capsized on striking a rock in heavy seas, 'down went thirty-six of our noble fellows, cheering as they sank; they were so loaded with ammunition, accoutrements, etc. that they went down directly; four only were saved of the forty in the boat – poor fellows! Not an hour before they were dancing reels to the bagpipes.'

Exposed as they were to cramped, comfortless conditions, to prolonged journeys by sea, to the risk of shipwreck and capture, and to the hazards of landings, the soldiers were likely to arrive exhausted at the scene of action. Every effort was made during the voyage to ward off the damaging effects of scurvy with remedies like lemon juice and to vary the salt meat and weevil-ridden biscuits by taking live poultry and fresh vegetables on deck, but these could easily be consumed almost before the transport set sail, and many a man could have written, as did John Shipp of the 22nd: 'my poor legs were as big as drums, and my gums swollen to an enormous size, and my tongue too big for my mouth.'

Far more serious were the diseases encountered once ashore. Between 1794 and 1796 alone it is estimated that some 80,000 soldiers were lost to the service in the West Indies, most of them from the deadly yellow fever or 'black vomit'. In that short period the 41st Regiment lost 17 officers and 1,500 men; in a single year the 32nd lost 32 officers and close on 1,000 rank and file in San Domingo; within three months of 1796 the yellow fever accounted for 9 officers and 436 other ranks in the 66th stationed on the same island; and of the flank companies of the 12th Foot which fought on St Lucia, Martinique and Guadeloupe in 1794, only one officer and two men survived to return home.

That the cavalry fared no better is shown by some dismal figures; whereas, during two and a half years in the West Indies the 13th Light Dragoons had one man killed in action, 19 of their officers, 7 quartermasters, 2 volunteers and 287 NCOs and men died

of disease. What is more, of the 52 who eventually returned to England out of 450, many were found to be totally unfit and were invalided at once, while some of the remainder had to be gradually discharged.

All in all, Government policy cost the British Army 100,000 men, dead or permanently incapacitated, in five years, and the 40,000 who perished in 1794–6 exceeded the total losses of Wellington's army in the Peninsular War. Only in the Walcheren expedition of 1809 were the depredations of sickness as appalling. One hundred and six men were killed in the campaign, but 4,000 died of fever, and when the island was finally evacuated, one third of the 35,000 survivors were in hospital.

The varieties of terrain almost equalled the number of countries in which the Army had to serve. In Holland the soldiers exhausted themselves either struggling up and down immense sand-hills or else crossing low meadows drained by deep ditches. In Calabria the soldiers made their way through marshes and skirted belts of coppice which concealed French sharpshooters. By contrast they scaled craggy slopes in Martinique, followed narrow tracks through dense forests, and dealt with sharpshooters firing at them from fields of sugar-cane. During Whitelocke's advance on Buenos Aires the troops, besides fording a river armpit-deep, pushed through a maze of narrow lanes and intricate high-fenced gardens; and they were already weary from floundering waist-deep through a veritable sea of black marsh mud, tripping over reeds and aquatic plants, and splashing most of the food they carried into an uneatable state. Seven years later, another British force, having been rowed up creeks through a forest of reeds, had to advance on New Orleans among orange groves, sugar-canes and cypress-swamps.

The landing of British troops in Egypt. Engraving of a painting by de Loutherbourg 1804

Above: French Chasseurs charging, unsuccessfully, a British square at the Battle of Fuentes de Oñoro

Below: The Battle of Castalla, March 1813. A good example of French columns attacking a British line. General Murray fought a creditable action against the French under Marshal Suchet. From a drawing by Lt Reeves engraved by Clarke and Dubourg

CHAPTER 12

The Era of Wellington;
The Peninsular War
and the Battle of Waterloo
1807–15

ANTONY BRETT-JAMES

CHRONOLOGICAL TABLE

If the last chapter appears to be a sorry recital, the British Army nevertheless improved steadily, in spite of and sometimes because of every setback. The new Commander-in-Chief, the Duke of York, made a major contribution to this improvement.

At the age of thirty-one he succeeded a general of seventy-nine and in the next few years carried out numerous important reforms. He appointed a Military Secretary; he increased the number of unpaid promotions, while retaining the system of

PENINSULAR WAR AND WATERLOO

Lt-Gen. Sir John Moore. An ensign in 1776, he had his first baptism of fire in the American Revolution. He was mortally wounded at the Battle of Corunna, but lived to hear that Soult, his opponent, had been repulsed. Soult chivalrously raised a monument to him. A painting by T. Lawrence

promotion by purchase; having called for a list of captains under the age of twelve and lieutenant-colonels under eighteen, he ruled that no officer could be promoted to field rank without at least six years service, or to captain with less than two. Officers in the Artillery and Engineers, controlled as they were by the separate Board of Ordnance, came under quite a different system.

The Duke of York also improved the lot of the other ranks by increases of pay and rations, by better clothing, including the provision of greatcoats, and by the gradual abolition of the pigtail. The medical service was reformed and hospitals were established. The Duke of York's School was opened in 1803 as 'an Asylum for educating one thousand children, the legal offspring of British soldiers.' In this and many other ways the Duke showed his humane interest in welfare, his sagacity and practical reforming zeal, based upon painful experiences while campaigning in Flanders.

Slowly, thanks in part to the translation of Continental manuals and treatises, the Army became more professional – a process to which John Le Marchant contributed notably by his proposals for 'the establishment of a Military College for the education of persons intended for the land service, which also comprised a course of instruction for officers intended for service on the General Staff.' His plans being accepted, and supported by the Duke of York, a senior department was opened in May 1799 at High Wycombe and two years later a junior department in Marlow: the forerunners of the Staff College and Sandhurst. Officers for the Royal Artillery and Engineers were already being trained at Woolwich.

A second vital breakthrough in the sphere of training occurred when Sir John Moore, veteran of Corsica, St Lucia, the Helder and Egypt as well as the American War of Independence, was appointed in 1803 to command a new experimental brigade at Shorncliffe Camp in Kent. The instruction given set out to provide the British Army with its own light infantry. Beginnings had been made before, though mostly with foreign corps, and when these dwindled through shortage of recruits, they were collected together into the 5th Battalion of the 60th – riflemen dressed in green jackets, but not British.

On several of the overseas expeditions the lack of riflemen had been serious, especially in Holland, so it was as well that in 1801 the 95th Rifle Corps was formed under Coote Manningham's command. Besides the 95th, Moore's brigade had the 43rd and 52nd, and they were ultimately to become the

famous Light Brigade, later expanded into the Light Division, which gained such distinction in the Peninsula.

Based upon translations of works like Baron de Rottenburg's *Regulations for the Exercise of Riflemen and Light Infantry* and General Jarry's *Instructions concerning the Duties of Light Infantry in the Field* as well as Manningham's own *Regulations for the Rifle Corps*, the training concentrated upon marksmanship. To encourage prowess, cockades were awarded to first and second class shots. The men practised at ranges between 50 and 300 yards. They learnt to patrol villages and woods, to do duty on picket and outpost, and to perform the role of rear-guard and advance-guard.

All this time the British Army increased steadily in strength, from close on 43,000 in 1793 to more than double that in the next year and 160,000 by 1801. Early in 1809, soon after the Battle of, and evacuation from, Corunna, the Army numbered some 200,000 effective rank and file, of which over half were stationed outside Britain, principally in the West Indies, in Ceylon and India, and in the Mediterranean. Approximately another 14,000 troops were in Portugal, near the Lisbon base which was to serve Wellington's Peninsular army from 1809 until the summer of 1813, when harbours along Spain's northern coast could be used to shorten drastically the line of communication by sea as well as overland.

Wellington never had more than 40,000 British troops under personal command. From the summer of 1810 onwards he had around 25,000 Portuguese, trainted and officered by the British under Sir William Beresford's able direction, and in several battles his force was swelled by Spanish troops, though after

Opposite: Fort St George Madras. *Overleaf:* The Battle of Fuentes de Oñoro, 5 May 1811. The picture illustrates one of the most famous feats of the Royal Horse Artillery during the Peninsular War. Isolated and surrounded by the French Cavalry, Captain Ramsay limbered up his guns and, at the gallop, charged right through the enemy horsemen to come safe away.

the let-down at Talavera in 1809 another four years elapsed before he had a sizeable force on one of his battlefields: 7,000 at Vitoria and nearly thrice that total in the battles among the Pyrenees at the end of 1813. Other British contingents operated latterly along Spain's Mediterranean coast, in particular at Tarragona, and in March 1811 General Graham's force, stationed in Cadiz, defeated a French army at Barrosa, one of the few successes achieved in the Peninsula away from Wellington's direct control.

With his comparatively small British-Portuguese army, which benefited from the fine regiments of the King's German Legion from Hanover, Wellington held his own against French troops whose numbers varied between 360,000 and a quarter of a million, but whose superior strength had to be dissipated in order to garrison the main roads and protect every convoy and courier from the revengeful attentions of guerrilla bands.

He achieved this by realising that the marshals commanding the several French armies were slow,

even reluctant, to help one another; that the more of Spain they conquered, the more territory would have to be held down by French troops against a disaffected population; and that they would seldom have enough troops left to take the offensive against him in Portugal. To concentrate a sufficiently large force to achieve this would produce two awkward results for the French: large tracts of Spain would relapse into revolt for lack of a quelling hand; and two French armies in the same area would quickly face shortages of food and be compelled to disperse again in order to avoid starvation. Hence Wellington's early assertion that with 30,000 British troops and his Portuguese levies – about equal in number – he would hold his own against any combination of fewer than 100,000 Frenchmen.

Wellington's first full-scale battle in Portugal was Vimeiro, fought in August 1808. Able to watch the Frenchmen's dusty approach, he disposed his troops on a hill and along a ridge. The French came on in the style which had succeeded so often in the

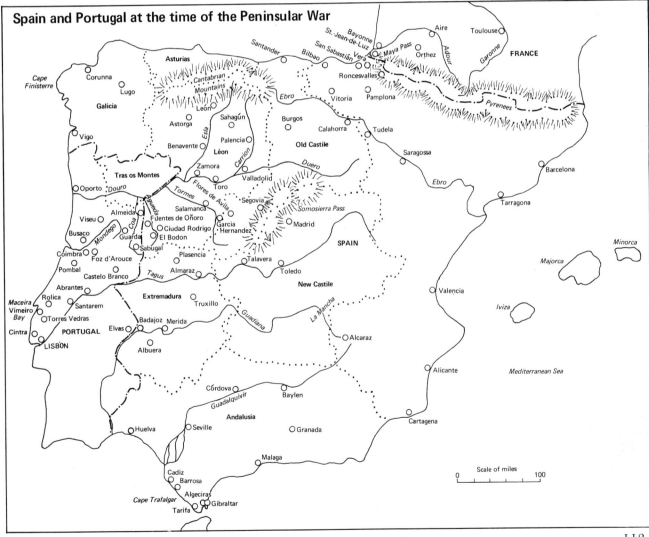

Spain and Portugal at the time of the Peninsular War

The Honourable East India Company's Army. *Opposite, above left:* Bengal grenadiers *c.*1815, sergeant and private. *Above right:* Bombay Horse Artillery officer, *c.*1845. *Below left:* 28th Bengal Native Infantry, Native officer and colours, *c.*1845. *Below right:* Officer of Bengal Light Cavalry in full dress, *c.*1845

past: infantry columns, some 30 men across the front and extending 42 ranks from the front to back, were accompanied by artillery, protected on the flanks by cavalry, and preceded by skirmishers. These were meant to distract the main British defence line by accurate shooting, but they had first to overcome or drive back Wellington's riflemen waiting down the slope. This they failed to do. Instead, the riflemen were able to shoot down so many French gunners and their horses that the infantry columns derived little support from their escorting artillery.

At this juncture the twelve British guns, masked till the last possible moment, fired one devastating blow, whereupon the British infantry unleashed one volley after another, starting at a range of 100 yards. The French had left it too late to deploy into line, and to do so under such a murderous fire was in any case impossible. They broke and ran. A similar fate overtook three other French columns: either the head virtually disintegrated as the British, in line two deep, fired their first volley, or it was caught by converging fire as Wellington's battalions wheeled and fired from a flank.

Wellington, besides protecting his infantry from the French skirmishers by use of his own riflemen, had spared his troops most of the poundings by French artillery by sheltering them behind the crest of the ridge, on a reverse slope. This became a familiar pattern.

The Vimeiro success of line versus column had been heralded by the small-scale victory at Maida two years before. In one of the battle's three main actions, 694 British light infantry, formed up in two-deep lines on a front of about 200 yards, had routed a French regiment, 1,600 strong, and had taken 430 prisoners besides inflicting the same number of casualties.

The passage of the R. Douro at Oporto, 12 May 1809. Wellington bamboozled Soult as to where he would cross and then using a few wine barges slipped a force over the river, which seized the Bishop's seminary (the large white building in the centre of the picture). A tardy French, attempt to retake the seminary failed and Wellington was in Oporto by nightfall

One can say that Vimeiro, followed by Talavera and Busaco, gave Wellington a reputation, among the French at least, as being predominantly a *defensive* general, though anyone who recalled his bold crossing of the Douro in May 1809 and his Indian victory at Assaye in 1803 would scarcely have limited him thus. However, it was at Salamanca in July 1812 that Wellington first convinced his opponents that he could attack with shattering results, for on this battlefield he suddenly, with masterly timing, went from the defensive to the offensive as soon as he saw that the French divisions had laid themselves wide open to such a blow by moving westwards across his front and, in so doing, becoming imprudently extended over four miles. The French, taken by surprise, were attacked by three of Wellington's divisions in turn, advancing in two-deep line except for one Portuguese brigade. This attack by infantry, with guns alongside and cavalry to the fore, wrecked the leading French division. The second one, though formed into squares and behind the crest of a ridge, was put to flight by British infantry in a two-deep line. The survivors, and then the next French division, were smashed and pursued by Le Marchant's brigade of heavy dragoons, which broke into hastily formed squares. Thus three divisions had been destroyed in half an hour.

The rest of the battle proved far more difficult and costly for Wellington's generals and their troops, but line continued to defeat column until victory had been achieved.

To see the British infantry facing one of the supreme battlefield ordeals, we can hardly do better than watch them at Albuera on 16 May 1811, when their commander, Beresford, left to himself without Wellington's guiding mastery, fumbled, disposed his troops inadequately, and was saved by the initiative of one staff officer and the superb valour of his soldiers.

Foremost in the fight were battalions from East Kent, Northampton, Berkshire, Huntingdon, Worcestershire, West Middlesex (who gained their honoured name of 'Die-hards'), and the Fusilier Brigade – the Royal Welsh and two battalions of the 7th. John Colborne's brigade, ordered forward at a run to support the Spaniards, gained ground until assailed by French hussars and lancers, and met disaster, suffering 1,400 casualties in the process. Hoghton's brigade, resolutely firing through the smoke at the advancing French columns, was continually ravaged by grapeshot, had to close the gaps in its dwindling line, and eventually found itself

A British division crossing the River Tagus by the rope ferry Wellington had established at Vilha Velha. The ferry cut two days marches off his communications with southern Portugal. From the painting by Major St Clair an officer who served with Wellington in the Peninsula

shooting at a range of twenty yards. Two thirds of the officers were killed or wounded.

Similar losses were incurred by Sir William Myers' fusiliers, who also fought a savage musketry duel, and closed the range until the French broke. Then, braving terrible artillery fire, they went in pursuit.

The English soldiers came through the test thanks to superlative discipline, to skilled handling of their weapons, and above all to sheer regimental pride and spirit. Small wonder that their performance inspired Napier to pen a noble and justly famous tribute which opens with the words: 'Then was seen with what strength and majesty the British soldier fights.'

Of cavalry Wellington never had enough in the Peninsula to copy the French pattern of launching several thousand horsemen with a massive frontal charge, as Napoleon could do in some of his central European battles. At Talavera he had under 3,000 of his own, at Fuentes de Oñoro in 1811 his cavalry numbered 1,864, while 3,880 British, Portuguese and Spanish horse were under Beresford's command at Albuera. The situation improved in 1812, because the battlefield of Salamanca saw over 3,500 British cavalry alone. Another year went by, and for the battle of Vitoria Wellington disposed of 7,424 British and nearly 900 Portuguese cavalry.

For the first three years at least he was kept very short, in part because much of the nation's cavalry was retained at home for police duties in case of industrial unrest or riot. One result of this domestic role was the splitting of regiments into small detachments, and this in turn diminished the amount of training – already most inadequate, above all in

French prisoners entering Salamanca after the battle

what was to be the cavalry's most regular task in Wellington's campaigns: outpost duty. This had to be learnt in Portugal and Spain, and the masters and models for this duty were the Hussars of the King's German Legion.

Other duties performed by cavalry off the battlefield included protection of foragers, finding river fords and sounding them, escort of prisoners, limited raids, pursuit, and capture of stragglers. All these were done with determination and considerable skill, but in pitched battles the cavalry frequently incurred needless casualties and Wellington's justifiable wrath. 'Our men could gallop', he declared acidly, 'but could not preserve their order.' To retain control of cavalry in attack was admittedly difficult, but too often squadrons galloped too fast and too far, found themselves attacked by French cavalry from a flank, and had to fight and escape when their horses were blown. This happened at Vimeiro to the 20th Light Dragoons, and as will be seen, the cavalry's finest achievement on the field of Waterloo was marred by the same failing.

To set against such ineptitude we have the superbly timed and executed charge of the Heavy Brigade at Salamanca, where reasonable control was maintained, though not as good as four squadrons (about 440 dragoons) of the King's German Legion displayed next day at Garcia Hernandez. Here they made a series of brilliantly handled charges against three French battalions, inflicted fourteen hundred casualties, and achieved the rare feat of breaking a properly formed infantry square.

Such a square, with the front rank kneeling to present a glinting hedge of bayonets, was a formidable target to deal with unless artillery had battered the infantry beforehand. Far worse was the fate of soldiers caught in the open without time to form square, as happened to the Sherwood Foresters at Salamanca. The French horsemen rode through them, cutting down all opposition with sabres, breaking the ranks, trampling men under hoof, and foiling every attempt to reform. Only the arrival of several British squadrons saved the battalion from destruction. Not surprising, therefore, that Colonel Wallace should have warned his Connaught Rangers to mind the square, for 'By God! if you are once broken, you'll be running here and there like a parcel of frightened pullets!'

In the campaigns against Revolutionary France the cavalry regiments had few if any veterinary surgeons. The first Principal Veterinary Surgeon was not appointed till late in 1796, and when Abercromby took his expedition to Holland in 1799 he had five veterinary surgeons – the first of the newly created branch to go on active service.

Even the provision of farriers had, like so much else, been inadequate, though by 1811 each troop was to have its own farrier, while another was attached to every squadron with the rank of corporal. This step was taken because regiments were so frequently scattered in small detachments. The farrier continued to perform such jobs as bloodletting, docking tails and branding, but above all he had to keep the horses shod, and this was by no means easy. For one thing, the roads across the Peninsula were so rough and rocky that in a regiment like the 13th Light Dragoons the stock of iron became exhausted in September 1813, and but for the fortunate discovery of a large supply of bar-iron at a foundry near Roncesvalles, the horses would have been in trouble. As it was, all were newly shod, and each man was supplied with enough iron to make a spare set of shoes.

The bad roads had another serious effect: it often proved impossible to keep the standard forge-carts near enough to the regiments for shoeing the horses. Consequently a small anvil and bellows were contrived for carriage on mule-back, with a second mule to take the charcoal and iron.

The practice varied a little in each regiment. Learning from bitter experience during the winter retreat through Galicia to Corunna at the end of 1808, the 7th Hussars provided every man with a set of spare shoes and a supply of nails, which he carried on the saddle. Furthermore, certain men in each troop were practised in putting on shoes, and several officers attended the farrier shop for the same purpose.

In a full-scale battle, horses, above all those ridden by senior officers and members of the staff, were exceedingly vulnerable, and at Waterloo the loss was huge. Major Cheney, for instance, commanding the 2nd Dragoons, had five horses killed under him in the space of twenty minutes; two generals and a colonel lost four each; and even an aide-de-camp ended the day with three dead mounts. As for the horse artillery, out of 200 horses in Mercer's battery, 140 lay dead, dying or severely wounded at the close of the battle. The sight of wounded horses running wildly around or plunging with pain affected every soldier who was there.

The army, in particular the cavalry and horse artillery, was time and again troubled by the difficulties of procuring forage in Portugal and Spain. In the words of Tomkinson of the 16th Light Dragoons: 'We were frequently 8 or 9 days without corn, and in consequence lost many horses. There was no straw in the country, and from the horses being so starved, they ate the withered grass with so much avidity that they swallowed many of the stones at the roots, and died in consequence.'

That was in October 1811, but it was usually the same. Of course the peasants hid their straw with care and cunning, this being the only chance they had of keeping alive through the winters their few remaining oxen required for agriculture. Once March came round, the regiments could generally

count on cutting green forage, for the horses, but even here snags arose, and we find one officer writing home for a scythe and whetstone, because his men had nothing to cut grass with except sickles, and he felt sure that with a scythe double the quantity of grass might be cut in half the time.

During the November retreat from Burgos in 1812, the artillery horses had no forage for four days, except, to quote Captain Dynely, 'the harness they ate off each other's backs, and the lids of the limber-boxes!' By the time the army reached southern France at the start of 1814, hussars had to be despatched in all directions to cut furze, which was first pounded with mallets into a sort of paste, and then fed to the horses, who devoured the result and often became ill.

Just as Wellington had less cavalry than the French, so too his artillery was inferior in numbers and weight, the batteries having mostly 6-pounders and the 5·5 inch howitzer. They gained, however, in ease and speed of handling. The Duke did not believe in using guns for shooting at the French artillery, and ordered them to support his infantry instead. Nor did he concentrate his artillery as Napoleon liked to do. At only one important battle – Vitoria – were the British guns concentrated; and this occurred almost by accident, due to the lack of roads. On this occasion, when 151 pieces were captured from the French, Wellington had 78 British and a dozen Portuguese guns in support of

The march of the baggage following the Army 1811. A water-colour by Major T. St Clair

61,000 infantry. His opponents usually had three or four guns per 1,000 men, whereas Wellington had only one or two; an improvement on Salamanca where 43,000 foot soldiers had 60 guns.

British artillery used three main types of ammunition. First round shot (solid iron balls), which could be most lethal. For instance, one French shot caught the 40th Foot in open column at Waterloo, took off a captain's head, and put *hors de combat* no fewer than 25 men – the most destructive shot anyone present had ever witnessed.

The next most widely used projectile was canister, or grape – a metal container which disintegrated to release small cast-iron balls. One limitation was the effective range of about 300 yards, since this compelled the artillery to be forward in line with the infantry. Next came explosive shells fired by the 5·5 inch howitzers.

In addition, Wellington had available shrapnel (or spherical case shot) and rockets. The former, invented by Colonel Henry Shrapnel and used successfully in 1804 at Surinam, could be fired at greater range, so the guns were not so liable to be charged by the enemy. The shell, being exploded by fuses, burst in the air and produced a widely dispersed fire. Shrapnel's spherical case had particularly destructive effects at Vimeiro, Busaco (1810) and Vitoria.

As for William Congreve's rockets, by 1806 their inventor was making 32-pounders with a range of three thousand yards. They were tried out that year from boats against invasion barges in Boulogne harbour, and again in 1807 and 1809 to bombard Copenhagen and Flushing. Consequently the generals tended not to think of their employment on the battlefield, and not until a British rocket battery performed so effectively at Leipzig in October 1813 did this weapon gain prestige.

Wellington, although the 12-pounder rocket produced in 1810 was infinitely more portable, had hitherto refused to have them in Spain. Even now he continued to view rockets with disfavour as being erratic; and in spite of their reasonable success when his army crossed the Adour early in 1814, he rejected the rocket troop sent to him for the Waterloo campaign, insisting that it be re-equipped as ordinary artillery. However, in response to great pressure he did allow the troop to carry eight hundred rockets.

Finally Wellington had siege artillery, though for years he had to manage without a proper siege train. Some idea of just how much ammunition was expended in a siege is given by the figures for San Sebastian, where 43,000 24-pounder round shot and

9,000 18-pounder shot, as well as another 18,000 shells and shot of various sizes were fired. In addition, 5,579 barrels of powder, each weighing 90 pounds, were used. Many of the eight-inch howitzer shells proved to be faulty, since they burst on leaving the howitzers. As some compensation, 6,000 12-pound shot were cast at foundries near Santander, and as at nearly every siege, sixpence was paid for each shot picked up and brought in.

Since the maximum effective range for 24- and 18-pounder size guns to batter a breach in a rampart was barely 700 yards, the batteries had to be well within range of the garrison's artillery. Consequently, not only did the gunners need protection, but all ammunition had to be brought forward along trenches dug by night and in zigzags. These 'parallels', as they were called, had then to be dug forward of the guns, so that when the final assault was ordered, the troops would not be exposed to French fire until the last possible moment. (*cf* chapter 2).

Some of the most costly endeavours of the entire Peninsular War were the five main sieges in which Wellington's army became involved: Ciudad Rodrigo in January 1812, when snow lay on the ground and ice was forming in the nearby rivers; Badajoz, another frontier fortress, which was twice besieged; Burgos, a failure in the autumn of 1812; and San Sebastian by the sea. On one occasion only did British troops have to withstand a siege: at Tarifa, the southernmost town in Europe. Despite thin walls, no ditch, and a commander who was

Sabugal on the River Coa. It was the scene of what Wellington called one of the most glorious actions British troops were ever engaged in, when on 3 April 1811 the Light Division engaged Masséna's rearguard. Here Major T. St Clair shows types of Wellington's Army in a setting typical of the country they traversed in the long Peninsular campaigns

keen to abandon the defence, the garrison held out against 6,000 French troops trying to get in. The Spaniards underwent sieges at Saragossa and Gerona by themselves, and, within Wellington's orbit, at Ciudad Rodrigo, which had to be abandoned after a resistance of 42 days. A Portuguese defence of Almeida, also a frontier fortress, was brought to a premature close by an accidental and devastating explosion in the main powder magazine.

When Wellington's men laid siege to Badajoz in May 1811, they were obliged first to turn aside and fight the Battle of Albuera when Marshal Soult arrived on the scene from southern Spain, and secondly to abandon the attempt for want of trained engineers, up-to-date siege artillery, equipment, and above all a proper battering-train.

Next time, in March 1812, Wellington did his best to ensure success. By 6 April three breaches had been battered in the formidably strong ramparts, and the town was stormed by night, as at Ciudad Rodrigo. Afterwards Wellington wrote: 'The capture of Badajoz affords as strong an instance of the gallantry of our troops as has ever been displayed, but I anxiously hope that I shall never again be the instrument of putting them to such a test as that to which they were put last night.'

The attack began at ten o'clock. For two hours the redcoats fought savagely in ditch and on glacis, on ladder and rampart. The 4th and Light Divisions were to storm the breaches, the 3rd Division would if possible scale a 100-foot wall and seize the castle, while the 5th and some Portuguese troops had orders to occupy the garrison with a demonstration. The defences had been so sharpened with mines, crow's feet (four-pointed irons strewn on the ground to hamper cavalry) and *chevaux de frise* – tree-trunks bristling with sword blades and chained together – that for all their gallantry the British could not penetrate the breaches, and after two hours of appalling slaughter, in which hundreds had been blown to pieces, dozens thrown down off ladders or drowned in the flooded ditch – all by the light of fireball, exploding powder barrel, fougasse and flaming carcase, a haggard Wellington called off the attack. But the 3rd Division, commanded by that intrepid, hard-swearing, blunt Welshman, Sir Thomas Picton, had fought their way at terrible cost into the castle and, with it, into the French reserves of food and ammunition. Meanwhile on the south side the 5th Division, after a struggle on the walls, had entered and virtually taken Badajoz, because their disconcerting appearance from behind the breaches caused the garrison to abandon the fight.

Badajoz had cost 4,000 British and 1,000

General Sir Thomas Picton. He commanded a division throughout most of the war, and died at the head of one at the Battle of Waterloo. Creasy wrote of him: 'Not even Ney himself surpassed in resolute bravery that stern and fiery spirit'

Portuguese casualties, and Wellington broke down when he read the lists.

The assault on a breach was always led by what was called 'the forlorn hope', consisting usually of a lieutenant, two sergeants and twenty-five men. Parties of sappers would carry bags filled with hay to lessen the depth of the ditch. Ladders, often too short and made from whatever materials were to hand, including the rails of Spanish waggons, had also to be carried forward. When, as happened at Ciudad Rodrigo, these ladders gave way, the soldiers coolly stuck their bayonets into the sod wall and climbed up on this ladder of steel. The front ranks had picks and axes for cutting down palisades and gates, and also knotted ropes on which to swing down into the ditch.

This account by Private William Brown of the 45th Foot, the old Sherwood Foresters, is typical of what the soldiers had to endure at Badajoz.

The point at which we descended into the ditch was between two bastions, from both of which we experienced a most dreadful fire of musketry, while from the body of the wall the enemy continued to pour, by means of boards placed on the parapet, whole showers of grenades, which they arranged in rows, and, being lighted with a match, the whole was upset, exploding amongst us in the ditch with horrid destruction. Coils of rope, in a friable state, strongly impregnated with tar, pitch and oil, were likewise employed by the enemy as a means of annoyance, which completely answered the purpose intended

by scorching and scalding numbers in a dreadful manner.
... Our men rushed up the ladders with the greatest impetuosity, but when near the top the whole broke down, and all that were on them were precipitated on the points of their comrades' bayonets, by which many received their death. We were then ordered to unfix our bayonets and sling the firelocks on our shoulders.

When, later in 1812, after the victory at Salamanca and his entry into Madrid, Wellington led part of his army north-east to besiege Burgos, he took risks which were scarcely justified in view of his crippling lack of artillery, ammunition, and engineers. Moreover, he seriously underestimated the strength of the place. As usual he was pressed for time, so he attempted to escalade the outer defence line without having recourse to the admittedly tedious work of mining. This having failed, the usual procedures had to be followed, and several galleries were dug beneath the wall and filled with barrels of powder. When the mine was fired, part of the wall collapsed, but the breach was smaller than hoped for, and the assault proved vain. After a month in the trenches and nearly 2,000 casualties, Wellington was obliged to retreat when relieving French armies approached the city.

There being so few engineer officers and no regular corps of sappers and miners, infantrymen had to be given a slight training in sapping and other field-work operations. Officers of the line would volunteer to serve as assistant engineers. Before a siege, fascines, gabions and pickets by the thousand were made by the infantry divisions, who also supplied miners and carpenters, the latter for laying gun platforms as soon as the emplacements were ready. Construction of the batteries was always difficult and expensive in casualties, being under fire from the fortress; consequently the earth parapets had to be at least 18 feet thick, and even half sinking the batteries could not produce so great a mass of earth if rock was soon reached. Indeed, at the first siege of Badajoz a large number of woolpacks had to be purchased, brought up, and worked into the parapet, where they resisted shot most successfully.

When the parallels were being dug and extended at night, the French garrison would keep up a heavy fire of musketry, shot and shell, and to discover the working parties would throw light-balls. Sometimes the French would make a sortie, but were usually driven back before they could do much damage, let alone reach the batteries and spike the siege guns. However, at Burgos they inflicted over three hundred casualties in two sorties. At Badajoz in March 1812 continual rain flooded the trenches and washed

The storming of the town and castle of San Sebastian, 31 August 1813

away the parapets; it also caused the river to rise so rapidly that the pontoon bridge was swept away. Consequently the siege-works were seriously delayed.

Delays could also be caused by poor quality tools: 'nearly all miserable country ones, too small for men, even when inclined to do much work with them, very easily broken, still easier buried and lost.' Wellington himself protested about the Storekeeper General: 'Everything in the way of intrenching tools and cutting tools supplied by his department is so bad as to be almost useless ... Is it not shameful that they [the French] should have better cutlery than we have?'

One other delaying factor was the marked lack of enthusiasm for siege preparations shown by the British soldier. Gallant and persevering as he was in the assault, he was too often a langorous slow-coach when it came to filling baskets with earth or excavating a trench. This uncomfortable work was, in the eyes of many, inglorious and unbecoming to true soldiers, especially when they were ill-trained and badly equipped for the job. Also they found themselves, at least in part, under the command of engineer officers, who did not know them and to whose ways they were unaccustomed. There were exceptions, of course, and no man could fail to respect the devotion and courage shown by the handful of engineers, whose casualties at every siege were always heavy: seven out of nineteen at Ciudad Rodrigo, thirteen of the twenty-four who served at Badajoz in 1812, three out of five at Burgos, as well as all the eight military artificers, and eleven out of eighteen killed or wounded at San Sebastian.

San Sebastian, built on an isthmus between harbour and river estuary, posed some different problems. For one thing, the British naval blockade was too weak to prevent French ships sailing in and out by night, with ammunition, food and medical supplies as well as fresh artillerymen and engineers. For another, the garrison could dominate the scene from a citadel perched four hundred feet up on a rock. The main assault had to be made across the tidal estuary, the storming party running over rocks slippery with seaweed. Even when the attackers reached the breach, they were confronted with a drop of twenty feet, and were forced back by grape-shot and musketry from the flanks. For lack of ammunition, no fresh attempt could be made until more guns, more shells and a reinforcement of engineers arrived from England.

Once again the troops waded knee-deep in water. Once again the redcoats, despite prodigies of valour, failed to mount the breach. The front ranks were almost annihilated. But then a master stroke turned the scales. Forty-seven guns, which had been laboriously tugged on to nearby sandhills, fired at a range of from six to eight hundred yards for 20 minutes just over the heads of the leading troops, aiming at the high curtain wall above the breach. Not a man was injured by an ill-directed shot. Suddenly fortune intervened to support audacity and accuracy. Large supplies of powder, shells and hand-grenades caught fire and exploded along the ramparts, killing and wounding many of the French and throwing the rest into wild confusion. At once the leading attackers took advantage of this accident, stormed impetuously ahead through the smoke, forced back the enemy in desperate close fighting, clambered down over the ruins, winkled the French out of loop-holed houses, fought their way past trap-pits, lines of pitch-fires, and breastworks made of sand-filled barrels placed across the narrow streets. The French garrison withdrew to the castle, where they surrendered a week later.

Although the troops who climbed and fought their bloody way into Ciudad Rodrigo, Badajoz and San Sebastian had to engage the French in the streets, such action was brief; and throughout the wars against France one rarely finds British troops involved in street-fighting as such. A little in the village alley-ways of Fuentes de Oñoro, and rather more in the last battle of the Peninsular War, Toulouse, where the French were driven from house to house, firing them as they withdrew. 'It is always ugly, dangerous work fighting in a town; so many holes

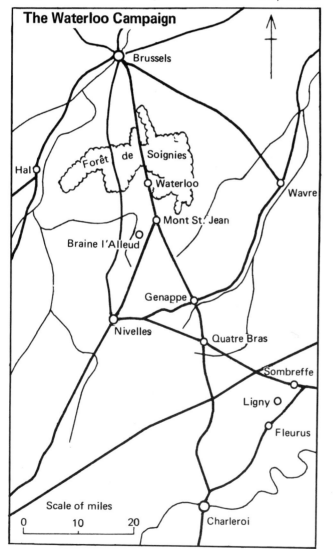

The Waterloo Campaign

Brussels

Forêt de Soignies

Hal

Waterloo

Wavre

Mont St. Jean

Braine l'Alleud

Genappe

Nivelles

Quatre Bras

Sombreffe

Ligny

Fleurus

Scale of miles
0   10   20

Charleroi

and corners, hiding-places and loop-holes, where one may be picked off by an unseen enemy' was George Bell's verdict.

Much more damaging was the ambush prepared by Albanian troops in Rosetta in 1807, when a British column blundered through the narrow streets without military precautions, and was badly shot up from trellised windows and specially prepared loop-holes. A worse blunder occurred in the same year, this time in Buenos Aires. Here Whitelocke's men not only advanced under a 'shower of musketry, hand-grenades, stinkpots, brickbats' hurled down by the population from behind the balustrades to the flat-roofs, but were trapped in streets with no outlets or driven off by artillery each time they tried to reach the rooftops. 'Every householder with his negroes defended his dwelling, each of which was in itself a fortress.'

When Britain faced the last and most decisive land battle of all those she fought against Napoleon's troops, it was not with the finest army she could have fielded. Wellington commanded once again, but many of the regiments which had brought him success against French marshals in Portugal, Spain and southern France were still in America or on their way home. After Waterloo the Duke more than once made remarks such as: 'If I had had the same army as in the south of France the battle would have been over in three hours.' And before the campaign he referred to 'an infamous army'.

He had only 31,000 British officers and men, many of them untried in battle. Of 16 cavalry regiments, no more than 5 had served with him in the Peninsula. The 4 infantry battalions which arrived from America just in time to fight on June 18th were veterans. Of the remaining 23 line battalions, 14 had fought under his command before, and 7 had campaigned briefly in Holland in 1814. But the 3rd/14th, comprised mainly of young recruits, had 14 officers and over 300 rank and file under the age of 20. Whereas the average strength of a line battalion at Waterloo was 640, a Guards battalion numbered close on 1,000 men. Most of the field and horse artillery had experience of war, but apart from a few officers and men who had been at the storming of Bergen-op-Zoom 15 months earlier, the engineers had not been in action.

For the rest, Wellington disposed of 16,000 Hanoverians, close on 7,000 Brunswickers, 29,000 Dutch-Belgian troops, nearly 3,000 from Nassau, and 6,000 infantrymen, hussars and light dragoons of the splendid King's German Legion, which had gained high distinction and regard in the Peninsula.

In the brief, bloody, decisive campaign of Waterloo Wellington had to fight two separate battles and conduct a retreat on the intervening day. The first battle, at Quatre Bras, was fought on ground not of his own choosing, and opened badly in that the Dutch-Belgian units holding this vital crossroads had been seriously shaken by the time he reached the scene. As the afternoon wore on, his own troops came hurrying to reinforce the position. Battalions had to be deployed as soon as they arrived. Helped by hedges and tall crops, the British lines repulsed French columns by superior firepower. Whenever cuirassiers attacked, the infantry formed squares and held the horsemen at bay – except for several battalions which were caught in line, thanks to inept interference with orders, and received a bad mauling.

Over and over again Marshal Ney's cavalry charged, milled round the squares, and then withdrew, leaving ramparts of dead and dying horses. Attacks came suddenly, heralded only by skirmishers running back for cover. French artillery battered the squares. The stalks of rye, as high as the Highlanders' bonnets, were trampled down and ceased to form a screen. Ammunition ran low. The Black Watch had four different commanding officers within a few minutes. Woods, hamlets, farms and fields changed hands during six hours of savage struggle.

Wellington, personally handling his troops, held Quatre Bras and prevented the unenterprising Ney from going to the aid of Napoleon, who was simultaneously engaged with the Prussians at Ligny, three miles to the east. But the Duke in turn was prevented from marching to the support of Blücher, whose army was worsted and compelled to retreat. Next morning Wellington did the same, to the ridge of Mont St Jean.

Torrential rain during the night before the Battle of Waterloo had effects far beyond subjecting the troops to extreme discomfort. It delayed the start, so that Napoleon's artillery could move more readily once the ground had dried a little. Even so, many of the French soldiers attacking up the slope had their shoes dragged off by heavy clods clinging to the soles. Gun-carriages sank up to the hubs in mud. Horses became unusually blown. One compensation was the reduced effect of shot and shell: many of the French howitzer shells with long fuses plopped into the mud and lay fizzing and flaring for several seconds before they exploded; and countless round shot, instead of hopping for half a mile or so, never rose from the place where first they struck the ground.

From a British viewpoint, the battle raged about three main positions. First the large farm of Hougoumont, surrounded by woods, a walled garden, an orchard and hedges, was attacked throughout most of the day, and was defended with outstanding devotion by companies of the Guards, a Nassau battalion and close on three hundred Hanoverians. The garrison shot at the French from upstairs windows and through loop-holes knocked in the garden wall. Twice the attackers forced the main gate and rushed into the courtyard. Twice they were knocked out by the Guards. Bayonet duels were fought above wall and parapet. Part of the buildings caught fire and not a few wounded soldiers were burnt to death.

Flames also took a hold of the second of Wellington's bastions – the high-walled farm of La Haye Sainte in the centre of his line along the ridge. This was smaller than Hougoumont, but also had a garden and orchard. A battalion of the King's German Legion, later reinforced by 100 Nassau troops, hung on doggedly until six o'clock, now repelling the French, now using chains of field kettles to extinguish the fire. Then the two score survivors of the garrison had to withdraw for want of ammunition.

At half past one that afternoon 80 French guns had bombarded Picton's division, positioned to the east of La Haye Sainte, then 18,000 French infantry had advanced in unwieldy formation up the long slope, only to be checked by the British volleys, charged with the bayonet, and then shattered by the timely charge of the Allied cavalry, in particular the Union Brigade comprising Dragoon Guards, Scots Greys and Inniskillings, with many a Highlander grasping the stirrups and dashing forward beside the horses into the fray. As had happened too often in Spain, this cavalry force, having brilliantly carried out its role, had marred the occasion and incurred excessive casualties through charging headlong at the French guns and being nearly overwhelmed and sent packing by enemy counter-attacks.

The Allied infantry, having emerged from this ordeal with success, were now subjected to some of the most formidable cavalry assaults of the war, when Ney launched 5,000 of Napoleon's finest horsemen, including cuirassiers, against the squares, where the infantry mostly had four ranks, one kneeling and one crouching with bayonets in line, and the third and fourth ranks firing for all they were worth. Prodigal, persistent, unco-ordinated, heroic, and vain were these attacks. The British horse gunners fired canister into the advancing host, and then ran

PENINSULAR WAR AND WATERLOO

for shelter to the nearest square. Whenever the French cavalry withdrew, their artillery fired with terrible effect into the serried British squares.

The graphic words of Ensign Gronow of the 1st Foot Guards indicate the grimness of the scene.

During the battle our squares presented a shocking sight. Inside we were nearly suffocated by the smoke and smell from burnt cartridges. It was impossible to move a yard without treading upon a wounded comrade, or upon the bodies of the dead; and the loud groans of the wounded and dying was most appalling.

At four o'clock our square was a perfect hospital, being full of dead, dying, and mutilated soldiers. The charges of cavalry were in appearance very formidable, but in reality a great relief, as the artillery could no longer fire on us: the very earth shook under the enormous mass of men and horses. I shall never forget the strange noise our bullets made against the breastplates of the cuirassiers. ...

The horses of the first rank of cuirassiers, in spite of all the efforts of their riders, came to a stand-still, shaking and covered with foam, at about twenty yards' distance from our squares, and generally resisted all attempts to force them to charge the line of serried steel.

Later still, an angry, frustrated Ney sent in 60 squadrons – 9,000 horsemen – on a front of barely 1,000 yards between La Haye Sainte and Hougoumont. Several British squares had to repulse a dozen assaults, and at least two squares had to be made up of two battalions each, or what remained of them. The butchery was dreadful, and mounds of dead horses protected Wellington's infantry while impeding Napoleon's cavalry.

Waterloo. A general view of the battlefield. Papelotte farm can be seen on the left; in the centre La Haye Sainte is obscured by a cloud of smoke, while to the right of the copse (right background) a black pall of smoke is rising from Hougomont hidden by the rising ground. The French have launched their first great infantry assault, and the British cavalry are forming to charge the French columns. The Highlanders, right foreground, are about to make their famous charge.

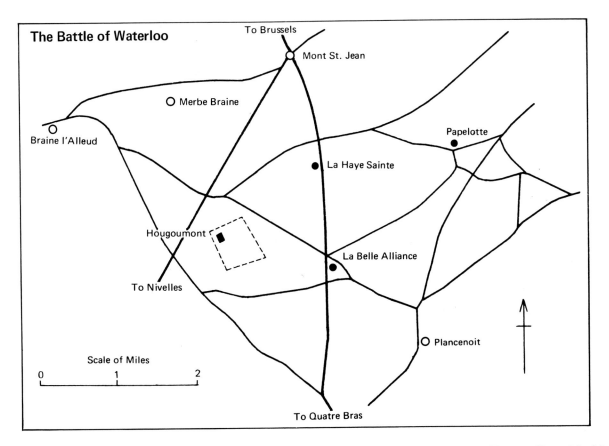

The Battle of Waterloo

To Brussels
Mont St. Jean
Merbe Braine
Braine l'Alleud
Papelotte
La Haye Sainte
Hougoumont
La Belle Alliance
To Nivelles
Plancenoit
Scale of Miles
0   1   2
To Quatre Bras

The final British battle on the ridge occurred soon after seven o'clock. Napoleon, doing what he should have done much earlier when the loss of La Haye Sainte caused a grave crisis in Wellington's line, brought up his precious reserve: six battalions of the Middle Guard followed by part of the Old Guard. These renowned veterans attacked the positions between Hougoumont and La Haye Sainte, and were seen off, first by grapeshot salvos and the steady shooting of Colin Halkett's brigade; next by Peregrine Maitland's brigade of Foot Guards, who, on being called to their feet by Wellington himself, fired one devastating volley at a range of 40 yards, a second which felled several hundreds more, and gave three British cheers prior to charging with the bayonet; and then by Colborne's 52nd, who wheeled parallel to the French left flank and fired to such effect that the death-knell verdict '*La garde recule!*' was heard, and Wellington unleashed two cavalry brigades to turn the enemy's centre into a mob beyond discipline and control.

Meanwhile, of course, Blücher's Prussians, who for various reasons arrived later than expected, had engaged first a French corps, then a division of the Young Guard, and finally part of the Old Guard in a desperate struggle centred upon the village of Plancenoit. Tenaciously the Young Guard held off the growing threat to Napoleon's right flank and rear.

After ten hours' fighting, the Allies had gained the day and made it one of the most fateful in Europe's history. But the cost had been heavy. On the British side alone, out of 63 commanding officers, 11 were killed and 24 wounded, several mortally. Nearly half the 840 infantry officers who fought at Quatre Bras and Waterloo were killed or wounded. The 73rd Highlanders lost 22 out of 26 officers, the Royal Scots 31 out of 37. As for the Cameron Highlanders, 32 officers, over half the 40 sergeants, and 424 out of 684 rank and file became casualties. Of 67 artillery officers 25 were killed or wounded, and the losses among the senior commanders and staff were of similar proportions.

Estimates suggest that the British guns fired 9,400 rounds at Waterloo and that the army expended 987,000 musket cartridges at Quatre Bras and Waterloo. To carry all this ammunition would have required close on 200 waggons, each drawn by four horses.

'It was', said Wellington, 'the most desperate business I ever was in. I never took so much trouble about any battle, and never was so near being beat.'

125

THE OLD SAUCY

SEVENTH,

Or Queen's Own Regt. of

Lt. Dragoons

COMMANDED BY THAT GALLANT AND WELL KNOWN HERO,

Lieut. General

HENRY LORD PAGET.

YOUNG Fellows whose hearts beat high to tread the paths of Glory, could n
ha e a better opportunity than now offers. Come forward then, and Enrol yourselve
in a Regiment that stands unrivalled, and where the kind treatment, the Men ev
experienced is well known throughout the whole Kingdom.

Each Young Hero on being approved, will receive the largest Bounty allowed by
Government.

A few smart Young Lads, will be taken at Sixteen Years of Age, 5 Feet 2 Inches,
bu' 'hey must be active, and well limbed. Apply to SERJEANT HOOPER, *at*

N. B. This Regiment is mounted on Blood Horses, and being lately returned fro
SPAIN, and the Horses Young, the Men will not be allowed to HUNT during t
next Season, more than once a week.

BOOTH AND WRIGHT, PRINTERS, NORWICH.

CHAPTER 13

Wellington's Army

ANTONY BRETT-JAMES

The spirit of the great majority of the soldiers is exemplified by the raw recruit in the 5th Foot who was wounded in the hand at the battle of Orthez and begged not to be sent to the rear. 'Though I can't draw me ramrod, I can shove with me bagginet', he said firmly. Or by a young soldier in the 73rd who, in the act of firing at Waterloo, had a foot taken off at the ankle by a rolling cannon ball. He did not fall, but advanced a step on his shattered stump and said: 'Damn you, I'll serve you out for that!' and promptly fired his piece at the enemy.

Not a few bemoaned the fact that war was a sad blunter of the finer feelings: 'the horrid sights always before our eyes make almost all callous' wrote one artillery officer. But humour at least was never far below the surface. The Irish, in particular – and there were many of them, not only in the Connaught Rangers and other Irish regiments – had a gaiety of spirit that never forsook them, a hilarity, a cheerful willingness. As George Bell of the 34th expressed it outside Toulouse in 1814: 'Everyone jolly, and the Patlanders in particular cracking their jokes.' 'How the devil are we to get over that big sthrame av a river to leather them vagabones out o' that,' says Paddy Muldoon. 'O, niver mind,' says another old cripple who lost an eye on the Nive, 'that country-man av yours wid the long nose will show you the way when he's riddy.'

This tribute to Wellington was typical of the immense confidence rather than affection that he aroused. 'The sight of his long nose among us was worth ten thousand men any day of the week' wrote another veteran. One must regret that, for all his supreme qualities as a field commander and administrator, he found himself unable to appeal to the better side of his soldiers. He could praise in his dispatches, but often indiscriminately, and some of his most blatant omissions kindled long-lasting disgruntlement. He admitted that they got him 'out of a scrape' more than once, but how much easier he found it to rebuke than to praise.

He had much to anger and exasperate him, but to declare, as he did: 'They are the scum of the earth. English soldiers are fellows who have enlisted for drink – that is the plain fact: They have *all* enlisted for drink' was a manifest exaggeration. Only in the aftermath of bloody siege and storming the breach did discipline disintegrate in orgies of drink, disorder, wild shooting, dressing up in costume, and outrage against the population.

To a lesser, if more prolonged degree, discipline cracked when the troops had to retreat to Corunna with Moore and from Burgos back to Portugal with Wellington – and in the hour of triumph at Vitoria, when part of the army disappeared in search of loot, and part wallowed in the prolific plunder abandoned on the field of battle.

After Badajoz, in particular, even the erection of gallows and triangles in the square did not subdue the indiscipline, to stop which many officers risked their lives. Of course the army had a proportion of criminals and drunkards, who were prone to plunder, straggle, skulk or desert. Recruiting parties often attended the quarter sessions and received men who, had they been tried, would mostly have been sentenced to transportation. 'Such men', wrote Sergeant Wheeler, 'when they joined the army set about their old trades and corrupted men of weak minds.' But they were most likely to commit crime when away from their units, either on detachment or while marching up the lines of communication to the front.

'There is no crime recorded in the Newgate

WELLINGTON'S ARMY

Calendar that is not committed by these soldiers' wrote Wellington. Yet the majority were men of zeal, loyal followers, exceedingly brave in attack and steady in defence, quick to volunteer for a 'forlorn hope' or some dangerous outpost duty. Many were intelligent men, as the long list of their memoirs and journals displays. Some were religious. Not a few were militiamen who had been tempted by bounties to transfer to regiments of the line. Others enlisted in order to escape from a bullying employer or from the consequences of getting a village girl into trouble. No doubt patriotism inspired few, but when Wellington asserted in later years: 'People talk of their enlisting from their fine military feelings – all stuff – no such thing' he was exaggerating once again.

Much of the indiscipline occurred whenever the Commissariat Department failed to overcome the manifold problems with which its members, at first very inexperienced, were faced. Whereas the French Army tried to live off the land, and in the ruthless way of so doing inspired more and more recruits for the guerrillas, the British established a proper supply line and paid for everything it took, even though a grave lack of specie obliged it to obtain many items on credit. The system improved with each passing year, but remained vulnerable to extremes of weather, to sudden changes of route, and to military setbacks like the long winter retreat conducted by Wellington at the close of 1812.

The Commander of the Forces was well aware of the need for sound administration. 'A starving army is actually worse than none', he wrote in 1809. 'The soldiers lose their discipline and spirit, they plunder even in the presence of their officers.' Meat marched on the hoof, and by 1813 the Army was consuming 300 bullocks a day, but these were often little better than skin and bone.

Verdicts differ on the quality of rations: 'ration leather (falsely called beef), and mouldy biscuit, hard and jaw breaking' wrote an infantry officer; 'the biscuit was frequently crushed to crumbs and mouldered to dust' complained a sergeant from Scotland; 'when a man entered a soldier's life, he should have parted with half his stomach', declared an officer in the Rifles. By contrast Sergeant Wheeler stands up for the achievements of the Commissariat: 'It is true we were sometimes badly off for biscuit, but taking everything into consideration no army could be supplied better. Indeed it is a mystery to thousands how we were supplied so regular as we were.'

That the range of crimes tried by court-martial in the Peninsula was wide is indicated by this random selection: absent from stable duty, selling equipment, insulting a Portuguese family, drunk on parade, speaking improperly to the corporal, stealing goats and honey, robbing a peasant of twelve pigs, and 'unmilitary conduct in making away with his ammunition to light his pipe'.

Punishments were savage by modern standards. Two privates were sentenced to 200 lashes each for 'destroying a pig', and actually received 170, while another man, though awarded 100, got 75 'on suspicion of killing a pig'. For plundering in Portugal four soldiers were hanged in 1810. Occasionally a sergeant would be reduced to the ranks and even flogged, but sometimes he was allowed to resign from the Army rather than stand trial; and for slight offences NCOs might be suspended from their rank for a period, receiving a private's pay the while. Now and then a soldier was permitted to volunteer for service in India, thereby saving himself and his regiment the dishonour of a court-martial.

As always, discipline and morale depended a great deal on the individual commanding officer. Many were most reluctant to order flogging, and would try solitary confinement or 'prescriptions of moderate diet, bread and water' as alternatives. Others copied Sir John Moore's policy of preventing rather than punishing crime, of encouragement, of fostering a better knowledge of men by their officers and a sounder relationship between officers, NCOs and men. Merit and good conduct were to be rewarded.

But official rewards were few. No medals came the way of junior officers and the rank and file. An officer might be promoted or obtain brevet rank for outstanding gallantry, but too many of the deserving did not, and the promotion was frequently into a West Indian or Ceylon regiment. One example is the notorious case of Ensign Joseph Dyas of the 51st, who twice led the 'forlorn hope' at Badajoz in 1811, yet remained a subaltern for a decade. A sergeant would occasionally be commissioned for distinguished conduct in the field. As for the men, a few were promoted on the spot. Several regiments established an order of merit with silver medals, often in three classes according to the number of battles in which a recipient had taken part. Several instances are on record of generals, even Wellington himself, giving a monetary award for an act of bravery, be it taking 31 prisoners or bringing boats across a river under fire. As one colonel put the matter: 'I like to reward bold fellows: it animates the rest.'

Such rewards came as riches when a foot soldier's pay was a shilling a day, and a sergeant was barely sevenpence better off. In fact a private, after 1797, received seven shillings a week, but stoppages for messing and 'necessaries' left him about threepence a day for himself.

When off duty, and especially in the winter months, officers and men took part in amateur theatricals, or learnt to dance the bolero and fandango. Coursing, hunting and games all found their supporters. There would be the occasional race-meeting and ball. We have the 18th Hussars playing shuttlecock and battledore, the 43rd playing at rackets with wooden bats against the side of a village church, and riflemen of the 95th pursuing a pig with his tail greased, the pig becoming the lawful prize of any man who could catch and hold it. Such activities helped to promote a good understanding between officers and men, and soldier writers often bear witness to this fact, among them Leach of the Rifles.

'Our gallant commander, Colonel Beckwith, was ever amongst the first to encourage these meetings, considering, no doubt, and very justly, that to divert and to amuse his men, and to allow them every possible indulgence compatible with the discipline of the battalion, whilst an interval of quiet permitted it, was the surest way to make the soldiers follow line cheerfully through fire and water, when the day of trial came.'

Most of the squadron and company officers appear to have been excellent men who learnt to take things in their stride and set an example of courage and resourcefulness to those who followed them. When at war the officers, having to share all dangers and privations, showed a greater degree of kindness than in peacetime with its harassing parades and lengthy drills. If an officer was liked and respected, his troubles would be shared by his men. Often the illiterate soldiers would ask their young officers to read and write letters for them, being reluctant to reveal private affairs to their better educated comrades.

Costello of the 95th put his finger on the heart of the matter when he wrote: 'Our men divided the officers into two classes: the "come on" and the "go on"; for as Tom Plunket in action once observed to an officer, "The words 'go on' don't befit a leader, sir".'

Regrettably certain officers were incompetent, slack, and inattentive to orders and to the welfare of those under their command. Drunkenness was too prevalent, though nothing like as bad as in 1794, for instance, when Sir Robert Wilson could write indignantly: 'What shocked me most was to see

The Recruit by J. Liversedge

courts-martial adjudging men to be punished for an offence of which the members themselves had often been guilty at the same time, and from which they had frequently not recovered when passing sentence.' And the mind of certain commanding officers never soared 'above the uninteresting minutiae of barrack-yard drill – the exact distance from button to button on the soldier's jacket, the width of his leather stock, and other matters of the kind.'

It is commonly said that commanders at this period were able to survey, and thus control, the entire battlefield. A general, by good use of his telescope and by cantering from one point to another, may well have been able to see what was happening, but for the junior officers and rank and file the reverse was true. Captain Mercer of the Royal Horse Artillery explains how at Waterloo: 'What was passing to the right and left of us I know no more than the man in the moon. ... The smoke confined our vision to a very small compass, so that my battle was restricted to the two squares and my own battery.' That cavalrymen were likewise hampered is shown by a brigade commander who wrote: 'We every instant expected to see the enemy appearing under our noses; for the smoke was literally so thick that we could not see ten yards off.' And we are assured by Rifleman Harris that the infantry felt the same. At Vimeiro in 1808, for instance, he soon found himself 'so hotly engaged, loading and firing away, enveloped in the smoke I created, and the cloud which hung about me from the continued fire of my comrades, that I could see nothing for a few minutes but the red flash of my own piece amongst the white vapour clinging to my very clothes. ...

Typical of the transport organised by Wellington for his Peninsular campaigns

Often I was obliged to stop firing, and dash it aside from my face, and try in vain to get a sight of what was going on.' And at Salamanca four years later Grattan of the 88th relates how 'the dry grass was set on fire by the numerous cartridge papers that strewed the field of battle, the air was scorching, and the smoke ... nearly suffocated us.'

Sometimes the fighting would be at such close range, almost muzzle to muzzle, that many of the soldiers' tunics were scorched all down the front by enemy fire. During a prolonged action the barrel became so hot from continual firing that a man could hardly bear to touch it and was obliged to grasp the stock beneath the iron. Private Brown of the 45th claimed that by the end of the battle of Orthez he had fired 250 rounds of ball cartridge, and his shoulder that night was 'as black as coal'.

And not the shoulder alone: the middle finger of the right hand too. The face would also be black. 'In biting off the ends of the cartridges, there are generally a few grains of powder left sticking to the lips and about the mouth; these, accumulated by the great quantity of ammunition each of us had fired, and with the profuse perspiration we were in during the heat of the day.... had caused the powder to run all over our faces.'

Most infantry regiments were armed with the Brown Bess, a smoothbore flint-lock musket which for accurate shooting could be relied on up to one hundred yards, though a volley was often effective at thrice that range. It fired a round lead ball, made up with a cartridge of stout paper, one end of which had to be ripped open by a soldier's teeth before he

placed it in the barrel and forced it down by means of an iron ramrod. A little powder was dropped in the pan to catch the spark when the flint was snapped.

Each soldier carried 60 rounds, but the greater part of these were expended in vain, it being estimated that only one shot out of two hundred took effect, whereas the rate for a rifle was one out of twenty. Certainly the Baker rifle, with a 30-inch barrel in which seven grooves made a quarter-turn, was accurate up to 300 yards and could be used at still larger range. Riflemen, however, found difficulty in ramming home the ball, on account of the grooves. Moreover, the 95th, the 60th and some of the Portuguese *Caçadores* to whom the rifle was issued had to carry 80, even 120, rounds per man. Sergeants were also armed with a rifle, but not in the line battalions and the Guards, where they had a seven-foot pike or halberd. An officer carried his straight sword, good for thrusting but too light a weapon when up against a French cavalry sword.

Whether he had a musket or a rifle, the soldier was invariably handicapped in wet weather. Even if rain did not dampen the powder, and render every shot a misfire, it could transform the priming-powder in the pan into a paste or wash it out altogether. However carefully a man had oiled his musket and inspected the flint, he could be in trouble.

Soldiers received most terrible wounds in battle, and the medical treatment, though it saved many lives, was primitive, relying much on amputation of limbs, and on bleeding in cases where the patient would now be given a transfusion. Many a man

Troops bivouacked near the village of Villa Tahas 1811

carried a ball in his chest, back or thigh for the rest of his life. Those who fought with lancers often had a dozen wounds, and one trooper at Waterloo 'had 17 or 18 about his person, and lived to tell the story.' Another who survived personal combat with French cavalry was Corporal Buchanan of the 13th Light Dragoons, who slew one opponent outright, wounded and put to flight a second, and wounded and captured a third. But in the process he had received fifteen wounds 'in the head, face, arms and body. His nose was cut off, and bone of the forearm cut through.' At the siege of Badajoz a soldier of the 30th Foot received 13 bayonet wounds when the French dashed the scaling ladders down. Yet he got well by good treatment.

Such soldiers had to be extremely tough, and tough they were, yet only when reinforcements arrived from Britain did the veterans realize their own suntanned, whipcord strength and quality. 'These fellows' rosy cheeks and plump appearance, with their new dresses, formed a bright-relief and amusing contrast to our fierce embrowned visages, covered with whisker and mustachio and our clothing patched and of all colours. … They, in fact, took us at first … for a foreign regiment.'

As long as the troops had their weapons and ammunition in good order, Wellington did not mind very much that their trousers – which replaced white breeches and gaiters in 1811 – were black, blue or grey, or that their tunics resembled Joseph's 'coat of many colours'. Since many regiments had to campaign for a year and more without replacement of uniform, one finds the overalls of the 13th Light

Dragoons in southern France 'patched with cloth of all sorts of colours and most frequently with red oilskin – fragments of the baggage wrappers.' And at one stage the 7th Fusiliers had more than a hundred men without shoes as well as 'ragged, shiftless, stocking-less'.

All in all, the British soldiers were contradictory beings, one week indignant, shocked and disgusted with the French for hamstringing several hundred donkeys and mules and violating and wantonly killing Portuguese women and children during a retreat in 1811, next week content to fraternise amicably with their enemies when the front lines were close. As well as frugal, they could be thriftless and ready to throw away ammunition to be rid of the weight. Once battle was over, they were quick to tend the French wounded and protect them from Spanish marauders. And at Copenhagen in 1807 and Flushing two years later they expressed horror at the bombardments which violated humanity by causing so many civilian casualties. Indeed the use of Congreve's rockets was widely condemned: 'We scarcely consider them as fair; they are more destructive than useful', was a typical comment. Men who displayed superlative gallantry in the morning could, by afternoon, have become a band of brigands, at once brutal and ridiculous.

Whatever their faults before and after, in the hour of testing 'a quiet but desperate calm replaced their usual buoyant spirits'; and General Foy, who commanded a French division in Spain, declared that 'The British soldier possessed the most precious quality in war: *le calme dans la colère*.'

131

CHAPTER 14

The Development of the Royal Artillery in the Eighteenth Century

WILLIAM V. CARMAN

The development of the British Artillery in the eighteenth century was very striking. At the beginning of the period 'traynes of artillerie' were specially raised each time a major conflict took place. By the end of the century a tried and well-organised force had been permanently established, including such advanced ideas as 'flying' or horse artillery. The improvement in design of equipment and the training of personnel were both reflected in a fine record of martial achievements in many countries.

In 1697 William III had established a regiment of artillery but this was disbanded within the year. Thus the new century began with the old system of a number of ancient gunners and staff attached to the Tower of London – the nation's arsenal – and to various castles and strongholds around the coast and in Scotland. In 1702 a train was raised for Holland, in 1703 one for Portugal and a third for Gibraltar in 1704. These trains took time to organise and equip. In fact the one raised to deal with the 1715 rising in Scotland was not completed until the troubles were over.

This emphasised the necessity for a permanent force to be created and in May 1716 two companies were established and marked the beginning of the Regiment of Artillery, still under the Master of the Ordnance who granted the commissions to the officers instead of the King. In 1722 these companies were grouped with the independent train in Gibraltar which had been formed in 1704 and with the train in Minorca raised in 1709. The Royal Regiment of Artillery was now firmly established with Albert Borgard, a Dane, as its commandant. Further companies were added and in 1744 the eighth company was formed – entirely of Gentlemen Cadets who trained to be future officers. It was at the practice camp at Byfleet in 1756 that brigades were first formed with four to six guns of a similar calibre in each, including three brigades of 24-pounders, three of 12-pounders, four of 6-pounders, one of 3-pounders and two of Royal Howitzers. In May 1755 a separate Irish Artillery was formed, not only for service in Ireland but later also to take a turn of duty in North America.

In 1757 there were sufficient companies to make two battalions and two years later a third battalion was formed. After a fourth battalion was formed in 1771, eight invalid companies were created from the old artillery out-pensioners, of which two companies were attached to each of the four battalions. In 1755 four companies left for Bombay and in 1791 two companies left Woolwich for Madras but each of the three Indian Presidencies developed its own artillery forces.

In 1788 the Master Gunner of the Ordnance, the Duke of Richmond, issued instructions to equip field guns so that they could accompany cavalry. It was in February 1793 that the Royal Horse Artillery was created and the mobility of warfare was increased. The slow and lumbering train of supply waggons had been under the control of locally employed civilians but in 1794 a step was taken to form a special driver corps which made for greater discipline and control. This body was named in 1806 the Corps of Royal Artillery Drivers. A fifth battalion of Artillery had been formed in 1794 and the sixth in 1799 while the Royal Irish Artillery was converted into the seventh battalion in April 1801.

The individual tasks of the artillery man were not clear cut and the men of a company were expected to cope with many tasks ranging from siege work to field work, either with infantry or in batteries, and

Opposite: Above: Royal Artillery in the Low Countries c. 1748. A painting by C. Morier in the Royal Collection
Below: Gibraltar 13 September 1782. General Eliott watches as the British guns, after a tremendous duel, set fire to the floating batteries of the Franco-Spanish besiegers. Painted by G. Carter 1784

also with the preparations of fireworks and fire-ships. Thus great versatility was expected, a trait which brought successful results on many occasions.

Early in the life of the artilleryman, siege work had been important and there was no lack of occasion in the eighteenth century for heavy guns of position to prove their worth, such as the taking of Vigo by Lord Cobham in 1719 and the capture of Barcelona in which latter occasion mortars and man-harness were put to good effect. The capture of Gibraltar by the fleet under Sir G. Rooke in 1704 led to the first successful defence where after six months siege by the French and Spanish troops the latter retired. British artillery and engineers had hurried out to this place of conflict where over 8,000 shells and 70,000 cannon shot were expended. The second siege of 1727 lasted four months with the Artillery as the principal defenders of the British forces.

In August 1708 Lille was besieged by an allied siege train, and Mons and Douai were two other cities which also fell to siege guns. The siege of Gibraltar in the period 1779–83 is also well known for the sterling work of the British Artillery.

The field use of artillery or the employment of guns in a moving and changing battlefield was limited by the mobility of the cannon. There was little difficulty in using cannon to support infantry. Early in the seventeenth century two 3-pounder guns had been attached to a battalion of infantry – a practice still continued at the Battle of Fontenoy in 1745 where the man-handled guns attacked within 30 yards of the French infantry, 6-pounder guns were also successfully employed in this battle for counter battery work against the French artillery.

At Minden in 1759 the British 12-pounders under Captains Macbean and Phillips overcame 30 guns of the enemy and later the Royal Regiment of Artillery gave valuable support to the allied forces in preventing the French cavalry reforming and by opening fire on the Saxon infantry. The artillery achieved its best results when acting independently and the 12 light 6-pounder guns attached to British infantry produced no striking results. Battalion guns did continue in use until 1799 but eventually lapsed.

At Culloden in 1746 Colonel Belford placed the ten guns in pairs at the intervals of the front line where after half an hour's cannonade the High-landers deemed it necessary to make a charge. Changing from annoying cannon balls to grape shot the guns repelled the Scots for a while and prevented the infantry from being entirely overrun. This was a successful use of artillery in the ranks, but earlier, at the Battle of Malplaquet, 1709, different tactics were employed. Forty guns were grouped in a supporting position and when the French cavalry were seen advancing Marlborough ordered the great battery forward. On reaching their position the guns opened a devastating fire of canister shot which wreaked havoc on the enemy.

An early example of mobility in the field took place at Blenheim in 1704 when Marlborough ordered Colonel Blood to march a battery of cannon across the pontoon bridge over a small river. When within half a musket shot of the enemy the guns proved deadly and checked a dangerous advance.

Artillery and 'cannoniers and bombardiers' at the funeral of the Duke of Marlborough. Detail from a print of the funeral published 1727

An example of improvisation rather than of massive attack took place in North America. The combined naval and military attack on Quebec was in the nature of a cautious advance up the St Lawrence River, and the steep Heights of Abraham which could only be scaled with difficulty permitted only a single artillery gun to be hauled to the top where even this slender support contributed strongly to the success of the British forces.

As the basic principles of gunnery had changed very little from the Middle Ages, it is surprising that artillerymen were able to advance their techniques at all. The field guns of the eighteenth century were the cannon and the howitzers. The lightest piece was the 1½-pounder gun. These could be mounted on galloper carriages as used in Germany in 1747. These carriages were made with the trail split in halves so as to make shafts for a single horse. In the main these guns were discontinued in 1748.

The 3-pounder guns served their purpose as battalion guns being placed in the intervals of the battle line ready to take up the fire when the musketry slackened. A battalion formed in charging order had a gun on each flank and in square had the two guns in opposite corners of the square. Light 6-pounder guns were also used as battalion guns. Man-harness was used for manoeuvring the pieces on the battle field. This particular weight of gun was popular in North America as the lightness permitted movement over difficult terrain.

Heavy 6-pounder and 9-pounder guns as well as 12-pounder were the usual weight of artillery for general field work and these the horses could move quickly enough when needed. The 24-pounder was used as a siege piece and proved unsuitable for America. The 32-pounder was a siege piece only used in Europe. The normal cannon could fire ball, grape shot, or canister shot directly at human beings but against fortifications and buildings the mortar and howitzer came into their own. The howitzers which had calibres up to eight or ten inches could throw shells with incendiary material by indirect fire over walls and buildings into the centre of otherwise protected areas. The heavy mortars could keep up steady bombardment during sieges, also using indirect fire.

In the eighteenth century all cannon were muzzle-loading and the priming was ignited by means of a 'port-fire' being applied to the vent at the rear end. Carriages were heavy at the beginning of the eighteenth century and had two heavy cheek-pieces to the trail. The British introduction of a block trail in 1792 by Sir W. Congreve did much to improve the weight and mobility. Regarding draught, the gun was originally attached to a pair of wheels by means of an upright pin but later the method of attachment was an iron eye on the trail and a hook on the limber (another English invention) which also served to carry ammunition.

Garrison guns did not need the same mobility and the fragile wheels were replaced by heavy wooden carriages somewhat similar to those used on board ship. By a system of blocks, pulleys, and cords the gun could be pulled back into place after the recoil of firing. Special carriages were developed from time to time, one of the most famous and successful being Koehler's 'depressing' carriage. Normally cannon could fire 'pointblank', i.e. absolutely horizontal, or at an elevation which enabled a wide range of shot. But the unusual position of the British artillery on the Rock of Gibraltar called for a weapon which could be fired at an object below the horizontal. Koehler produced a carriage with extra arcs at the rear which enabled that end to be raised and the front depressed to fire at the enemy and their shipping. It was also at this 1779–83 siege of Gibraltar that the use of 'red-hot' shot was most effective. Special tools and holders permitted the heated iron balls to be moved swiftly from the red-hot fires to the waiting cannon. The opposing fireships of the French and Spanish navies failed to achieve their objects and suffered severely when they caught fire.

In 1784 Colonel Shrapnel developed a type of spherical case. The hollow shell well known many years before was so made that it exploded into fragments, thus reaching a wide zone of fire. Grape

rs.

The grand attack at Valenciennes 1793

shot – many small shots on a circular base and bound in position – was popular against massed troops for the cord burnt away and the shot dispersed over a wide front. Canister shot was somewhat similar in effect having the shot within a metal case where the explosion ejected the shot with greater force.

In India the use of war rockets against the British troops at Seringapatam in 1799 killed at least 50 men. Congreve was inspired to experiment with these war rockets for use in Europe, but he did not develop a suitable weapon until the turn of the century. Rockets had been used by artillery men at the beginning of the eighteenth century but these were only display rockets and made by the fireworkers for special occasions.

The artillery at this period came under the control of the Board of Ordnance which was not considered part of the Army but rather a State department, which situation caused jealousy and strife between the officers of the army and those of the Board of Ordnance. King George II eventually ruled that the commissions granted by the Master Gunner were equal to those of the army. Gradually the Royal Regiment of Artillery took precedence of place over the infantry, dragoons when dismounted, and when the Royal Horse Artillery was created, even before cavalry. This precedence was brought about by the need of the quick-moving troops to be in front of the slow-moving ones.

Because the work of artillery was considered a science, special training was necessary. The specialists – both officers and men – in a train all had specific and arduous tasks to perform. Besides the requirements of the gun itself, there was the work of the engineers who planned the sieges and attacks, the pioneers who carried out the saps, earthworks, and embankments, the fireworkers who were responsible for the gunpowder, the shells, the bombs, and other explosives. The great lumbering train had to have its own carpenters, tin-men, pontoonmen, sail-makers, corders, etc., as the train had to be self-sufficient on the march and in the field. The conductors and commissaries saw to the actual movement and provisioning while for music the train had its own distinctive kettledrum-carriage. The artillery did not carry standards or colours as in the case of cavalry and infantry. It was said that the actual guns took the place of regimental colours and thus they were defended with the utmost tenacity.

The kettledrum-carriage or 'chariot' supplied the necessary pomp and the two large kettledrums were on a light four-wheeled carriage. Up to six white horses drew this unusual vehicle. A postillion sat on the near horse of the leading pair, a driver sat on the front of the carriage while the kettledrummer was at the back wielding his drum sticks to great effect. The drums were draped with special embroidered banners and those of the Georgian period can still be

Royal Horse Artillery at the gallop

seen at Woolwich. When in the artillery park on service the kettledrums beat each evening at tattoo and of course the carriage was prominent in processions, one famous occasion being the funeral of the Duke of Marlborough in 1722.

It may not be realised that the early dress of the artilleryman was the red coat lined with blue, the Royal livery as worn by other soldiers of the Sovereign's army. This uniform was worn by the trains of Marlborough's wars but with the coming of the Hanoverian dynasty the uniform changed to dark blue with red linings. The drummers retained the scarlet coat suitably laced and the kettledrummer wore a State coat similar to that worn by the State trumpeters.

The officers had gold lace on their hats and garments and besides being armed with a sword had a fusee or fuzil, a better type of lightweight musket. In April 1770 officers were no longer to have fuzees but were to carry and salute with swords the same as the dragoon officers. The sergeant, corporal, and bombardier also had gold lace of varying widths to indicate their ranks; later shoulder-knots were used for this purpose. Their arms were halberts and brass-hilted swords, the former being taken from the corporals and bombardiers in 1754 when they adopted carbines like the gunners. Sergeants are said to have carried a polearm up to 1845. The gunners carried field staves and brass hilted swords.

The field staff was said to have been laid aside in 1748 but in 1757 it was known that the gunners marched with their guns slung and a linstock over the left arm, this item holding the match to fire the gun. Gunners carried powder horns for priming and wires for clearing the touch-hole as late as 1792. The matrosses, a lower grade of artillerymen, had muskets and bayonets. In 1748 the common muskets were discontinued and both gunners and matrosses carried carbines and bayonets. The title of matross was abolished in 1783 and all privates were called gunners.

Just before the end of the eighteenth century the cocked hat began to go out of fashion and broad-brimmed hats were worn. At the turn of the century gunners adopted shakos and the coats which had been worn open for so long were now closed across the body. The breeches and hose which had been worn since the beginning of the century were now being covered by overalls, at first for training and fatigue duties and later for active service.

The introduction of horse artillery brought a new dress to this arm of service, based on the light dragoon dress. The headdress was the black leather helmet as worn by the light cavalry with a red turban and gilt fittings. A red lapelled jacket was soon changed for a braided hussar type. As befitted a mounted branch trumpeters were introduced instead of drummers.

CHAPTER 15

The Conquest of India; The Wars against the Sikhs 1806–53

JAMES P. LAWFORD

Throughout this period British power expanded unchecked until by 1850 it was supreme on the Indian sub-continent. During the first Afghan War, the Honourable East India Company suffered a defeat of some magnitude; but the great struggle for power was with the Sikhs, and with them the Company experienced probably the hardest fighting of its two hundred and fifty year life. Other campaigns there were, but in none was British military power seriously threatened.

In 1806 some inane orders on dress and turn-out were issued by the Madras government, beards and caste marks in particular being prohibited. All armies suffer from this type of stupidity, normally with resignation. At Vellore the sepoys suspected an attack on their religion. They suddenly mutinied, and massacred two companies of Europeans who shared their station. Gillespie with a small force galloped up from Arcot, blew in the gate of Vellore fort, cut down many of the mutineers and captured the rest. The order causing the mutiny was rescinded. Notice, however, had been served that, while the sepoy was normally docile and loyal, if trouble did come it was likely to be explosive and murderous.

In 1812 the Governor General, Lord Hastings, resolved to put down the Pindaris. These were bands of freebooters who had been accustomed to loot and plunder in the wake of the Mahratta armies. Before, however, the Company could dispose of them it found itself embroiled with the Gurkhas. Towards the middle of the last century the Gurkhas had conquered Nepal, and had then gradually extended their sway over much of the Himalayan foothills. They, in common with many other hillmen, suffered from an inveterate desire to supplement the spartan resources of their mountain fastnesses by raiding into the rich and enticing plains nearby, and the nuisance eventually became intolerable. In 1814 the Company declared war. After hard fighting and not a few reverses, General Ochterlony captured the province of Kumaon, defeated the Gurkha armies, and advanced on Katmandu. In 1816 a treaty was signed delimiting the Gurkha borders; it

Opposite above: Rangoon. The storming of the principal stockades 8 July 1824. These stockades were an unusual type of fortification much used by the Burmese. Painted by J. Moore
Below: The 3rd Light Dragoons charge into the Sikh encampment at Ferozeshah

was faithfully observed by both sides until 1947. Gurkhas, having forcibly demonstrated their martial qualities, were enlisted into the Indian Army, and Gurkha regiments have given Britain magnificent service ever since. As an interesting footnote to that campaign, the sepoys had on occasion to face volleys of arrows; they found it very disconcerting to advance against missiles they could see.

When he had settled the Gurkha problem, Hastings at once turned his attention back to the Pindaris. In 1817 he deployed one hundred and twenty thousand men over an enormous area of Central India in the hope that he would succeed in finally extirpating the scourge. The Mahrattas were not prepared to watch their brethren subdued without a final tilt at the British, and his campaign provoked the Third Mahratta War.

In the autumn of 1817 Baji Rao, the Peshwa, launched a treacherous attack on the British Resident at Poona, but a nearby British brigade, although heavily outnumbered, so roughly handled his men at the battle of Kirkee that he fled to become a homeless wanderer. Berar and Holkar joined the Peshwa, but their armies were easily overthrown at the battles of Seetabaldi and Mehidpur, and, although punitive columns continued to chase fugitives for the following year, the revolt, for it was little more, was broken by Christmas. The campaign against the Pindaris was also brought to a successful conclusion, the last of the Pindari chiefs being eaten by a tiger which presumably failed to recognise a blood brother. By 1819 two thirds of India had come under the Company's rule.

In 1824 a campaign had to be waged against the Burmese who had conquered Assam and threatened Bengal. An expedition to Rangoon, despite administrative mismanagement, compelled a Burmese withdrawal. The expedition was the occasion of a serious sepoy mutiny at Barrackpore near Calcutta. For the high-caste Hindu a journey overseas violated his caste. Madras overcame the difficulty by enlisting special regiments with a specific overseas liability. But the Bengal Army had made no such provision, and when the 47th Native Infantry Regiment of that Army was ordered to join the expedition it refused to march. A badly handled parade to disarm the regiment led to many of the sepoys being shot down where they stood.

Punishments in the sepoy regiments at that time were, by European standards, remarkably lenient. As in most armies, mutineers received no mercy, but a sepoy could quit the Army by giving a month's notice, and flogging was very rare.

The matter of caste caused many problems. Previous conquerors in India had often forcibly converted their new and unwilling subjects to their own faith. The Indians forever suspected that the British intended to make Christians out of them, probably first by defiling their caste. How much caste meant to the sepoys perhaps this anecdote from the memoirs of Subedar Sita Ram of the Bengal Army will show.

Sita Ram had been serving with a column chasing Pindaris. In an engagement he had been severely wounded and left for dead in the jungle. He eventually managed to drag himself to a well. Here he

The retreat from Kabul. Near Gandamuk the last remnants of the 44th Foot, the only unit still to retain its order, formed square, and here most of them died. Only one man, Doctor Brydon, managed to ride on and, badly wounded, tell the garrison at Jellalabad of the disaster.

General Gough. He was later created First Viscount and Field Marshal

found a young girl from a low caste jungle tribe and nearly dead from thirst, persuaded her to draw him some water. Sita Ram was a Brahmin, a Hindu of the highest caste. After some vicissitudes he succeeded in rejoining his regiment, and was sent on leave to convalesce. What happened in his village is best told in his own words:

One evening ... I chanced to mention the incident of the little girl ... when a Brahmin priest declared ... that from having drunk the water drawn by her I was defiled. Everyone now shunned me, no one would now smoke with me ... I was not allowed even to enter my father's house.

Through the influence of my father a Panchayat (a council of five elders) was held ... who sat in judgment on me, and after the priests had performed many ceremonies over me and ordered me to fast many days – after which I have to give them gifts and other things – I was declared 'pak' (clean) ... All the money I had saved during five years was thus spent.

In 1838 the first Afghan War broke out. The British government in England fearing the Russian drive southwards through central Asia, wished to have a British puppet on the Afghan throne and thereby seal off the Himalayan passes.

This policy failed disastrously. A British Army occupied Kabul and placed Shah Shujah, the British candidate, on the throne. It soon became apparent that Shah Shujah's rule depended on British bayonets, and a British Army of occupation had to remain.

Then in November 1841 as the bitter Himalayan winter closed in the Afghan tribes rose in a general revolt. British leadership was irresolute and in January 1842 the army of occupation withdrew. In the high, snow-choked passes, the tribesmen destroyed it. Only one man escaped; Dr Brydon, desperately wounded, rode into the fort at Jellalabad and announced the catastrophe. In the autumn British Armies occupied Kabul and avenged the defeat, but all plans for turning Afghanistan into a protectorate were abandoned and all British forces were withdrawn.

In 1843 Sir Charles Napier invaded Sinde with the ultimate aim of bringing the waters of the Indus under British control. He defeated the Baluchis at the battle of Miani and Sinde was annexed. The victory was proclaimed by a single word despatch, the Latin word *Peccavi* – 'I have sinned'. It was true in both senses.

Now the arena was clear for the final trial of strength, the war with the Sikhs, the 'lions of the Punjab'. The Sikhs above all things prized bodily distinction and martial prowess. Under their great leader, Ranjit Singh, they had conquered the Punjab, Kashmir and most of north-west India. Ranjit Singh avoided conflict with the British, and the River Sutlej was accepted by both as the border between them. The Sikh army that he trained, often known as the 'Khalsa', consisted of highly trained infantrymen and artillerymen; not for him the gaily caparisoned elephants and masses of wild horsemen beloved by so many Indian rulers.

Ranjit Singh died and six years of intrigue, assassination and treachery followed, years in which the Khalsa played a leading and often discreditable part. Slowly it became plain that internal dissension could resolve itself only by external aggression, aggression that inevitably would be directed against the British.

The British Commander-in-Chief, General Gough, was an Irishman, impetuous, hardy and very brave; but his orders were seldom clear and his staff had a genial habit of not only keeping no record of the instructions they issued, but frequently of forgetting what they were. Gough's battles tended to be gallant but somewhat muddled affairs. His 'Tipperary tactics' came in for a good deal of criticism at the time; yet under his leadership the power of the Khalsa was broken, and his men, always the best judge of a general, would follow him, as the saying was, 'to the gates of Hell' – they knew he would be the first to enter.

In the autumn of 1845 Gough recognised the

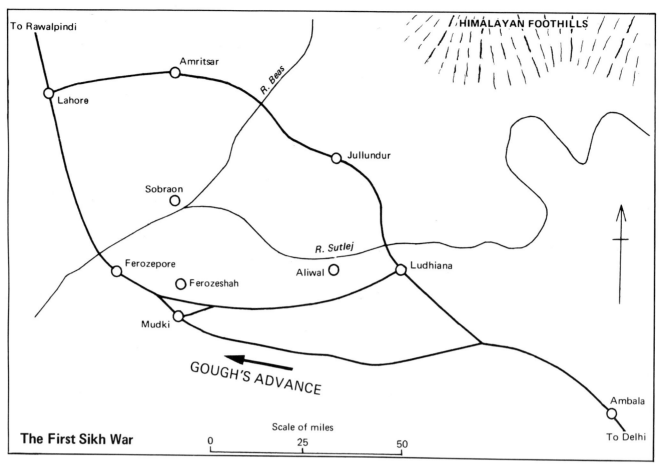

The First Sikh War

Scale of miles

0   25   50

dangerous situation developing in the Punjab and concentrated an army at Ambala. Then with the incredulity that comes from an event long prophesied but not wholly expected, the British learnt that the Sikh army had crossed the Sutlej.

The Sikhs advanced to Ferozeshah and prepared an entrenched camp there while detached forces blockaded the forward British bases at Ferozepore and Ludhiana. Gough at once moved forward to relieve Ferozepore and destroy the Sikhs.

At Mudki, after his men had completed a long and fatiguing march and were about to camp, a Sikh army came into view. Gough at once attacked. His guns silenced the Sikh artillery and his cavalry drove off the Sikh horsemen in disorder. The Sikh infantry, however, who had taken post in broken scrub-covered ground stood firm, and a desperate and bloody combat ensued. As daylight faded clouds of dust and smoke from the musketry obscured the battlefield. The battle swayed uncertainly, then General Harry Smith seized a colour of HM 50th Foot and plunged into the thick of the Sikh infantry. The 50th followed with the bayonet. Now the combination of night and dust cloaked the whole battlefield in impenetrable darkness. In the black chaos it became impossible to tell friend from foe, and regiments fired on both impartially. The firing began to slacken and suddenly bright moonlight

bathed the whole scene. The Sikhs, with the loss of some guns, fell back on Ferozeshah. The exhausted British formed camp by Mudki village.

On 19 December Gough rested his men. On the 20th he laid plans for assaulting the main Sikh army at Ferozeshah next day. He sent orders to General Littler, who with his division was facing a Sikh army under their General Tej Singh at Ferozepore, to slip away undetected and join him for the attack. This would give Gough a total of eighteen thousand men supported by fifty-four guns and organised into four divisions. His divisions were each two infantry brigades strong, each brigade normally consisting of one British and two sepoy battalions.

At four o'clock on a cold winter morning, Gough's army marched for Ferozeshah. At about 10.30 a.m. in bright bracing sunlight, Gough halted out of gunshot range of the encampment and his men ate a hearty breakfast, the last many were to eat. There was no sign of Littler. Now occurred a curious incident. The Governor General, Lord Hardinge, himself an able soldier, had accompanied Gough, and, anxious not to miss the fighting, had volunteered to serve under him as second-in-command.

After the men had breakfasted Gough wanted to attack at once. Hardinge disagreed violently, and insisted that he should wait for Littler. Gough, once he had formed an opinion, rarely altered it.

142

Hardinge at last dropped the mantle of second-in-command and as Governor General ordered Gough to wait. That fiery general had no alternative but to comply.

Littler did not arrive until after midday, and the attack did not go in until 3.30 p.m. This was to have serious consequences.

Gough's plan, like the man, was simple. He lined up three divisions along the length of the Sikh encampment and held his fourth, under General Harry Smith, in reserve. Harry Smith, an outspoken critic of Gough, commented acidly that the plan ensured that every Sikh gun had a target, while the British artillery was spread too thinly to be effective.

Littler's division on the left, for some unexplained reason, possibly owing to a light-hearted staff officer, attacked somewhat earlier than the other two. It was met by a fearful cannonade. HM 62nd, the only British regiment, lost three hundred men, about half its strength, in ten minutes. Before this appalling and deadly hail his division broke and ran back in disorder leaving the ground dotted with their dead and wounded, while the Sikhs gave a great shout of triumph.

Hardinge led the centre division forward. With great gallantry the men rushed the guns to find lines of steady Sikh infantrymen behind them; volley thundered against volley, neither side prepared to give way. On the right, where Gough himself led, HM 29th and 80th Foot advanced with parade-ground precision, charged over the Sikh guns, and with a few fierce volleys dispersed the Sikh infantry behind. Darkness was now falling. Suddenly there was a tremendous noise and the 3rd Light Dragoons with superb dash jumped the breast-works, sabred down the remaining Sikh gunners, and charged right through the camp cutting down Sikh infantrymen as they went. But they left half their number on the ground behind them.

In the centre things were critical. Littler's failure had exposed the left flank of Hardinge's division. The Sikh infantry showed no signs of giving way. Hardinge's British battalion, the 9th Foot, was being shot to pieces. Hardinge called upon Harry Smith. Harry Smith, owing to some curious dispositions by Gough, could only muster one brigade. He hurried them forward; with an irresistible impetus they crashed through the Sikh infantry into the heart of their camp.

Darkness, enhanced by rolling clouds of musketry smoke, fell on a scene of immense confusion. The Sikh camp had caught fire, tents flared up briefly in the blackness igniting any ammunition near them, a Sikh magazine blew up with a report like a thunderclap scattering the 1st European Light Infantry who had charged with Gough. Firing continued in all directions. The noise was prodigious.

Harry Smith, sweeping up men from both Hardinge's and Gough's divisions, rushed on and stormed Ferozeshah village. Here he halted and tried to restore some order among his wildly excited and confused mob of men.

Gough's position was now very dangerous. He was out of touch with Littler and only knew that his attack had failed disastrously. Harry Smith and his men had been swallowed up by the darkness and none knew their fate. The regiments of the centre and right were inextricably mixed up. He realised control was impossible while his men roamed the Sikh encampment in disorganised bands.

He decided he must pull his men back out of the encampment and reorganise them. He appointed assembly points for the regiments about three hundred yards from the Sikh breast-works, and had their buglers blow incessantly their regimental calls and the 'Assembly'. Gradually some sort of order was restored, while Gough and Hardinge peered anxiously through the gloom. Hardinge had with him Prince Waldemar of Prussia as a volunteer. He thought it prudent to send him back to a place of safety. Then from the abandoned breast-works a Sikh gun suddenly opened fire on him point blank. He gathered together men of HM 80th and 1st European Light Infantry and they silenced it with their bayonets. By now it was midnight, and after the charge quiet descended on the men outside the encampment, while away in the distance inexplicable volleys of musketry revealed a battle raging somewhere in the darkness. The night was bitterly cold; unfed and without greatcoats the men lay down to seize what rest they could. The situation was one to unnerve the stoutest heart, but Hardinge and Gough were agreed on at least one point, come what may they would fight the battle to a finish. There would be no retreat.

Meanwhile Harry Smith in Ferozeshah looked vainly for support. Realising he was isolated, he grouped his men round the ordered and unruffled ranks of HM 50th Foot. The Sikhs attacked from all sides, yelling out in Hindustani and broken English that the British were surrounded and must all die. Harry Smith's men confined their reply to musket balls. As the firing in the rear faded and died, the moon broke through shedding an eerie light. It was now about 2 a.m. Harry Smith knew it was hopeless

Ferozeshah, the second day. Gough's weary men storm the Sikh encampment

to stay where he was. He noted a gap in the encircling Sikhs. He feigned an attack to make them draw back, then with masterly skill, slipped away with his men through the gap. He marched back to the British lines guided by the dead and the wounded that marked his line of advance.

As dawn broke Harry Smith reported back to find his indomitable old chief busy arraying his exhausted regiments in some form of battle order.

As the light came up a heavy mist for a brief time obscured the Sikh encampment. As it thinned and disappeared the Sikhs could be discerned once again manning their guns. The British guns spoke out, then Gough's buglers sounded the advance; the hungry, weary line surged forward. It was too much for the Sikhs. They drew back, and with a tremendous cheer the British poured into the encampment. There they captured seventy cannon; almost all the Sikh guns had been abandoned.

But the battle was not entirely over. As the tired men were taking up their new positions, a great cloud of dust could be seen approaching. Tej Singh had belatedly discovered Littler's disappearance and had followed him up. Gough's peril now was great. His men were bone weary, their ammunition almost all fired. The Sikhs began a long range bombardment and their cavalry threatened Gough's flank. The 3rd Light Dragoons or what was left of them, supported by the 4th Bengal Lancers, flogged their stumbling mounts forward, and undaunted rode into their new foe. The Sikh cavalry gave back. Then suddenly the Sikh bombardment ended and Tej Singh marched off. There has been no clear explanation for this withdrawal, but he could not have known how critical was the state of Gough's army and probably hesitated to attack the main British army on his own.

Now the men could rest and the wounded be tended. The Army had suffered some 2,400 casualties and these were particularly heavy among the European regiments. The 9th Foot had lost some

330 men, and the others had lost almost as many.

The Sikhs withdrew across the Sutlej leaving a fortified bridgehead on the British side of the river close by the village of Sobraon. Gough rested his men. For the moment he could do no more.

In January 1846 a Sikh force crossed the Sutlej and threatened Ludhiana. On the 29th General Harry Smith with ten thousand men brought them to action at Aliwal village with their backs to the river. In a brilliant action he utterly routed them. The cavalry executed some spirited charges; HM 16th Lancers charged right through a Sikh infantry square, reformed, and charged through them again. The fugitive Sikhs suffered terribly as they tried to cross the Sutlej to safety. For the first time the sepoys saw the backs of the Sikh infantry; it had a tonic effect on all the sepoy regiments.

To celebrate the victory Gough ordered a royal salute to be fired and the regimental bands to play 'The Queen'. The Sikhs across the river promptly fired a royal salute themselves, and then to the amazed ears of Gough's men came the strains of 'The Queen' played by the Sikh bands!

In February General Gough received a full siege train; he needed it as during this time the Sikhs had been busily fortifying their bridgehead, at Sobraon and it now contained the whole Sikh Army.

On 10 February Gough attacked. For two hours the British guns endeavoured to silence the Sikh artillery without success. Gough, on being informed that his guns were running out of ammunition, is reported to have said: 'Thank God, then I'll be at them with the bayonet', and ordered the advance. The struggle was long and bitter. In places the Sikh entrenchments were so high that men had to stand on each other's shoulders to climb in. At last the Sikhs gave way, and, as at Aliwal, paid dearly for fighting with a river at their back. The 3rd Light Dragoons following into the camp charged the retreating masses. Guns came up and played upon

Opposite: The Battle of Aliwal, 29 January 1846. Twice at this battle the 16th Lancers broke a Sikh square
Overleaf: Waterloo. Before the British fire the Old Guard recoils. On the left near La Haye Sainte, Wellington sees victory within his grasp. Far right, wreathed in gun smoke, Napoleon watches his last throw fail. Painted by Sir William Allen

144

Sobraon. The infantry surge over the high Sikh earthworks

the only bridge. It collapsed. The Sikhs had mutilated some British wounded, and the British troops were merciless. It is estimated some ten thousand Sikhs perished during the fighting or trying to cross the river. All their guns were captured. The first Sikh War had been won.

THE SECOND SIKH WAR

The Khalsa licked its wounds and resolved on a final throw. A Sikh army revolt in Multan touched off the war. Gough advanced from Lahore and on 13 January 1849 fought a typical chaotic night battle at Chillianwala without securing a decision. As orders for his supersession were on the way he fought at last a deliberate and skilful action at Gujrat. In the main the British artillery won the day and for once British casualties were light. The remnants of the Sikh army surrendered at Rawalpindi on 14 March. Thereafter for nearly a hundred years the Sikhs displayed their splendid martial talents in the service of the Crown.

The fighting had been brutal and merciless, atrocities were on occasion committed by both sides, yet through it all ran a curious streak of chivalry, a streak which must be recorded if the spirit of the times is to be understood.

Early in the campaign Lieutenant Biddulph, riding to join his regiment at Ferozepore, was surprised and captured by a party of Sikhs. He was placed in the charge of a Sikh gunner officer. Biddulph got on so well with the Sikh gunners that after the battle of Mudki they sent him with an escort back to the British camp. Hardinge refused to allow Biddulph to fight at Ferozeshah, as he thought it would be unfair to a generous enemy!

In the assault on the Sikh encampment at Ferozeshah, Lieutenant Sievewright, HM 9th Foot, fell with his leg shattered by grape. The battle flowed by and Sievewright lay in solitary agony through the long cold night. Shortly after dawn he saw a Sikh soldier approaching. He drew his pistol and challenged him. The Sikh replied: 'Salaam Sahib'. After a few more words the Sikh picked Sievewright up on his back and carried him, at no small risk to himself, two miles to the rear, where he put him on a cart which carried him to Ferozepore. Unhappily Sievewright died a few days later.

In less than ten years the Bengal Army that had carried the colours of Britain from the delta of the Ganges to the snows of the Himalayas, that had just broken the famous Khalsa on the plains of the Punjab, was to turn on its creator. In part the opportunity for this possibly most famous of mutinies came from the war in the Crimea which had drained India of British troops.

Opposite: The Siege of Delhi, the storming of the Kashmir Gate, 14 September 1857. The gate has just been blown in, and the 52nd are leading the assault, followed by the Kumaon Battalion and the 1st Punjab Infantry

CHAPTER 16

Peacetime Economy and the Crimean War 1815–56

PHILIP A. WARNER

In the period which followed the Napoleonic wars the British Army, which had fought so long and so well, was treated with short-sighted ingratitude. Essential units, such as the Wagon Train and Staff Corps, were abolished entirely. The Army's numbers were reduced to 225,000 in 1816 and to 100,000 in 1821. Of the latter figure about half were overseas, 20,000 in India and the remainder scattered over the world in small colonial garrisons. After 1824 the numbers began to rise again and by 1854, when we required troops for the Crimea, there were 140,000 men with the Colours. Fortunately, the Militia which had been abolished at the end of the Napoleonic Wars was reconstituted in 1852, and therefore provided a form of reserve. But in general the numbers were hopelessly inadequate for the tasks they were expected to perform.

The explanation of this drastic cut-back was at first that the country was exhausted by the Napoleonic wars, and that crippling taxation must be reduced as soon as possible; this was succeeded by the belief that armies would be an expensive superfluity in the era of universal peace which was rapidly approaching. The Army is, of course, thoroughly accustomed to being venerated in wartime and scorned and neglected during the peace its efforts have won, but has seldom been treated as stupidly as it was between 1816 and 1854. This was a time of great expansion both at home and overseas and an efficient army was a vital necessity. Abroad it was the protection for expanding trade; at home it had the unenviable task of maintaining law and order under extremely difficult conditions. Until 1829 there was no Metropolitan police force. In consequence the first resort of Parliament when threatened with mob violence was to turn out the Army.

The task at home was exacerbated by Parliament's attitude to any concession to social reform. In the period after 1816 the Prime Minister, Lord Liverpool, and the Foreign Secretary, Lord Castlereagh, were firmly convinced that any move to improve the conditions of the working class would be to open the doors to an English version of the French Revolution. Any assembly or meeting was seen as a prelude to national insurrection. As wages were low, working conditions extremely bad, and unemployment widespread, it was hardly surprising that some of the assemblies produced dangerous situations. In 1816 a mob tried to seize the Tower of London and distribute arms among its followers; the courage of the Lord Mayor and a handful of supporters saved the day. In 1819 30,000 people assembled at Manchester to listen to an inflammatory orator. The situation became dangerous and was handled unwisely. Thoroughly alarmed, the magistrates ordered a cavalry regiment to disperse the crowd, in the course of which action there were some seventy casualties. The following year saw a plot to murder the whole Cabinet. It was betrayed, but four of these 'Cato Street conspirators', as they were called, were subsequently hanged

Opposite: Cardigan, 'the last of the Brudenells', leads the charge of the Light Brigade at Balaclava. Engraved by H. Cousins after A. F. de Prades

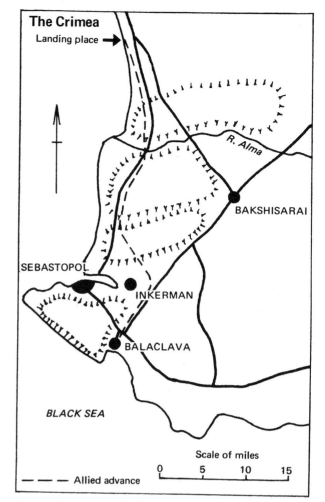

The Crimea
Landing place →

R. Alma

BAKSHISARAI

SEBASTOPOL

INKERMAN

BALACLAVA

BLACK SEA

Scale of miles
0   5   10   15

— — — Allied advance

and decapitated. Fear was widespread; in the towns no one knew where the next riot would lead; in the country landowners never knew whether the next night would see their ricks and barns burnt.

Against this tide of dissatisfaction and lawlessness 50,000 ill-organised men were little enough protection. It might have been thought that their small numbers would be compensated for by great efficiency and good conditions. The reverse was the case. Pay was low, overcrowding was universal, food was bad, and recreation did not exist. Like their counterparts outside, soldiers found relief from their conditions in drink, but as this frequently led to indisciplined behaviour the final outcome was often a flogging. The severity of punishment seems almost inconceivable today; a man might be flogged brutally for a mistake on parade or a blemish on his turnout. The problem of discipline was, of course, far from easy; it was a harsh age and if punishment was to act as a deterrent it had to be in accord with the ideas of the times. Unfortunately, many of the 'crimes' were minor offences by modern standards, and most of them would not have occurred at all had Parliament been a little less parsimonious towards the Army, and improved its conditions slightly. Neither the appointment of the Duke of Wellington as Prime Minister in 1827, nor the threat of Civil War over the Reform Bill in 1832 made the lot of the soldier any easier. The Duke believed that what was good for the Napoleonic Wars was good for ever, and the Government was much too involved in its own affairs to pay any attention to the soldiers, on whom, if they but knew it, their lives and liberty depended. It is therefore all the more remarkable that this small, overstrained, and neglected force was able to provide troops for home and overseas security, to occupy Aden in 1838 with a small force drawn from our Indian Army; to send 7,000 troops to China to fight successfully in the war between 1839 and 1842; to win the Ashanti campaigns of 1824 and 1831; and to provide an efficient fighting force in South Africa for the sporadic wars between 1834 and 1852.

Shortage of money and neglect were not, of course, the only things wrong with the Army. The system which had worked reasonably well in the past was now obsolete. The practice of purchasing commissions had once been a useful means of ensuring that officers looked after their men as an investment, if for no other reason, but in the nineteenth century had become an absurd anachronism. Children held Colonel's commissions in certain regiments, and they (or their parents) were therefore

able to obtain the lion's share of any plunder which came the regiment's way. Meanwhile the path to promotion for poor but able officers was permanently blocked in peacetime. This situation was to continue until the 1860s but be swept away by the Cardwell Reforms in 1870, of which we shall have more to say later.

The war with Russia which broke out in 1854, and was not concluded till 1856, is rightly known as a grim occasion for British arms. In view of what we have already seen of the conditions of the army which was pitched into it this is not surprising. It is famous for being the setting of the most remarkable cavalry charge in history, for the hideous conditions in the hospitals, and for the magnificent examples it provided of unit and individual courage. What is less well known is the fact that in the course of two agonizing years the neglected British Army was so reconstituted that it finished the war as a highly efficient fighting force.

The nominal cause of this war was a dispute over rights of access to the Holy Places in (what was then) Palestine. The outcome was that Russia decided to support the Greek churchmen, and France the Roman Catholics. Motives lay rather deeper. Turkey had long been in a state of decline, and the ambitious Russian Emperor, the Czar Nicholas, felt the time was opportune to take control of that country whose territories enveloped Russia's shortest route to the sea. He hoped to placate France, Britain, and Austria by sharing out portions of Turkish territory; Britain was to have Egypt and Crete. Such calculations were naïve in the extreme. Britain was certain to be apprehensive about the implied threat to her interests in India, and the French Emperor, the self-appointed and ambitious Napoleon III, was looking for cheap prestige in thwarting the country which had defeated his great namesake in 1812.

Having made up his mind, the Czar demanded to be regarded as the Protector of all Greek Christians within the Turkish Empire, and showed that he meant business by sending troops to occupy Moldavia and Wallachia, later to become part of Roumania, but at that time vassal states of Turkey. This was July 1853. From then on events moved fairly rapidly and led to the complete destruction of the Turkish fleet by the Russians at Sinope in November 1853. All but two of the Turkish ships were sunk, and three out of every four of their sailors were killed or drowned. Russia now controlled the Black Sea. Even now England was slow to realise the threat to her communications, and it was not until Palmerston threatened to resign that an

ultimatum was sent to the Russians. Eventually England and France declared war on 27 March 1854.

With considerable, but hardly surprising, difficulty an expeditionary force was assembled and put under Lord Raglan, who at the age of 66 was now receiving his first independent command. Approximately 25,000 men were embarked and eventually landed at Varna, a port 300 miles from the Crimea, on the western shore of the Black Sea. There they were joined by some 30,000 French. All had suffered greatly on the journey out and it was no surprise that sickness began to take its toll immediately after they arrived. Fortunately they were not required to take immediate action as the Turks had already succeeded in driving the Russians out of the areas they had occupied the previous July. Now, and later, cholera proved the greatest killer of the war. It is a disease of terrifying swiftness. A man can be alive and well one day but dead by the following morning. A waterborne infection, it spreads easily.

In consequence, when the expeditionary force re-embarked for the Crimea on 7 September, cholera and dysentery travelled with it. The force, which now consisted of 27,000 British, 30,000 French and 7,000 Turks, landed on the western coast of the Crimea thirty-five miles north of Sebastopol. Had it

A plan of the Battle of Alma

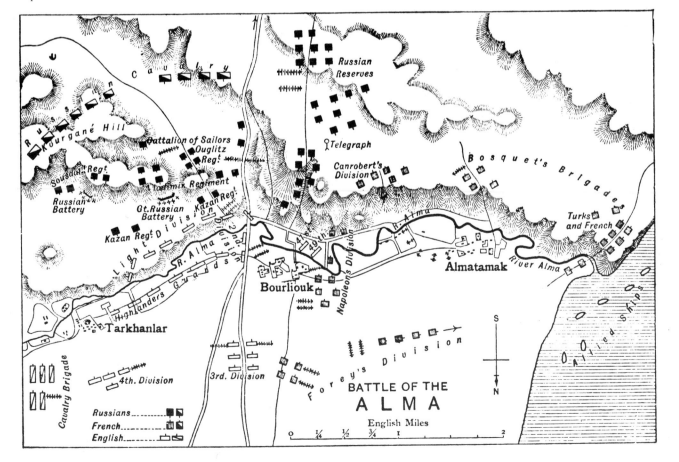

arrived in July, as originally intended, the Russians would have been caught unprepared, but by September Prince Menschikoff, the Russian commander, knew very well what was in prospect, and had taken appropriate measures. When therefore the Allies began a painfully slow advance towards Sebastopol, Menschikoff was waiting with an army deployed along the heights overlooking the River Alma. It consisted of 3,400 cavalry and 33,000 infantry supported by 106 guns; including artillerymen it numbered 39,000.

THE BATTLE OF THE ALMA

The Russian commander did not know the ground well but had a considerable advantage in that the Allies would be attacking up difficult slopes against a force with adequate cover. His outworks consisted of a 300 × 10 yard earthwork, 600 yards back from the river, which contained fourteen heavy (i.e. 32- and 24-pounder known as the great battery and a smaller battery further to the east. The battle ended in victory for the Allies but was handled with considerable ineptitude by both sides. The Allies had continued landings until the 18th and on the 19th had set off, a magnificent sight in scarlet, white, blue, green, and gold, with bearskins, bands, and feathered bonnets but no forward patrols and only the scantiest provision against flank attack. The column was $1\frac{1}{2}$ miles long and the British contingent marched as on a parade ground, constantly checking its dressing, until the roughness of the ground made this impossible. Raglan and St Arnaud (the French commander) knew that the Russians had moved nearly 40,000 troops out of Sebastopol and stationed them along the Alma, so they conferred together and formulated a very simple plan. The French, who had less sickness in their ranks than the British, would move along the sea shore, and scale the cliffs in a flanking movement. The British would be in the centre. In theory the French would engage the majority of the Russian force but in fact, as everyone well knew, this was unlikely as the main Russian force would be in the centre.

There is not, unfortunately, space to give a full account of this remarkable battle but certain features must be mentioned. From the earliest stages, when the troops executed the difficult manoeuvre of turning from column into line, formation was observed with meticulous care. Whatever the faults of this neglected army they did not include weakness or indiscipline; on the contrary all ranks showed high morale and amazing courage. The higher command was sadly ineffective, St Arnaud was a sick man – he died soon after – and Raglan was so vague

he probably never fully understood what was going on. He even lost touch with his own men and at one point took up a station behind the Russian front line. He thought it would be a good observation point, and indeed it was; the Russians were so amazed to see him there that they concluded the rest of his army must be near and that it would be a waste of time to try to capture him. Cavalry was scarcely used at all, and the task of turning a defeat into a rout which could well have been done was prevented by direct order; in consequence the Russians were able to save much for the strengthening of the defences of Sebastopol. The French army, although full of dash and courage, was so mishandled that it did little fighting, although what it did do was extremely effective. The honours of the battle really went to the British infantry who advanced with the utmost steadiness, reached and captured the Great Battery, and then received an order from an unknown source to retire. The bugler who had been given the order blew the appropriate call, and the Battery which had been won at great cost in lives was promptly abandoned. It was equally promptly occupied by the Russian infantry.

There was nothing else to be done except fight the battle over again. Although the guns from the Great Battery were now silenced those from the eastern battery were firing to full capacity. Furthermore the fire from some eight Russian infantry battalions swept the glacis in front of the Great Battery. And up those blood-soaked slopes there marched the steady lines of the British infantry, stopping occasionally to check their dressing and to make sure that formation was perfect, and then moving on again in perfect and unhurried order.

Once more the Great Battery was captured. The Russians lost just under 6,000, the British 2,000, and the French 500. The victorious army had the dubious pleasure of holding the waterless heights on a battlefield which there were no facilities to clear. The Russians were able to move back to Sebastopol shaken but scarcely damaged. Even so, victory was still within grasp. Menschikoff had so little faith in the ability of Sebastopol to resist capture that he had retired from it with his army, leaving a skeleton garrison of sailors and militia. The former were from the ships which Menschikoff had blown up and sunk in the entrance to the harbour, having first removed their guns to the town defences. The Allies, completely unaware that the town was theirs for the taking, pondered on what to do, whether to attack on the north where the defences were incomplete but where there was no harbour for a base, or

The Battle of the Alma. Highlanders and the Guards storm the Russian battery

whether to move around to the south to the Khersonese where Balaclava Cove could be used by shipping. Eventually they decided on the latter plan, and in fact crossed the rear of Menschikoff's army as it too was moving to the open country; both sides were so surprised that only minor clashes occurred. An enormous advantage had now been presented to the Russians; they were able to re-enter the citadel from the north side and they had a field army well placed to harass the British lines.

But the greatest advantage the Russians possessed at this juncture was a young engineer of genius called Todleben. Thirty-six years old and only a junior Field Officer he was nevertheless a person of genius and authority. Taking full advantage of the interlude in fighting he built a screen of earthworks around the town. On the north side was a construction known as the Star fort (a strong permanent fortification containing 47 guns) and within ten days this was surrounded with an impressive screen of outworks and trenches. On the south-west work was proceeding on the Malakoff and the Redan, of which more was to be heard later. Todleben was a genius of the quality of Vauban, and until 20 June 1855 directed the defence in person. His great attribute was his flexibility of outlook, and unlike many he believed that defensive works should serve the strategy of the army and not vice versa. The siege was, of course, purely nominal for the Allies were only on the landward side while the Russians were able to pour in reinforcements from across the estuary. To add to their troubles the British camp was over six miles from its base, which could easily be harassed by the Russians. There was no transport and stores had to be carried over indifferent roads. The Khersonese was dry and waterless in summer and terribly cold in winter.

At this point the Russians decided it was time for them to take the initiative, which meant destroying the main Allied supply base at Balaclava. It was guarded by two understrength cavalry brigades of some 750 each, a Highland regiment, and 3,000 Turks. A Russian force of four times that number bore down on them, cleared the Turks from the outer redoubts and seemed unstoppable. At this point there occurred the famous stand of the 93rd Highlanders commanded by Colin Campbell. This was the 'thin red line' (consisting of a single battalion drawn up two deep), and it was the only defence between the Russian cavalry and Balaclava harbour. (In a brief account such as this it is not possible to mention all the examples of superb courage produced by individuals or by units and it may seem invidious to mention only a few; where they are mentioned it is because the unit and event is already well known. However it should be remembered that equal though less well-known deeds were performed on the hills behind the Alma, and before the defences

155

of Sebastopol.) As the Russians drew back General Scarlett launched the Heavy Brigade on to Russian cavalry who outnumbered them by three to one. This action though less celebrated than its successor, was almost as gallant, and considerably more useful for it turned the check into a defeat.

Unfortunately, as the Russians fell back, Raglan sent a message which was intended to prevent them from carrying off the Turkish guns from the redoubts they had overrun that morning. Such an action might be interpreted as a Russian victory. The message, taken down by General Airey, contained the words 'Lord Raglan wishes the cavalry to advance rapidly to the front, follow the enemy and try to prevent the enemy carrying away the guns.' When the message reached the Light Brigade in the valley below, the guns in question were assumed to be a battery of Russian guns at the end of the North valley where the Russians were firmly established. The sides of the valley and the surrounding heights were covered with Russian guns and troops. It was a perfect death-trap a mile and a quarter long and into it rode 700 men. They reached their objective, but could not of course hold it without support; they thereupon turned round and rode back again. Of the original 700 only 195 returned. The entire action had taken twenty minutes. Raglan was furious at the way his orders had been misinterpreted, but Lord Cardigan who had led the charge was convinced he had understood his orders and obeyed them correctly. The outcome of all these events was that the Russians had captured some redoubts and some guns and felt satisfied with the results, while the Allies had saved Balaclava and were fortunate to have done so. Less satisfactory for the Allies, the Russians were still in a position to continue harassing the communications between the Allied camp and Balaclava (25 October 1854).

Menschikoff thereupon decided to try a further attack and decided that the best point was the siege lines to the right of the English position. The attack was planned as a dawn operation and approached the English lines in two columns of approximately 20,000 men each. The Russians set out in darkness and aided by a dense fog and drizzle were into the British position almost before either side realised the fact. Taken by surprise the British soldiers rushed out of their tents and tackled the Russians without plan or orders. Because of the absence of higher control the Battle of Inkerman became known as the 'soldiers' battle'. It lasted six hours and for the loss of just over 2,000 men the British army, assisted in the final stages by some French reinforcements, accoun-

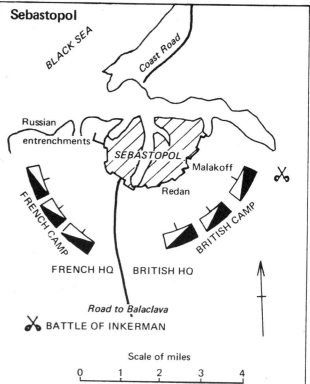

Balaclava. The charge of the Light Brigade. Lord Cardigan is leading the charge with the 17th Lancers and 13th Light Dragoons immediately behind him. These two regiments have broken into a gallop. Echelonned back behind them are the 11th Hussars, then the 4th Light Dragoons, and finally the 8th Hussars. In the far distance on the right the Heavy Brigade can be seen moving forward to help extricate their comrades. On the far left of the picture the Russian cavalry are calmly awaiting the British charge

ted for some 10,000 Russians. This was 5 November 1854 and once again, if followed up, could have decided the campaign then and there. But once again the opportunity was lost.

The folly and incompetence of the planning staff was now clearly shown, but it was not of course the guilty who suffered. No one at home had visualized anything but a brief campaign, and no thought had been given to any longer term arrangements. No one apparently had been aware that the Crimea was hot and arid in summer and had exceptionally severe winters. In consequence there were soon more men sick than were fit for duty, and the nearest hospital was at Scutari, 300 miles away. All the horses and mules died, and the wretched troops had to hump all their supplies the eight miles between Balaclava and their position. With no shelter except light tents, with scanty food, and with hopelessly inadequate medical services conditions were soon appalling. A further crushing blow was the loss in a freak storm of the ships bringing supplies of warm clothing. The French were in no better condition but their plight was less obvious because their numbers were kept up by steady reinforcement.

Fortunately for the Army there was one important new element on the scene, the presence of war correspondents. As a result, the scene in the Crimea was fully reported in a number of newspapers, and the outcry at home produced results. The stories of incompetence which now came to light were almost unbelievable. As a result the Prime Minister, Lord Aberdeen, and the Minister for War, the Duke of Newcastle, both resigned their offices. They could however hardly be blamed for not being able to put right forty years of neglect within the space of a few months.

K

Camp and soldiers of the 4th Light Dragoons. The officer
and soldiers are outside an improvised hut. At this period it
was normal to permit about six wives per squadron or
company to accompany the troops on a campaign. They were
usefully employed as laundresses, cooks and nurses.
Photographed by Roger Fenton

But the removal of Aberdeen made way for the
forceful Palmerston who all along had been trying
to have the war prosecuted effectively. Soon the
situation was greatly changed. Men and materials
were soon moving towards the front in huge quantities; at long last a railway replaced the inefficient
roads between Balaclava and the front; and the
hospital service was transformed by the drive and
energy of Florence Nightingale. The numbers of
men at the front had increased steadily, the British
being 40,000, the French 100,000, and the Italians,
who were anxious to cultivate French friendship,
had now come in with 40,000.

It should be remembered that the Russians were
in little better condition than the Allies. For one
thing Sebastopol was hundreds of miles from
Moscow, and was not linked by a railway, but only
by indifferent roads. In point of time the Allies were
nearer to the Crimea than the Russians were. However the Russians did not have to compete with being
completely ignorant of the surrounding countryside,
which the Allies did. Even so it was said that one

quarter of the Russian troops despatched to the
Crimea failed to arrive, which is hardly surprising
considering that many of them had to march through
the Steppes during the Russian winter. Czar
Nicholas died on 2 March 1855, sent into decline it
was said by the failure of his army. His successor
Alexander II was not so much an enthusiast for the
war as too proud to sue for peace. The only bright
spot on the Russian horizon was the situation at
Sebastopol where Todleben had worked so
effectively that the place seemed almost impregnable. This was certainly how it must have seemed to
the Allies who launched a tremendous assault on
18 June 1855 but only succeeded in sustaining crippling losses.

From then on it was a gun duel. The British had
heavy Lancaster guns which were far superior to
anything the Russians possessed. The Russians
fought with great courage and constantly replaced
their battered units; they were said to have lost
100,000 men in the war, most of them at Sebastopol.

But the tide, none the less, was turning in the
Allies' favour. Lord Raglan, although much liked
and respected, was much too old for his post. When
therefore he died in July 1855 and was replaced by
General Simpson, the British Army was more in
touch with current events. In the French Army
Canrobert, an extremely cautious general, was replaced by Marshal Pélissier, who, if anything, went
to the other extreme. With this new blood at the top
a general assault was ordered on 8 September.

In this attack the French were assigned to the
Malakoff and the English to the Redan, these being
the two forts which held the key to the citadel. The
British force reached the Redan, and even got inside
it but had not the manpower to hold their gains.
Meanwhile the French stormed the Malakoff with
20,000 men, and captured it. The loss of this important key point convinced the Russians that they had
lost Sebastopol so they set fire to the town and
abandoned it.

At this point it might have seemed that the war
was over, but in fact it was six months before the
Treaty of Paris was signed in March 1856. Most of
this time was spent by the Allies in quarrelling between themselves, the French wishing to treat the
Russians mildly and make friends of them, the
English wishing to remove the Russian threat from
their lifeline to India. In the event the situation soon
reverted to what it had been before. The Russians
soon recovered from the disabling effects of the war
and broke all their agreements, the Turks continued
to sink into decline, and Anglo-French relations were

The Siege of Sebastopol. In the foreground are an allied battery and parallels, or trenches. On the high ground in the background is the Malakoff redoubt. Photographed by James Robertson

no better or worse than they had ever been.

But the war had far-reaching effects on the British Army. The Civil Board which had controlled Artillery, Engineers and Ordnance now became the War Office. Clothing would be supplied by an Army factory and no longer by Regimental Colonels. A small arms factory was set up at Enfield. A Staff College was built at Camberley so that officers could receive further professional training in mid-career. Training camps were established at Aldershot, the Curragh, and Colchester. A School of Musketry was established at Hythe, and a School of Gunnery at Sheerness. Above all, certain lessons had been learnt and did not appear to be forgotten. The first was that it was necessary to have a Commander-in-Chief, the second that plans must have flexibility, the third that an Army must know something about the terrain it was expected to fight over, and fourthly there must be adequate medical services if a fighting force was to be maintained in the field.

It was in the medical services that perhaps the most far-reaching changes were made. At the outbreak of the war there was a small Army Medical Department under a Director-General with 163 officer surgeons and this was expected to cater for the needs of troops spread all over the world. There

was nothing at all for transport of the wounded apart from a few stretchers. The Hospital Conveyance Corps consisted of such ancient and feeble members that few could ever be used in battle areas: in consequence the surgeons and bandsmen usually carried the men to safety.

Battle casualties were, however, the least of their troubles. Names like cholera, typhus and dysentery are too unfamiliar nowadays to strike the chill they once caused but those who know the devastating killing power of these diseases will wonder how anyone at all survived in the Crimea once they had obtained a grip.

Those whose wounds or ailments caused them to be evacuated to Scutari (opposite Constantinople) had a hazardous journey in overcrowded ships on which many of the sick and wounded died. Once in the so-called hospital they were so overcrowded that they lay in lines on the floors along the passages and in the wards. So great was the overcrowding that limbs were amputated in the wards watched by a dispassionate audience. All medical supplies were desperately scarce while at home clerks and inspectors quarrelled about the amounts which should be issued. Nursing, such as it was, came from those lucky enough to be able to move around among their

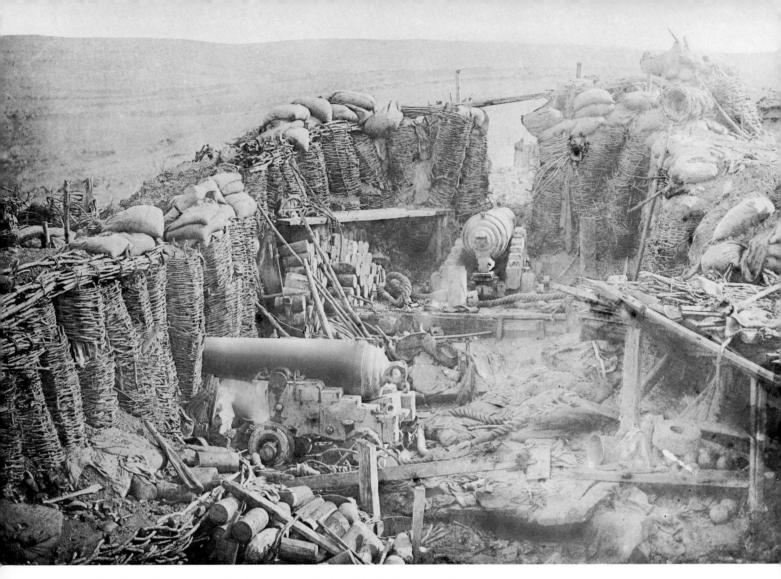

The Siege of Sebastopol. The Redan, the objective of the British attack. It is interesting to see how the Russians have used gabions to build up its parapet. Photographed by James Robertson

less fortunate comrades. In consequence it was not surprising that of the 28,000 men who had landed in the Crimea in 1854, 10,000 were dead of disease six months later.

Conditions in the Crimea were mainly brought home by W. H. Russell, *The Times* correspondent. The indignation in his articles spread to the public and ultimately to Parliament. Reforms were soon under way. Florence Nightingale, who is sometimes thought of as a sweet gentle nurse wandering among the sick with a lamp, carried in fact a different sort of torch. Well connected and of iron determination, she used all her influence in high places to achieve vitally needed reforms. Fortunately she was a friend of Lord Herbert of Lea, the Secretary for War, and later of Queen Victoria herself, but even then her task was a long and arduous one. She never spared herself. In the winter of 1854 she had worked twenty hours a day on many days, often on her feet the whole

time, and always inspected the wards personally every night. In 1857 she was given the authority to enquire into the health of the Army which meant a thorough investigation of such matters as food, housing and clothing. Her findings, published in 1858, became a manual for reform. In 1860 she opened the Nightingale Training School for Nurses at St Thomas's Hospital, and in the same year the Army Medical School was transferred from Fort Pitt to Netley. But years were to elapse before these reforms were fully effective.

Appalling though the Crimea story is it is at the same time heartening. In spite of the incompetence and blunders the war was a triumph of British fortitude and endurance. Heroism and self-sacrifice were widespread, not only by the British but also by their Allies and opponents. Grim though it all was, the world learned much about human courage and dignity from this campaign.

Opposite: Crimean heroes of the 42nd Highlanders. Gardner, Mackenzie, and Glen. Colour sergeant William Gardner won the Victoria Cross, subsequently, in the Indian Mutiny when on 5 May 1858 he bayonnetted two of the enemy who were attacking his CO, Lt-Col. Cameron. Photographed by J. Cundell and R. Howlett

CHAPTER 17

The Indian Mutiny 1857–58

JAMES P. LAWFORD

CHRONOLOGICAL TABLE

1856–57	War with Persia. Outram defeats the Persians at Kush-ab
1857 10 May	The Indian troops at Meerut mutiny
7–26 June	Siege of Cawnpore (Kanpur)
8 June	Battle of Badli ki Serai, British troops start siege of Delhi
30 June	Lucknow besieged (Naklao)
14–20 September	Delhi stormed
25 September	Havelock relieves Lucknow
26 September	Second siege of Lucknow begins
17 November	Colin Campbell relieves Lucknow and evacuates it
1858 11–19 March	Colin Campbell recaptures Lucknow
3 April	Sir Hugh Rose storms Jhansi
22 May	Sir Hugh Rose defeats Tantia Topi at Kalpi

In 1857 with the Crimean War scarcely ended and the strength of Her Majesty's troops in India at its lowest for many years, the Bengal Army, one hundred and fifty thousand strong, mutinied.

The causes of this mutiny, if not the greatest certainly the bloodiest of recorded history, were plainly far from trivial. For some time one or two far-sighted officers had prophesied the possibility of a sepoy revolt only to have their views received with derision. The causes were deep-rooted, various, and to the average European at this time, completely hidden.

The original sepoy companies had been commanded by Indian officers called subedars, who in many cases had raised them. British officers commanded a group of such companies to meet the requirements of a particular situation. As the Bengal army expanded permanent regiments were formed and the British officers took over command of individual companies, but the Indian officer, with the rank of subedar or jemadar, remained as a link between the British officer and the Indian soldier, the sepoy. In the early days of the Company, the British officers spent their whole lives in India, often took Indian wives or mistresses, frequently relatives of their sepoys, and understood not only the language of the sepoy but how he felt and thought. At the same time something was always happening, there was some little war to fight, promotion to be sought, a field allowance to be gained.

With the coming of the steamship much was changed. European women and missionaries started to arrive in substantial numbers, home leave became a possibility. The British officer still learnt his Urdu, the universal language of the Army, but very often failed to learn the invariably different mother tongue of the men of his regiment. The vast expansion of the Bengal Army had led to a lowering in the general standard of officers, and the period of peace that followed the Sikh wars was spent by many wining, dining, and hunting, rather than with their men.

Yet no major mutiny was conceivable without the connivance of the Indian officers, the sirdars, as they were known. Why did these sane, mature, hard-headed men who had so much to lose revolt?

No certain answer can be given. Subedar Sita Ram called it a collective madness. Undoubtedly the financiers of the Company who looked on their army as an unfortunate and possibly largely unnecessary expense, did much damage by withholding allowances the troops had every right to

Opposite: The Siege of Delhi. The siege train approaching that city. From a contemporary sketch by G. F. Atkinson

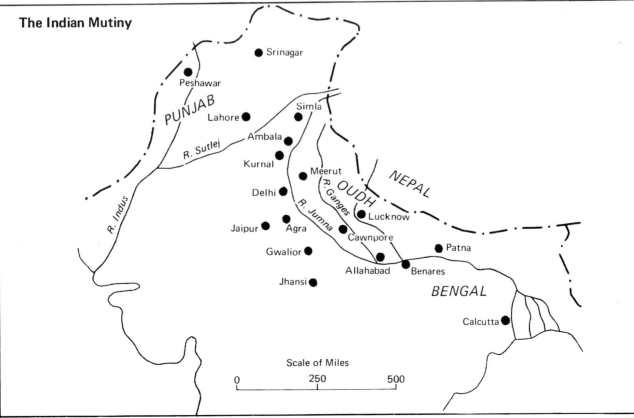

The Indian Mutiny

Srinagar

Peshawar

PUNJAB

Lahore

Simla

R. Sutlej

Ambala

R. Indus

Kurnal

Meerut

NEPAL

R. Ganges

OUDH

Delhi

R. Jumna

Lucknow

Jaipur

Agra

Cawnpore

Patna

Gwalior

Allahabad

Benares

Jhansi

BENGAL

Calcutta

Scale of Miles

0   250   500

expect – but financiers do that the world over.

Something more there must have been. No evidence of an actual conspiracy has ever been produced, and the actions of the mutinous regiments seem to have been very little planned, but regiments revolted in sympathy with each other and some general understanding must surely have existed. One can imagine the sirdars on leave, and many came from the province of Oudh, smoking a communal hookah in the cool of the evening discussing their grievances, and one might say:

'Brothers, the *John Company* (East India Company) treats us like dirt, they cheat us of our money, but who made the *John Company*? Who won the battles? The English regiments are few, if we had but the courage we could overwhelm them, and then brothers, then think of the pickings!'

And his listeners might nod approvingly but without committing themselves, or perhaps one might say, 'but what of the *Iqbal* what of the luck of the Company, who can stand against it?'. Then the British disasters in Afghanistan and rumours of catastrophes in the Crimea might be recalled.

Whatever the cause at the beginning of 1857 the Bengal Army was deeply discontented, but the British officers were blissfully unaware of the feelings of their men. They were not to remain much longer in ignorance. Early in that year the Enfield rifle was introduced. The cartridge had to be rammed down and was greased to make ramming easier. Owing to an incredible error the grease was made from a mixture of pig and cow fat. Since the cartridge had to be bitten, any sepoy using it tasted pig, if a Muslim, and cow, if a Hindu, the animals forbidden to them by their religion.

When this was discovered there was an immediate outcry. It was rumoured that the British intended to make the sepoys outcaste, so that they would all be forced to become Christians. Had there been trust or a proper understanding between the British officers and their men, the matter would have been solved without trouble. As it was, although orders were at once given to change the grease and discontinue the biting of the cartridge, they were too late.

Near Calcutta in March the 19th Native Infantry (N.I.) mutinied and were disbanded. Then in April a sepoy named Mangal Pandy of the 34th N.I. ran amok and shot his adjutant while the Quarter-Guard stood idly by. General Hearsey, commanding in Calcutta, fearlessly rode at the sepoy whereat he ran off and shot himself. The Indian officer and his guard were courtmartialled and the regiment disbanded. But on 10 May, in the intense heat of the Indian hot weather, tragedy came to Meerut. Here there were the 3rd Light Cavalry and two Native Infantry battalions, HM 60th Rifles and the Carabiniers, a British cavalry regiment. The proportion of British to Indian troops was higher than almost anywhere else in India.

The almost unbelievable mixture of harshness and weakness displayed by the British commanders in Meerut precipitated the terrible events of the mutiny, events that, given time, and a more understanding high command, might perhaps never have happened. The following letter written by nineteen-year-old Lt McNabb, of the 3rd Light Cavalry on the fateful Sunday, 10 May describes clearly the feelings and fears that led up to that tragic day.

Meerut May 10, 1857.

My dear Mother,

... We have had a mutiny in this regiment, like several others, on the cartridge question. Of course you have heard in England that the 19th N.I. had refused to bite the greased cartridge because they said they had pigs' fat on them. The 19th are disbanded. Some other regiments made a fuss about it, so an order was issued that the men were to tear the top of the cartridge off with their fingers, instead of their teeth. Our Colonel, Smyth, most injudiciously ordered a parade of the skirmishers of the regiment (85 picked shots) to show them the new way of tearing the cartridge. I say injudiciously, because there was no necessity to have the parade at all or to make any sort of fuss now. No other Colonel of Cavalry thought of doing such a thing, as they knew that at this unsettled time their men would refuse to be the first to fire their cartridges, but that by not asking them they would not give their men the chance of refusing, so that next parade season when the row had blown over, they would begin to fire as a matter of course and think nothing of it.

The night before, Captain Craigie, who knows everything that is going on in the regiment, wrote to the adjutant to ask the Colonel to put the parade off, as he had got information that the men would refuse to fire. The men themselves humbly petitioned the Colonel to put the parade off till this disturbance had gone over, in fact pointing out to him what he ought to have seen for himself. He was half inclined to indulge them and sent for the adjutant and asked him what he advised ...

The adjutant who is always severe to the men said it would look like being afraid of them, and that he had better abide by what he had ordered. He might have countermanded the parade without seeming afraid of the men, and then, if they took advantage of it, have pulled them up sharp. But the great mistake was ordering the parade at all.

... (The skirmishers refused to fire the new cartridges) ... They did not want to be the first regiment who had fired. But the real cause is that they hate Smyth, and if almost any other officer had gone down they would have fired them off, for Cragie told me that from what he knows of the men in his own troop and in the regiment he would have guaranteed that they fired them five minutes after he had spoken to them.

... The men of course had *no* real excuse for not doing what they were ordered, and they knew what these cartridges were made of, as they had fired them off privately in riding school since the 19th N.I. were disbanded, and they would have continued to do so if they had been left alone, instead of paraded and addressed and all that humbug.

... A day or two afterwards these eighty-five mutineers ... were tried by Court-martial and sentenced to ten years on the roads in chains! They could not have hit on a more severe punishment as it is much worse to them than death.

... The sentence was carried out yesterday morning. We were paraded at 4 (a.m.) on foot and marched up the grand parade ground where all the troops in the station were paraded. It is lucky that this happened in Meerut where there are so many European troops for if it had been in a smaller station I would not have given much for the officers' lives.

... When the irons were put on them, they were marched past the whole parade, and when they passed us, of course, they began to cry and curse the Colonel. It was very sad to see these fine men in such a condition. One handsome young man said 'I was a good sepoy and would have gone anywhere for the service, but I could not forsake my religion'.

It was the last letter Lt McNabb ever wrote. That Sunday evening all the native regiments rose and he was shot down while galloping to his regiment's lines. Many other British officers were murdered by their own men. The 3rd Light Cavalry rode to the gaol, freed their comrades and released all the criminals. The scum of Meerut then joined in, massacring and looting the European bungalows nearest the city. But by the time the 60th and the Carabiniers were under arms and had marched to the Native Infantry lines they were dark and deserted, except for Captain Craigie. He had turned out with his troop perfectly in hand and properly dressed and accoutred. He and his men saved the lives of many European and Eurasian wives and families. Inexcusably, that night and the next day the British troops in Meerut did nothing but safeguard the lives and property of the European population.

Meanwhile a terrible morning had dawned at Delhi. In the palace of that city, quite bereft of power, the heir of the Moguls, the eighty-two year old Bahadur Shah, still resided with the title of king. There were no European troops. The garrison consisted of a native infantry brigade with a light field battery. In Delhi itself was one of the largest arsenals in India.

At about 8.00 a.m. on 11 May over the bridge of boats and on to the palace clattered some troopers of the 3rd Light Cavalry. There they called for the king and proclaimed him their sovereign. Others as they arrived rode round the city sabring any Europeans they could see. The dregs of the city joined in, while the native infantry guards stood by

General Wheeler's encampment at Cawnpore. It can be seen that the walls were far from shot-proof. Photographed by Felice Beato shortly after its recapture

refusing to act. Troops sent in to restore order mutinied and joined the mob. Many Europeans of both sexes were murdered, and the rest escaped to the cantonment situated on a ridge outside the city.

At the arsenal occurred one of the epic actions of the Mutiny. Lt Willoughby had charge of it. He had with him Lieutenants Forest and Raynor, conductors Buckley, Shaw, Scully and Crow and sergeants Edwards and Stewart, all of the Commissariat Ordnance Corps.

When Willoughby learnt of the tumult in the city, he realised an attack on the arsenal was certain. He at once barricaded the gates and placed guns loaded with grape at salient points. Knowing that an attack could have but one end and resolved at all costs to prevent the magazine falling into the hands of mutineers, he laid a trail of gunpowder into the centre of the magazine. He had not long to wait. A disorderly crowd of sepoys surged up to the entrance shouting to be admitted in the name of Bahadur Shah, Emperor.

They received their answer in grape shot. For some three hours Willoughby and his gallant few maintained their unequal battle. Then at about 4.00 p.m. when the gates had been forced and capture was imminent, Willoughby gave the order to fire the magazine. With a tremendous roar it blew up. Those waiting anxiously on the ridge heard the heavy boom of the explosion and saw a black pall of smoke mount over the city. Many of the attackers perished, but by a miracle, Willoughby with four companions survived. Blackened and filthy they escaped their appalled assailants and found their way to the ridge. There, as night came down, the Commander of the Delhi brigade ordered the Europeans anxiously sheltering on the ridge, and the handful of still loyal sepoys to escape as best they could. Delhi had fallen.

Now it was apparent that a crisis of the greatest magnitude threatened British rule in India. The Governor General, Lord Canning, was in Calcutta, his Commander-in-Chief, General Anson, had gone to Simla, in the distant Himalayan foothills, a separation that made the proper framing of plans well-nigh impossible. It was however obvious that many would be watching the course of events pondering the outcome, anxious to join the successful. The speedy recovery of Delhi was vital to the British cause.

General Anson strove to assemble a British force at Amballa, but a long period of peace had played havoc with the supply services. On the 27 May the weary worried old gentleman died. Command of the Field force was taken over by General Sir Henry

A panorama of Delhi. On the right British troops can be seen on the Ridge. The bridge of
boats which came into Delhi by the Emperor's palace has been broken, and the British breaching
batteries are in action against the Water Bastion and the curtain wall next to it

Barnard, described as a 'nice considerate little man'. It was not until 7 June that the British Army came within sight of Delhi, drove in a superior force of mutineers at the battle of Badli-ki-serai, and encamped on the low ridge near the city, ever after known as 'The Ridge'. But the 'army' was little more than three thousand strong, it had no proper siege train and faced a strongly fortified city manned by a superior force. The young officers wanted an immediate storm but the generals, perhaps wisely, demurred. The little force settled down on the Ridge to become besieged as much as besiegers.

The Indian Army at that time was divided into three, the Bengal army to which more than half of all the Indian regiments belonged, the Bombay army and the Madras army. Throughout the mutiny the Madras army stationed in southern India remained loyal. The Bombay army experienced some mutinies but kept them under control from its own resources.

But in early June the flame of mutiny flared through the Bengal army stationed across the length of India from Calcutta to Peshawar. The delay in dealing with the mutineers at Delhi had proved fatal.

In the newly annexed province of the Punjab the great John Lawrence had a number of European regiments at his disposal, and calculated he could rely on his newly raised irregular Punjabi Corps. Acting with speed and decision he set about disarming his Bengal Army units. At the same time he formed a movable column under the legendary John Nicholson to hunt down any mutineers that escaped. Although the Bengal army in the Punjab numbered over thirty thousand, Lawrence, despite some dangerous crises, never lost control.

But in Oudh to the south-east, the situation was very different. Between Lucknow and Calcutta there were only two European regiments. Oudh itself had been newly annexed by Dalhousie. The new administrators, by endeavouring to ameliorate the lot of the peasants and by a heavy-handed approach, had alienated many of the great landlords. The far-seeing Henry Lawrence had recently been appointed governor, but the peril in Oudh was very great.

Canning recognised the danger but had virtually no resources available. He sent Colonel Neill with his regiment, the 1st Madras Fusiliers, 'Neill's blue caps', up the Ganges. Neill, one of the titans of the mutiny, displayed a ruthless energy. At Benares he disarmed the 37th N.I., then secured Patna. From

The mutineers make an assault on the Ridge, and are repulsed here with three hundred men he pressed on to the crucial city of Allahabad. Now cholera broke out among his men. Nevertheless with the help of the loyal Ferozepore Sikh battalion he reimposed British rule on the city. Sick himself, an uncertain city in his hands, his men suffering from cholera and sunstroke, Neill could not advance to Cawnpore.

At Cawnpore Sir Hugh Wheeler had some four hundred women and children, an assortment of European military details and volunteers, numbering about two hundred and forty men, and the Cawnpore Native Infantry Brigade. On 5 and 6 June the Cawnpore brigade quietly mutinied and marched away, ostensibly to Delhi.

Sir Hugh Wheeler withdrew the Europeans into a hastily extemporised entrenchment he had had constructed. Then on 7 June the mutineers, now under Nana Sahib, the adopted son of the last of the Peshwas, reappeared and besieged the encampment.

Despite entrenchments that were barely bullet-proof, the little European garrison put up a superb defence, for 18 days beating back all attacks. Then Nana Sahib, under a flag of truce, offered them boats and a safe conduct to Allahabad. The offer was accepted, and on 27 June the garrison and the women and children embarked. As they started to pull down the river, the mutineers fired on them from the river bank. The boatmen leapt overboard and, amid a scene of wild confusion, the boats grounded. Five men escaped, but the remainder were either shot down in the boats or captured and executed. The women and children were confined for two weeks then, quite literally, butchered in cold blood. The sepoys would have nothing to do with this final atrocity, and Nana Sahib had to call in butchers from the Cawnpore bazar. The news of the massacre roused the British troops to fury, and for the rest of the war it banefully affected their attitude towards the mutineers.

At Lucknow Henry Lawrence knew that, if Cawnpore were attacked, his turn must come. By mid-June most of Oudh was in revolt, and many of the Europeans in outlying stations had been murdered. Lawrence steadily fortified his Residency area and collected provisions. Bands of mutineers began to rove in the neighbourhood and on 29 June Lawrence fatally allowed himself to be persuaded into attacking a large body near Chinhat.

A badly planned, badly executed British attack resulted in a near disaster. A victory might have saved Oudh, the defeat turned every waverer into an enemy. As the British forces sought refuge in the Residency, the victorious mutineers swept down to

Above: General Havelock. He died of dysentery a week after General Colin Campbell relieved Lucknow. From an engraving by C. Holl. *Below:* The Residency at Lucknow after the siege; some troops from Havelock's force encamped outside. From a sketch made by an officer with the relieving force

invest it. On 30 June the siege of the Residency at Lucknow, one of the most famous sieges in the annals of British military history, had begun.

At first the mutineers showed little desire to come to close quarters. On 1 July they began shelling, and the noble Henry Lawrence was one of the first to be killed. Brigadier Inglis took command. The fortifications at the Residency were no more than low earthworks linking together a number of far from round shot-proof buildings. Its garrison consisted of HM 32nd, a company of the 84th Foot and a number of volunteers totalling in all about nine hundred Europeans and about seven hundred loyal sepoys of whom 250 came from the 13th NI. There were also about five hundred women and children. To the siege flocked most of the mutineers in Oudh and many discontented land-owners with their retainers. The besiegers never numbered fewer than six thousand and at times their numbers were probably swollen by ten thousand more.

Brigadier-General John Nicholson

They kept up a constant artillery and musketry fire on the Residency from houses only a stone's throw away. Through the steaming rains of July and August the struggle continued. Smallpox and cholera broke out among the garrison, but their inflexible resolve never faltered. Enemy mines were driven in by counter mines, nearby houses were carried by sortie and then blown up. The besiegers made four abortive attempts at a storm; in beating back the last the 13th NI particularly distinguished themselves. Nevertheless from wounds and sickness the strength of the garrison steadily declined. Brigadier Inglis never lost his air of cheerful confidence, but in September matters were becoming serious. Then on the 25th of that month a tremendous noise of firing burst out in the city. High above it could be heard the skirling of the pipes. At 6 o'clock that evening amid the heartfelt cheers of the garrison Havelock brought his weary men to the Residency.

But to turn back to Neill and his handful of Madras Fusiliers desperately striving to succour Cawnpore. Although mutinies and disturbances were widespread all over northern India, Canning recognised that the twin centres of the mutiny were at Delhi and Cawnpore-Lucknow. To Allahabad he sent forward Brigadier-General Havelock, a small greying man, but a skilful tactician and a bold leader, and all the troops he could spare. By 7 July Havelock had the Madras Fusiliers and elements of HM 64th and 84th Foot, the 78th Highlanders and the Ferozepore battalion of Sikhs amounting in all to about a thousand men.

With these Havelock drove on to Cawnpore, routed Nana Sahib outside the city, and uncovered the dreadful facts of the siege and massacre. Reinforcements came in, and now, some one thousand five hundred strong, Havelock marched on Lucknow. At Unao he beat from the field successively two armies of mutineers numbering altogether about nine thousand. But his small force had dwindled to 850 effectives and reluctantly he fell back on Cawnpore.

In mid-September river steamers brought up the 5th Fusiliers and 90th Light Infantry, and, equally important, three batteries of guns. Once again, this time with three thousand men, Havelock took the road to Lucknow, and on the 25th after a day-long battle in the city fought through to the Residency near which the brave Neill was shot dead. Here Outram, his senior, took over command. Large numbers of mutineers yet remained and Outram and his men were besieged in turn, but the Residency and the women and children within it were no longer in any real danger.

Meanwhile, outside Delhi, the small besieging army, glumly awaiting a proper siege train and more men, watched brigade after brigade of mutineers march into the city with colours, British colours, flying and drums beating. After each accession of strength the mutineers sallied out to drive their sullen besiegers off the ridge, and each time were chased back within the ramparts of the city.

The summer wore on. On 5 July General Barnard died of cholera; his successor General Reed lasted but a fortnight before his health broke down. Brigadier Wilson, a methodical conscientious man, took command.

Then in August John Lawrence, confident he had pacified the Punjab, sent troops and his dynamic subordinate, Nicholson, to the Ridge. A cold wind from the north-west now blew to dissipate the inertia and stagnation.

On 2 September a large siege train of heavy guns rolled in. Still Wilson hesitated, but Nicholson would brook no delay. Wilson acquiesced and the engineers drew up plans for a storm.

The walled city of Delhi resembled a capital 'D'. The stem of the 'D' ran north and south along the banks of the Jumna, and the curved side projected westwards.

At the northern end the water bastion secured the junction of the curved ramparts and the river. About four hundred yards west of this bastion was the Kashmir gate and nine hundred yards further west the Mori gate and bastion. Here the walls curved away southwards and about three hundred yards further on were pierced by the Kabul gate. From this gate the walls ran south for about one and a half miles before curving back to the river.

The assault was planned to go in at the water bastion, the curtain to the west and the Kashmir gate, with a subsidiary thrust at the Kabul gate.

At 8.00 a.m. on 11 September the heavy breaching batteries began to roar, bringing great slabs of masonry crashing down from the water bastion and the wall linking it with the Kashmir gate. By the 13th practicable breaches had appeared.

Five columns were detailed for the storm. One against the water bastion, one to carry the breach to the west of it, and the third to rush the Kashmir gate after it had been blown in. The fourth column was to assault the Kabul gate and come in on the rear of the defenders facing the other three columns. The fifth was held as a reserve.

The regiments that took part in the storm were HM 60th Rifles, 8th, 52nd and 61st Foot and the Company's 1st and 2nd Bengal Fusiliers, 1st, 2nd and 4th Punjab Infantry, 4th Sikhs, Sirmoor Rifles, Baluch and Kumaon battalions and the Guides Infantry. They numbered about four thousand seven hundred men, while the latest figures on the Ridge for the mutineers showed them some seventeen thousand strong.

At about 9 o'clock on the morning of the 14 September Nicholson gave the word and the columns charged home. The mutineers let loose a hail of fire, but as the attackers closed in their nerve failed and they bolted. By the Kashmir gate a small party of engineers won undying fame.

Lieutenants Home and Salkeld, with eight British and Indian sappers carrying explosives, rushed to the gate and, before the amazed defenders knew what was happening, piled their load against it. Then the mutineers, at point blank range, blazed away. Two of the small group were immediately hit. Lt Salkeld tried to light the fuze but was struck down. Corporal Burgess seized the slow match from his nerveless fingers and applied it. He fell mortally wounded as the charge blew up and the great gates caved in. A bugler with the party now sounded the 'Advance'. The waiting column did not hear his thin notes, but, seeing clearly enough what had happened, the men sprang forward to find that the survivors among the mutineers had fled.

But the fourth column met with disaster at the suburb of Kishenganj outside the ramparts and never reached the Kabul gate. Although the British were within the city, lacking the flank support expected from the Kabul gate, the attackers were halted by bitter street fighting. By the end of the day a thousand men had fallen in the storm and but a quarter of the city was captured. Nicholson had been mortally wounded. General Wilson contemplated a withdrawal. The dying Nicholson threatened personally to shoot him if he gave any such order, and his subordinates backed him up. The battle continued. The mutineers, however, were utterly disheartened by their failure to prevent a British entry. Large bands of them began to drift away from the city. Despite their heavy losses the British troops were eager for battle and confident of victory. Systematically the remainder of the city was reduced. On 20 September the deserted palace was captured and resistance in the city ceased. Hodson, the beau sabreur of the Ridge, found the last of the Moguls hiding in Humayum's tomb three miles outside the city, and brought him back captive.

The war was to continue for another year and more, but the crisis was over. In Calcutta Sir Colin Campbell, the new commander-in-chief, was forming a strong balanced army as British reinforcements at last began to pour in. From Nepal a Gurkha army marched to help.

On 16 November Campbell fought his way through to Lucknow and brought off the women and children, but it was not until the spring of 1858 that he managed to subjugate Oudh. Thereafter, over the Lucknow Residency the Union Jack, the flag the defenders never struck, flew by night as well as by day, until at last on 14 August 1947 it was finally hauled down.

In central India during the spring and early summer of 1858, Sir Hugh Rose with an army from Bombay conducted a brilliant campaign. He recaptured Jhansi which had revolted under its ex-rani and routed Nana's henchman, Tantia Topi, at the Battle of Kalpi. Thereafter the mutiny became an affair of small columns hunting down fugitive bands of mutineers.

In November 1858 India came under the Crown and the East India Company was dissolved. Many reforms were undertaken and the Indian Army was to give distinguished and devoted service for another ninety years. The great sepoy mutiny was not a satanic conspiracy as some Victorian historians suggested nor a nationalist uprising as have others. It was the tragedy of a joint stock company that had outgrown its strength.

Thus ended the last serious military threat to British rule in India until in 1942 the armies of Japan fought their way to the eastern border.

CHAPTER 18

Colonial Wars
and Punitive Expeditions
1856–99

BRIAN BOND

    * A complete list of expeditions to the north-west frontier is given by Captain H. L. Nevill, *Campaigns on the North-West Frontier*. London: Murray, 1912. p. 404.

In the second half of the nineteenth century the British Empire achieved its commercial and industrial apogee, and enjoyed a brief period of clear supremacy before encountering the challenge of new potential Great Powers such as Germany, the United States and Japan. The Royal Navy, despite periodic 'scares', maintained an all-round superiority

Opposite: Field Marshal Lord Wolsely. Garnet Wolsely was one of the foremost exponents of colonial warfare. He was Commander-in-Chief of the British Army, 1895–1900. Painted by A. Bernard 1880

COLONIAL WARS

"IT IS BETTER TO INCUR A SLIGHT REPRIMAND RATHER THAN PERFORM AN UNPLEASANT DUTY"

FROM FRANK WILSON/66

Not all military service was devoted to colonial wars

not merely over its nearest rivals, but over all the fleets of the world should they possibly combine. Britain's maritime supremacy also came under challenge in the last decade of the century, but in the period covered in this chapter it remained the fundamental assumption behind British strategy.

In contrast to the Royal Navy, the British Army was almost constantly in action, yet by Continental standards it was small and ill-organised. Isolation from Europe, though not always 'splendid' or even desirable politically, was accepted as a military fact of life between the Crimean and South African Wars. Indeed as late as 1905 the Prime Minister, Balfour, gave the Russian threat to India a higher priority than possible military intervention in Europe. In practice then a European expeditionary force took a poor third place after imperial policing and defence against invasion. Successive governments proved reluctant to compare the Army's possible uses with its capabilities, so that leading soldiers – such as Lord Wolseley in the 1880s – justifiably complained that they were obliged to plan and train in a political vacuum.

The 'scramble for Africa' notwithstanding, the British viewpoint in the late Victorian era may be broadly described as one of imperial satiety. It was widely recognised that trade did not follow the flag, nor was it necessary for the flag to follow trade. British business interests concentrated increasingly in Europe, the Americas and India rather than in more recently acquired colonies. In terms of defending the enormous empire already held, the

outstanding themes were the security of India's frontiers, and of the strategic routes linking India with Britain via the Suez canal (opened in 1869) and the Cape. The Indian Mutiny, though ruthlessly suppressed, was not quickly forgotten by the Raj; while after 1870 Russia's overland expansion in Central Asia seemed to be directed against India. Rivalry with France, and from 1894 France in concert with Russia, posed a threat to Britain's dominance in the Mediterranean and the Middle East. Consequently much, though not perhaps quite so much as suggested by some recent historians, of Britain's interest in the partition of Africa was strategic rather than commercial.

India, however, played a far greater role in the history of British colonial warfare than even this strategic summary suggests. Throughout the nineteenth century India had constituted the hub of British power in the East or, as Lord Salisbury bluntly called it, 'an English barrack in the oriental seas'. The Indian taxpayer not only bore the cost of his country's occupation but also maintained the British garrison of some 70,000 troops – approximately a third of the standing army. Though of doubtful constitutional legality British colonial campaigns, even outside the Indian continent, were fought to a remarkable extent by British and native troops of the Indian Army. They were used for example in China (1859–60) New Zealand (1860–1), Abyssinia (1867–8), Egypt (1882), the Sudan (1885 and 1896–9) and Mombasa (1896). Thus there were ample nineteenth century precedents for India's great sacrifices on behalf of the British Empire in the two World Wars.

The 1860s witnessed a dramatic change in British military policy that in many respects resembles that of the 1960s; namely the 'withdrawal of the legions'. The colonies had for years been under verbal attack, particularly from Radical politicians, as military and financial encumbrances which did not pay for their upkeep. British responsibility for protecting white colonists against dissident Maoris, Kaffirs and other indigenous peoples was seen to be not only a thankless task but one that had no logical conclusion short of the conquest and annexation of vast unwanted territories. The white colonists should therefore be encouraged to govern and defend themselves. In time, some visionaries hoped, the Dominions might even contribute to 'imperial defence' (a new concept in the 1870s).

Thus, by 1870, the policy of colonial self-help was far advanced. All British troops had quitted Australia, New Zealand and Tasmania, and the last were soon to leave Canada, except for the garrison at the naval base at Halifax. South Africa proved to be the great exception, for after 1870 the British garrison was reinforced first to fight the natives and then the Boer farmers of the Transvaal and Orange Free State. Indeed South Africa, together with the North-West Frontier and Egypt and the Sudan were to constitute the three main theatres of war in the late Victorian era.

Before discussing the outstanding characteristics of Victorian colonial warfare it will be useful to say something of the military system that had to cope with these infinitely varied campaigns.

A professional and recognisably modern Army only began to develop as a result of harsh experience in the Crimea. The 1870s for example witnessed the abolition of purchase of commissions for the officers and of flogging for the troops. Concern for the better professional education of officers was exemplified by the foundation of the Staff College at Camberley in 1858. Much of the muddle, waste and suffering before Sebastopol stemmed from the fact that Army administration was in the hands of no fewer than thirteen departments with ill-defined responsibilities. These were reduced during the war, and by the War Office Act of 1870 Cardwell vested control in two great offices; those of the Secretary of State for War and of his principal military adviser, the Commander-in-Chief.

Unfortunately the Crimean war had virtually no immediate impact on practical training. Popular enthusiasm for military preparedness, fanned by the French invasion scare of 1859, found expression in the Volunteer Movement, but this was a poor substitute for regular training. Indeed only after the Franco-Prussian War of 1870–1 were annual manoeuvres instituted, and these revealed that there was virtually no Army ready to take the field. Gradually however the land forces ceased to be a mere aggregation of scattered regiments and semi-independent corps and began to resemble a unified army under a single politically responsible minister.

Cardwell's period at the War Office from 1868 to 1874 certainly constituted the watershed in the history of the Victorian Army. By linking the infantry battalions in pairs he hoped to equalise the periods of home and overseas service, and also to reduce the length of colour service to six years. These reforms and the localisation of units were designed to introduce a system where there had been none previously, to improve recruiting, and to create a substantial trained reserve.

The Cardwell system however was undermined

by serious weaknesses from its inception, and none of his nineteenth century successors had the insight, energy or political authority to remedy them. There were three major and related problems: finance, recruiting and providing drafts for India. Intense Parliamentary criticism of military expenditure all too frequently resulted in reducing the establishments of home battalions below the minimum necessary for military efficiency. Similarly pay and

Abyssinia, 1867, the Chella Ravine. A good example of the rugged country the British Army had to traverse

terms of service could not be improved to keep pace with civil developments, and hence the recruiting problem remained unsolved. The uncertain flow of recruits, and also extra overseas commitments for which Cardwell had made no allowance, meant that the balance of battalions at home and abroad was never attained. Lastly the maintenance of the Indian garrison proved an insurmountable obstacle both to really short service and the creation of a large reserve. In short the efficiency of the units at home was sacrificed in order to maintain the flow of replacements to India. Thus Colonel G. F. R. Henderson, describing the Army before the South African War, remarked that 'a man must have been east of Malta before he is qualified to sit in judgment on the regular army of Great Britain. The beardless regiments of Aldershot or the Curragh can no more compare with the masses of strong men … who hold India and Egypt, than the lazy routine of English quarters can compare with the vigilance and stir of the restless East'.

Perhaps the Victorian Army's most serious deficiency was the lack of a General Staff which could study possible future military commitments in peacetime; train officers for staff duties; supervise mobilisation on the outbreak of war; and select qualified officers for the headquarters staff in the field. Not least important, a General Staff would have been responsible for co-ordinating military policy with that of the Royal Navy. Considering the frequency of warfare in this period it is astonishing that combined operations received so little attention.

The absence of a General Staff entailed that each expeditionary force had to be hurriedly improvised. Much depended on the officer chosen to command. Sir Hope Grant's expedition to China, Sir Robert Napier's to Abyssinia, and Sir Frederick Roberts' to Afghanistan and Burma provide examples of successful improvisation from the Indian base. The prince of improvisers in the 1870s and 1880s however was generally held to be Sir Garnet (later Field Marshal Viscount) Wolseley, so that 'All Sir Garnet' became a music-hall catch-phrase as a synonym for efficiency. Wolseley was recklessly brave as a young officer, and became an able administrator. His reputation was established by his speedy and economic conclusion of the operations in Canada in 1870 and Ashanti in 1873-4. In the Egyptian War of 1882, commanding some 20,000 troops, he achieved strategic surprise by moving his base from Alexandria to Ismailia, and won a decisive victory at Tel-el-Kebir after the daring expedient of a night march. Yet Wolseley's 'personal method' of command and

his habitual reliance on a favoured 'ring' of personally selected officers had its drawbacks. These became painfully evident, despite Wolseley's attempt to lay the blame elsewhere, in his bungled attempt to relieve Gordon at Khartoum in 1884-5. As Dr Adrian Preston has recently shown in his edition of Wolseley's campaign journal, *In Relief of Gordon*, the commander and his 'ring' were gravely at fault both in the unsystematic way they plumped for the Nile route against the advice of most experts, and in their actual handling of operations. One can only conclude that although generals such as Napier, Wolseley and Kitchener appeared to flourish in their highly personal and pragmatic approach to minor campaigns, even they would not have prevailed against sterner opposition.

It was perhaps indicative of this pragmatic approach that no systematic study of colonial warfare was undertaken until 1896 when Captain C. E. (later Major-General Sir Charles) Callwell R.A. published *Small Wars: Their Principles and Practice*.

What at once strikes one in this study is the diversity of the terrain on which British soldiers campaigned, and the extremely varied equipment, tactics and fighting qualities of their enemies. Then, as more recently, the appropriate form of training and acclimatisation presented almost insoluble problems. It was nothing unusual for a regiment like the 92nd (Gordon Highlanders) to be on active service in Afghanistan in 1880, in Natal in 1881 and Egypt in 1882. Thus Callwell pointed out that although small wars differed markedly from regular operations in certain respects, the practical lessons derived from the former must either be very general or seriously qualified by exceptions.

Britain's colonial wars were of three broad, though not always distinct, types: campaigns of conquest or annexation; campaigns for the suppression of insurrection and lawlessness (imperial policing); and punitive expeditions designed to avenge a wrong or wipe out an insult. Campaigns clearly in the first category are hard to find in this period, though the First South African War was directly caused by Britain's annexation of the two Boer Republics in 1877. The other two types are commonplace however, and frequently brought the same result of more or less permanent occupation. The China War of 1860 and the Abyssinian expedition exemplify punitive expeditions in which permanent commitments were wisely avoided. The Ashanti War of 1873-4, by contrast, was only temporarily effective and led to eventual annexation; while the occupation of Egypt after 1882 became permanent

Sudanese battalions of the Egyptian Army, raised and commanded by British officers, in action
against the Dervishes, 3 August 1889

despite the government's genuine intention to withdraw. In Burma, West Africa, Egypt and on the North-West Frontier Britain was faced with the recurring dilemma; less than Draconian victories only dispersed the enemy and inevitably led to further trouble, while decisive victories – such as Tel-el-Kebir – effectively destroyed the indigenous government and posed the alternatives of a British take-over or leaving the country in anarchy.

Perhaps the most interesting feature of Victorian colonial campaigns is the colourful variety of the opposition. Some of Britain's enemies displayed a curious mixture of primitive habits and civilized culture: the unusually chivalrous Maori warriors, for example, were avid students of the English Prayer Book; and the Ashantis, who practised human sacrifice on the grand scale, adorned their royal palace with Bohemian vases, Persian rugs and engravings of the Duke of Wellington. Nor could the fighting qualities of people like the Zulus, Afghans or Dervishes be underestimated with impunity.

No two enemies were alike in their weapons, tactics or military organisation. At one extreme Colonel Arabi's Egyptian force most closely resem-

bled a regular European army, which was hardly surprising since it had been trained and armed by French and British officers. At the Battle of Tel-el-Kebir Arabi commanded nearly 30,000 men with between 60 and 70 guns. But the Egyptians lacked the cohesion, discipline and manoeuvrability of a European army so that Arabi was obliged passively to await Wolseley's offensive in a fortified position. Surprised by a dawn attack, the Egyptians put up a poor fight and the army disintegrated within hours. Wolseley sent Drury Lowe's Indian cavalry brigade dashing ahead to Cairo and by this bold stroke ended the campaign. British losses were only 57 killed and 382 wounded.

At the other extreme were the primitively armed and tactically unsophisticated savages encountered in the West African forests and the Sudanese desert. Between these extremes the Zulus, for example, displayed unique tactics, neglect of which resulted in the disaster at Isandhlwana. Their *impis* comprised highly disciplined 'divisions' with an astonishing capacity for rapid manoeuvre on the open veldt. Yet their weapons were those of savages and their tactics were too inflexibly offensive to succeed

An incident on the North-West Frontier of India. At Nova Kili in Swat, on 17 August 1897 Lieutenant Lord Fincastle and Colonel Adams rescue a wounded comrade under point blank fire from Pathan tribesmen and earn the VC

against alerted British troops. The heroic defence of Rorke's Drift perfectly illustrated the superiority of British firearms and discipline over reckless Zulu courage. In the same campaign, at Zambula, Colonel Evelyn Wood defeated the *impi* opposing his column by a simple ruse. Wood sent a group of mounted infantry to fire dismounted at the enemy at close range. Zulu discipline was powerless to resist this challenge and they were drawn in a running fight close to the British laager where rifle volleys took a heavy toll. A third of the force was thus routed before the main Zulu attack began.

The Maoris, by contrast, lacked Zulu mobility and offensive spirit, but were better armed – with assorted muskets – and became formidable defensive fighters behind their elaborate earthen strongholds or *pahs*. Crimean tactics of infantry assaults in close order proved costly and ineffective. A particularly inept operation was that at Rangiriri on 20 November 1863. General Sir Duncan Cameron, who had led the Black Watch up the Heights of Alma, first bombarded the enemy stronghold with three Armstrong guns, and then ordered three successive frontal attacks which resulted only in a futile loss of life.

The Dervish followers of the Mahdi – and his successor the Khalifa – in the Sudan were true religious fanatics. Though they possessed a few rifles and obsolescent guns by 1885, the Dervishes continued to rely mainly on spears and knives, and attempted to overwhelm the enemy by reckless mass charges. By such tactics they did succeed in annihilat-

ing Hicks Pasha's thirsty, lost and demoralised force in the jungle on his march from the Nile towards El Obeid in 1883. They also achieved a brief tactical success by breaking into Sir Herbert Stewart's square at Abu Klea when he was marching to the relief of Gordon. As a rule however these primitive tactics were suicidal against European rifles, not to speak of machine guns. In the actions of Atbara and Omdurman in 1898 Kitchener's Army massacred the Dervishes as easily as partridges. In the latter action for example, 11,000 enemy corpses were counted on the battlefield while Kitchener lost only 48 killed.

Finally mention must be made of the Boers, by far the most sophisticated enemy encountered by the British in this period. In 1881 the Boers, though lacking artillery, possessed a good firearm in the Westley Richards rifle; they were all basically mounted infantry and as such were more mobile than the British. Also, as the Battle of Majuba demonstrated, they possessed fine marksmen and some highly enterprising leaders. Yet they had no permanent military organisation and their *commandos* were simply 'bodies of determined men acknowledging certain leaders, drawn together to confront a common danger'. In 1881 they boldly confronted Colley in pitched battle on the Transvaal frontier and three tactical successes were followed by Britain's political capitulation. It is interesting to speculate whether, had the campaign continued, the Boers could have resorted to guerrilla warfare as successfully as they did in 1900–2.

In assessing British military efficiency in these small wars it must never be forgotten that poor communications imposed enormous handicaps. The only campaigns fought within the vicinity of railways were probably those in Egypt in 1882 and the Sudan in 1896–8. All-weather roads too were rarely available. Indeed the trait which most distinguishes small wars from those fought between regular armies is that the former tend to be chiefly 'campaigns against nature'.

One of the most fascinating campaigns in this respect was the Abyssinian War of 1867–8. Napier's Army had first to establish piers and quays on a harbourless marsh in the Red Sea and then construct about 12 miles of railroad across the salt flats to the mountains. Then at Koomayli the march to Magdala began through nearly 400 miles of roadless mountains intersected by innumerable ravines. Napier's policy was to reduce the pack train to the minimum and concentrate on pushing a striking force to within range of the enemy capital as quickly

The Battle of Omdurman. By this battle, fought near Khartoum in the Sudan, Kitchener destroyed the Dervish Armies and re-occupied Khartoum. The illustration shows the charge of the 21st Lancers, in which the young Winston Churchill took part. Painted by T. Berkeley

as possible. Fortunately the Emperor Theodore reserved his force for the defence of Magdala and did not seriously harass the line of communications. His troops were no match for European infantry and artillery in pitched battle. Napier's triumph owed more to logistics and engineering than to orthodox military skills.

Napier's campaign illustrates another interesting aspect of this type of warfare. Commanders had frequently to race against time as well as overcome immense natural obstacles. Napier had to rescue the European captives from Magdala, punish the Emperor, and return before the spring rains swelled the river gorges and blocked his retreat. A summer spent in the fever-ridden marshes around Zula would have cost far more lives than the actions before Magdala. In fact Napier lost only 35 men from an army of 13,000. Wolseley had a similar problem, though in completely different terrain, in 1873 when he had to reach Kumasi, the Ashanti capital, and extricate his army before the rains thickened the jungle barrier and decimated his troops with fever. Shortness of time presented the same general with an agonising problem in 1884 in his mismanaged effort to relieve Khartoum: the cataracts had to be passed while the Nile waters were still high, and of course Khartoum had to be reached before it was stormed by the Mahdi. Although Sir Charles Wilson's column arrived only two days too late, it is far from clear that Wolseley had a large enough striking force within range to

have broken through the besiegers. Furthermore he had lost touch with both his column commanders.

These illustrations underline the point that, in sharp contrast to most of their opponents, Victorian generals could seldom afford to dispense with a line of communications. Such a line was necessary to bring up supplies, reinforcements and information to the front. Secondly, in event of defeat and an enforced withdrawal a protected escape route could avert a total disaster such as occurred in the First Afghan War. Thirdly, provision had to be made for removal of the sick and wounded, who could not be left to the tender mercies of such opponents as the Pathans or Dervishes. There seem to be only two examples of British generals in this period emulating Sherman in his famous march through Georgia to the sea by entirely cutting free from their communications. Both occurred in the Second Afghan War. In 1880 Sir Donald Stewart took six weeks to cover the 260 miles from Kandahar to Haider Kel, where he met the Kabul field force and linked up with the Khyber line of communications. A few months later Sir Frederick Roberts made his more famous march in the opposite direction from Kabul to Kandahar. His force comprised 10,000 soldiers and nearly as many followers. The baggage was carried by 2,800 ponies, 4,500 mules, and 950 donkeys. No wheeled vehicles or heavy guns could be taken. Roberts' men suffered severely from the dust storms and the extremes of climate but, unlike Stewart, they were not seriously attacked en route.

179

On the other hand Roberts had to relieve a beleaguered fortress and it is therefore easier to understand why his march became famous while Stewart's was forgotten.

Communications could be interpreted in quite a different sense with reference to the relations between Victorian field commanders and their political superiors. In the Crimean War Lord Raglan had tended to allow his authority to command to be undermined by the telegraph link with London. Yet in Afghanistan a quarter of a century later generals with large armies could be completely out of touch with the outside world for six weeks. The extension of the telegraph, and then railways, to India, Australasia and the Far East in the last quarter of the century gradually transformed the strategic environment in which colonial wars took place, but for much of the period under discussion field commanders inevitably enjoyed great scope for personal initiative. Napier suffered from bureaucratic interference in India in 1867 while building up his expeditionary force, but once he arrived in Abyssinia he was his own master. Wolseley too seems to have received only broad political directives in all his campaigns. The Maori Wars provide the clearest example of the freedom of the man on the spot. The two-way passage of an enquiry to Whitehall might take eight months, while communications between the islands of New Zealand were so poor that the quickest way to get a letter from Auckland to Wellington was often to send it via Australia. Reinforcements rushed out from the Curragh in 1860 took 82 days on what was considered a fast passage.

The slow transmission of orders from England might also allow commanders to turn a deaf ear to unwelcome news. After the disaster of Isandhlwana Lord Chelmsford was superseded in the command by Wolseley, but he feigned ignorance of his replacement, even when Wolseley arrived in Natal, and went on to salvage at least part of his reputation by the crushing victory at Ulundi which, to Wolseley's chagrin, ended the war.

Britain's humiliating capitulation in the First Boer War is only comprehensible if it is appreciated that Sir George Colley, and his successor Sir Evelyn Wood, were closely circumscribed by government instructions telegraphed to Newcastle in Natal. Colley, in short, was forbidden to press on his advance into the Transvaal pending a reply to truce terms offered to the Boers. Wood likewise was forbidden to avenge the defeat at Majuba so long as Kruger delayed his reply. Politically, Gladstone's government could justify its actions; but there can

be no doubt that militarily the British commanders were handicapped by this attempt at remote control and – in Colley's case – by the ambiguity of the instructions he received.

If, as Callwell observed, the conduct of small wars must differ radically from some of the traditional principles of regular warfare, it follows that tactics and weapons which are obsolete among European armies may yet continue to be highly effective against irregulars. The outstanding illustration of this point in Victorian colonial warfare is the survival of the square as a tactical formation. After Waterloo steady developments in firepower made it increasingly suicidal to bunch men together on the battlefield, and by the time of the Franco-Prussian War loose skirmishing lines were becoming normal. Against irregular opponents, other than the Boers, however, various types of 'square' remained indispensable right to the end of the century. It should be explained that 'squares' had become infinitely more adaptable than the rigid eighteenth century formations of infantry and artillery. Indeed 'squares' took on various shapes according to the terrain and the military situation; for example large loose formations for crossing open country when the enemy was distant, and small compact ones for resisting attack. Sir Herbert Stewart's advance from Korti via Abu Klea to the Nile illustrates the square's uses both in moving through desert scrub and in resisting a fanatical attack. Even in the Ashanti jungle Wolseley adopted a loose square formation during the advance to prevent the enemy falling upon his rear.

Secondly, volley firing, which was obsolescent in European warfare due to the development of more sophisticated weapons and tactics from the mid-nineteenth century, remained the most effective way to stop native rushes, as the British demonstrated in such actions as Abu Klea and Rorke's Drift. Even at Isandhlwana the defenders exacted a fearful toll before they were eventually overwhelmed when one corner of their perimeter collapsed.

Lastly, one of the few tenable defences of the cavalry in its traditional *arme blanche* role of the charge with lance or sabre was, that although of very dubious value in European warfare, it was still potentially the decisive instrument against irregulars. Callwell instances the successful use of lances or spears at Ulundi, Kambula and El Teb, and Winston Churchill – a participant – immortalised the charge of the 21st Lancers at Omdurman.

Evidently British colonial warfare in the second half of the nineteenth century cannot command the same kind of interest as conflicts between reasonably well-matched European powers. Command of the sea insured Britain against hostile intervention, while tactically superior weapons and discipline frequently rendered the contest one-sided. On the other hand British troops were operating far from their home base and in unfavourable terrain. Her overworked battalions consequently did not always triumph easily, and occasionally they did not triumph at all. Clearly good or bad leadership and staff work could make all the difference between a victory such as Tel-el-Kebir or a defeat such as Maiwand.

Even minor campaigns moreover could exert a far-reaching influence on national or international politics. In Egypt, the Sudan and the Transvaal British military intervention provoked early nationalist movements. Wolseley's failure in the Sudan in 1885 emboldened the Russians in their encroachment on the borders of Afghanistan since it was clear that Britain had no strategic reserve available to meet another crisis. The defeat at Majuba caused a crisis within the Liberal Government in which appeasement eventually triumphed over coercion.

A study of these small wars will also throw interesting light on that strange phenomenon: the Victorian military mind. Although civilian critics of the 'imperial idea' were never lacking, they seem to have made little impression on the serene, pre-Freudian self-confidence of the majority of generals in Britain's right – or duty – to impose her superior civilisation upon 'lesser breeds' – if necessary by force of arms. As always, however, there were interesting exceptions. Sir William Butler, like so many distinguished British generals an Irishman, was an eccentric champion of the underdog – or rather of some underdogs – and eventually sacrificed his career in 1899 rather than be the executor of the Milner-Chamberlain policy of coercing the Boers.

Finally, a modern student of Victorian colonial campaigns must be impressed, as Callwell was in the 1890s, by the enormous difference between the characteristics of this but slowly changing type of warfare, and the rapid transformation simultaneously taking place in the art of war in Europe. While Britain's leading generals were gaining unrivalled experience, albeit on a small scale, on the veldt or on the north-west frontier, Germany was perfecting her General Staff, mass conscript armies were being raised and intricate preparations were being made for their movement to the frontiers by rail on the outbreak of war. The tremendous increase of firepower foreshadowed a revolution in tactics by giving great advantages to the defender. Britain observed these developments at a safe distance but did not follow them: in 1899 the Army was still utterly unprepared to fight on the Continent. Fortunately the South African War to some extent exposed this military weakness to the government, and both soldiers and statesmen came forward with perceptive ideas on reform. From 1905 the Army began seriously to prepare, for the first time since Waterloo, for possible participation in a great war in Western Europe.

The Tirah campaign on the North-West Frontier of India. The Afridis held the heights above Dargai to prevent a British column penetrating into their territory. On 20 October 1897, after a bitter struggle, the Gordon Highlanders finally took the heights at the point of the bayonet. Piper George Findlater (VC), although wounded, continued to play and cheer the men on. After this action the Afridis avoided pitched battles and devoted themselves to guerrilla warfare

CHAPTER 19

The Army at the End of the Nineteenth Century and the Development of the Services

WILLIAM Y. CARMAN

After the Crimean war the main reorganisation was not so much in the fighting forces as in the supply and administrative corps although the processes of producing an efficient fighting machine continued to develop. An opportunity did occur to increase the number of fighting regiments, for the reforms after the Indian Mutiny permitted many European soldiers to leave the 'John Company' and add to the cavalry, artillery, and infantry of the Queen's army.

The 1st, 2nd and 3rd Bengal European Cavalry in 1861 formed the nucleus of the 19th Princess of Wales' Own Hussars, the 20th Hussars, and the 21st Hussars. The Horse and Foot Artillery of the Bengal, Madras, and Bombay Presidencies all added troops and batteries to the Royal Regiment of Artillery. The three Bengal European Infantry regiments became in 1861 the 101st, 104th and 107th Regiments of Foot, taking in 1881 the new titles of 1st Royal Munster Fusiliers, 2nd Royal Munster Fusiliers, and 2nd Royal Sussex. The three Madras European Regiments were numbered 102, 105, and 108 and were named in 1881 as the 1st Royal Dublin Fusiliers, 2nd King's Own Yorkshire Light Infantry, and 2nd Royal Inniskilling Fusiliers. The three Bombay European Regiments were numbered 103, 106, and 109, later taking the titles of 2nd Royal Dublin Fusiliers, 2nd Durham Light Infantry, and 2nd Prince of Wales' Leinster Regiment.

The 18th Hussars had been re-raised in 1858 when they were formed at Leeds and were permitted to carry the honours of 'Peninsula' and 'Waterloo' previously borne by the old 18th Hussars disbanded in 1821. The 21st Hussars noted above served with distinction at Omdurman where two officers and a private gained the Victoria Cross and for this brilliant action the regiment was converted to Lancers and also named 'Empress of India's'.

In the infantry the old 100th Foot was re-raised at the time of the Indian Mutiny from Canadian volunteers who wished to serve in India; later they became the 1st Prince of Wales' Leinster Regiment (Royal Canadians).

The problem of keeping up strength in regiments serving overseas was met by having a second battalion at home. This linked system which began in 1873 produced the two-battalion regiment which was also localised with its own recruiting area. The final linking took place in 1881 when the County Militia battalions were associated as the 3rd and 4th battalions. The regular battalion system worked satisfactorily in time of war but it was found that the militia battalions did little but garrison duties and that the volunteers were not really part of the war machine. A war scare had brought about a vast voluntary movement and many volunteer rifle corps were formed from 1860 onwards. These volunteer units could vary from a handful of men to a complete battalion; thus it was necessary to organise the many corps into administrative battalions. Later these were numbered volunteer battalions and attached to the linked battalions of 1881 but their services were entirely for home defence. Depots had been established for the linked battalions but this was more a man-producing idea rather than a grouping for major warfare.

The method of finding sufficient fighting men at this time seemed satisfactory. Local and colonial engagements saw the deployment of troops ranging from a battalion to a brigade and up to an undefined 'force'. However, the advent of large campaigns like those in Egypt and South Africa brought for-

Opposite above: Life Guards. Coloured lithograph by G.H.Thomas. *Below:* Regiments of the line.
From left to right: Bandsman 41st Foot, drummer 10th, private 35th, rifleman Rifle Brigade, private 29th pioneers, sergeant 32nd Light Infantry, piper 78th Highlanders, corporal 78th Highlanders. Coloured lithograph by G.H.Thomas *c.* 1860

183

Left: King's Royal Rifle Corps (formerly 60th Rifles) in marching order. A colour print by F. Dadd
Right: Foot Guards. A print by F. Dadd

Royal Artillery. Royal Horse Artillery and Foot Artillery. Coloured lithograph by G. H. Thomas *c.* 1860

ward the need of established brigades and divisions. This aim was not achieved until the next century although cavalry and yeomanry brigades were established. Large formations created in the field were broken up at the end of hostilities.

In the field of armaments after the Crimean war there were great strides and the whole concept of firearms and artillery changed. Although on the continent the needle-gun had been accepted by the Prussians and the French, the British were slow to think in these terms. It had been realised that the muzzle-loading musket was not the best of weapons and the War Office asked for ideas to convert the Enfield rifle, pattern 1853, into a breech-loader. The ingenuity of Jacob Snider produced a stop-gap weapon which lasted until 1871 when the Martini-Henry rifle was adopted. The next step was to get away from the single-shot weapon and the adoption of a magazine allowed the rifle to fire five cartridges one after another without reloading.

In the cavalry, experimental issues were made of the Terry and Westley-Richards breech-loading carbines, both from British inventors. The American Sharps carbine was also tried but a Snider-type carbine replaced all these until 1877 when a Martini-Henry version caused the Snider itself to be relegated to yeomanry, volunteers and the Irish Constabulary. The cavalry sword was little used in battle but the long lance was found of value in Africa.

Hand weapons had not at this time reached the peak of automatic fire but the weapon that did was the machine-gun invented by Hiram S. Maxim. It was successful in its trials of 1884 but the high rate of fire which cost £5 a minute was not popular with all

observers – in fact the King of Denmark decided that such a weapon was much too expensive for his country. The Gatling gun and the Hotchkiss gun were two multiple-fire weapons also invented by Americans and used in British service, the former not too successfully and the latter at a later date.

The opposing artillery in the Crimean war slowly crashed away at each other with cast guns, muzzle-loading and firing round cannon balls – all principles used in the Middle Ages. But great changes were on the way. In 1854 W. G. Armstrong, an English civil engineer, had the idea of gun barrels made of wrought iron. He further produced a rifle-gun which also was breech-loading and threw a projectile five miles. The shape of the projectile was now elongated and had modifications to engage with the rifling of the piece. But in 1864 the British Government decided not to continue with breech-loading cannon even though they had been successful on the continent. It was not until 1885 that it was considered that the day of the muzzle-loader was over. The wooden gun-carriage was now replaced by one of steel or iron and recoil devices were adopted. In battle the black smoke of the gunpowder not only hampered vision but gave away the position of men and guns. The introduction of cordite charges at the end of the century not only improved the charge but the smokeless explosion helped to conceal the whereabouts of artillery.

Realistic changes were also taking place in the uniform of the ordinary soldier. The red coat had been the mark of the English soldier since Elizabethan times and the fighting man was expected to wear a colourful and imposing uniform when fighting, with no thought to comfort or practical reasons. It was the war in the Crimea which brought the realisation that a strikingly dressed automaton did not ensure that victory was at hand. Several misfortunes and much tribulation eventually brought a drastic change in dress.

The cavalryman as well as the infantryman dashed at his Russian counterpart in the first months of the Crimean campaign in a tight and restricting full dress uniform which made concessions to warfare only in such trivia as the discontinuance of plumes in the headdresses. Warm clothing was not available. The hussar was expected to wear his pelisse as an overcoat, a situation not improved when a ship carrying these was sunk in Balaclava harbour. The rigours of the campaign soon wrought havoc with the clothing which was slow in replacement. No wonder that hasty repairs were made and local garments pressed into service, producing a common soldier whose appearance was quite unlike the rosy image which was given in the woodcuts at home. The short-waisted coatees afforded little protection to the guardsman and the infantryman. The artistic shakos soon showed that they could not stand up to the hard knocks and rough weather of a continuing campaign. Thus overcoats of local purchase and fur garments made the soldier look like a kind of animal. Long boots were sought and the knitted woollen cap was much more sensible than the vulnerable shako.

With such trying conditions it was obvious that the authorities had to make some concessions and improvements even during the war. The short infantry coatee with the useless tails at the back was replaced in 1855 by a double-breasted tunic with deep skirts which afforded protection to the body. This pattern was changed to a single-breasted tunic but still with the deep skirts. The cavalry also were given the tunic, the hussars having less braid than previously across the chest. The new tunics were cut quite full and were more comfortable. The collar was much reduced in height and in 1862 the leather stock which had so restricted the neck was abolished and replaced by a small black leather tab which sufficed to close the gap. The Highland troops adopted their own body garment, a doublet with elaborate cuffs and skirt flaps piped with white braid. The highland stockings of stitched tartan were replaced by softer knitted hose. The infantry overcoat was improved in quality and in 1869 had the addition of a detachable cape.

The tall Albert shako of the infantry and light dragoon was reduced in height and size – whether as a concession to comfort or in imitation of the current

Cavalry. *From left to right:* Sergeant 6th Inniskilling Dragoons, corporal 6th Dragoon Guards (Carabiniers), corporal Scots Greys, corporal II P.A.V.O. Hussars, sergeant 17th Lancers, trooper 7th Queen's Own Hussars. Coloured lithograph by G. H. Thomas

French style is not clear. With the passing of the years there was a continuing reduction in the height of the shako (or chaco as it was later known) until 1878 when a change of style took place. The French képi had suffered a defeat by the Prussian Pickelhaube in 1870–1 so obviously a new head-dress based on the German head-dress was needed. A blue cloth helmet with a spike on top was introduced and remained in use as the last full dress headgear for infantry of the line despite attempts to return to the shako.

The field artillery abandoned its fur cap for the blue helmet with a ball instead of the spike on top. Incidentally the artillery were successful in returning to the fur cap or busby before the full dress disappeared. Engineers also surrendered their fur cap with the distinctive garter blue bag for the spiked helmet and they too regained the fur cap in later days. Other headdress remained more or less the same. The hussar busby and the lance cap had minor alternations in size and the heavy cavalry helmet was simplified in its decoration although coloured plumes were adopted instead of the black which had been a common issue. Rifle regiments wore the helmet for a short period before acquiring a black fur cap, lambskin for officers. Highlanders retained the feather bonnet but the expansion of Lowland regiments eventually saw the introduction of a stiffened bonnet called the Kilmarnock for the Royal Scots and the King's Own Scottish Borderers. The Scottish Rifles and the Highland Light Infantry retained versions of the shako.

Apart from supplying the immediate needs of the

185

soldier with an eye to ornamental additions, thought was now being directed to clothing in other less temperate climes. The fierce fighting during the Indian Mutiny had brought about a loosening of regulations, and comfort in battle was sought. When one troop of Bengal Horse Artillery galloped outside the range of staff inspection the first task was to remove the high restricting collars from their jackets. The Royal Munster Fusiliers when they were the 1st Bengal European Fusiliers campaigned without their coats in their grey shirts which earned them the nickname of 'the Dirty Shirts'. Special sun helmets had been worn by officers and now men were allowed to wear them at their own expense. The introduction of khaki in India brought not only a suitable colour but a lighter weight clothing. Cold weather was not overlooked and troops in Canada had fur caps and mitts as well as warm coats.

While these changes in the organisation, weapons and uniform of the fighting soldier were taking place, some thought was also being given as to how best he and his weapons could be provided with the wherewithal to fight, and also as to how the wounded soldier might be better cared for – an obvious way to economise in man-power.

In the early days fighting units were expected to be self-contained and self-sufficing, but as warfare became more complex special services were necessary to supply the needs of the soldier. At the time of the establishment of the standing army it was considered that the task of the colonel, as father and proprietor of the regiment, was to find all the necessities of his troops. Being given a bulk sum of money he was responsible for the men's pay, their clothing, their food, quarters and such comforts as light and heat, in fact the management of a regiment was similar to that of a commercial undertaking with all its profits and losses.

The Board of Ordnance was in the nature of a departure from the colonel-proprietor system. With guns and associated supplies kept in such arsenals as the Tower of London, the Board was also responsible for the artillery, engineering projects and for arms in general. As time passed the store department grew in complexity and the advent of barracks, instead of local requisitions or tentage, brought forth the barrackmaster's department in the Board of Ordnance.

Even on the regimental level the civilian 'tail' was increasing. The Parliamentary Army had seen to it that chaplains or preachers were attached to regiments, not only for their spiritual aid but also to promote special political aims, in fact an early use of propaganda. Surgeons were necessary at battalion level in order to keep as many men as possible in fighting condition. Quartermasters and solicitors made sure that the allotment of material and money was not mishandled.

The creation of larger specialist bodies was only a matter of time. Even the movement of supplies and material depended on local improvisation and the precarious employment of civilian yokels not to be relied on in actual combat. The artillery partly solved this problem by creating its own corps of drivers in 1794. In the same year was raised the Corps of Waggoners consisting of five companies who accompanied the Duke of York on his unsuccessful expedition but were soon disbanded, in August 1795. A second corps was raised in 1799 and this time they were named the Royal Waggon Corps. Once again they went on active service almost at once. Their establishment included 100 bread waggons, 100 forage carts, 20 hospital waggons and 10 forge carts but these were not all ready in time for the actual conflict. Later waggons were specified for bread, hay, oats and luggage as well as spring waggons and forge carts. In Portugal and Spain pack mules and bullock waggons were employed by the Royal Waggon Train. One forge waggon was attached to each regiment of cavalry and spring waggons were used to carry the sick and wounded. Despite its obvious use in time of war the Royal Waggon Train was gradually reduced until in 1833 it disappeared entirely.

It needed another major conflict like the Crimean War to bring back an efficient transport system and eventually in 1855 the Land Transport Corps was formed. Even this body had a short life and in August 1856 was replaced by the Military Train, now an established and not just a war-time formation. The men were stationed all round the world and gained honour as far away as India during the Mutiny. A further reorganisation took place in 1869 when a Control Department was created with several small sub-departments including one called the Army Service Corps. Into this volunteered men from the Military Train, the Commissariat Staff Corps, the Military Store Staff Corps and part of the Army Hospital Corps. This Control Department lasted but six years and in 1875 the supply and transport service was known as the Commissariat and Transport Department, while the Ordnance Store Department became a separate branch. In 1881 yet another reorganisation brought forth the Commissariat and Transport Corps and the Ordnance Store Corps. Another change came in 1888 when the Commissariat and Transport Corps became the Army Service Corps, the honour of 'Royal' being added in 1918.

It has been noted that the Board of Ordnance had been responsible for many supplies and services, but when the Board was broken up at the time of the Crimean War certain aspects were continued by the men who eventually were known as the Ordnance Corps. The old Board had been responsible for issues and accommodation. A special Barrack Department was formed in 1792 and in 1797 also took over army hospitals. There existed in the nineteenth century such departments as those of the Storekeeper General, the Quartermaster General, the Paymaster General and the Commissary General but in 1855 with the end of the Board of Ordnance, new bodies appeared. In 1857 the Storekeepers formed into the Military Store Corps and in 1863 the Barrackmasters broke away from the Stores to make a new War Office unit. To produce men to actually handle the stores, a Military Store Staff Corps was made in 1865.

It was thought that the Control Department created in 1870 would eliminate many small units and create an effective overall command. Here were grouped the Commissariat, Military Transport, Military Store Department, Barrack Department and Purveyors Department, with the Army Service Corps doing actual work in the field. But in 1876 the Control was considered too unwieldy and was split up. The Ordnance Store Department now had a separate entity and in 1896 the Ordnance Store Department (the office side) and the Ordnance Store Corps (the working or labour side) changed to Army Ordnance Department and Army Ordnance Corps, not making the final marriage until 1922 when they became the Royal Army Ordnance Corps.

Baggage wagons, 1802. A contemporary water-colour by W. H. Pyne

Above: Commissariat wagons on the way to Sebastopol, 4 November 1854
Below: Doctor Smith's new hospital wagons at the Siege of Sebastopol. *The Illustrated London News*

In the eighteenth century each regiment besides having its own surgeon and mate, had to make its own hospital arrangements. In 1801 the Medical Officers of the Royal Artillery formed a separate medical establishment but for the actual movement of wounded personnel in time of war there was no provision until 1854 when the Hospital Conveyance Corps was formed. This in 1855 became part of the Land Transport Corps and was disbanded in 1856.

A Medical Staff Corps came into being in June 1855 and provided the staff to run hospitals – stewards, cooks, ward masters, orderlies, etc. but when the Crimean War was over a new body appeared, the Army Hospital Corps which undertook hospital and ambulance duties. In 1884 the officers were taken into the Medical Staff and the men into the Medical Staff Corps but in 1898 they were again united into the Royal Army Medical Corps. Such female nursing as had been needed was supplied regimentally in a more or less unofficial manner by soldiers' wives, but during the Crimean war the need for a nursing service was obvious and Florence Nightingale laid the foundations which later developed into the Army Nursing Service.

In the eighteenth century the works services in the army were undertaken by the regiments or the artillery but the needs of a wider service were not attempted until 1800 when a Corps of Pioneers was established to undertake field works. About the same time the Royal Staff Corps attached to the Quartermaster General's Department was created to deal with bridging, road-making and survey including map-making. Even communications were the responsibility of the Royal Staff Corps who sent messages by semaphore. Despite useful work in the Peninsular War and a post-war life the Corps only

Above: Army Service Corps, 1914. A painting by C. C. P. Lawson
Below: A plough for laying the new electric telegraph, 1854. *The Illustrated London News*

lasted until 1837 when it was disbanded and its tasks transferred to the Ordnance.

Another attempt was made to establish a labour corps in the Crimea when the Army Works Corps some 450 strong (mechanics and labourers) sailed from London Bridge in 1855 to swell the force of some 3,000 men engaged in this work. Peace brought the abolition of the Corps and it needed the advent of the First World War and the Second World War to see the revival of a Labour or Pioneer Corps.

The signal side of the Royal Staff Corps was most important on the battlefield. The short range of the drum or bugle might be satisfactory for the transmission of very local orders but the increase of battle fronts and the complexities of warfare brought the need for long-distance apparatus like semaphore. It may not be realised that as early as the Crimean War there was an 'Electric Telegraph'. At this time two waggons each drawn by six horses provided the necessary instruments, batteries and telegraph apparatus with enough wire to set up telegraphic communication over a distance of ten or twelve miles. This branch of signalling became the responsibility of the Royal Engineers and in 1870 the first regular mobile telegraph troop was established with two officers, 133 other ranks and twelve four-wheeled waggons. Volunteer telegraph corps had been on manoeuvres before this date.

Apart from these more important services the nineteenth century saw the development of such specialised corps as the Army Pay Corps, the Corps of Army Schoolmasters (later to become the Education Corps), the Police, and many others which had a slow growth and are too complex to be covered in this chapter.

M

CHAPTER 20

The Boer War
1899–1902

JOHN M. SELBY

In 1877 the Independent Transvaal Boer Republic was surrounded by warlike Bantus and was neither stable politically nor viable economically. It seemed a kindness for Britain to suggest annexation, and the offer was gratefully received by the majority of the Transvaal burghers. A few years later, however, several leading Boers had second thoughts and began to take action to regain independence. Paul Kruger, the late vice-president, led two delegations to London; Piet Joubert joined the protesters; Piet Cronje stirred up trouble in the town of Potchefstroom; and the culmination was a great patriotic assembly of burghers at Paardekraal. At this historic meeting a fight for freedom was decided on, and in the ensuing rebellion the British garrisons in Pretoria, Potchefstroom and elsewhere in the Transvaal were surrounded.

Troops under General Colley were sent from Natal to relieve the British garrisons. Colley occupied Majuba Hill, a key point in the mountain barrier between Transvaal and Natal, but his scratch force was driven off in disorder following a surprise Boer attack, and he was killed. The British Government had been trying to come to terms with the Boer rebels even before and during Colley's operations. Now, after Majuba, they were adamant on peace at almost any price; and as a result of the negotiations which followed the Transvaal obtained virtual independence again. A few strings, however, remained: a vague British suzerainty; some restraints on external treaty-making; and some even vaguer guarantees of European residence and citizens' rights. Paul Kruger who became the leader in the Transvaal set about making these void by paying no attention to them; but there were other matters which could not be dealt with in this way. The Boers

wanted room to expand, and when Cecil Rhodes's British South African Company seized Matabeleland and Mashonaland to their north, and West Griqualand and the diamond fields were annexed in the west, they felt hemmed in and robbed. The most serious difference, however, arose over demands for citizens' rights from British and other European immigrants to the Johannesburg goldfields, demands which the British Government felt called upon to support. There followed the planning of a raid by Dr Jameson's mounted police from Rhodesia to help these Johannesburg *Uitlanders*; but when the time came they were too disorganised to co-operate in the coup; and Dr Jameson's horsemen were cleverly surrounded and made prisoner by Piet Cronje's commandos. 'The Raid' caused Kruger to prepare the Transvaal for armed conflict against the *Uitlanders*' outside supporters, and led in turn to Britain reinforcing the garrisons in her colonies of the Cape and Natal. Then came an ultimatum suggesting British suzerainty must end and demanding that Britain withdraw her armed forces from the Transvaal's frontiers. Britain's refusal led to the war which began on 12 October 1899. In this Second Boer War, unlike the first, the Transvaal had the burghers of the Orange Free State as allies.

Militarily the war fell into three phases of unequal length. In the first which lasted from 12 October 1899 to the end of the year, the initiative was with the Boers. Although defeated at Talana Hill and Elandslaagte in Natal and at Modder River in the West, they besieged Mafeking, Kimberley and Ladysmith, and in the second week of December, 1899 – 'Black Week' as it was known in Britain – defeated General Gatacre at Stormberg, holding the line in the centre, Lord Methuen at Magersfontein,

Opposite: Field Marshal Lord Roberts (VC) at Cape Town, 1900

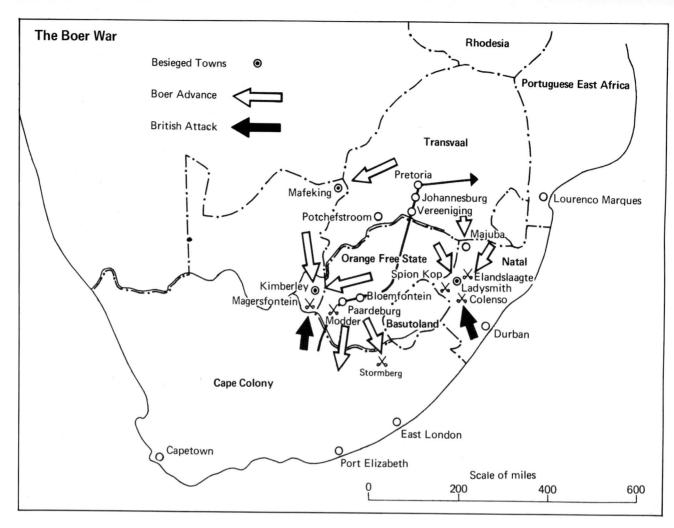

The Boer War

Besieged Towns ◉

Boer Advance ⇦

British Attack ⬅

Rhodesia

Portuguese East Africa

Transvaal

Pretoria

Mafeking

Johannesburg
Vereeniging

Potchefstroom

Lourenco Marques

Majuba

Orange Free State

Spion Kop

Natal

Kimberley

Elandslaagte
Ladysmith
Colenso

Magersfontein

Bloemfontein

Paardeburg
Modder

Basutoland

Durban

Stormberg

Cape Colony

East London

Capetown

Port Elizabeth

Scale of miles

0   200   400   600

trying to relieve Kimberley, and General Buller, the commander-in-chief, at Colenso, trying to relieve Ladysmith. In this period, as at Majuba, the Boers proved to be good soldiers. They shot straight and made good use of cover. When natural protection was absent, they were adept at digging deep narrow trenches which not only gave them protection from shrapnel, but, aided by smokeless powder, hid them almost completely from the British. These were not fieldworks with great mounds of earth to serve as rangefinders for their enemies, but holes cleverly camouflaged with grass and twigs, curved to obviate enfilade fire on them, and with covered rear approaches to bring in reserves. Such trenches, like those produced under General de la Rey at Modder River and Magersfontein, gave the Boers great advantages. The Boers also had the benefit of all being mounted on ponies and could move around quickly in attack or in retreat. The British did not shoot as well as the Boers, nor were they good at making use of cover; on the other hand, they were better disciplined. The Boers were alternately cowardly and brave, panic-stricken and confident. Because there were no penalties for disobedience, they did what they felt like doing and no more: thus it was said that

'every Boer was his own general'. It might be added, however, that he proved a pretty good general too.

Failure to relieve Kimberley and Ladysmith led to the appointment of Lord Roberts as commander-in-chief, and Lord Kitchener as his chief-of-staff; and with the arrival in South Africa of these two great leaders, the tide of war soon changed. Lord Roberts planned a great march on Bloemfontein and Pretoria, and set Lord Kitchener the task of organising a vast animal transport system so that they could leave the restricted routes provided by the railways and cut across country. His supplies assured in this way, Lord Roberts abandoned his lines of communication, outflanked Kimberley to the east and sent off General French and the cavalry to relieve the besieged town on their own. This task General French carried out to perfection, demonstrating as he had at Elandslaagte, a battle to be described later, the generalship which led to his being chosen as commander of the BEF in 1914. General Piet Cronje's besieging army, meanwhile, had moved east to escape being cut off from base; but, slowed down by cumbersome oxwagons, he was not fast enough to escape Lord Roberts' forces. He was trapped under the banks of the Modder River at Paardeburg, and shelled into surrender with 4000 men on 28 February 1900, the nineteenth anniversary of Colley's defeat at Majuba. Bloemfontein was now occupied, and a large part of the Orange Free State army was pinned against the mountains of Basutoland and surrendered. After pausing for seven weeks in Bloemfontein, largely because of a serious outbreak of enteric fever among the troops, Lord Roberts resumed his march to the north, occupied Johannesburg and Pretoria, and shepherded the Transvaal forces eastwards down the railway leading to Portuguese East Africa and Lourenço Marques from which port President Paul Kruger sailed away to Holland, an old and broken man. Meanwhile, General Buller, after failures at Spion Kop and Vaal Krantz, had pushed through at last at Colenso and relieved Ladysmith. It seemed, with the second phase of the war over – that of the great British counter-offensive – the war was over too. It was not so, however; there was to be a third phase, the longest of all, lasting eighteen months.

The Boer governments had been dislodged from their capitals, but, peripatetic though their existence was, they retained their authority. President Steyn of the Orange Free State had been loth to start the war, but, with his seat of government wherever he happened to be, was tenacious in carrying it on; and Vice-President Shalk Burger who had replaced Kruger in the Transvaal carried on the war as well. To begin with, General Botha in eastern Transvaal and General de la Rey in Western Transvaal led the largest forces to harass British communications. Later, General Christian de Wet and General Smuts also showed themselves particularly aggressive and elusive in carrying out raids, the latter ranging almost up to Cape Town itself.

Lord Roberts had given up command at the end of 1900. During the period of the guerrilla operations mentioned above Lord Kitchener commanded the British forces. Displaying his customary efficiency, thoroughness and tenacity he eventually won through. By burning the farms which supplied the recalcitrant Boers still on commando, and by confining their women and children in camps, he disorganised the rebels' sources of supply. Next, he divided the country with wire fences covered and guarded at strategic points by manned blockhouses, and then carried out sweeps within the confined areas so produced to clear them of warring Boers. These severe methods were eventually successful; but they increased the odium under which Britain already lay in world opinion. By the beginning of 1902 both sides were tired of war. In May of that year peace was signed at Vereeniging under which the Boers

were promised eventual self-government.

Usually a battle to illustrate the nature of the fighting in the Boer War is chosen from one of the great British disasters, like Spion Kop, the most bloody, or Magersfontein, the most humiliating. In this chapter, however, for a change, an early British victory has been selected. This not only shows how the Boers fought, as do the examples above, but also indicates that the British could be successful if well led. The battle selected is Elandslaagte, and it took place north of Ladysmith near a railway station of that name on 21 October 1899.

From 12 October 1899 onwards, Boer commandos had poured into North Natal from all directions, and General White vc, the British commander at the time was in the unfortunate strategic position of having one brigade isolated at Dundee in the north-east while the bulk of his force was at Ladysmith further south. Two Boer forces approached Dundee and were held there in the battle on Talana Hill; but old General Koch's levies[1] in the meantime moved down the centre of North Natal. These reached the Biggarsberg Mountains on 19 October, and their forward patrols advanced south as far as Elandslaagte on the railways halfway between Dundee and Ladysmith. Dashing into the station they attacked and captured a supply train steaming through on its way

[1] Germans and Hollanders, but also a Johannesburg commando and the Vrede Free State commando.

Cronje surrenders at Paardeburg. A painting by Henri Dupray

Above: Carrying a wounded Boer from the firing line
Below: A block house

Infantry storming a kopje

to Dundee, and then occupied the hotel and the buildings around the railway, completely cutting rail, road and telegraphic communications between Dundee and Ladysmith. Appealed to for reinforcements, Koch hesitated, for he knew Joubert's wish for caution and being old himself shared it. Then he reluctantly agreed and rode all through the night with the rest of his force to reach Elandslaagte. He rested the next day, while the battled raged at Dundee; but in the evening held a smoking concert in the hotel, to which the English prisoners captured on the supply train were invited, and where 'God Save the Queen' and the Transvaal 'Volkslied' were sung with equal impartiality, a curious prelude to the morrow's battle, for General White, not knowing of the reinforcement, had already ordered General John French to move north from Ladysmith 'to clear the neighbourhood of Elandslaagte of the enemy and cover the reconstruction of the railway and telegraphic lines'. At this stage he wanted to clear communications by road and rail to Dundee so that General Yule might fall back on Ladysmith unimpeded; and he fought the Battle of Elandslaagte on 21 October to clear the route.

General French began with two reconnaissances, the second in force. Moving north along the New-

castle road from Ladysmith he drew up on the higher ground west of the station and sent patrols forward on either side of the line. As the mist lifted parties of Boers were seen around the station and colliery buildings, and when the cavalry scouts approached, some of these rode off to the kopjes south-east of the station (the scene of the main battle to follow). French now brought into action his Natal Volunteer Field Battery of 7-pounders and the gunners, after sending a shot by mistake through a Boer ambulance, skilfully hit the tin outbuildings of the station. This evicted Boer and British alike. The latter made off in the direction of their compatriots' guns and the former galloped away to the kopje. Then the Imperial Light Horse entered the station yard, captured the remaining Boer guards and released further British prisoners including the stationmaster and some colliery officials. But the Boers among the kopjes now came to life, and shells from their guns fell among the 7-pounders and smashed up an ammunition wagon. French considered there were too many Boers on the kopjes for an immediate attack with his small force. Abandoning the damaged wagon, he fell back to a position four miles south of Woodcote Farm, where, having covered the armoured train which had followed him out, he tapped the telegraph wire and sent back a message to General White in Ladysmith reporting on the encounter and asking for more troops to enable him to complete his task. Then he fell back further still to where Modder Spruit crossed the route, and awaited the arrival of his promised reinforcements.

At the start of the main operation which followed, French again advanced up the Newcastle road, this time leading with squadrons of the 5th Dragoon Guards and the 5th Lancers. Besides the 7-pounders he now had the 21st and 42nd Field Batteries of 15-pounders which had galloped out from Lady-smith with double teams. Half a battalion of the 1st Manchesters was following by train, and seven companies of the 1st Bn the Devonshire Regiment, and five companies of the 2nd Bn the Gordon Highlanders reached him in the same way.

Opposition was soon encountered. A force of Germans under Colonel Shiel opened fire from a point south of Woodcote Farm. After a brush with the 5th Dragoon Guards they were dispersed by the 42nd Field Battery and made their way eastwards, north of Elandslaagte station, to rejoin the force on the kopjes and play a further part in the battle at the end of the day. On the nearer ridge east of the railway the 5th Lancers, and later the Imperial Light Horse, brushed with Field Cornet Pienaar's scouts. These were more tenacious, and although pushed back by the 5th Lancers continued to skirmish on the British right flank until the main assault was well under way.

About 3 o'clock in the afternoon when all the re-inforcements had arrived, although only a few hours of daylight remained, French decided to attack. The battle area south of the railway station had the general form of a plain surrounded by a horseshoe of hills with the toe to the south. The western arm, from which Pienaar's scouts had been driven off, was to form the start line of the attack. The eastern arm con-sisted of a nest of kopjes in the north changing to a longer hogsback ridge, 300 feet above the plain and steep on the British side but sloping down more gently to the east. Between the kopjes in the north lay the Boer laager, and their two guns were placed in front of the northern summit of the hogsback.

General White gave command of the infantry to his AAG, Colonel Ian Hamilton, who was at Majuba, and in whom he had great confidence. Hamilton showed his qualities from the start. Before the attack he gave his men an inspiring 'pep' talk and put them right 'in the picture'. He told them the Devonshires would attack frontally while the Man-chesters and Gordons worked round the curve of the horseshoe and rolled up the Boer line from the south.

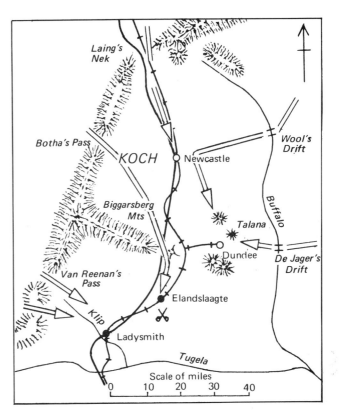

He said he knew they would 'shift' the Boers from their hills before sunset, and that the newsboys on the streets in London would be calling out the glad tidings of victory next day. The men cheered and cheered, waving their helmets, and running out of the ranks and crying, 'We'll do it, sir! We'll do it!' It was a wonderful scene, not easily forgotten by those who took part in it. Moving off from the neigh-bourhood of the railway with squadrons of the 5th Dragoon Guards and 5th Lancers on their left and another of the 5th Lancers with four of the Imperial Light Horse on the right, the infantry advanced eastwards, and by 4 p.m. had occupied the western arm of the horseshoe. The 21st Field Battery galloped up and came into action between the Devonshires in the north and the Manchesters and Gordons in the south and were soon joined by the 42nd Field Battery; and the artillery preparation for the attack began. Pienaar's scouts opened on the gunners who had to turn their pieces and drive them off with shrapnel. Next some mounted Boers passed across the front as if leaving the field in panic. Some Boers did leave the field early on, but their particular move was probably a feint to draw off the British cavalry. It caused the 5th Lancers to move off after them.

As the attack started, an anxious Sir George White arrived with an escort of Natal Mounted Rifles to watch from the heights behind the British line.

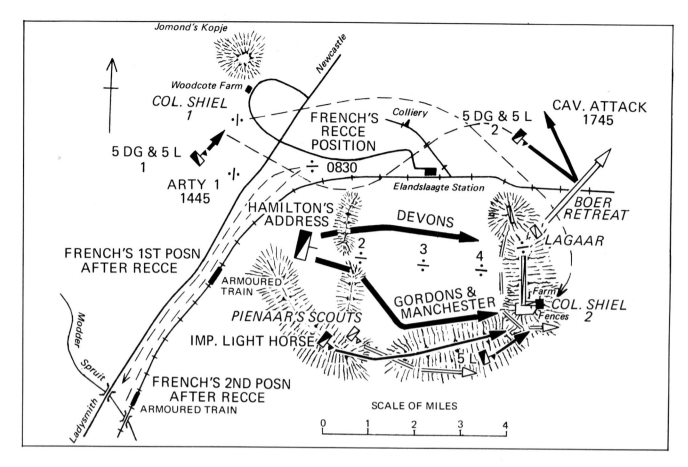

Satisfied with General French's plan and Hamilton's handling of the infantry he remained only a spectator, and when the success of the engagement seemed assured, rode back to Ladysmith in the darkness.

A huge bank of thundercloud edged by the rays of the fast sinking sun overhung the sky behind the Boers, its blackness making every puff of bursting shrapnel clear. Flashes of lightning revealed as sharp lines the summit of the hogsback, and amid the crash of shells, the rattle of rifle-fire and thud of the hooves of the gun teams galloping to the rear came peals of thunder which at times dwarfed the din of battle. Night was being hastened by the storm and the light

was fading, so after a mere half-hour's artillery bombardment, French ordered Hamilton to advance.

The Devonshires went forward in open formation, well spaced frontally between individual soldiers and with wide gaps in depth. Hamilton introduced these formations as a result of his previous experience of fighting the Boers, although it was contrary to continental practice at the time; and he achieved good results thereby: there were only three casualties until the Devonshires reached to within 120 yards of the Boer position. Here, with only eighteen-inch anthills as cover, they came under severe rifle-fire which stopped them in their tracks. Meanwhile the

Opposite: The Boer War, the advance of the cavalry to relieve Kimberley, General French's cavalry brigade approaching the Modder River, 13 February 1900. In the right foreground a helio signalling mirror in being operated. From the painting by G. D. Giles.

Overleaf, above: China, the taking of the Taku forts, 21 August 1860. The forts commanded the entrance to Tientsin; as a result of the failure of the Chinese government to meet their obligations, a mixed Anglo-French force besieged the North Fort. In the picture the 44th and 67th are shown storming the breaches in front while the French (in the blue uniforms) are attacking the ramparts forming the right-hand face of the fort. Painted by Lord Charles Hardinge

Below: The Fight at Abu-Klea 17 January 1885. General Stewart was leading a column about eleven hundred men strong to rescue General Gordon at that time besieged in Khartoum, when, near the Wells of Abu-Klea, some ten thousand Dervishes charged down on his men. The Martini-Henry rifles of the British had no magazines and the Dervishes, fighting with a fanatical disregard of their lives broke into the British square. After a desperate conflict General Stewart's men won the day, but his column was too late to save Gordon. From the painting by W. B. Wollen

Right: The Guards at Landrecies, 25 August 1914. On 25 August during the retreat from Mons the 4th Guards Brigade, supposedly screened by a rearguard, halted for the night at Landrecies. At 8.00 p.m. a strong German force burst into the town. Surprised but undismayed the Guards met the invaders with the bayonet and after a ferocious night action drove them back with heavy loss. From the painting by W. B. Wollen

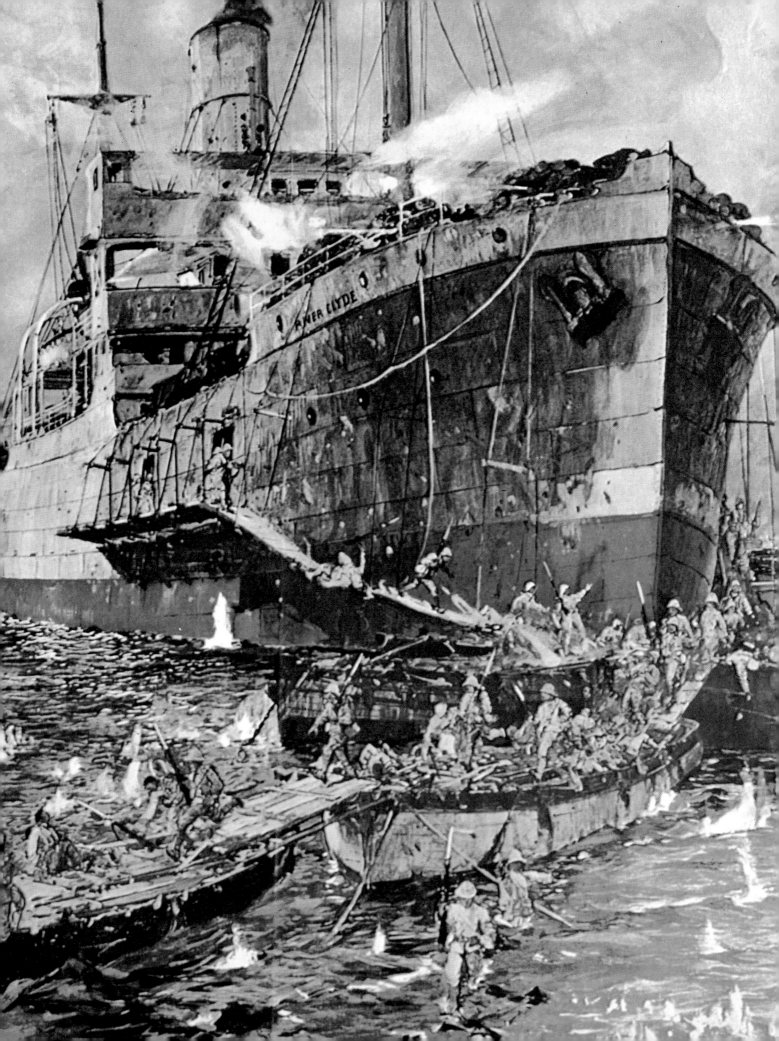

A cavalry patrol. A water-colour by F.J.Waugh

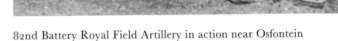

82nd Battery Royal Field Artillery in action near Osfontein

Manchesters and Gordons rounded the bend of the horseshoe, and, facing northwards, were joined by the dismounted Imperial Light Horse. These consisted largely of Johannesburg men, the same *Uitlanders* for whom the war was being fought, and whose failure to go to Jameson's aid had earned them accusations of cowardice and their city the name of 'Judasburg'. They had waited a long time to vindicate their honour, and as the opposing force consisted of Boers from Johannesburg and detachments of the detested Hollanders and Germans, they were eager to storm the position. Doubling forward on foot, they extended the right of the Manchesters. Still further to the right the same squadron of the 5th Lancers that had followed the mounted Boers watched the flank and waited to take up the pursuit. As the Boers eventually retreated northwards, this opportunity came instead to the 5th Dragoon Guards and the other 5th Lancer Squadron to the north.

The assault on the southern flank of the Boers on the hogsback was a difficult one to carry out. The troops had first to cross a grassy open downward slope swept by fire; next came a dip under cover; and this was followed by a rough rock-strewn glacis, full of Boer sharpshooters, and intersected at intervals by the barbed-wire fences of the neighbouring farm. It was, moreover, commanded from positions on the north of the hogsback 'as a butt would command a rifle-range'. The storm broke as the Manchesters reached the dip and for a time the drenching rain blotted out friend and foe alike, but it cleared as they mounted the slope towards the wire fences. Stumbling forward among the boulders, blundering over the bodies of their comrades, they pressed on. Men stopped, lay behind boulders and fired; then rose from cover and rushed forward another few paces. Many fell. The slaughter was worst as they bunched to cut gaps in the wire fences; but after a while the rain of Boer bullets did this job for them. When half the glacis was covered, Shiel's Germans suddenly emerged from among the farm buildings in a flank attack. The Imperial Light Horse shot them down almost to a man; but their bold attack put life into the defenders ahead, and they shot down the Imperial Light Horse in their turn. Half the officers of the Gordons were dead or disabled, and the Manchesters were decimated. Then Ian Hamilton, having ordered the staunch Devonshires to move forward again, as a diversion, rode over to the right to rally the rest. Sweeping forward by encouraging words the skulkers in the rear, he ordered the 'Advance' to be sounded. The drum-major of the Gordons himself stood up to sound the call. It was taken up by all the other buglers left alive, and in the distance could be heard the Devonshires' buglers sounding too. Then with bayonets fixed the British infantry surged forward and swept from the hogsback all the Boers except those manning the two guns, who gallantly went on serving them until the end.

Opposite: Gallipoli, the disembarkation from *The River Clyde*, 25 April 1915. *The River Clyde*, the clumsy forerunner of landing ships, was nothing more than a collier with sally ports cut in her sides. Carrying the Munster Fusiliers and two companies of the Hampshire Regiment, she was run aground about a hundred yards out from 'v' beach. Under a heavy fire barges were positioned to link her with the shore. Turkish machine guns turned the sally ports into a death trap, and few reached the shore alive before nightfall. From a coloured print of the painting by C. Dixon

It was now that Boer white flag tactics were used to British disadvantage. Down in the laager a few Boers stood holding a flag of truce prominently before them, and Ian Hamilton ordered the 'cease fire' to be sounded. For a moment there was a lull, and then suddenly forty or fifty Boers who had lain unseen below the rear of the crest dashed up the slope and emptied their magazines point blank into the un-suspecting groups of British soldiers crowded on the summit. Old General Koch in a black frock-coat and top hat was at their head. Believing the fight over the bewildered British were driven off the crest again, and the guns were retaken and fired at the Devon-shires still climbing stolidly up the front of the hill. Again Hamilton rallied his men, this time with the help of French's ADCs and other officers near the summit. Even General French himself rode up and drove back the waverers. The retreat was stopped. The men charged forward as the Devonshires emerged from the plain below. In a wild three minutes the combined assault overwhelmed the defenders. 'Majuba! Remember Majuba!' the Gordons roared as they charged back. An honest cease-fire now sounded, and the pipes of the Gordons skirled a paean.

A quarter of an hour before the infantry gained the crest the majority of the defenders had begun to stream away to the north. Now was the turn of the 5th Dragoon Guards and 5th Lancers waiting con-cealed east of Elandslaagte Station. As the Boers passed into the gloom across their front the order was given to charge. With levelled lances and bared sabres the two squadrons dashed forward and rode over and through the panic-stricken burghers. Great was their punishment. Two burghers riding on one pony were speared together; another received sixteen lance wounds. The Boers opened out and tried to save themselves by flight; but their little ponies were no match for the big-striding cavalry horses. Some tried to snap their Mausers from the saddle, others threw themselves on the ground vainly imploring mercy. For a mile and a half the cavalry over-rode their flying enemy. Then they rallied and rode back to complete the havoc. It was dark now, and raining again. The troopers were wet through but generously gave their cloaks to the wounded Boers; after which they rode back through the thickening darkness with their little knots of prisoners. Not far from the guns old General Koch was found fatally wounded.

Although small in scale it was a great British victory. It was exceptionally well conducted, and from it, and other successful operations in the war, General French won the reputation which led him to be chosen as Commander-in-Chief of the British Expeditionary Force in 1914. Had there been a few more victories like Elandslaagte early on in the war it might never have assumed its ultimate proportions. During the battle the infantry, gunners and cavalry combined successfully as well as carrying out their separate roles to perfection – the final cavalry charge was a model. The Devonshires fought staunchly and and the rest, though having skulkers, rallied in their bad moments to their officers – and to Hamilton and General French. The high proportion of killed and wounded officers testifies to their gallantry. A lieuten-ant of the Gordons who fell rallying his men and two captains of the Imperial Light Horse gained VCs, and French recommended Hamilton for the VC, but he was considered too senior to receive it.

The Boers fought typically at Elandslaagte. They shot straight, used cover well, hung on till the last moment, and then mounted their ponies and gal-loped away before the final bayonet charge. Their gunners on this occasion were particularly staunch. At Talana and in almost all subsequent engagements in which they were worsted, they removed their artillery long before the assault was pushed home. The white flag was certainly used to advantage by the Boers; but it is possible that General Koch may not have known about the first cease-fire when he staged his counter-attack. The cavalry charge offended the Boers who vowed they would shoot lancers in future if they captured them. According to their rules, they should be able to lie down and fire at an enemy to within twenty yards and then demand and receive individual quarter. Such conditions precluded cavalry and bayonet charges; yet almost only in the use of cold steel were the British superior to the Boers. It is therefore greatly to the credit of the British that they later yielded this advantage and fought the war generally in the Boer way[1].

The British fought exceptionally well at Elands-laagte. Not until the advent of Lord Roberts were they to do so well again. They fought and lost many times: in Natal at Nicholson's Nek, Colenso, Spion Kop and Vaal Krantz; in the west at Stormberg and Magersfontein; but even in defeat much gallantry was displayed; and also many lessons were learnt in this so-called 'last of the Gentlemen's Wars'. The Boers taught the British some 'tricks of the trade', in shooting, in using cover, in camouflage and in digging trenches; and the British were able to put this to good effect in their mightier struggle with the Germans in 1914.

[1] The British discarded the lance and sabre for their cavalry after the first year of war.

Opposite: Above: Lord Kitchener and his staff at Johannesburg, 1900
Below: Botha returns from a raid on Klip River

China. The Boxer revolt. British troops are seen in action against the Chinese rebels. Khaki has replaced the red coats of the previous expedition against the Taku forts

CHAPTER 21

An Interim
1902–14

ANTHONY H. FARRAR-HOCKLEY

Kitchener handed over his command in South Africa in June 1902, and landed at Southampton on 12 July. From the moment of his arrival, he was mobbed and fêted, much as Roberts had been almost eighteen months before. But whereas Roberts, in his modest way, had been able to curtail the round of receptions and dinners in London by pointing out that the war against the Boers continued, Kitchener had neither this reason nor the inclination to reduce the celebration of his triumphal return. Having been created a viscount and promoted to general, with the onset of autumn he departed to India to become Commander-in-Chief.

At this time, Kitchener was 52; Roberts 70. When Kitchener came to say goodbye to his old chief, Roberts remarked: 'You have a great deal to do in India; the whole organisation of the Army there needs overhauling to make it fit for war.' He sighed and added, 'And so does the Army here.'

If any soldier in Britain knew what was needed in training, organisation, not least in arms and equipment to bring the British Army into the twentieth century, it was Roberts.

In 1902, with the war won and Roberts established in the War Office as Commander-in-Chief, it might have seemed that his knowledge, inclination and power to accomplish reform must succeed to the limit of his ambition. Unfortunately, prospects were not what they seemed.

Though Roberts certainly had the knowledge and inclination, he did not have the power. Financial power was vested in the Secretary of State – very properly, since he was answerable to parliament for expenditure – an arrangement fully accepted even by the autocratic Wellington in his time. But over the years, ministers had encroached on many other military departments including operational requirements, organisation and discipline; departments in which Wellington would not have tolerated interference by a politician.

Widely admired though he was, Roberts did not possess Wellington's reputation as the saviour of national independence, and he was less ruthless, less jealous than the Duke in maintaining personal authority. Obliged to work with two successive Conservative ministers, Brodrick and Arnold-Forster, each of whom meddled in details they did not understand, Roberts and the Army might have fared ill but for two factors. The Commander-in-Chief was the most open and generous of men; and he was naturally charming. He thus won his way often.

In armament, Roberts introduced a heavy gun – the 60-pounder – and two new quick-firing guns: the 13-pounder for the horse artillery, the 18-pounder for the field batteries. The short-magazine Lee Enfield, an improved version of the long rifle currently in battalion use, was ordered and adopted for the cavalry as well as infantry. Several committees were organised to examine the transport organisation. A dress review was begun to simplify and reduce the cost of uniforms, particularly the officers'. New barracks were designed, the canteen service was overhauled and the soldiers' pay reviewed. Impatient to begin teaching the tactical principles he had seen ignored or abused in South Africa, Roberts demanded an expansion of training areas.

Willing to indulge Roberts' measures, so manifestly beneficial, Brodrick was nonetheless obliged to remind the little military 'chief' that there were limitations to what could be afforded. '... Remember that in order to provide the improved barracks which you consider necessary and the training grounds in other localities than Salisbury Plain, we still have to press on the Exchequer a loan for at least £10,000,000 beyond the £4,000,000 granted last year.

Your most recent proposals to add 6 officers and 18 non-commissioned officers to each battalion and to raise 8,000 mounted infantry etc. would add £3,500,000 to this loan, besides £2,000,000 of annual expenditure …

I am quite convinced that any further large addition to our Estimates would not only meet with vehement opposition in the Cabinet, but would bring the Government into serious danger in the House of Commons.'

This minute was written by the Secretary of State in reply to proposals made by Roberts almost a year before the war in South Africa ended. After the armistice, there was even less inclination by Government or parliament to spend substantial sums on the armed forces. The Treasury began to press for retrenchment, pointing out that the quantities of war stores remaining should tide the Army over for some time before it resettled to its pre-war level of stocks.

This sanguine view was soon in question. It was only a matter of months later that Lord Elgin's commission on the war in South Africa accumulated evidence to show that peace stocks prior to the war had proved unable to meet the demands of the campaign. There was disquiet, too, in matters of organisation and staff duties. The evidence of Lord Roberts that he was still unable to make the necessary changes due to the opposition of the Secretary of State and Cabinet astonished the commission. One member, Lord Esher, reported to the King: 'It would appear strange that upon a question of purely military organisation, within the Army, involving no expense, the most experienced and eminent soldier of Your Majesty's Empire should have to yield to civilian authority.'

This type of criticism by persons independent of Army or Government assisted the slow movement of reform. A general staff was created, the office of commander-in-chief was abolished and an Army Council instituted, chaired by the secretary of state with the chief of the general staff as his senior professional adviser with direct access to the Cabinet on matters of principle. Ironically, there were those who thought Roberts would resist the changes and, partly due to the temporary absence of the Prime Minister, in bed with influenza, the old field-marshal was dismissed by default.

The 60-pounder gun. Here it is seen being manhandled into action near Ypres

Perhaps it was as well for him; the cabinet had decided that the cost of the Army must be reduced by £5,000,000. Economy could only be achieved by scrapping or reducing the scale of new projects and by a reduction in manpower. Roberts' waning influence was sufficient to prevent the cancellation of the contracts for the new weapons but in or out of office he was not strong enough to defeat the combined weight of Cabinet and Treasury in any other particular.

Quite apart from defence policy, the government was struggling to maintain its authority. At Christmas 1905 the Conservative ministry resigned and the Liberals succeeded.

The new Secretary of State for war was a lawyer, Richard Haldane. His quick mind, energy and ambition combined to master the problems of the ministry but, in the first hour at his desk, he silenced the general staff by asking a key question which none had specifically pondered:

'Yes, this is all very interesting; but what is the Army *for*?'

The answer might have been: to defend the home islands and the Empire; and *(sotto voce)* to keep the Irish under control. There had been no thought of

taking part in war in Europe for decades; but now there was some public opinion that Germany was rearming for war. The cabinet were agreed that the occupation of French Channel ports by the Germans would be unacceptable. To prevent this, Haldane gave instructions to Grierson, Director of Military Operations, to open staff talks secretly with his contemporaries in Paris and Brussels towards British defence assistance. Notwithstanding a cool reception by the Belgians, anxious not to compromise their neutrality, there was a general Anglo-French agreement that in the event of a German attack on France or Belgium a British Expeditionary Force of six infantry divisions, a cavalry division, two corps and one army headquarters and a supporting base should be sent to their aid.

It was realised that this contribution would be a small one against the tens of divisions that France or Germany would be able to mobilise for war; but at least the British contribution would be one of quality. For unlike the great continental armies, the British units composed of long service volunteers were able to undertake advanced training over the years and, for the most part, had already a degree of experience in battle. Yet the War Office staff were apprehensive at providing even seven divisions. The demands of the Empire were still considerable; home defence could not be neglected; and the Liberals were obliged to continue the Conservative plan to cut the regular Army whose numbers had become swollen during the Boer War. Thirty-five thousand men were to be reduced in the establishment – though, as units were under-recruited, this was to a great extent a paper transaction and there was little redundancy.

Haldane decided to compensate for these cuts by raising a new and improved home defence force in place of the old militia. After some difficulties, county associations were organised to raise and administer the volunteers and, in April 1908 the Territorial and Reserve Forces Act became law. It enabled the War Office to raise for the first time a citizens' reserve army, comprehensively organised as fourteen divisions and a cavalry brigade, grouped concurrently for command, training and administration in convenient sectors of the kingdom. Professional skills were to be imparted by a tiny cadre of regulars and they had a gigantic task to train the flood of volunteers. Uniforms were adequate but arms and equipment were from stocks too antiquated or unserviceable for the regular Army. Nonetheless it was the beginning of a solution to Britain's lack of reserve military forces.

Throughout this time, Lord Roberts was campaigning for National Service. Some inside the War Office, like Henry Wilson, believed that conscription was both a necessary and practicable policy for the country. Others, like Douglas Haig, Director of Staff Duties and later of Military Training, believed it to be desirable but could see no hope of gaining public support for it. Thus he supported Haldane and gave him a good deal of assistance in launching the Territorial Army. By 1910, almost 300,000 men had begun simple training in the new reserve.

The training of the regular army was also prospering; partly due to Roberts' arrangements begun in 1902, partly to the ideas and energy of officers who had seen service with Roberts in South Africa. It was at its best in the regiments where, year by year, the subtle skills of fieldcraft and shooting were enhanced. The problem was to train senior commanders and their staffs. Expense limited the scope and duration of annual manoeuvres; hence, the higher direction never lived without camp comforts and were never taxed to exhaustion.

Typical of the British system, but untypical of the fashion in the remainder of Europe, the British Army remained outside politics. The struggles of the Conservative Party to regain power and the Liberals to retain it at Westminster occasioned little interest, although the majority of officers were by tradition Conservative. Apart from the most senior officers, the distant political adventures in the Balkans or Africa that threatened war in Europe made little impact on their lives. One persistent matter of domestic dispute, however, pulled officers and men at home suddenly into the cockpit of party politics in the early part of 1914: Home Rule for Ireland.

Determined to do what seemed to be wanted and needed by the Irish people in this ancient issue, the Prime Minister, Asquith, led a united party towards a Home Rule Bill. Moved much by the wish to destroy the Liberal Government and a little by anxiety for Protestant Ulster as a minority in Catholic Ireland, the Conservatives encouraged the people of Ulster to resist Home Rule by force. The 'Ulster Volunteers' were said to number 100,000. Slowly, the government were obliged to consider the use of troops to support the civil power. Mr Churchill, First Lord of the Admiralty, expressed a more extreme intention than Asquith's when he warned the Unionists publicly at Bradford on 14 March, 1914, not to threaten rebellion. 'If that is what is to be done,' he remarked, 'let us go forward together and put these grave matters to the proof.' Warships were ordered to Irish waters: there seemed no doubt of naval loyalty. But for the Army, containing so many Protestant Irishmen and Unionists – some of whom were Ulstermen – it was another matter.

Colonel Jack Seely had succeeded Haldane at the War Office. The former reported to the Prime Minister on 20 March:

'I discussed the question of officers' resignation with Chief of the Imperial General Staff[1] (Sir John French), Adjutant-General and Sir A. Paget (Commander-in-Chief, Ireland) yesterday. Paget strongly urged that ... where officers have direct family connections ... in Ulster, so that in the event of serious trouble arising their future private relations might be irretrievably compromised if they were engaged with our troops, they should be permitted to remain behind on leave or with details ... In all other cases, he wished to be able to say that any officer hesitating to comply with orders or threatening to resign should be removed ...'

Paget crossed to Kingstown by the night boat on 19 March and sent for all local formation commanders on Friday morning, the 20th. Prominent among those who attended the meeting in the Royal Hospital in Dublin were Major-General Fergusson, commander of the 5th Division and Hubert Gough, 3rd Cavalry Brigade commander from the garrison at the Curragh. General Paget opened by a review of the situation. Unintelligent and emotionally confused, what he said was misleading. The need for precautionary moves was mentioned, the necessity for restraint, but there were intermittent references to the country being imminently 'ablaze'. Eventually, he made his listeners an offer: for themselves and, through them, to their officers. Excepting the men domiciled in Ulster, would they accept orders to march to Ulster or would they refuse and be dismissed?

This was an extraordinary option to offer, not at all what had been intended by Seely or French whose instructions had been meant to cover the eventuality of a refusal following substantive orders. Unhappily, Fergusson went away to put the matter to his officers, as did Gough. But Gough had no doubt of his own intentions.

'If I had been ordered north, I should have gone,' he said afterwards. 'As I was given a choice, I refused.' The bulk of his officers joined him. Asquith received the news while playing bridge after dinner and he hurried away to order Gough and his regimental commanders to London.

In London on Sunday the 22nd, first Ewart, the Adjutant-General, then French, finally Seely attempted to get Gough to withdraw his resignation.

[1] The word 'imperial' was added in 1909.

Peacetime life might be enervating. Here a Connaught Ranger officer is adding to the gaiety of an officers' Mess dinner by jumping his horse over the dining room table

At hand always was Henry Wilson, Director of Military Operations, who had exacerbated the crisis by secretly telling the leader of the Unionists what the War Office were doing. Gough would not be browbeaten by Ewart and Seely or persuaded by French. The only terms on which he would withdraw were written assurances from government that they would not use the Army to coerce Ulster. Anxious to correct matters, Asquith personally drafted a note to this end, the principle of which was weakened by a late addition of Seely's and an endorsement by French. Gough returned in triumph to the Curragh. Asquith published a disclaimer concerning Seely's postscript, and Seely, French and Ewart resigned.

Ireland remained the direct responsibility of Westminster.

Now began a memorable spring and summer of glorious weather. A grand exercise was planned for September, when the main Army would withdraw across the river Severn under pressure of a numerically superior enemy. Much preparation was complete when the murder of the Austrian archduke, Franz Ferdinand, at Sarajevo in June became suddenly, through July, an international issue. Russia and Austria-Hungary were at enmity in the Balkans. Germany could not afford to see Austria crushed by Russia. France was committed to assist Russia; and Germany would not guarantee to respect Belgian neutrality in war against France. The British Government felt obliged to fight for Belgian integrity. In this way, at the beginning of August 1914 war began between the powers of Europe.

N

CHAPTER 22

The Outbreak of the First World War 1914: Into Battle

ANTHONY H. FARRAR-HOCKLEY

On Monday, 3 August, a Bank Holiday, telegrams were sent out to mobilise the British Army. Weapons and equipment not permitted to be in service in peace time were issued from the mobilisation stores depots; live ammunition was broken out. Regular infantry battalions, cavalry regiments, gunner batteries, engineer companies and the administrative corps took in their reinforcements of men and horses and made ready to move by train to the ports of embarkation. Territorials and Yeomanry assembled at their drill centres.

In London, the Prime Minister sent an urgent telephone call to Kitchener at Dover to prevent his departure to Egypt. Two days later, Field Marshal Earl Kitchener (as he had become) was appointed Secretary of State for War, the first serving soldier to sit in a cabinet since Monk in 1660. At once, his political colleagues and military subordinates had an indication of his methods. Prophesying correctly that the war would be a long one and that millions of men would be needed to take the field, he announced his intention of raising immediately the first 100,000. The Territorials were set aside: '... useless, no better than the militia.' The Special Reserve was discounted: '... half-baked and out of date.' All the careful work of Haldane and his staff was set aside and soon posters of Kitchener appeared everywhere, his finger pointing with uncanny directness at the onlooker, impressing on him the caption above: 'Your King and Country need YOU'. From the land, the factories, the shops men poured in to the recruiting centres, some afraid that the war might be over before Christmas. There were no billets, no blankets, no weapons, no instructors or administrators to receive them. Chaos ensued.

Meantime, Sir John French, restored to the Army

by the demands of war, was passing over to France as Commander-in-Chief of the British Expeditionary Force. With him went Archibald Murray as his chief of staff, Henry Wilson as the sub-chief and the gruff 'Wully' Robertson as quartermaster-general. Kitchener had withheld two of the divisions for home defence, the 4th and 6th, sending the 1st Corps under Haig with the 1st and 2nd Divisions from Aldershot and Smith-Dorrien's 2nd Corps with the 3rd Division from Salisbury Plain, the 5th from Ireland. Allenby commanded the cavalry division. Despite his wish to 'cancel all arrangements and begin again', Kitchener was defeated in his proposals for the BEF. He was obliged to release the 4th Division and to concede that Sir John's command should deploy forward to Maubeuge and Le Cateau rather than in rear at Amiens. Sir John was not sorry to leave England and be free of Kitchener.

The French Army had mobilised more than a million men on its frontiers, about a quarter of these covering the northern Ardennes while the remainder prepared to hurl themselves across into Germany. This simple strategy might have succeeded but for two factors: the Germans had guessed what the French would do and had made excellent preparations to throw them back again. By 23 August, France had lost the battle of her frontiers and 300,000 men.

The German plan was to hold the French with rather less than half their divisions while wheeling the remainder through Belgium into northern France. On 23 August, as the French attempted to recover from their defeat, the British Expeditionary Force was in the mining town of Mons, a few miles inside the Belgian border. On their right was the French army covering the Ardennes and Sir John

Opposite above: 16th Lancers on the march, September 1914
Below: 'J' Battery Royal Horse Artillery in open positions, 1914

211

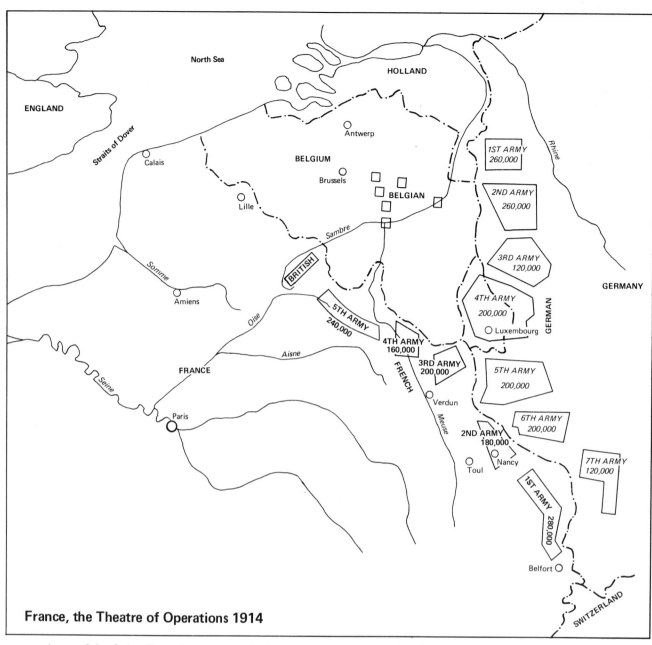

France, the Theatre of Operations 1914

was mistrustful of the French commander's intentions. He knew, too, that a large German force was approaching thanks to the watch kept by his cavalry and aeroplanes. The two British corps were told to cancel all plans for advance and to make a defensive line. Quite early in the morning of the 23rd, the leading corps of the German First Army blundered unawares on to this.

As it happened, Haig's corps remained unengaged, the collision having been made with Smith-Dorrien's men along the line of the Mons canal. Here and amongst the pit gear and slag heaps, mean mining houses and alleys, the British expert riflemen fired with accuracy into the advancing lines of German infantry. Even when a second German corps came up and the numerous enemy guns and howitzers were doubled, the British 2nd Corps did not break. But by

evening, the German commander, von Kluck, had discovered that the northern British flank was open and he had only to march round it with a third corps to envelop the British line. The BEF were facing 260,000 men. Moreover, Sir John received news late in the evening that the French on his right were withdrawing without regard for his position. He ordered his own force to withdraw.

The staff work in his headquarters, 30 miles behind the troops, was poor; and little better in Smith-Dorrien's corps. While Haig's fresh divisions drew back unscathed, the 3rd and 5th had to break contact and inevitably a number were left fighting until they were overwhelmed. All the troops were tired; they had been marching for days in an unusually hot summer; many were reservists. Two days later, the 1st Corps returned to Landrecies, where a minor incident unnerved Haig and he called for assistance. But it was not he who was threatened. Again, it was towards Smith-Dorrien that von Kluck's army was moving directly and late at night on the 25th, at Le Cateau, Allenby found 2nd Corps commander to warn him that, unless he moved his men on at once, they would be attacked at dawn.

Smith-Dorrien's battalions and batteries were scattered over a wide area at Le Cateau. They were very tired. He did not believe that he had time to find and wake the sleeping units in the darkness, issue fresh orders and move them off before daylight. The alternative, which he accepted, was to let them sleep and then fight it out before they marched again next day. Allenby agreed that his cavalry division should fight with him and, a reward for Smith-Dorrien's decisiveness, out of the night came the 4th Division, newly arrived and the 19th Brigade from the rear.

When von Kluck attacked next morning, in great strength, he was ill-informed about the position of the shallow British trenches and his assaults and supporting bombardments were delivered at an oblique angle to his waiting enemy. The first assault was thus a failure but more followed and gradually the run of the British line became known and there was very heavy fighting. By the late afternoon the Germans were no longer pressing their advance with vigour. Unit by unit, 2nd Corps began to withdraw, many battalions succeeding in slipping away with that skill and discipline in fieldcraft which they had practised so often over the years. As at Mons, a few units did not receive the order to pull back or could not do so and they remained to fight to the end in the dusk.

If the fighting skill of the regimental officers and men was evidence of their long and detailed training, the actions now of Sir John and his staff proved how much they had needed tuition and practice in the higher direction of war. Sir John could think of nothing else but a withdrawal to the coast and evacuation from France. He deemed the campaign to be lost. He did not realise – few realised – however, what reserves of strength had been tapped in the French now that the aggressor was on their soil; or how resilient and resourceful were the French staffs in the regrouping and movement of their forces. Joffre, the massive, inscrutable French Commander-in-Chief began to form a new army on the left of the BEF while sacking the general on their right. In London, Kitchener read Sir John's gloomy reports and decided, with cabinet approval, to meet him in Paris. They had a painful interview but the upshot was to keep the BEF in conformity generally with

their ally. Fighting, marching, skirmishing, the weary British soldiers continued on their way along the dusty French roads, among deserted villages, through fields unharvested, picking up rations from dumps placed out at random by the resourceful 'Wully' Robertson, until they reached the Marne and Joffre was ready to turn to fight a decisive battle.

Here Joffre appealed to Sir John to join his offensive.

'Monsieur le maréchal, it is France who begs you to help her,' he said. Next day, slowly, under orders given grudgingly by Murray, the BEF turned back.

The weaknesses of the German plan were now apparent. Their distant general headquarters had insufficient communications to control seven armies in France. The soldiers could not march and fight over 25 miles each day for weeks without relief; the Belgians would not leave their railways and canals undamaged for the carriage of supplies.

Remote from general headquarters, von Kluck began to make strategic plans of his own devising; his colleague alongside would not conform. The weary German soldiers did not expect the French to counter-attack with such ardour and they began to lack ammunition. On the night of 9 September, in drizzling rain, the German armies began to draw back.

If the French and British forces had followed quickly and fallen on their enemy again, they would have scattered them, perhaps for ever in that campaign. But they could not: the French were too weary; the British inadequately directed. In these circumstances, the Germans withdrew without diffi-

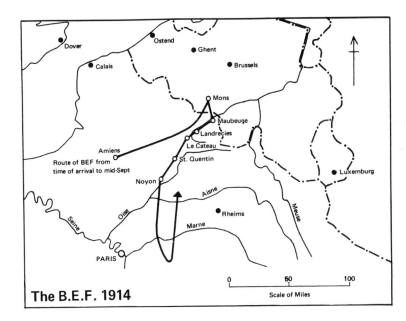

The B.E.F. 1914

The 1st Battalion the King's Own (Royal Lancaster) Regiment manning a front line trench at Ste. Marguerite, 22 September 1914. The trench is a rudimentary forerunner of the trench systems that were to spread across France. It is shallow and without a fire-step; it lacks bays and so would be vulnerable to fire from a flank; however, left foreground, there is an entrance to a crude form of dug-out. *Right:* Officers of the 1st Battalion the Cameronians conferring at the Battle of Le Cateau, 25 August 1914

culty to the heights on the right bank of the Aisne and there, reinforced by a corps released from the siege of Maubeuge, rebuffed the British when they attacked across the river.

The intensity of the Germans' struggle for a quick victory, the desperation of the French defence had drawn the bulk of the armies towards the river Marne. The weak counter-offensive returned the allies to the Oise and Aisne. Then, as the ferment diminished, and the commanders on either side considered what they should do next, it became apparent to each that the expanse of France between the Oise and the Channel coast was empty of troops. At once, the French began to transfer divisions to this western zone, to exploit the enemy's open flank. But the Germans did exactly the same and so, by a continuing process of confrontation, the line extended through Arras and northward again towards Flanders.

In this process, the BEF became sandwiched between the French armies. Their Commander-in-Chief and many of his staff wished to return again to the extreme left of the allied line where, close to the Channel ports and the Royal Navy, they might engage in open warfare once more. A transfer was proposed to Joffre and, after some demur, he agreed.

'I believe the decisive battle of the war is going to be fought here,' Sir John said to his staff as they assembled in Flanders. 'And we are going to play a major part in it.' He was in a cheerful mood. A meeting on 10 October with General Foch, the aggressive French northern army group commander, had resulted in agreement that the BEF should advance at once. The French believed that the only opposition was 'a cloud of cavalry'. Against this, the British army

was now a formidable body: Pulteney's 3rd Corps – 4th and 6th Divisions – was added to Haig's and Smith-Dorrien's; and from Ostend and Ghent, Rawlinson's 4th Corps – the 3rd Cavalry and 7th Divisions – was marching to join the BEF at Ypres. Allenby's cavalry had also expanded to two divisions and was now spread out to screen the British deployment into Belgium.

'The enemy's advanced cavalry appear to have fallen back,' was the opening remark of the British operation order for 12 October. 'It is the C-in-C's intention to follow the enemy tomorrow with a view to bringing him to action.'

Next day, orders for the 13th noted that 'It is the Commander-in-Chief's intention to continue the advance, passing the Army to the north of Lille and driving the enemy before it.' On the 17th, 'The main force of the enemy's cavalry is reported to have fallen back ... Lille is reported to be entrenched and strongly held ... The Commander-in-Chief intends to carry out a vigorous attack against the enemy in conjunction with the French forces on the right and left of the British Army.'

This succession of orders gives the impression of a week of steady progress, such as would justify the confidence of Sir John French and his colleague, Foch. What both men were doing was to ignore the evidence of a deteriorating situation. Their forces were not advancing steadily; and though this was initially due to the inability of a number of formation commanders to take advantage of their opportunities they were now inhibited by the resistance of the enemy. Agents and refugees told of many troop trains arriving in rear. British Intelligence intercepted a German wireless message referring to 'Fourth Army', which was believed to be many miles to the south. French and British air reconnaissance reported dense marching columns in the east. On 20 October, the accuracy of these various pieces of information became clear.

Falkenhayn, the Chief of the German General Staff, had decided on one final offensive for 1914 which aimed to clear Belgium and capture Calais. He had brought into the line from Germany eight new divisions of young men who had had little training but were ardent to join the battle. These with a corps of veterans formed the new Fourth Army under Duke Albrecht of Württemberg. Simultaneously, Crown Prince Rupprecht of Bavaria was attacking with his Sixth Army from Arras to the Belgian border. The armies locked for a second great struggle.

The British trenches were shallow and badly placed. The Germans had little shrapnel for their artillery but quantities of high explosive which demolished trenches, often burying their occupants alive. Massed German infantry advanced behind this shellfire, the soldiers singing, sometimes accompanied by their bands. The skill of the British riflemen was backed by a highly trained artillery but shell stocks soon began to dwindle. There were few reinforcements to replace the dead and wounded; companies shrank to the size of platoons. After a week of fighting for 10 to 12 hours a day, the German offensive ceased.

Falkenhayn had not finished, however. Transferring yet more divisions from the south, he had formed a special force, General Fabeck's Group, to break through the BEF's positions, while Crown Prince Rupprecht and Duke Albrecht continued to press the French and Belgians on either side.

At 5.30 on the morning of 29 October, a silent attack began out of the darkness. Aided initially by surprise, subsequently by their mass of infantry, the Germans began to force their way into the trench lines, continuing with fresh forces on the 30th. Some of the British battalions were reduced to fewer than 50 men in this fighting and had to be withdrawn. On the 31st the weight of the German numbers – 7 to 1 – proved too much. At noon the last British position in Gheluvelt village was lost and the road to Ypres was open.

Behind the line was confusion. Shells had landed on the buildings shared by the headquarters of 1st and 2nd Divisions, killing or wounding the commanders and staffs. Fortunately, a nearby brigade commander was able to find the one reserve battalion, 2nd Worcesters, which he committed to counter-attack Gheluvelt. Three hundred and fifty men

The Battle of the Marne. First line transport of the 1st Battalion the Middlesex Regiment under shell-fire at Signy Signets. The watercart has been riddled with shell splinters and the soldier in the centre foreground has been wounded

set off across open country, were scourged by shells until they reached the woods round the chateau, where they assaulted and destroyed a force of 1,200 Germans relaxing after their victory. The line was resealed. Sensing crisis, Haig rode forward into the foremost sector, quietly, deliberately, his presence calming the remnants of the battalions holding the line. Sir John had gone to Foch to ask for French reinforcement, 'otherwise', he said, 'there is nothing left for me to do but go up and be killed with 1st Corps.'

Of the 84 British battalions on 1 November, 18 had fewer than 100 men, 31 fewer than 200, 26 had 200–300, 9 only exceeded 300 but none had more than 450, that is, half strength. Foch responded loyally and relieved a further sector of the British line to permit the regrouping of the British force. Some of these reliefs were still in process when Falkenhayn attempted one last attack on 10 November with thirteen divisions between Messines and Gheluvelt. Of these, the most successful was Winckler's Guard which, 'grey ghosts coming out of the clouds of morning fog,' forced a breach between British and French positions on the morning of 11 November and pierced the line. But the numbers of German guardsmen who survived the action were few and a sweeping action led by the 52nd Light Infantry cleared them completely. A wet night followed, the rain cold and driving, during which each side resited their lines and the battle ended.

It was also the end of the old Army. Believing that an army of so few divisions was worthless, the German emperor had described the BEF as 'a contemptible little army'. In the defence of Ypres it fought and held the line at a mighty disadvantage in numbers which was never to be suffered, never to be matched by any army again in the war.

CHAPTER 23

1915: The Realities of Trench Warfare Revealed

ANTHONY H. FARRAR-HOCKLEY

It was a bitter winter in Flanders in 1914. The seasonal cold, the reeking damp of the low-lying Flanders plain were keenly felt in the harsh circumstances of war.

In mid-November, there was snow. 'Wully' Robertson, quartermaster-general to the BEF, wrote to his counterpart in the War Office,

'There are many cases of frostbite … The men never grumble at having too large boots, as they can always put on two or three pairs of socks.'

Supply of uniform clothing was still inadequate but the British public had responded generously to appeals for woollens of all types. Without them, it is doubtful if the battalions could have remained in the trenches; for the frost was succeeded in December by rain and positions on the low ground were at once swamped.

There was, unfortunately, nowhere else for the men to go, except to withdraw altogether from Flanders, thereby making the Germans a present of Belgium and rendering Calais unusable. Yet defence was not only a matter of manning the trenches, but of having the means to fight if attacked. Trained men were still lacking, so were barbed wire, grenades, mortars, and above all, shells. 'It is sad to think,' Robertson remarked on 24 November, 'that we have provided guns which fire ten or more rounds in a minute, while our output is less than ten rounds (per gun) in 24 hours.' At the BEF Base at Le Havre, the workshops were set to manufacturing makeshift grenades with jam tins, gun-cotton, nails and safety fuse.

The French and German armies were, of course, similarly short of war material but less critically than the British. Asquith's government was now paying for the mistake of allowing Kitchener to appeal in-

discriminately for volunteers. On 1 September, for example, 30,000 men enlisted and day by day thousands more clamoured to be taken. A high proportion were skilled artisans from all industries; hence, factories were drained of labour at the very moment that government was ordering huge quantities of war stores. Thanks to their excellent mobilisation arrangements, the Germans actually had a surplus of labour in 1914 which they were able to direct to industry, agriculture or the military depots as needed. By December, Kitchener had been obliged to make use of the despised Special Reserve to obtain instructors and administrators for his new armies; and to employ units of the Territorial Force and Yeomanry – almost all of whom had volunteered for service overseas – to reinforce the BEF or to relieve regular troops in distant garrisons. On 26 December, the BEF reorganised into First Army under Douglas Haig, and Second Army under Smith-Dorrien with a total of eleven British and Indian infantry divisions, excluding Allenby's cavalry corps and the Indian cavalry. The fresh and eager Territorials gave just sufficient easement to the thin ranks of the regulars for the short rest and refitting they needed.

Hard frost returned at Christmas, more readily borne than the floods in the trenches. The catholic spirit of the Christian feast, the arrival of special comforts for Christmas, the lack of malice between the opposing soldiers caused officers and men at many points among the forward trenches to cross spontaneously to the other side quietly to shake hands, sing a few carols together and perhaps pose in a group photograph.

The new year brought sterner policies.

With problems on the Russian front, the Germans were obliged to remain on the defensive in the west.

Opposite: Douglas Haig, afterwards Field Marshal Earl Haig

Recruits of the Royal Fusiliers on the march at Battersea Park

Joffre was determined to breach his enemy's line and began a series of offensives in Artois and Champagne. Sir John was not reluctant to take his share of the attack but preferred independent action. Thus he persisted in March in attempting to capture Aubers ridge, towards Lille, even though the French had postponed their complementary operation. The village of Neuve Chapelle was taken but the ridge was not: the cost was 12,000 casualties over three days. Ammunition stocks were depleted. The prospect of full replenishment was poor as the cabinet in London had approved the opening of a new front at Gallipoli to capture Constantinople. Troops and ordnance were withdrawn even from Flanders for the venture.

This diversion of effort was understandably resented by those directing the BEF. 'Wully' Robertson had succeeded Murray as Sir John's chief of staff and his shrewd mind saw that, given the leadership and material necessary, the Territorials and volunteers swelling the remnant of regular soldiers were capable of breaking through the enemy defences. He began to husband resources towards a second operation against Aubers Ridge and Festubert in cooperation with the French Tenth Army in Artois.

Before plans were complete or stocks concentrated, however, the Germans took a sudden initiative and obtained an unexpected success.

Believing, like his opponents, that decisive victory was to be found only on the western front, von Falkenhayn had supported an offensive against Russia with reluctance. Unable to mount a spring offensive against the French and British, he was not content to leave them in peace. Short of men, he had a new weapon which he hoped might facilitate the initial assault: poison gas.

Throughout 22 April, the German artillery shelled the British and French trenches in the Ypres salient, the mighty 320-mm. guns concentrating on the old city through which came almost all allied supplies. At 5 p.m., amongst the black smoke of the bursting German shells, there arose 'two curious greenish-yellow clouds on the ground on either side of Langemarck ... These clouds spread laterally, joined up, and, moving before a light wind, became a bluish-white mist, such as is seen over water meadows on a frosty night.'

It was chlorine. Duke Albrecht of Württemberg and his Fourth Army had waited almost ten days for a favourable wind. Lightly blown, the toxic mixture

dispersed over and descended into the dugouts of two French divisions – one Algerian, the other of home defence reservists. Then, 'men streamed past me, reeling and retching, eyes bloodshot and weeping, some with blistered flesh.' This British observer saw the opening of four miles of the line between the left of Smith-Dorrien's Army and the Belgians to the north. Despite continuing releases of gas, the 1st Canadian Division filled and held the gap with a thin line of men, though the effort was to lose them

Christmas Day 1914. Two German officers are fraternising with a British private at Ploegsteert

a third of their infantry. Even this effort would have been unavailing but for the failure of the Germans to follow up their advantage. '... Leaders and troops regarded with mistrust the still untried means of offence ...' Too late, they committed their reserves but captured only small features, local defences. None were of importance but, in company with the French, whom Foch ordered to 'recapture every metre lost and add a kilometre more,' the British became engaged in the same fruitless endeavour. Simply to maintain the line, much of it already directly exposed to German observation, over 2,000 officers, more than 57,000 soldiers fell dead or wounded.

The second battle of Ypres ended in mid-May. Then Smith-Dorrien proposed to withdraw up to a mile or so for tactical advantage and Sir John, giving way to numerous petty, personal grudges, dismissed him.

Persisting in attack, Foch launched the delayed Tenth Army offensive at this time, seeking to capture the long crest of Vimy Ridge. While still struggling at Ypres, Sir John loyally tried to help his ally once more at Aubers Ridge and Festubert, achieving a trivial success for the loss of 27,000 men. The French artillery gave extensive support to compensate for the

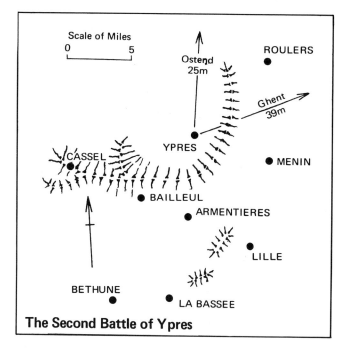

The Second Battle of Ypres

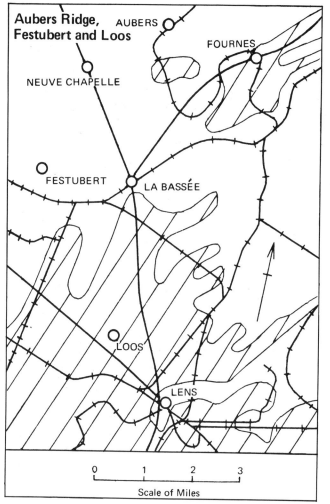

Aubers Ridge, Festubert and Loos

lack of British shells. At last, Kitchener's secretive and personal authority in armament production was withdrawn and the dynamic Lloyd George became minister of munitions. Shortly, shell production rose dramatically.

The spring fighting – Aubers Ridge, Neuve Chapelle, Festubert and the deadly struggle at Ypres – had cost the BEF more than 100,000 casualties. Sir John, Robertson and his assistants in the operations staff at GHQ, were not without compassion for those lost but believed still in an early victory. At Festubert, the deception plan had permitted a successful surprise attack. Might this concept not succeed equally on a grander scale with a wider success?

What troubled Robertson now was the inexperience of troops, commanders and staffs; and the fact, disclosed by air reconnaissances, that the Germans were constructing complete trench systems as much as three miles behind the established line. Sir John's vanity and extremes of mood worried him no less. The British Commander-in-Chief and Kitchener were at enmity; the army commanders in the BEF did not trust their chief's judgement. Robertson was relieved when Asquith and Kitchener came to France on 6 July to discuss strategic policy with French ministers and Joffre. The latter was persuaded that the BEF would not be allowed to join his next offensive until the outcome at Gallipoli was known. Exactly a month later, the final advance against the Turks failed by a narrow margin. Kitchener returned to France on 16 August to announce that henceforth the western front would have first call on resources. Joffre followed with a pressing request for action to support his Tenth Army in September.

As at Aubers Ridge and Festubert, Haig was given command of the offensive. The chosen zone was from the La Bassée canal south to the mining villages of Loos and Lens. Unhappy at the width of front and lack of time to prepare and train his troops, and aware of the enemy's advantage in artillery, Haig accepted that poison gas might compensate him. 'Without gas,' he wrote to Robertson, 'the front of our attacks must be reduced to what our guns can satisfactorily prepare, with the results normally attendant on small fronts; namely, concentration of hostile guns at point of attack, large losses and small progress. In my opinion, under no circumstances, should our forthcoming attack be launched without the aid of gas.'

Early in the morning of 25 September, Haig stepped outside his headquarters, from which could be seen and heard the flash and roar of his guns in bombardment. Holding up a Turkish cigarette, he watched the light wind blow the smoke slowly towards the enemy.

It was enough; but only just enough. In the northern sector, the wind backed, containing the gas over British lines. In the centre and south its effect was successful and the assault divisions advanced easily over 8,000 yards of the line, the 15th Division almost breaching the German defence zone round Hill 70. The moment had come for the reserve divisions to pass through.

Astonishingly, Sir John was 25 miles in rear without even a telephone to Haig's forward headquarters. The reserves were directly under GHQ contrary to

Robertson's advice and Haig's request. When at last the two divisions were sent forward from a concentration area far in rear, the Germans had recovered. The new, unfledged infantry arriving in darkness to exploit the first success were shelled and scattered. The Guards Division, underpinned by veterans, saved Sir John from a serious counter-attack.

It was too much to be borne. Under pressure from the King, Kitchener and his colleagues in cabinet, and much to the relief of his subordinates, Sir John was posted to command the Home Forces. Long ambitious to succeed him, Haig became Commander-in-Chief of the BEF.

A wiring party setting out

CHAPTER 24

The Somme and Passchendaele: Ordeal by Fire 1916–17

ANTHONY H. FARRAR-HOCKLEY

Well aware that Joffre would return to the offensive as soon as possible and that the British armies were receiving in growing numbers the tens of thousands of Kitchener's new divisions, Falkenhayn asked himself, late in 1915, what strategy might offer him victory in the west. His appreciation led him to the view that he must bring about the collapse of the French Army by forcing it into a battle of attrition. Seeking a sector which the French would defend to the death, he chose Verdun.

Thus he began on 21 February 1916 to shell the ring of largely disarmed fortresses shielding the citadel on the Meuse and the interconnecting trench systems. Throughout March, April and May, the French defended their positions unstintingly as Falkenhayn had predicted.

A Franco-British offensive had been under consideration prior to the opening of this immense German offensive. Joffre's choice was the area of the river Somme. Personally inclined towards a separate British operation in Flanders, Haig agreed for the sake of unity to join his ally. But the persistent demand for divisions at Verdun soon made it plain that the role of sponsor on the Somme had passed to the British with limited co-operation from one French army, the Sixth. July had been agreed as the earliest period for opening operations but Haig did not believe that his unfledged troops would be trained adequately before 15 August. Mentioning this date to Joffre on 26 May, he was astonished by the reaction of the habitually impassive French chief. 'If you do nothing until then, the French Army will cease to exist,' he shouted.

The pressure on Haig was acute: Verdun might fall and the French public were asking everywhere for British intervention; the Russians in the east, the Italians in the south were about to open great offensives.

Reluctantly, he agreed to assault on 1 July.

There were now no shortages of anything necessary for war-making by the BEF, with one important exception: experience. The consequences of the lean years in training higher commanders and staffs were now to be seen: generals at all levels and their assistants struggled to learn as they operated. Administrative work, particularly work of preparation for a great offensive, was undertaken successfully by men brought in from great commercial and industrial concerns. They had comparable experience on which to draw. But no civilian and few professional soldiers knew how to conduct the refined tactical training needed to breach the formidable German defences. The art of controlling several hundred thousand infantry soldiers was certainly not known by any general under Haig's command. At regimental level, commanding officers were burdened with responsibilities which their officers were too raw to accept. As a late, desperate measure, Haig wrote policy notes as to the minor tactics his infantry should adopt when they advanced. But his advice presupposed standards in leadership, fieldcraft, weapon training achieved only by long service regular soldiers. On the morning of 1 July, the trenches were packed with men unused to bearing arms, about to be launched in the most hazardous operation of war: a deliberate frontal attack.

The guns, howitzers, mortars had pounded the German line for 7 days – two more than planned due to poor visibility and recognition that the enemy wire was not cut. Just after 7 a.m. on 1 July they lifted and the infantry went forward '... in line, the easiest formation for control, the safest in ensuring that no

Opposite: A scene in a communication trench just before an attack, July 1916

one is caught in our own shellfire.' But it was not the safest. Almost everywhere the Germans managed to ascend from the deep shelters underground to man their broken defences. The German machine guns swept the ranks of British infantry, often impeded by uncut barbed wire; the German shellfire raked those coming behind in support and the packed reserves crowding up into the British trenches. By that night, 57,470 soldiers were casualties, 20,000 being dead.

Neither Haig nor Rawlinson knew immediately what had happened. Telephone cables in the forward area were frequently cut by shellfire and there was a reluctance in the higher headquarters to accept the horrible news that began to pour in. Thus for two days, the attacks continued. On 3 July Joffre and Foch called on Haig, the latter telling the French Commander-in-Chief that he planned to halt the offensive until he had exploited his limited success on the right. 'At this,' Haig recorded, 'Joffre exploded in a fit of rage. *He* could not approve of it. He *ordered* me to attack ... I quickly explained ... I am solely responsible to the British Government for the action of the British Army.'

On 14 July Rawlinson mounted a silent night attack which had great success. The German main line was breached and there was panic behind their line, the more so as Falkenhayn's orders were that every metre of ground lost must at once be recaptured. The British arrangements to exploit the night success were, however, cumbersome; there was ample time for the Germans to draw in reserves and reseal their line. Heavy fighting followed at one point and then another. Australians, Canadians, Indians, New Zealanders, South Africans were drawn in to join the British regiments.

With over 30 divisions employed, Haig appointed Hubert Gough to command the left sector of the Somme battlefront. His clash with the War Office over Ireland temporarily forgotten, Gough had been promoted to command an army of cavalry positioned to exploit the expected breach in the first week of July. Believing that, if nothing else, he was relieving the pressure on Verdun and preventing the Germans from sending divisions to fight Russia or Italy, Haig ordered Rawlinson and Gough to make a major attack once more in September. This time they had a new weapon. 'I hope,' Haig wrote home to Robertson at the end of August, 'the Tanks prove successful. It is rather a desperate innovation.'

'Tank' was a name aptly given to the steel box with caterpillar tracks which, it was hoped, might carry men in safety across the enemy wire and trenches: the guns of the 'male' and the machine guns of the 'female' should open a way through for infantry and cavalry. While Gough was to draw off the Germans by attacking the high ground immediately on either side of the river Ancre, Rawlinson was to push with infantry and the bulk of the tanks to make a wide breach in the enemy line. Five cavalry divisions were ready to pass through this breach.

In early September, a series of 'minor' attacks were made to secure a good assault line for the main offensive. Typical of these was the dogged action of the 20th Division, formed originally of Kitchener's volunteers with a sprinkling of regulars and Territorials, who now as veterans clawed their way forward down the terrible road into Guillemont, straight, desolate, swept by fire; the Fourth and Fifth Armies had scarcely recovered from these terrible endeavours when, on 18 September, the main offensive began.

The pattern was almost time-honoured: a prolonged bombardment rising in a crescendo as the sweating, laden infantry packed the trenches. The guns lifted, whistles blew, the infantry rose up to cross the pitted earth of No Man's Land. The enemy manned their positions and opened fire with rifles, machine guns and artillery. The size and force of the assault captured a few trenches, then lost cohesion and momentum.

There was one difference, however, due to the

A 6-inch gun in a camouflaged emplacement near Albert, July 1916

A tank being used to tow a 60-pounder gun into a position near Ypres

presence of the tanks. For although these strange, noisy, unwieldy machines, dispersed amongst several divisions, became bogged or bellied, broke down or were hit by shells, a few crossed intact into the enemy lines, where nothing else could have survived in the intense fire. By Courcelette on the main road to Bapaume, two tanks caught up the Canadians and persuaded numbers of Germans to surrender – '... not war but bloody butchery,' was a German officer's opinion of the machines. At Flers, on Rawlinson's front, the circling pilots of the Royal Flying Corps saw, amazed, the collapse of the German defences as four tanks swept into and round the shattered village.

These notable events on the first day were not, however, a victory but local successes; signs of what tanks could achieve. The infantry were unable to exploit, the tanks were too scattered – and soon disabled – to make immediate further use of their breaching capabilities.

The Germans were nonetheless greatly alarmed and feared a tank onslaught. Though Falkenhayn had been dismissed and his policy of immediate counter-attack overruled, the Germans reinforced the sector continuously and sought to recapture everything lost. Urged on by Joffre, believing correctly that the Germans were suffering irremediably and that he was preventing them from transferring troops to Russia, Haig persisted into the winter. A minor success on the Ancre in November seems to have convinced him that there would be no major victory in 1916. In sleet on the morning of the 19th,

the British soldiers heard that they were to stand down. The line was, at best, 4 miles from its starting point on 1 July, the casualty figure for the sector being 415,000.

As the offensive ended, the allied chiefs, political and military, met again to consider what they should plan for 1917. But Joffre was not to direct France's armies on the western front. His enemies in Paris triumphed, replacing him with the flashing Nivelle. In London, Lloyd George succeeded Asquith as Prime Minister and openly declared that he preferred Nivelle's to Haig's methods.

Nivelle might have succeeded when he attacked on 16 April 1917 but for his lack of secrecy. Arrogant and confident, he had told his plans to many dinner parties for weeks beforehand. 'Wully' Robertson remarked that Nivelle would 'fight with a halter round his neck' and so it proved. The French Army lost about 180,000 men but, more importantly, Nivelle's promise to his divisions that they would now win and end the war if they attacked with all their might was seen to be false. In May, there were mutinies in the trenches, some regiments killing their officers and deserting the line. Nivelle was dismissed; Pétain, the defender of Verdun, was appointed Commander-in-Chief. Correctly, he told his government that he would not put the Army to an offensive. The Americans had entered the war in April and, in Pétain's view, they must bide their time until this powerful and fresh ally deployed its strength.

The sudden collapse of French offensive power had

o

Passchendaele. Canadians of the 2nd Division laying a duckboard track. Wounded and prisoners can be seen coming from the front line, 6 October 1917

left Haig with the task of maintaining operations jointly begun round Arras. But he did not believe it was a sector which promised victory. With the initiative in his hands alone now, he returned to the idea of a break out through the extreme northern flank in Flanders where the Royal Navy might assist. Thus as the summer of 1917 drew on, the focus of action for the BEF returned for a third time to the region of Ypres.

The offensive was to be mounted in the summer in secrecy. Yet even in the summer it was known that there was frequent rainfall and now that the intricate drainage system was destroyed this water must lie in the flat countryside. The gigantic preparations were not well concealed and, in any case, the Germans

were alerted by a premature operation. No minor consideration was the fact that the Russian revolution, which had brought to an end all hope of offensive action by the allies in the east, permitted Germany to thin out its armies there. In the face of these circumstances, Haig set his soldiers to assault at 3·45 on 31 July.

They attacked across a quagmire of black slime. Progress was in feet rather than yards; success, such as it was, was due to dogged courage and perseverance. The tanks were committed but sank even more quickly than infantry, artillery and engineers. Fearing the effects on the French if he should desist, concerned that the Germans might yet gain an armistice while they were in possession of most of Belgium

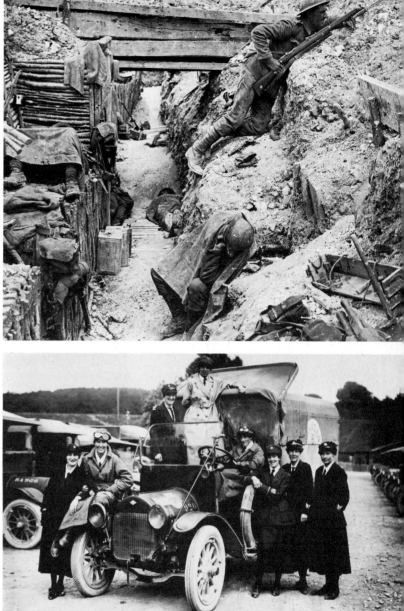

Above: The front line, Ovillers, July 1916
Below: The women join up. Members of the F.A.N.Y. with an ambulance at Étaples, 27 June 1917

and much of France, unaware of the true state of the fighting in process, Haig felt it his duty to keep attacking, until, in November, the Canadians took Passchendaele on the top of the low Ypres ridge and faced still an unbroken enemy line. The situation was then too plain to be ignored. A winter defence line was established.

The regulars had seen out the first battle of Ypres; the Territorials and Kitchener's volunteers had filled out their ranks until, almost in their own right, they had fought through the Somme and now to Passchendaele. They were experienced in trench warfare; knew how to patrol, how to bomb, how to wire, assault or defend. They had mastered the new weapons: the Mills grenade, the Lewis light-machine-gun, the varieties of trench mortar and the latest novelties in gas. But the professional application of the regulars, the eager bravery of the Territorials and Kitchener's volunteers were passing. Amongst the rank and file there was readiness to do their duty but, above all, after the winter of 1917, to endure. It was not alone the cumulative terrors of the fighting which was sapping their spirit but the privation of trench life through the scourging winters.

The day of the volunteer was past – regular or citizen. Conscription had begun in Britain after many attempts to do without it. As 1918 approached, it remained to be seen whether the British Expeditionary Force would sustain its fighting power towards a fifth year of war.

CHAPTER 25

The Battle of Cambrai and the Final Offensive
1917–18

JOHN D. P. KEEGAN

What had made the reverses of 1917 all the harder to bear was that they had been inflicted by an enemy inferior in numbers and resources; by implication therefore, an implication which the public seemed increasingly ready to note, superior in strategic skill. General Sir Henry Wilson, an enthusiastic critic of his fellow soldiers' shortcomings, summarised the prevailing mood of disillusionment in a diary note of 30 October, comparing 'the different strategies – ours and the Boches': 1. We take Bullecourt, they take Rumania: 2. We take Messines, they take Russia: 3. We *don't* take Passchendaele, they take Italy'. Passchendaele; there was the crowning misfortune. By the beginning of October, it could no longer be disguised that the operation 'to clear the Belgian coast' had failed: failed tactically, leaving a decimated and dispirited British Army floundering in the man-made swamps east of Ypres; failed strategically, leaving unfulfilled all the grand promises Haig had made the Cabinet in June. He now needed a victory as no one else on the Allied side.

Conventional methods were unlikely to win him one; nor had he any longer the necessary reserve of infantry. Cavalry he had, but it was unusable until the front had been broken, and artillery too, but experience showed that it created almost as many obstacles as it destroyed, besides always betraying an attacker's intentions. His only other offensive arm, the Tank Corps, was unproved. Committed prematurely in the Somme it had done well in places at Arras, failed at Passchendaele (as its commanders had predicted). Haig, however, was now ready to try any expedient and when reminded in mid-October of a Tank Corps scheme rejected by his staff in August, had ordered detailed planning to begin. It was now nearing completion and he pinned his hopes

on its successful outcome to offset his failures of the spring and summer.

Detailed planning had unfortunately confused the aims of the original scheme. Its author, Colonel J.F.C.Fuller, had projected no more than a giant tank raid, designed to confuse and humiliate the enemy, not to win ground. Third Army staff, drawn in because his chosen sector lay on their front, had insisted on planning for a breakthrough and Haig had accordingly sent down five divisions of cavalry – though none of the infantry necessary to sustain the momentum of a major attack. That, in Fuller's view, made a breakthrough unlikely. But of a successful 'break-in' he was optimistic. For the first time the Tank Corps, now at a strength of nine battalions, was to operate together on dry and uncratered terrain with infantry trained in tactics of co-operation and without surprise compromised by preparatory bombardment. For the artillery, though powerful, was to use a new map-shooting technique and open fire only after the infantry had moved off. Since the enemy deployed only 2 divisions against 7, 150 guns against 1,000 and no anti-tank weapons, there was an excellent chance of overwhelming them. But if the battle zone was still in their hands after 48 hours, Haig planned to close down the offensive, since enemy reinforcements, which he could not match, would by then certainly have arrived. It was thus to be a race between the tank and the railway.

The distance the tanks had to cover to gain open country was short, only 7 miles from the outposts of the Hindenburg line to the town of Cambrai. But the battlefield was extremely constricted, deep canals bounding each flank, and the exit was dominated by the woods of Bourlon ridge. Its slopes would have to be gained in the first rush. The crucial first step – the

Opposite above: Armoured cars setting out on reconnaissance, Biefvillers, 25 August 1918
Below: The village of Ribecourt near Flesquieres two hours after its capture, showing prisoners brought in and men of the 11th Battalion the Leicestershire Regiment

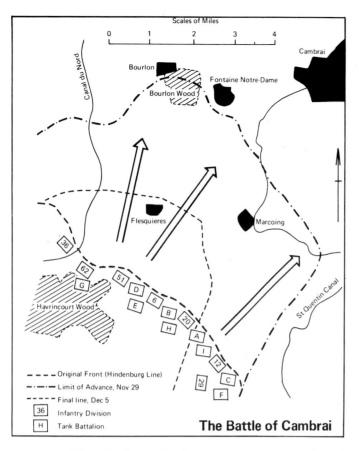

Scales of Miles
0   1   2   3   4

Canal du Nord

Cambrai

Bourlon
Fontaine Notre-Dame
Bourlon Wood

Flesquieres

Marcoing

36

62
G   51   D
E   6
B   20
H
A
I   12
29   C
F

St Quentin Canal

Havrincourt Wood

- - - - Original Front (Hindenburg Line)
- · - · - Limit of Advance, Nov 29
- - - - Final line, Dec 5
36 Infantry Division
H Tank Battalion

The Battle of Cambrai

assembly of 480 tanks in secrecy – was achieved successfully however and the morning of 20 November dawned without any sign of counter-preparation by the enemy. By early afternoon it seemed that the plan was on the point of succeeding. The Hindenburg line had been breached on a seven mile front, 16,000 prisoners taken and the leading troops, advancing almost unscathed in small columns behind tanks in triangular formation, were 4,000 yards from their start line. Only in one place had the attack failed; that was at Flesquières where the 51st Highland Division, on its commander's orders, had hung too far behind the tanks. He had feared they would draw fire. So they did; but had the infantry been with them, the German field gunners would have been driven from their pieces. Unsupported, the tanks were picked off singly and the infantry, when they got forward, mown down by machine gunners. It was a brutal object lesson in the necessity for close infantry-tank co-operation. It was also a tactical set-back, for Flesquières lay at dead centre of the battle-field and a delay there meant a postponement of the attack on Bourlon.

The Germans grasped the importance of Bourlon, though it lay to the rear of their support line, as soon as they recovered from their initial shock, which they did with commendable speed. By the worst of bad luck, moreover, the first of the divisions to be transferred from Russia had detrained at Cambrai the day

before and by late afternoon was hurrying to seal off the British break-in. It was joined next day by units from the northern front. Haig's forty-eight hours were now up but he resolved nevertheless to fight on for Bourlon. Most of the tanks were now out of action, chiefly for mechanical reasons and the battle, which was to drag on for the rest of the week, resolved itself into a conventional and increasingly savage infantry affair. Its outcome was decided by a counter-stroke of Ludendorff's. He, having contained the break-in, had continued to reinforce the Cambrai front and on the morning of 30 November surprised the British divisions on the quieter right flank and drove them back beyond their old positions. Haig abandoned Bourlon to shorten his line which, by the end of the battle of 5 December, ran in two un-comfortable little salients across the original front.

Cambrai, which had begun more promisingly than any battle of the war, thus ended much as any other. In terms of the history of war in general and of the British Army in particular its disappointing outcome may be overlooked, for it marked the arrival of a major new weapon and crowned the work of the British tank pioneers. But in December 1917 it was difficult to stand back from events. The public had heard the church bells rung on 21 November to herald a victory. It now wanted an explanation, as did the war cabinet, and a commission of enquiry was appointed. Haig, anticipating trouble, dismissed one of the three corps commanders involved before it convened and subsequently persuaded it to lay the blame on 'untrained troops'. Lloyd George, who perhaps rightly felt that but for Passchendaele Haig would have had trained troops to spare, would not however let him off so lightly. He did not dare to dismiss him, could not indeed think of a successor, but determined instead to break down his circle of protective subordinates. Within the next weeks his Chief and Deputy Chief of Staff, Intelligence Officer (Charteris, who had wept at his first sight of Pass-chendaele mud) and Quartermaster-General were all taken from him. And in February the Prime Minister moved against his principal ally, Robertson, the Chief of the Imperial General Staff.

Robertson typified for Lloyd George that sort of general to whom, Clemenceau was saying, the war was 'too important to be left' – a view Lloyd George had held since 1916 but had not found the means to act on. He had recently come to hope that the Supreme War Council, a committee of Allied prime ministers and military advisers set up after Caporetto to co-ordinate strategy, might serve to curb the independence of the generals. It had not. In February, therefore, he sprang on Robertson a plan to transfer to the Council control of the Franco-British reserves and asked him to join it as British military adviser. Robertson refusing, out of loyalty to Haig's known opposition to the scheme, he too was dismissed, and replaced by Wilson, a man loyal to no one.

These changes in the high command were justifiable but not timely. For they left Haig, who had always needed help in making a case to the politicians, without a persuasive voice at the moment of dire crisis. Lloyd George perhaps had reason not 'to trust Haig with men'. But the BEF needed men in the spring of 1918 more than it had done since first Ypres, not to launch some dubious offensive but simply to hold its line against a German attack which certainly impended, probably in overwhelming strength. The War Office, however, had now begun to restrict its supply of manpower, in any case rapidly scarcening, and had had in consequence to order a reduction of divisional establishments from twelve to nine battalions. Haig failed to convince the cabinet what risks these reductions entailed.

They were heightened by the way in which the War Office ordained they should be implemented. For it laid down – and here one catches a reflection of how strong is the grip of regimental tradition on the British Army – that no Regular, First-line Territorial or Yeomanry battalion should be disbanded. But since those that might – the second-line Territorial and junior Kitchener battalions – were scattered unevenly throughout the Army, the disbandments, 134 in all, entailed a host of exchanges between brigades, divisions and even Corps at a moment when all should have been consolidating their organisation against the trials ahead[1].

To compound the BEF's difficulties, this contraction (one, it must be added in fairness, copied from the French and Germans) coincided with the largest of its regular extensions of front, by which since 1915 it had progressively relieved the French of stretches of line. When in December Haig had agreed with Pétain to take on an additional 30 miles between the Somme and the Oise, it had been in the belief that a German attack was most likely east of Rheims. But by February all the signs were that they would attack the British. For though the French still held twice as

A tank crossing a trench on its way to take part in the Battle of Cambrai

much line with 100 divisions as the British with 60, the latter were now faced by almost half the German divisions on the western front, now nearing 200 in number and swollen at the rate of 10 a month by transfers from Russia. Many of those transferred clearly came to form an offensive reserve and that a large one. The Allies, whose ultimate reserve was the American Army, as yet beyond the Atlantic, could muster only 23 between them. It was for fear of losing the use in a crisis of the few each possessed that Haig and Pétain had opposed the Supreme War Council over the General Reserve. But the substitute arrangement they had come to – that each should assist the other as needed – was scarcely satisfactory. Wilson warned Haig that he would 'have to live on Pétain's charity and would find that very cold'. Wilson judged Pétain aright, as events proved.

The weakest of Haig's Armies was the Fifth, which he had saddled with the new stretch of line below the Somme and yet starved of reinforcements to maintain his strength in Flanders. That was undoubtedly the more sensitive front since the Channel ports lay so close behind it that 'elastic defence' was ruled out, but any sort of manoeuvre was likely to overtax the stretched Fifth. It certainly lacked the men to repair its newly acquired and typically makeshift French trenches or to organise that triple front – Forward, Main and Rear lines – which a new GHQ directive ordained. GHQ in any case had misunderstood the

[1] The establishment of a division in 1918 was therefore much changed from 1914: only two-thirds as strong in artillery and in infantry (though it had acquired a pioneer battalion). But its battalions were much stronger in automatic weapons, with 36 Lewis guns against two Vickers (those were now brigaded, as were the new light and medium trench mortars) Corps, Army and GHQ troops – tanks, medium and heavy artillery and aircraft – were of course incomparably stronger.

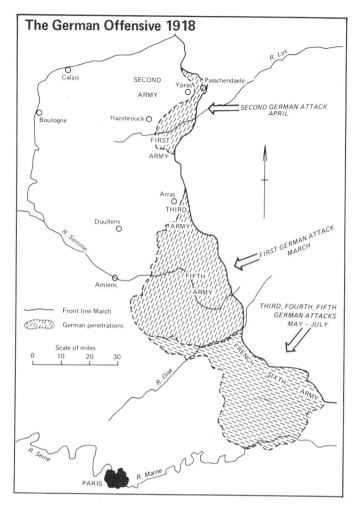

The German Offensive 1918

SECOND GERMAN ATTACK
APRIL

FIRST GERMAN ATTACK
MARCH

THIRD, FOURTH, FIFTH
GERMAN ATTACKS
MAY – JULY

Front line March
German penetrations

Scale of miles
0   10   20   30

German handbook on which its new defensive directive was based, advising that over a third of the infantry be left in the Forward Line, which the Germans held only with pickets.

These mistakes were to prove disastrous. For though Ludendorff indeed intended to make his major effort in Flanders, the weakness of the Somme front had decided him to attack there first. Only when he had drawn off the reserves from the north would he strike for the Channel ports; and not until the destruction of the British Army had been accomplished would he turn on the French. Tactically, he put his faith in a new system of infantry-artillery co-operation which bore similarities to that adopted for Cambrai. The artillery, of which he had an enormous preponderance, was to 'neutralise' the British infantry by a short but intensely heavy bombardment on a wide front; trained teams of storm troops from the élite divisions were then to infiltrate the stricken front. These tactics had worked splendidly against the demoralised Russians and Italians. It remained to see what they could do to the British.

In practice, they worked devastatingly well. In the early morning of 21 March, 6,000 guns opened up without warning on a 70 mile front between Arras and the Oise, their heaviest weight falling along the 42 miles held by Gough's Fifth Army. Four hours later the infantry attack began, 43 divisions moving forward to assault Gough's trenches, and nineteen the right wing of Byng's Third Army, with fourteen. Most of Gough's divisions had been badly mauled at Passchendaele and the majority of their infantry, in any case, were in the badly prepared forward zone. Many battalions in consequence were overwhelmed in the first minutes, some engulfed without trace in the thick fog which covered the battlefield all morning. Surrounded units fought on in strong points until overrun or out of ammunition, but they did little to delay the German spearheads, which had been trained to leave pockets of resistance to the support waves.

By 24 March it was evident that the Fifth Army, whose centre had been driven back 15 miles, was on the verge of collapse – a collapse which would separate the British from the French armies and open a gap through which the Germans might reach the sea. This was the supreme crisis of the war, threatening Haig and Pétain with defeat in detail and promising Ludendorff almost immediate and total victory. The prospect struck all three supreme commanders simultaneously and the decisions they took that day determined the war's outcome. Ludendorff, ever an opportunist, decided to press forward rather than roll up the flank of the British Third Army. Pétain decided to husband his reserves against an attack on Paris, even if that meant abandoning the British. Haig decided to petition for unity of command.

On 26 March, he, Pétain, Lloyd George, Clemenceau and Foch met at Doullens, a little town north of Amiens from which they could hear the rumble of the battle. By lunchtime they had agreed, as they had failed to do during three years of war, on a supreme commander: it was to be Foch, as much an optimist as Pétain was a pessimist, and his instrument of power was to be the reserves, now mainly French. Clemenceau, who on entering had heard Pétain refer to Haig as 'a general about to be beaten in the open field' told Foch on leaving, 'Well, you've got the job you so much wanted'. Foch answered, 'A fine gift. You give me a lost battle and tell me to win it'.

In fact, the battle was not yet lost, nor was it to be won by Foch's reserve. By 28 March the very success of the Germans was wearing them out. As in 1914 their infantry had had to make enormous marches, this time across the wastes of the old Somme battlefield. Their support and transport had failed to keep up, they had stopped to plunder supplies and on the outskirts of Amiens they had met fresh British troops. By the beginning of April their advance had petered out. They had won an enormous salient, come within 30 miles of the sea, inflicted 160,000 casualties on the British but now could go no further.

Ludendorff, though disappointed, did not despair. Because French reserves had scarcely intervened in the battle but British divisions from Flanders had, he reckoned still to be dealing with an unco-ordinated defence and switched his remaining reserves, still very numerous and enormously superior in artillery, to the River Lys, south of Ypres. There, on 9 April, the hurricane burst again, this time opposite Hazebrouck, principal rail junction of the northern front whose loss would bisect the supply line of the BEF. By inexplicable negligence, the point of impact was held by a Portuguese division, which decamped almost to a man, leaving undefended a gap through which the storm troops poured. Fortunately the British troops on their flanks were less tired than Gough's had been and occupied much stronger positions. The Germans made four miles on the first day but all that they could do during the next fortnight won them only another eight. And this despite Foch's calculated parsimony with French reserves, which he was witholding for a deliberate counter-stroke.[1]

By the beginning of May Ludendorff's strategy was wearing thin at the elbows. It had been based on using his reserve, which if lost he could not replace, to knock out the stronger of his enemies before their reserve – the United States Army – could take the field. British losses for the last 40 days now numbered 240,000 but his own had mounted to 350,000. His siege train was still intact but his infantry strength failing. He decided therefore to transfer what was left (some 30 divisions of an original 45) to the French front, which he had always regarded as the softer option and hoped might have softened further during the spring. On 27 May therefore the by now familiar sequence of hurricane bombardment and lightning infantry assault unrolled across the stricken ridge of the Chemin des Dames, northern bulwark of the old Marne battlefield. Yet not even in this battle was the BEF wholly to escape for by an ironic stroke five of its divisions exhausted in the previous months' fighting had been sent there to rest. They took the full

[1] A subsidiary attack in the Somme front, 24 April, was notable for the first tank versus tank fight in history, in which a 'male' Mark IV knocked out one German tank and drove off two others. Appropriately the British tank was No 1 of No 1 Section, A Company, 1st Battalion, Tank Corps.

brunt of the German attack and with the rest of the French Sixth Army were swept southwards to the banks of the Marne. For the second time in four years Paris was threatened with siege and the government prepared again to evacuate.

But by 6 June the danger had passed. The advance had been halted, as before, chiefly by its own loss of momentum, no commander in that pre-mechanised age having the means to feed his spearhead at a rate sufficient to overcome the frictions of the battle, however feeble the resistance in its path. But a contributory factor were the counter-attacks launched on 6 June at Belleau Wood, significantly by the American 6th Division. Pershing, though steadfast in his determination to command a united American army, had agreed at President Wilson's insistence to commit his units piecemeal during the crisis.

They were to intervene again in what was to prove the most spectacular, if not the most decisive battle of 1918, the Second Marne. On 15 July Ludendorff launched his 'Peace Offensive' across the Marne towards Paris. He had assembled 56 divisions, while still keeping a powerful force in Flanders, and expected either to reach Paris or to finish the French army, perhaps both. But he was to be counter-bluffed by a French command which had learnt well the lesson of secretly assembling a reserve. On 18 July

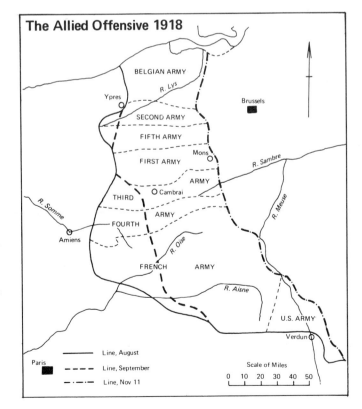

The Allied Offensive 1918

Mangin struck with 18 divisions and 321 tanks into the Germans' right flank, caught them off balance and tumbled them back across the Marne. By 4 August they were back across the Vesle and almost on their May startline.

The Germans' situation was now very grave. They occupied two enormous salients and had inflicted grievous loss on the Allies but had nowhere broken their line. Worse, they had lost a million of their own soldiers and the spirit of those who remained was so depressed that it seemed doubtful if Ludendorff could commit them again to the offensive. The Allies, in any case, were not to allow him the chance. Haig had used the breathing space given him in June and July to reconstitute most of the ten divisions he had had to reduce in May with cadres from Egypt, Italy and England and to make good the vast losses of material incurred in March and April. The Tank Corps in particular was now stronger than it had been before Cambrai and in late July he approved plans to engage it in a similar enterprise against the tip of the German salient at Amiens. On 8 August the Fourth Army assaulted in the most perfect set-piece attack of the war. The Canadian and Australian Corps, advancing behind 500 tanks and beneath 800 aeroplanes, intervening directly in the battle on a scale never before attempted, broke clean through the German front. There was no Flesquières to mar the achievement and though the advance petered out on 12 August, partly because of disagreements between Haig and Foch, partly because of the onset of that familiar factor, 'the diminishing power of the offensive', Amiens was unmistakably a victory.

As in all great victories, the moral results of Amiens counted for more than the material. Ludendorff called 8 August the German army's 'black day' because for the first time in four years the spirit of the troops had noticeably failed. The defence had given ground more rapidly than the power of the attack merited and the retreating divisions had insulted those moving up with cries of 'blacklegs' and 'war prolongers'. On 11 August, Ludendorff offered his resignation. It was refused but the Kaiser agreed that his army's capacity to resist was waning and that 'the war must be ended'.

Exactly three months later it was. During those months the British Army had continued to engage, as since early 1917, the greater balance of German divisions in the west. It had fought, by the Battle Nomenclature Committee's post-war reckoning, six major offensives and a host of smaller actions, broken the Hindenburg line along its whole length, retrieved all the territory the original British Expeditionary Force had lost in 1914 and suffered in the process nearly 350,000 casualties. All the Allied armies, the American not excluded, had contributed to the final victory, but the British forces had played perhaps the major role.

Cambrai. Men of the 51st Division crossing a German communication trench, near Ribecourt

Royal Engineers repairing a bridge, 20 September 1918

CHAPTER 26

The War
outside Western Europe
1914–18

JOHN D. P. KEEGAN

'He who commands the sea is at great liberty and may take as much and as little of the War as he will.'

Francis Bacon.

The first great land battles were fought in France and East Prussia, but when Turkey and later Bulgaria entered the War on the Austro-German side and Italy joined the Allies the fighting spread right across Europe and into Asia.

Britain's traditional policy, since the days of the first Lord Chatham and the Seven Years' War, had been to leave the main fighting on the Continent to her European allies, and to exploit her sea-power to turn, as it were, her adversaries' sea flank.

It had been a complete break with this tradition when the newly formed British General Staff achieved their understanding with the French. No longer, if the soldiers had their way, would a British Government be free to use the oceans as 'a barrier not only of space but of time', allowing it 'to go to war unarmed and build up its strength at leisure'. In any future war, the home army was to be despatched forthwith to the Continent, there to risk its existence in the opening encounter – an encounter which all military theorists were convinced must be decisive. This concept was not one which all cabinet members accepted with forthright enthusiasm when the moment was upon them in August 1914 and the full implication glimpsed. For a 'battle of decision' was an uncomfortably relative concept. The decision might go to Britain and her allies; on the other hand, it might not. Faced with such drastic alternatives, the Cabinet divided. Even after the most timorous had resigned, it could not bring itself to meet the General Staff's pledges in full and sent the BEF to France with five instead of seven divisions.

What no one in high places foresaw was that a decision might elude both sides. Yet that was the undeniable outcome of the first great clash of arms. There was much else unforeseen besides, notably that Britain in consequence would have to raise an army of millions and keep it in the field, if Kitchener was right, for three years. Little wonder therefore that by Christmas 1914 opinion in the same high places was inclined to favour an experiment in the traditional alternative to mass warfare. The First Lord of the Admiralty, Winston Churchill, argued the case for amphibious operations with special fervour. The case was an unpopular one with the commanders in France, who daily cried out for more troops, but more troops were on their way. The first of the New Armies were in the training camps, the Territorials were ready to leave and the last of the regulars had returned from the colonies. Most were owed in honour to the BEF but the stalemate in France was a powerful argument for withholding some to use elsewhere. The Navy was equipped, perhaps as never before, to 'embark (an) army and land it'. The question increasingly debated that Christmas was where might it 'do the most mischief'?

It could clearly *prevent* mischief by capturing the German colonies. Not only were they valuable in themselves as bargaining counters at some future peace but they also offered, through their ports and wireless stations, aid and succour to the German commerce raiders presently at loose on the high seas. Yet, acquired as they had been purely for reasons of national prestige, they were of insufficient material importance for their loss decisively to hinder Germany's power to make war. Moreover, the very effectiveness of the Royal Navy's blockade scuppered any chance that Germany would weaken herself by trying to defend them. Left to fend for themselves,

Opposite above: Kitchener at Suvla. He is on Karakol Dagh, looking towards the Salt Lake, Koja and Chunuk Bair, November 1915. With him are generals Birdwood and Cunliffe Owen
Below: Gallipoli. Australians charging at Anzac, 17 December 1915. Owing to the lack of artillery, despite the utmost gallantry, attacks by either side achieved little success

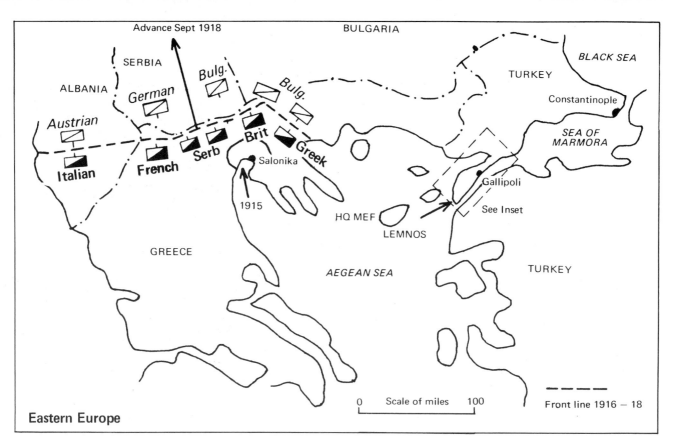

Eastern Europe

therefore, the German colonies fell swiftly. All those in the Pacific had been captured by the end of September, either by Royal Naval, Australasian or Japanese forces. Of those in Africa, Togoland had gone under as early as 27 August and resistance in the Cameroons had been almost overcome by Christmas. The fall of German South-West Africa, delayed by the outbreak of rebellion in the Union, remained only a matter of time. Once achieved, the South African forces engaged there could be transferred to German East Africa (Tanganyika), whose garrison could certainly not resist long[1].

If not in the colonies, where else could the whale do the elephant mischief? Certainly not in the Baltic though Fisher, at his most lunatic on this topic, for a time persuaded Churchill that it was the right place. They persuaded no one else. It would have then to be on the Central Powers' southern flank, either in the Adriatic, to take Austria in the rear, or in the Aegean, to disable Turkey. Those who argued for striking against Turkey had the stronger case.

The facts were these. Austria was more than fully occupied by the Russians on her own front door step while her Balkan backyard was trackless and boulder-strewn. It was therefore unlikely that she could harm

[1] In fact the campaign in German East Africa was to prove the longest and relatively the most costly of the war. The German Commander, von Lettow-Vorbeck, a guerrilla leader of genius, was to elude the pursuit of an Allied force, eventually numbering 150,000, for four years, and cause it to suffer a sickness rate of 2,024 per 1,000. His own force was never stronger than 15,000. He surrendered it on 23 November 1918.

the Allies or they her. Turkey on the other hand presented a genuine military menace in the Mediterranean, where she was already preparing an attack, abortive as it turned out, on the Suez Canal from Palestine. Yet the vast extent of her possessions also laid her open to amphibious retaliation. An expedition had already been mounted by the Government of India, acting more or less on its own account, at the head of the Persian Gulf, which had secured Basra and the outlets of the Royal Navy's oil supply. But Mesopotamia was too far distant from the principal theatres of the war for success there decisively to influence its outcome. Turkey-in-Europe was not. An expedition to the Aegean might bring Greece and perhaps even Bulgaria, both Turk-hating nations, in on the Allied side, and would extend help both to the Serbs and to the Russians in the Caucasus – help for which the latter urgently appealed in January 1915. There were two obvious fronts: Salonika in northern Greece and Gallipoli, at the mouth of the Dardanelles. A force landing at Salonika would do so unopposed. But it would thereafter lack a clear-cut objective. The route through the Dardanelles Narrows, on the other hand, led directly to Constantinople, whose capture might knock Turkey out of the war, to the Black Sea shores of the Balkan states, which once in direct touch with the Allies might turn on Austria, and to Russia's ice-free ports, through which her armies, so vital to the Allies in the struggle with Germany, might be revictualled and rearmed.

238

It could be argued moreover, as it was by Churchill, that the Dardanelles would fall to naval attack alone.

By the end of January the Cabinet had accepted his arguments and a fleet of obsolescent British and French battleships was assembling to put them to the test. After it sailed, second thoughts persuaded Kitchener that landings might nevertheless prove necessary to secure the Dardanelles shore in the wake of the bombardment and on 12 March he appointed Sir Ian Hamilton to command a Mediterranean Expeditionary Force. The troops to fill it out were not found without difficulty. After much havering, Kitchener released the 29th Division, last of the three formed from the regulars returned from the colonies; the Admiralty added the R N Division; the Australian and New Zealand Governments, whose contingents had landed in Egypt to complete their training, contributed what was to become famous as ANZAC; and at the last moment the French sent a division to demonstrate solidarity.

'Too little too late' is a summary of the reasons usually advanced to explain the failure of the Dardanelles expedition and is true enough of the military operations. But 'too much too soon' more aptly applies to the naval preliminaries. The fault was perhaps less that of the commanding admiral than of the Admiralty, whose First Lord could not restrain his impatience. Hence the first bombardment was begun before the weather had settled and had to be broken off for a month. When resumed on 18 March, the Narrows were found still largely undefended and the damage done in February unrepaired but on retiring as darkness fell the fleet lost three ships on a stray row of mines. De Robeck therefore declined to try again without the army.

But where in February there had been only one Turkish division, there were then four. By the time Hamilton was ready on 25 April, after preparations which had alerted every Turkish spy in the Mediterranean and were yet inadequate, there were six. Two it is true were on the Asiatic shore, where no more than a feint by the French was intended. But the rest were deployed opposite the chosen beaches: those at Cape Helles, labelled by the staff S, V, W, X and Y, and that on the western shore of the peninsula, ever since known as Anzac Cove. At all the beaches the landings went disastrously, either because the Turks shot down the troops as they left the water, as at V where the *River Clyde* grounded, or because elsewhere the inexperienced troops settled down to consolidate their footholds instead of enlarging them. By the end of the day, the invaders were almost everywhere reduced to scratching for cover on the lower

Preparing for the evacuation of 'W' beach. A shell from the Turkish Asiatic batteries has just exploded in the sea. The evacuation was carried out skilfully and with amazingly few casualties

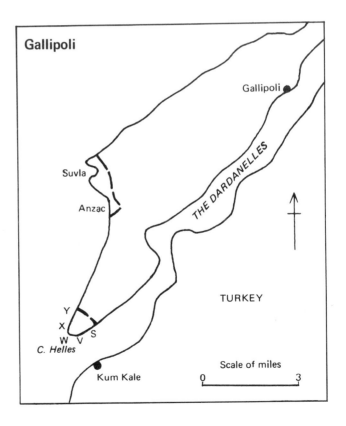

239

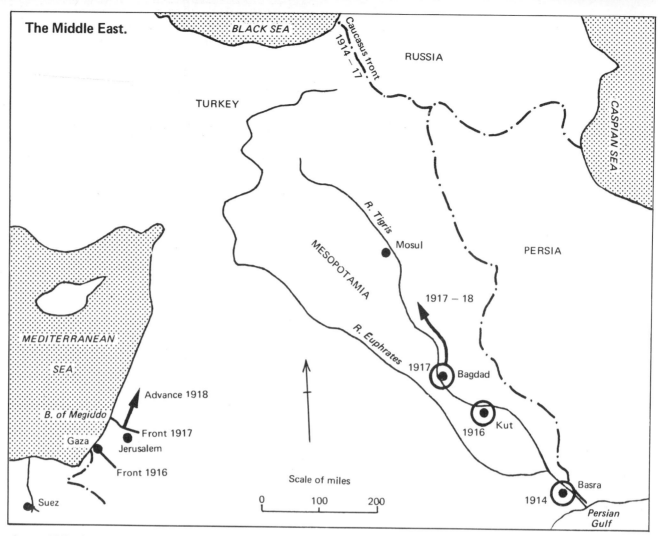

The Middle East.

slopes. Within a week the trench line was as impenetrable as that in Flanders.

Subsequent reinforcement, which the Turks matched, merely heightened the stalemate and a secondary landing at Suvla in August failed, like that at Y in April, for want of push. By October, the Gallipoli affair was shaking the government to pieces. Hamilton was dismissed and Monro, who succeeded him, recommended evacuation. Churchill opposed it stridently, but with a lonely voice, and Kitchener, of whom his colleagues now wished to be rid, was sent out in November to gather impressions on the spot. It was hoped he could be persuaded to go on to Egypt and stay there. When he returned, without clear recommendations, he found Churchill gone, French going, and Haig and Robertson in charge of higher strategy. Both believed that the war could be won only in France and detested the diversion in the Dardanelles. Confronted by these determined 'Westerners', the Cabinet first faltered, then ordered immediate evacuation. It was completed by 8 January 1916. The campaign had cost 200,000 casualties and ended any belief in 'a way round'.

It did not, however, put an end to sideshows.

Lloyd George, soon to be Prime Minister, had always preferred Salonika to Gallipoli as a backdoor into Europe, a view which the French had come inexplicably to share, and thither troops had already been sent from the Dardanelles. More arrived to join them in 1916; they were to spend all but the last few months of the war in passive discomfort, watched by Bulgarians half their number.

Meanwhile, as Gallipoli drew to a close, another campaign, equally disastrous but lacking any comparable motive, was reaching a climax in Mesopotamia. Encouraged by the ease with which it had seized Basra in 1914, the Government of India decided in early 1915 on an attempt to extend its conquests up the Tigris towards Baghdad, the capital. By September a riverborne force under General Townshend had arrived not far short of the city and the Cabinet, anxious for a 'striking success in the East' to offset the reverses at Gallipoli, approved an attempt to capture it. But Turkish reinforcements and German advisers had now arrived and Townshend, checked outside the defences, was forced to fall back on his advanced base at Kut. There he was invested in December and on 29 April 1916, after several efforts at relief had failed, surrendered. The garrison of 10,000 died in captivity almost to a man. Townshend, an unstable and unattractive figure, survived. Baghdad was captured at a second attempt and the campaign kept alive to the end of the war but its returns never justified the outlay.

The conduct of the parallel campaign in Egypt and Palestine attracted less controversy and its inception none, for it was the Turks who provoked it by attacking Suez in February 1915. They were repelled without difficulty by the permanent garrison but no thought was given to retaliation until the evacuation of Gallipoli brought in abnormal reinforcements. It was then decided to advance across the Sinai desert and in March 1917 an attempt was made to capture Gaza. That, and a second in April, failed. At the end of the year Allenby, a commander of vision and energy, arrived with orders from Lloyd George to take 'Jerusalem by Christmas'. He also brought fresh troops and in October took Gaza by an encircling movement with his cavalry. Deprived of two divisions to make good the losses of March in France, he made slower progress during the following summer and not until September 1918 was he able to complete the destruction of the Turkish Army, by then collapsing from within, at the Battle of Megiddo. Once again his success stemmed from an encircling movement through the desert, which has been held to anticipate *blitzkrieg* methods but really demonstrated his mastery of traditional cavalry tactics. On 30 October, Turkey made a separate peace with the Allies.

The war outside Western Europe cost Britain 850,000 casualties, not counting those incurred during the interventions in Russia. Were these losses justified? At Gallipoli without doubt, for success there would have transformed the character of the war. The government's mistake was in acting too hastily, before it could provide sufficient troops, co-ordinate their operations with the Navy or make available the munitions with which to supply Russia,

Allenby riding into Jerusalem in triumph. To avoid appearing as a conqueror, he dismounted later at the Jaffa gate

supposing the way had been opened to her Black Sea ports. But the sideshows proper were clearly a wasteful diversion. However well-established the tradition of extra-European operations, the strategy which would have had Britain devote herself to their prosecution during the First World War was ill-founded. For it rested on the assumption that Turkey, Austria and Bulgaria in some way supported Germany and that in attacking those countries Britain was 'knocking away the props'. Precisely the opposite was true. Germany supported her allies and did so largely because in attacking them the British played her game. The 'Easterners', in short, ignored the first rule of amphibious strategy: that if the elephant stays at home the whale must open his front door. Unfortunately the 'Westerners' who remembered the rule, had lost the key.

However it was on the Western Front that victory finally came. In a railway carriage standing at a forest siding near the town of Compiègne in France, the military chiefs of the warring nations signed an armistice that brought the 'War to end Wars' to its conclusion. That war had shown the appalling devastation which powerful nations can wreak, when their peoples are dedicated to a fight to a finish. A short 20 years later the lesson had to be learnt again. But for the British, at least, the recollection of that ghastly roll of death was to influence many military decisions in the Second World War.

Men of the New Zealand Mounted Rifles galloping into Jericho, 21 February 1918. Allenby's handling of his cavalry was one of the features of the Palestine campaign

CHAPTER 27

The Development of the Royal Engineers

JOHN H. S. LACEY

It was in the second half of the nineteenth century and the beginning of the twentieth that the Royal Engineers, or 'sappers' as they have always been called in the Army, came into their own. Young officers travelled much of the world and, although their work might be concerned initially with engineering, it could take strange turns; General Gordon for instance commanded for a time, and very successfully, a Chinese Imperial army. It was no coincidence that two of the most outstanding British soldiers of that period, Gordon and Kitchener, were both sappers.

But the history of the Royal Engineers is a long and full one. It spans over 900 years of history, for the sappers can trace an unbroken record of permanent employment by the Crown to the military engineers of the 1066 Norman conquest. Furthermore, they have taken part in every major battle fought by the British Army. They have often been the 'forlorn hope' and the first in during an assault, and their demolition parties the last out during a withdrawal. They have produced five Field Marshals and have never failed to provide officers who have reached the highest ranks and directed the affairs of the Army. They have made valuable contributions to the art of war by the development of scientific discoveries for military purposes. The development of almost every country now forming the British Commonwealth owes much to the sappers who were often the only professional engineers in the land during their early days, and many of their towns, public buildings, roads, bridges, railways, telegraphic communications, harbours, irrigation schemes and surveys are a lasting monument to their work. Even to this day the sappers' skills and equipments are employed on the betterment of living conditions, water supply and road and air communications in under-developed countries and are constantly being called upon to help in disaster areas.

The Norman and Plantagenet Kings selected as their military engineers those skilled in castle building, for the castle was then a most important military and administrative centre and a powerful instrument for enforcing obedience to the Crown. To this skill had to be added the ability to devise and operate 'engines of war' to breach the walls of a hostile stronghold and to drive tunnels below its ramparts to bring them tumbling down. They had also to survey, set out and build roads and bridges to give mobility to punitive expeditions sent to quell insurrection. Thus in those early days the traditional sapper tasks began to evolve: Fortifications and Works, Survey and Combat Engineering.

British sappers were first employed overseas in 1346 at the siege of Calais and the Battle of Crécy, and a primitive form of cannon was first used in those operations – a landmark in British military history and in the sapper story. The gun gradually replaced the cumbersome engines of war of the Middle Ages, and it also revolutionised the design of fortifications. To deal with this technological advance a Board of Ordnance was set up to administer in peace all matters connected with fortifications and works, survey, guns, arsenals and military stores, and in war to raise Ordnance Trains of artillery and engineers. These trains were disbanded at the end of hostilities and, except for the engineer and gunner officers held on the Board of Ordnance's permanent establishment, the personnel comprising them were discharged. Thus Marlborough's powerful trains were disbanded after the Treaty of Utrecht and two years later no guns could be provided to oppose the Jacobite Rising of 1715. As a result the Board formed

Opposite: A Royal Engineer officer and a private in the Royal Sappers and Miners *c.* 1815. A painting by Hamilton Smith

General Charles George Gordon. An officer in the Royal Engineers, he first achieved fame in China where he commanded a Chinese army and helped to put down the Taiping rebellion. He was made honorary mandarin. Sent by Gladstone to evacuate the Sudan, he was besieged by the Dervishes under the Mahdi, and died when the Dervishes stormed Khartoum, 1885

company was commanded by sapper officers and a second company was formed later. Both companies more than proved their worth during the Great Siege 1779–83 and constructed the famous galleries from which guns could be fired against the Spanish lines.

The threat of invasion after the French Revolution showed how vulnerable our coast line was, and in 1787 a Corps of Royal Military Artificers was raised to strengthen the country's defences. Companies were also sent to fortify overseas possessions, and in 1797 the Gibraltar Soldier Artificer Companies were absorbed into the new Corps for which the Corps of Royal Engineers provided the officers.

Although Wellington's sappers of the Peninsular War 1805–15 were highly skilled in the art of fortifications they lacked experience in siege operations. The impregnable Lines of Torres Vedras, constructed by them, were an excellent example of the former: the crippling casualties they suffered in the storming of fortified Spanish towns resolutely defended by French troops, a tragic object lesson of the latter, and on Wellington's insistence the Board of Ordnance set up an establishment for the instruction of junior engineer officers and soldiers in the 'duties of Sapping, Mining and other Military Field Works'. Furthermore, to stress their combat engineering role, the Corps of Royal Military Artificers was renamed the Corps of Royal Sappers and Miners.

The Field Works Establishment set up at Chatham exists today as the Royal School of Military Engineering, and its scope has widened over the years to include instruction in every branch of military and civil engineering the sappers have ever undertaken.

The sappers' main task during the Crimean War 1854–6 was the construction of batteries, trenches, saps and rifle pits steadily dug towards the walls of Sebastopol which it was planned to storm by escalade. It was the sappers who best knew their way about this maze of trenches and, with a white ribbon around their headdress to distinguish them, they were used as guides. 'Follow the Sapper: Quick March' became a well-known order to Infantry parties moving to positions allotted to them. 'Follow the Sapper' was also the cry when, at last, the order for the assault was given and the sappers rushed forward with their scaling ladders.

In the reorganizations that followed the Crimean War the Board of Ordnance, which had controlled the gunners and sappers for almost 450 years, was abolished and these two Arms came directly under the control of the Commander-in-Chief, while the Royal Sappers and Miners were incorporated into the Royal Engineers, thus ending the long-standing

the Royal Regiment of Artillery on a permanent basis. However for the next 150 years the Board's Engineer officers remained the architects of offensive siege operations responsible for siting and constructing the batteries from which the artillery fired their guns.

At that time civilian labour had to be hired for engineer tasks in peace. This system broke down when it became necessary urgently to strengthen the defences of the Rock of Gibraltar, and in 1772 a company of Soldiers Artificers – the first regular engineer soldiers of the Army – was raised there. The

anomaly of military engineer officers and soldiers belonging to separate corps.

The newly constituted corps shortly received a further dramatic infusion when, after the suppression of the Indian Mutiny 1857–8, the British officers of the East India Company's Engineers were transferred to it. These officers brought with them a remarkable tradition of achievements in war, and their vast irrigation schemes and other civil works carried out for the betterment of her people were a testimony of their long service to India. The company's three Indian other rank Corps of Sappers and Miners were retained in the newly-established Indian Army for which the Royal Engineers supplied officers and NCO instructors. British sappers also became responsible for the Indian Military Works Service and the Survey of India, and many were seconded to the Public Works Department, the State Railways, Telegraphic Services and other departments. A new era had dawned but the past traditions were preserved and the Royal Engineers continued to lead Indian sappers into battle and to serve the Sub-Continent until India and Pakistan became independent countries of the British Commonwealth in 1947.

For over 150 years the Royal Engineers built barracks for the Army and due to their training for this responsibility many became outstanding architects and town planners in both the military and civilian field. Three examples only of the latter must suffice. Captain Francis Fowke, sponsored by the Prince Consort, was the architect of the Dublin National Gallery, the Edinburgh Museum of Science and Art and London's Victoria and Albert Museum and Royal Albert Hall. Between 1826–32 Lt-Col. John By was engaged on constructing the Rideau Canal. As his headquarters he built the township of Bytown which has grown into Canada's capital city of Ottawa on the lines its far-seeing founder visualised when he first set out the original site. Many years later Sergeant Ellis RE, employed on the construction of the East African Highway, chose a site for a base camp and laid it out with such imagination that it has become Kenya's capital Nairobi.

The Jacobite Rising of 1745 gave birth to the Ordnance Survey of the United Kingdom. After the Battle of Culloden the Board of Ordnance sent its sappers into Scotland to build military roads and survey the Highlands. Later the threat of invasion from Revolutionary France necessitated a national survey. The Ordnance Survey, which produces maps of the United Kingdom to this day, is no longer a military organization, but its Director General is a

The blowing in of the Kashmir gate at the Siege of Delhi, 1857. An example of a typical engineer 'forlornhope'

serving Sapper Major-General and it still employs many Royal Engineers. The original mapping of almost every country of the British Commonwealth was carried out by sappers, and they have been employed on numerous International Boundary Commissions. The sappers also produce and distribute all maps and aeronautical charts required for military operations.

In 1825 the sappers began experimenting in firing electrically-detonated underwater charges to demolish wrecks in navigation channels and from this the art of submarine mining evolved. Later RE Companies were employed at home and overseas to lay and fire electrically-controlled minefields placed in

The Boer War. The Camp of 17th Company Royal Engineers with *Searchlight* at Frere

time of war to protect naval bases and important commercial ports. In addition they operated an underwater guided missile, the Brennan Torpedo, which could be directed against a hostile ship from a directing station ashore. When the Royal Navy took over submarine mining duties in 1906 the sappers turned their attention to coast defence searchlights to illuminate hostile craft by night, and then to anti-aircraft searchlights. Later the infra-red beam and radar made searchlights obsolete, but sappers still man searchlights for battlefield illumination.

A traction engine known as a 'steam sapper' towing a train of trailers, used extensively during the Boer War 1899–1902, was the parent of mechanical transport in the British Army. Although the tank of World War I was the child of many brains, two sapper officers, Major-Generals Sir Ernest Swinton and Sir John Capper, were largely responsible for its practical development, and a sapper Brigadier-General (later Lt-Gen.) Sir Hugh Elles led 350 tanks victoriously into action at the Battle of Cambrai in 1917 flying his pennant in the foremost tank. With the introduction of armoured warfare came the anti-

tank mine, and with it the sapper tasks of both siting and laying defensive mines and breaching enemy minefields to allow our armour to pass through.

For 50 years between 1862 and 1912 the sappers were responsible for military flying. This at first was limited to the use of balloons and man-carrying kites. Later the powered airship and aeroplane were introduced into the service and aerial navigation equipment, wireless communications, aerial photography and bomb sights developed. The pioneering days of military aeronautics were over, and in 1912 the Royal Engineers gave birth to the Royal Flying Corps, organised into a Military and a Naval Wing, from which the Royal Air Force and the Fleet Air Arm are descended, and from the R E Balloon Factory at Farnborough has grown the present Royal Aircraft Establishment.

A primitive form of military railway was first used in the Crimean War. The success of Kitchener's reconquest of the Sudan in 1895–8 rested largely on the railway laid and operated by sappers across a waterless desert. The sapper-operated railways and armoured trains played a vital role in the Boer War

Bridging, a typical Royal Engineer task. Sappers have laid a bridge across the River Marne at La Ferté sous Jouarre 10 September 1914. 'D' Company 1st Battalion. The Cameronians are crossing it.

1899–1902, and the vast armies of both World Wars could not have been maintained without the backing of the RE Transportation Service that operated the ports, railways, inland waterways and coastal craft in every theatre of operations.

The Germans first used poison gas in World War I against our troops in April 1915. The sappers were given the task of providing methods to retaliate, and by enlisting the assistance of the best physicists and meteorological experts the sappers were able to launch their first gas attack as a preliminary to the Battle of Loos in September that year.

The need for large scale concealment against ground and air observation became essential as operations on the Western Front stabilised into a long period of static trench warfare, and it became yet another RE task to provide the answer. By enlisting this time the services of artists and theatrical scenery painters, the sappers raised camouflage units and factories were set up to produce camouflage materials. RE Camouflage units were raised again in World War II, their task being not only counter-surveillance but also the production of dummy tank and vehicle concentrations, gun positions, pipe lines and landing craft, placed to mislead the enemy.

The German air raids on Great Britain during World War II called for an organization to deal with unexploded bombs, many of which buried themselves deep in the ground. The sappers were given the task of dealing with them, which was a grim and deadly game since nothing was then known of the mechanisms of German fuses nor ways of steaming the explosive charge out of the bombs they had located. RE Bomb Disposal units were later employed in every theatre and today they are still dealing with unexploded German bombs found in this country and Japanese bombs in the Far East.

When asked almost a hundred years ago to define a sapper Captain and Quartermaster T.W.J. Connolly, RE replied: 'He is a man of all work for the Army and the public, astronomer, geologist, surveyor, draughtsman, artist, architect, traveller, explorer, antiquary, mechanic, diver, soldier and sailor, ready to do anything or go anywhere; in short he is a sapper.'

The definition holds good today.

247

CHAPTER 28

The Inter-War Years 1919–39

THE LATE SIR BASIL LIDDELL HART

The most significant feature in the history of armies between the two World Wars, particularly that of the British Army, is the development of armoured forces and their operational technique. The tank had been brought into war, and by the British Army, in 1916. Two years later it played a great part in winning victory for the Western Allies. In the years immediately following the war it was developed from a slow-motion vehicle, which could only operate at an infantryman's pace, into a fast vehicle that could move at more than 30 m.p.h. Moreover, a new technique of fast mechanised operations was thought out, and worked out in practice, by a group of forward-thinking officers in the British Army.

Twenty years after the close of World War I, this technique became the most decisive in the next great war, particularly in the opening stages, which shaped the course of all that followed. But it was applied so strikingly not by the British Army, but by the German Army, which had adopted it – and much quicker than the British.

That was one of the supreme ironies of history. How did it come to pass? Partly it was due to the pressure of economy, and the usual reluctance to spend money on the armed forces that is a characteristic of peace-desiring countries. But that is by no means the whole explanation.

Victory tends to induce complacency, and satisfaction with things as they are. After victory had crowned their efforts in 1914–8, the military chiefs of the Western powers were dangerously content with the instruments they had possessed in the final stages. They were even inclined to go back to the instruments of 1914. Since several of them were cavalrymen they exalted the virtues of an arm for which they had a sentimental attachment, regardless of the small part that horse cavalry played in comparison with its scale.

That was illustrated in an important speech made as late as 1925 by the most highly respected British soldier of the time – Lord Haig, the Commander-in-Chief of our armies in France in World War I:

Some enthusiasts today talk about the probability of horses becoming extinct and prophesy that the aeroplane, the tank, and the motor car will supersede the horse in future wars. I believe that the value of the horse and the opportunity for the horse in the future are likely to be as great as ever ... I am all for using aeroplanes and tanks, but they are only accessories to the man and the horse, and I feel sure that as time goes on you will find just as much use for the horse – the well-bred horse – as you have ever done in the past.

Nevertheless, the advocates of the new idea prevailed so far that in 1927 the first complete mechanised force that the world had seen was experimentally formed on Salisbury Plain. Its trials were so successful that the then Chief of the Imperial General Staff, Sir George Milne, spoke of creating 'armoured divisions'.

But a conservative reaction soon set in, and in 1928 this first mechanised force was disbanded – a high officer announcing to the Press at the time: 'Cavalry are indispensable. Tanks are no longer a menace.'

In 1929 the War Office was persuaded to approve the issue of the first official manual of mechanised warfare, and it made sufficient impression to lead to the revival for trial of an armoured force in 1931. A year later this was dropped. A step forward, a step back – such was the fluctuating course of progress.

Despite much opposition, the new technique was by degrees worked out in practice during these years. Among those who took a leading part in its develop-

Opposite: A mixed tank battalion on training during the Thirties. In the foreground there is a Vickers medium tank, mark II

ment, special tribute is due to the far-ranging theoretical vision of Colonel Fuller, and then to the important practical contributions made by Colonels Lindsay, Broad, Pile, Hobart, and Major Martel. It was Hobart who, after being chosen to command the 1st Tank Brigade in 1934 – our first permanently established armoured formation – brought its operational technique a long jump ahead of that in any other army.

At that moment, when our rearmament programme was about to be launched, following the unmistakable signs that Nazi Germany was rearming rapidly, we had both the minds and the means to maintain our original lead in mechanised warfare. Unhappily, the heads of the War Office, in a pronouncement on policy, declared their obstinate conviction that 'We should go slowly with mechanisation.' Thus the Germans were given the chance to leap ahead. Meantime, the mechanised experts of the British Army were hobbled or shelved, apparently as a check upon their inconvenient persistence.

This treatment was the more unfortunate for Britain's prospects because the knowledge gained in developing the new offensive technique had led to the discovery of an effective counter-technique. But it had taken fully ten years to gain official acceptance for the former, and even then in a half-hearted way. So it was perhaps too much to expect that the antidote could have been approved and prepared in time.

A survey of the basic factors in the problem which faced us led me towards certain conclusions, mutually linked. First, that, in face of the growing strength of anti-tank defence, the best chance for applying the new offensive technique lay in starting with the advantage of surprise and a superiority in tanks and aircraft. Second, that the peace-seeking policy of France and Britain would inevitably deprive them of this opportunity. Third, that in these circumstances, their only hope lay in developing the capability for a 'defensive-offensive' strategy – and in providing the necessary modern means for it.

After a spell in the doldrums, a new impetus towards military reform and modernisation came in the summer of 1937 when Mr Leslie Hore-Belisha was appointed Secretary of State for War. The new Prime Minister, Mr Neville Chamberlain, had sent him to the War Office on the express ground that he wished to see 'drastic changes' – writing that 'the obstinacy of some of the Army heads in sticking to obsolete methods is incredible.'

At that moment – acting upon a suggestion from Sir Thomas Inskip, then Minister for the Co-

ordination of Defence – I was occupied in preparing a paper to show how the Army might be reorganised to meet modern conditions, and how, even within the limits of its existing scale, a more powerful type of force could be produced. This immediately aroused Mr Hore-Belisha's interest and, on his instructions, it was circulated throughout the War Office.

From this time onwards I was in close association with him, as personal adviser – and drafted a programme of reforms, which he approved. But as official progress became all too slow compared with the imminent risk of war, I gave up this advisory role the following summer in order to be free to press the urgency of the needs publicly – in the hope that the pressure of public opinion might help to overcome the constant obstruction that he had suffered from the 'old school'.

The weight of military authority was against any reorganisation, and content to proceed merely with the existing programme for a 1914-like Expeditionary Force of four to five infantry divisions and a solitary mobile division. Yet it had just become known that the Germans had formed their fourth armoured division, and that they were planning to equip such divisions with a more heavily armoured tank mounting a field gun.

A similar attitude was shown towards the proposals in a supplementary paper on measures that might be taken to improve the flow of promotion and the conditions of service in other respects. Since these steps would have the effect of quickening the advancement of younger men, it was natural that they should have been resisted by those who were then at the top. Moreover the idea of giving preference to officers who had grown up with the mechanised arm was repugnant to a still wider circle – of those whose whole service had been spent in practising the old style of warfare. While the opposition was thus quite understandable, the consequences were unfortunate for the country.

A variety of improvements were achieved during the next three months, especially in regard to the Regular soldier's conditions of service and in paving the way for the development of the Territorial Army. But much time was wasted in a prolonged argument as to whether the command of our first armoured mobile division, now being formed, should be given to a cavalryman or to a tankman – in other words, whether the choice should be determined by tradition or by reason.

In November 1937 I had reverted to the broader issues in a paper written, at the War Minister's request, on 'The Role of the Army'. In this, a survey

9th Lancers in light tanks while on manoeuvres. A light tank, mark V, is in the foreground

of our various strategic problems in the event of war with the Axis powers led to the conclusion that, even apart from any call to support France on land, it was beyond the capacity of our existing field force to cope with them.

To provide adequate security against the contingent dangers in the Middle East alone would, if we continued to rely on infantry divisions, require more such divisions than we had available altogether. Even if they were available they would not be the best type of force for operations on those far-stretching desert frontiers. A solution, I argued, could only be found by exploiting the potentialities of mechanised mobility, and increasing the proportion of such new-model forces – at the same time developing the resources of India as a means to furnish a modernised strategic reserve for the Middle and Far East.

I went on to emphasise that: 'A wider point worth attention is that the readjusted proportions of our forces would fit alternative Continental needs better than the present proportions. If circumstances should cause us to regard support to France as the more urgent contingency, the most effective type of support would be by armoured mobile divisions rather than by infantry divisions – the French have plenty of the latter but few of the former. Because of their value for rapid and powerful riposte in emergency, if any breach should be made in the French frontier defences, these would be a considerable asset – probably greater than if the whole Field Force of the present pattern were available.'

The views expressed in this paper proved extremely unpalatable in the higher military quarters, and the idea of any radical alteration in the ratio of armoured units to infantry was vigorously rejected.

No less stubborn was the resistance to an adequate

expansion of our anti-aircraft defences – which were the War Office's responsibility. The prevailing attitude was that money and resources applied to this purpose – on which depended the security of the army's national base – was an inconvenient diversion and virtual subtraction from the needs of the army proper.

The opposition offered to the adequate development of the anti-aircraft forces and of the mechanised forces did much to produce the decision to make radical changes in the Army Council, the existing military heads being replaced by officers half a generation younger. The result of these changes, however, fell short of anticipations. They brought only a modest development of ideas and plans, especially where the mechanised and anti-aircraft forces were concerned.

This may be accounted for by the fact that the new members of the Army Council were officers who had grown up in the older arms of the Service, though known as progressive members of them. Their choice was indicated not only by their personal ability but by the necessity of avoiding too great a shock to conservative opinion in the Army and in Parliament.

The new War Minister ran no small political risk in making such sweeping changes, and he was not so secure in his office that he could afford to give them too revolutionary a complexion. The predominant

importance of mechanised forces may seem obvious to all now, when it has been proved by bitter experience, but in 1937 'mechanisation' was still a suspicious term. Anyone who pressed its claims too strongly was apt to be labelled a 'tank-maniac' or 'military Bolshie'.

The effects of past environment and prolonged submission to a series of 'go-slow' regimes now became manifest. Twenty years of such a humid atmosphere had been enough to blunt the edge of the keenest minds, save when tempered by constant and direct contact with the mechanised arm. Where there is an incipient tendency to conservatism, nothing is more apt to develop it than sudden accession to authority.

At the same time, it became more difficult for the personally dynamic War Minister to apply a spur or press a differing view as strongly as he had done previously – lest it might be felt as showing a lack of confidence in the new team that had just been installed. The changes recently made could not be lightly repeated.

In the effort to speed up progress a natural but regrettable friction was generated. And from it developed a fresh 'heresy-hunt' against those who preached the gospel of armoured mobility. Their most prominent representative on the General Staff, Major-General P.C.S. Hobart, who had been made

The new style forces organised and trained after the precepts of Major-General P.C.S. Hobart.
British tanks in the Western Desert 1940

Director of Military Training just before the changes in the Army Council, was pushed out of the War Office at an early opportunity. With some difficulty, the continued use of his special knowledge was preserved, in a more limited sphere, by sending him to command the newly formed armoured division in Egypt. From this post he was in turn pushed out, and home, not long after the outbreak of war – six months before the Germans vindicated these ideas in the process of conquering France, while nearly a year before the new-style forces which he had trained won the battle of Sidi Barrani, and then swept through Cyrenaica, reducing the much larger Italian force to a state of paralysis. Because of his strong conviction that his ideas were right, he was doubtless a trying subordinate – but the test of war proved that he was right, and that his resentful superiors were out of date.

It would be unjust to belittle the progress that was made during the two years before the war. In numerous directions, steps were taken that had been overdue for twenty years – since the last war. The soldier's conditions of service and the prospects of the officer were greatly improved. In such respects, fresh and better foundations were laid. By comparison with the performance of any of its predecessors, its achievements were most notable. But by comparison with the needs of the situation and the pattern of the coming war it fell short.

Although the creation of an armoured division in Egypt had been agreed on, it was not until the Munich crisis in September 1938 that hasty steps were taken to improvise such a division in an incomplete form – and, after that, nothing more was done for a long time towards completing it. As for the second armoured division proposed for the Middle East, this remained in the realm of discussion, while little sense of urgency was shown about the formation of one in India. And not until the spring of 1939 was a definite decision taken to form a second armoured division at home.

The reorganisation of the Territorial Army was likewise delayed until after the Munich crisis, and then its new pattern field force was so designed as to provide nine infantry divisions of the revised pattern, three motorised divisions, and only one armoured division – instead of two.

There was a wide gulf between these measures and the 1937 project of three Regular armoured divisions at home, three abroad, and two more to be created in the Territorial Army. By May 1940 only the first of the armoured divisions destined for the Expeditionary Force was trained and equipped. Worse still, it was not sent to France before the German offensive was launched, and thus was not available when needed for the 'rapid and powerful riposte in emergency' visualised in 1937.

CHAPTER 29

The Second World War: The Years of Retreat 1939–42

HUBERT ESSAME

On 3 September 1939, while the air raid sirens, a lugubrious and unnecessary addition to his speech, wailed in the background, Neville Chamberlain announced that Hitler had invaded Poland; Britain with her ally France was at war with Germany.

Now Britain had to pay a heavy price for the follies of the past years. The German Army not only had a lead of at least three years over the British in armament and equipment but in mental preparation as well. Ironically the Germans, lacking guidance in their own country, had found it in the doctrine of *blitzkrieg*, the breakthrough by the armoured mass and deep penetration supported from the air propounded by Liddell Hart and Fuller in the early thirties and virtually ignored by the higher British military and political authorities at the time. It was this system of tactics which achieved the annihilation of the Polish Army in the short space of 18 days in September 1939.

The French Army and the BEF of four infantry divisions organised as two corps which now occupied the Maginot Line and its extension to the north along the Belgian frontier were still for the most part wedded to the ideas of the 1914–18 war. From September 1939 to May 1940, the so-called period of 'phoney war', they did virtually nothing except work on the inadequate defences and bombard the Germans with propaganda leaflets. By the latter date the BEF had been built up to ten divisions now organised as three corps and a solitary tank brigade. Its equipment however was incomplete, ammunition was short and many of its officers and men were only half trained. To sustain their morale the British had little more than their traditional discipline: some of the French divisions lacked even this prop.

First to pay the penalty for inadequate preparation

mental, moral and material were the three unfortunate Territorial brigades despatched without adequate air support to Namsos and Andalsnes when the Germans invaded Norway in April 1940. Ill-equipped and badly trained, although they fought bravely they were no match for the Germans and were only extricated with difficulty. In the north, 24th Guards Brigade, a demi-brigade of Chasseurs Alpins and a Polish Brigade sent to Narvik had more success but had to be withdrawn when France collapsed. In this short campaign political direction and inter-service cooperation reached an all-time low. Each service thought and planned in a world of its own. It is not surprising that it brought about the fall of Chamberlain's government and its replacement by a coalition under Churchill. The campaign therefore stands high in the long list of blessings in disguise with which the Army's history is studded.

The extent to which the Allies were outclassed in tactical method and leadership was now demonstrated on a much grander scale in the Low Countries and north-east France. Here in fact the Allies had a slight superiority in numbers and equipment and some of their tanks were of better design. They were however dispersed on a wide front with no reserves. When the Germans invaded Belgium on 10 May the BEF immediately advanced to the River Dyle only to fall back behind the Scheldt when the main German armoured thrust of seven Panzer divisions through the Ardennes virtually cut the Allied armies in half. This thrust reached Abbeville on 20 May. Thereafter the Allies in the north were steadily pressed inwards from three sides. On 27 May Gort was ordered to save as much of the BEF as possible through Dunkirk. The actual evacuation over the beaches lasted nine days – a splendid achievement

Opposite above: Dunkirk. Troops waiting to embark. *Below:* Girls of the Auxiliary Territorial Army ATS manning the controls of an anti-aircraft gunsite during a night action

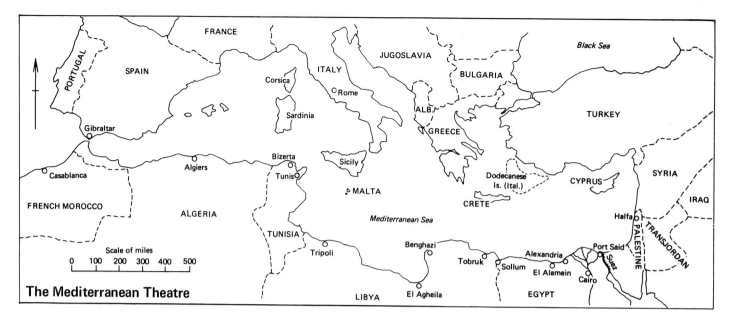

The Mediterranean Theatre

for which virtually the whole credit goes to the RN and RAF. Eight hundred and eighty-seven ships of all sizes were used: the RAF in a period of four days shot down 179 enemy aircraft for the loss of 29. Altogether about 225,000 British and 110,000 French were taken off. Skilful propaganda at the time painted the evacuation almost as if it were a victory; the truth was that the BEF, although its discipline remained intact, had been defeated in battle and had lost practically all its equipment. As Churchill said, wars are not won by evacuations. The only consolation was that the nucleus of the Regular Army, upon which new armies could be built, had been saved.

The decisive event in the history of the Army, and indeed of the nation in 1940, was the Battle of Britain. Thanks to the victory of the RAF in which Anti-Aircraft Command played a secondary rôle, Alanbrooke, the Commander-in-Chief Home Forces, was able to begin to reorganise and retrain the Army on more realistic lines for mobile warfare, passing over responsibility for coastal defence progressively to the Home Guard as the danger of invasion receded. In the evolution of new training doctrines Paget, Alanbrooke's successor as Commander-in-Chief Home Forces and Montgomery played a prominent part. Britain's full productive capacity was now turned towards the re-equipment of the Army: much material came from the United States despite the fact that they were neutral. The expected German invasion never came. Nevertheless the Germans remained in occupation of the whole of Western

Europe from France to Norway and, in the eyes of the world outside Britain, were there to stay. In the grim winter of 1940 Britain, under nightly air bombardment but sustained by the leadership of Churchill, stood alone.

At this dark time came the first good news of the war – victory in Africa. In June, on the collapse of France, Italy had entered the war. In September, Graziani with seven divisions began an advance from Libya towards Egypt, took Sollum and reached Sidi Barrani. Here he halted in a series of fortified camps on a fifty-mile front for administrative reasons. Opposing him Wavell had only the Western Desert Force of 4th Indian and 7th Armoured Divisions

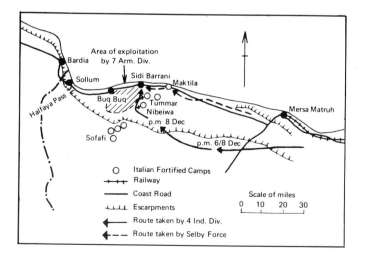

256

The Western Desert. Matilda tanks passing an abandoned Italian gun position, 19 December 1940

under O'Connor. Outnumbered five to one, he decided to attack. His armour fortunately included the Matildas of 7th RTR sent out by Churchill via the Cape at the height of the Battle of Britain and when invasion seemed imminent. Although the British did not know it, the Italians had no anti-tank weapons capable of piercing the armour of these particular tanks. On the night of 8–9 December, O'Connor's force penetrated the rear of the line of Italian fortified camps and rolled them up in succession. Two nights later they cut across the desert to the sea west of Sidi Barrani to block the Italian retreat. Altogether five divisions were destroyed. O'Connor pushed boldly on. Bardia fell on 5 January and Tobruk on the 22nd. At Beda Fomm on 8 February the last of the Italians were defeated. Altogether a British force of two divisions had destroyed an army five times its own size, taken 130,000 prisoners, 380 tanks and 845 guns for the loss of 500 dead and 1,400 wounded. It had been a triumph for brilliant generalship, high morale, mobility, improvisation and speed.

Meanwhile other smaller forces consisting mainly of Indian and African troops under Platt and Cunningham had started operations against the Italians in East Africa, Eritrea and Abyssinia, culminating in their final defeat in May.

In October 1940 the Italians had invaded Greece but by February 1941 had got themselves in such difficulties that the Germans had to intervene on their behalf. With Wavell's concurrence the decision was now taken to send the 1st New Zealand, the 6th and 7th Australian divisions and part of 2nd Armoured division to help the Greeks. This involved reducing the garrison of Cyrenaica to what remained of the 2nd Armoured Division and the 9th Australian Division which was partially trained and also incomplete. Rommel had arrived in Tripoli on 12 February with the leading elements of the Afrika Korps. He soon found out how weak the British were and by a ruthless advance along the coast and across the desert chased the Australians back into Tobruk and reached the Egyptian frontier in a lightning campaign lasting only 14 days. O'Connor, who had come forward as an adviser, was captured: Tobruk, however, resisted all Rommel's efforts to take it.

Meanwhile there had been disasters in Greece and Crete resulting in the rapid expulsion of the troops and severe losses to the Navy and RAF. Pressed by Churchill to stage a counter-offensive in Cyrenaica and to relieve Tobruk, Wavell attacked prematurely in June with the XIII Corps consisting of 7th Armoured Division, 4th Indian Division and 22nd Guards Brigade. In this battle, known by the code name of 'Battleaxe' Rommel, by the skilful use of his anti-tank screen of 88s and by using his forces concentrated, massacred our armour and forced us to withdraw to our original start line. The truth was that in armoured warfare we had everything to learn, that our command system was inflexible, our wireless procedure and equipment bad, and our recovery system inadequate. Wavell's transfer to India and his replacement in the Middle East by Auchinleck

R

followed this defeat.

During this period Wavell had had to deal with a dangerous rebellion in Iraq and a very awkward situation with the Vichy French in Syria. Auchinleck therefore reorganised his forces as 8th Army in the Western Desert, 9th Army in Palestine and Syria and 10th Army in Iraq. Eighth Army under Cunningham now consisted of two Corps, the XIII under Godwin-Austen and XXX Corps under Willoughby-Norrie.

Churchill's impatience and pressure for a quick victory at this time are understandable. The air and naval situation in the Mediterranean was deteriorating rapidly, the USSR was *in extremis* and the threat of war in the Far East was increasing. Tobruk was still under siege and placing a very heavy strain on our sea and air resources. Cunningham's opening gambit with XXX Corps, which included most of the armour, was an advance on the desert flank designed to bring Rommel's armour to battle. Rommel did not react as expected. Our armour therefore pressed on to Sidi Rezegh. Three days of intense fighting followed in which we lost two thirds of our tanks and Rommel staged his celebrated raid into our rear areas. At this crisis Auchinleck came forward, took personal command and eventually turned the tables on Rommel. The Tobruk garrison now broke out: Rommel was driven back first to Gazala and then pursued by XIII Corps to Agedabia. Eighth Army's supply line was now stretched to the limit. This prolonged battle, called by the code-name

'Crusader', had been an expensive victory. The 8th Army had fought well but as will be seen, had developed an inferiority complex with regard to its own equipment in face of the German tanks. In fact, Rommel's strength lay in his anti-tank guns and his superior technique.

With the start of intense Axis air attacks on Malta and the arrival of 25 U-boats in the Mediterranean, the situation both in the air and at sea now took an adverse turn. Rommel's recuperation was rapid. In January 1942 he once again launched a spoiling attack, found out how weak and dispersed we were in Cyrenaica and soon hustled XIII Corps 300 miles back to the Gazala position. At the crisis of the battle a difference of opinion between Ritchie, the Army Commander, and Godwin-Austen, the Corps Commander, resulted in the wrong decision being taken.

Now came a lull of three months in the Western Desert with Auchinleck building up supplies for the resumption of the offensive to recapture the airfields in Western Cyrenaica, now a matter of over-riding urgency owing to the attacks on Malta.

The Gazala position, held by XIII Corps on the right and XXX Corps on the left stretching from the sea to the old Turkish fort at Bir Hacheim, was in fact a series of brigade localities too far apart to be mutually supporting. There were extensive minefields between them, but not all were under the close fire of the defenders. Numerically we had superiority in tanks. True to form, Rommel struck first on 26

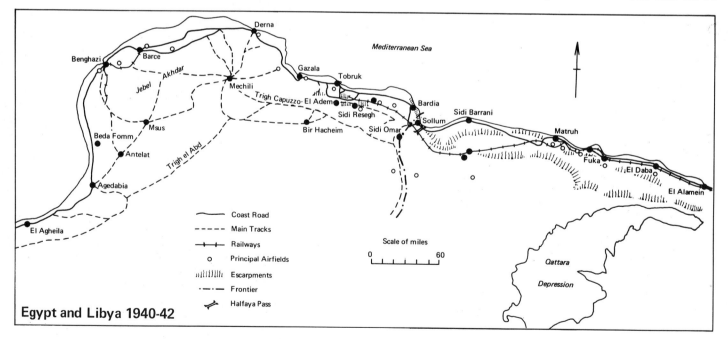

Egypt and Libya 1940-42

Coast Road
Main Tracks
Railways
Principal Airfields
Escarpments
Frontier
Halfaya Pass

Scale of miles
0   60

Opposite above: The siege of Tobruk. A British 25-pounder field battery in action, 13 September 1941. Note the wide dispersion of the guns, a precaution against enemy air attack
Below: Eritrea. The Battle of Keren. An armoured car in difficulties 7 April 1941. The photograph shows the mountainous nature of the country where the 4th and 5th Indian divisions decisively defeated the Italians

British troops advancing in open order at the Battle of Alamein, after the night bombardment, 26 October 1942

May with a great sweep by the Afrika Korps, the XX Italian Corps and 90th Light Division, combined with an attack in the centre designed to create a corridor through the positions held by 50th Division. There followed ten days of chaos and on our part abortive operations in the 'Cauldron' battles, ending with the fall of Bir Hacheim. Rommel now struck his final blow. Tobruk fell into his hands on 21 June with 32,000 prisoners and sufficient supplies and petrol to carry him all the way to Alamein. Rommel pressed on with lightning speed against Auchinleck, who had now taken over command from Ritchie, and bounced him out of the Matruh position. By 30 June, 8th Army were back at the Alamein position only 60 miles from Alexandria.

The truth is that we had been out-generalled. We had in the Gazala battle more tanks than the Germans, but Ritchie never had his finger on the pulse of the battle: he dispersed his efforts while Rommel concentrated his.

The first Battle of Alam Halfa (or El Alamein) fought by the 8th Army under Auchinleck's direct command is now seen as the turning point of the war in Africa. Rommel, with troops on the verge of exhaustion and down to 55 tanks, attacked again on 1 July in the hope of achieving another breakthrough. This time he was held, counter-attacked and finally driven back (3 July). There was no pursuit. The supply pendulum had now swung against the Germans: Rommel was now 680 miles in advance of his main base at Benghazi with his communications under continuous attack by the RAF under Tedder. Three hundred Sherman tanks and 100 self-propelled

guns were soon to reach 8th Army from the United States. Furthermore 8th Army was now within less than 100 miles of the vast Middle East Base and reinforcements were arriving in the theatre.

In mid-August Churchill saw fit to replace Auchinleck by Alexander and to give Montgomery command of 8th Army. The latter was not slow to make clear to all concerned that he intended to knock the Axis forces 'for six' out of Africa and that, if they could not stay alive in the Alamein position, they would stay there dead. He was equally determined not to resume the offensive until he had built up the necessary supplies and ammunition and a large reserve of tanks. His immediate problem was how to deal with Rommel's attack now known to be imminent. Montgomery reached the conclusion that Rommel's objective would be the Alam Halfa Ridge. He therefore moved up the newly arrived 44th Division to hold it aided by the dug-in tanks of 22nd Armoured Brigade. Up to this time Rommel's tactics had been to induce us to make our first attack against his armour which he protected by a screen of anti-tank guns. Having knocked out the bulk of our armour, he then counter-attacked with his own supported by maximum possible fire. Montgomery decided to try these tactics on Rommel for a change. Duly on 30 August Rommel's expected attack came in round the southern flank. It soon ran into trouble on our minefields, got behind schedule and was caught in daylight by our anti-tank guns and the artillery on the Alam Halfa Ridge. Under continuous hammering from the RAF, Rommel had to call the battle off. Montgomery did not pursue

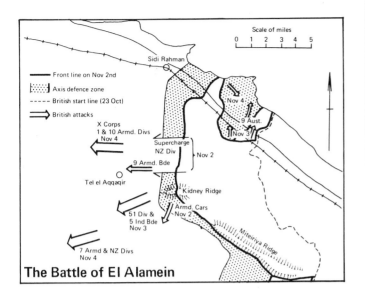

The Battle of El Alamein

Front line on Nov 2nd
Axis defence zone
British start line (23 Oct)
British attacks

Scale of miles
0 1 2 3 4 5

Sidi Rahman

Nov 4

9 Aust.

Nov 3

X Corps
1 & 10 Armd. Divs
Nov 4

Supercharge
NZ Div   Nov 2

9 Armd. Bde

Tel el Aqqaqir

Kidney Ridge

Armd. Cars
Nov 2

51 Div &
5 Ind Bde
Nov 3

Miteiriya Ridge

7 Armd & NZ Divs
Nov 4

Alamein. British Infantry are rushing a strong point,
26 October 1942

because he considered that his armour was insufficiently trained for a mobile battle in the open and because his administrative arrangements for the conquest of Libya were not yet complete. He had inflicted a severe reverse on Rommel and revived the morale of 8th Army. Thus ended the Second Battle of Alam Halfa.

At Alamein Rommel had secure flanks: his defensive positions were protected by minefields in considerable depth and all were covered by fire. It was therefore necessary for the attack to be delivered by night to enable the infantry and engineers to pick up the mines. On 23 October there was a full moon. By this date, the RAF under Tedder had already won the battle in the air and now outnumbered the Germans by three to one. Montgomery also had numerical superiority in troops and tanks. He now had three Corps, XXX Corps on the sea flank and XIII Corps on its left. X Corps, Montgomery's *Corps de Chasse* contained all the armoured divisions. In brief he planned to punch two corridors through Rommel's position on XXX Corps front and then immediately to launch the armour of X Corps close on the heels of the infantry thus forcing Rommel's armoured divisions to attack his tanks in position. Meanwhile the infantry divisions would defeat the enemy infantry by what he described as 'crumbling' operations on their flanks and rear. The cover plan with dummy installations and diversions conveyed the impression that the main attack would come in the south.

The attack duly went in at 21·40 hours on 23 October supported by concentrated artillery fire,

reminiscent of the great battles of World War I. German resistance, particularly in the north, proved formidable. For the first week there was bitter fighting. Montgomery therefore switched his main effort to the north with 9th Australian Division and thus attracted much of Rommel's armour in that direction. He now pulled out his armour for the decisive blow known as 'Supercharge'. This went in on 2 November a little to the south of the original breach. This choice was most fortunate as it struck the junction point of the Germans and the Italians. 51st Division and the 2nd New Zealand Division broke out and X Corps finally reduced Rommel to 35 serviceable tanks. The battle was over. Altogether it had lasted 10 days: we took 30,000 prisoners of war including 9 generals.

Few battles have been the subject of more criticism than El Alamein. It may be that it was an error to superimpose the armour of X Corps on the infantry in the corridors; there may have been delay in mounting the pursuit. The fact remains to use Montgomery's own words: 'I won: there can be no argument about that.' As Churchill said of another battle, 'The gleam of victory had caught the helmets of our soldiers. For the Germans in Africa it was the beginning of the end and for the British the end of the beginning.'

By now thanks to the efforts of the whole united nation, the Commonwealth and our Allies under Churchill's inspiration, the Army in the United Kingdom, Africa and South-East Asia had reached 2½ million of whom 175,000 were women. The days of retreat were at an end.

General (later Field Marshal the Viscount) Montgomery in conversation with General Brooke (later Field Marshal the Viscount Alanbrooke) Normandy, 12 June 1944

CHAPTER 30

The Years of Victory
1942–45

HUBERT ESSAME

After Alamein Rommel abandoned his Italian allies but still regained control of what was left of the Afrika Korps. Such was the state of confusion in the area of the break-in after the battle that the pursuit took some time to develop. Rommel succeeded in evading Montgomery's attempts to cut him off by hooks towards the sea. Heavy rain then slowed down operations. Rommel was thus able to conduct a skilful 1,500 mile withdrawal to the Tunisian border.

Alamein had a political aim: to induce the French in North-West Africa not to oppose the Anglo-American landings known as 'Torch'. When these duly came off on 8 November at Casablanca, Oran and Algiers there was virtually no resistance. Admiral Darlan under American pressure was induced to order a cease-fire. Unfortunately Eisenhower had no troops immediately available to intervene in Tunis. A few British troops from the leading elements of First Army reached Bone and Bougie on 11 and 12 November but by this time the Luftwaffe had already taken over the major airfields in Tunisia and reinforcements intended for Rommel were arriving. By the end of November the Axis had over 17,000 troops including part of 10th Panzer Division in the area. The leading troops of Anderson's First Army thus lost the race to Tunis although they got within 15 miles of the city. By the end of February Axis troops in Tunis had been built up to 4 armoured divisions and 10 infantry divisions under Rommel. At this time, Eisenhower could only muster in the forward area three and a half British Divisions, three US divisions and two ill-equipped French divisions.

From the east Montgomery reached the port of Tripoli on 23 January and, having thus solved his administrative problem, pushed on towards the Mareth Line, a strong system of fortifications on the southern Tunisian border. Rommel thus enjoyed the advantages of the central position or 'interior lines'. On 17 February he flung his weight against the inexperienced United States II Corps, broke through and threatened to outflank the British First Army in the north. This attack, which looked very serious at the time, was eventually held by a mixed force of British armour and American and British artillery at the Kasserine Pass.

At this stage Alexander took over command of all Allied land forces in North Africa. When Rommel turned on Montgomery on 6 March at Medenine, he was induced to throw all three of his armoured divisions against 500 anti-tank guns and was pushed back with very heavy loss. As at Alam Halfa Montgomery had sited these guns to kill tanks to protect the infantry. His concentrated artillery fire was devastating. He now proceeded with his meticulous preparations to smash the Mareth Line.

This battle, which started on 20 March, has all the characteristics of the Montgomery technique in its most effective form. The enemy's position on the seaward flank was immensely strong owing to wadis and concrete defences: in the centre stood the rugged and intricate Matamata Hills: the west flank rested on the waterless desert. The Long Range Desert Group however had found a way round this flank via the Tebaga Defile. Montgomery opened the battle on 20 March by attacking on the coastal flank to draw the enemy reserves in that direction. This attack, though repulsed, attracted von Arnim's reserves, and Montgomery now attacked in the centre to keep them there. Having done this, he swung Horrocks X Corps round the west flank. This attack went in at the unusual hour of 4·00 p.m. on 26 March when the sun was in the Germans' eyes. It was supported by 22

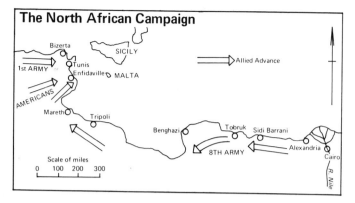

The North African Campaign

fighter squadrons of the Desert Air Force in a low flying rôle laying a moving carpet of bombs. It continued throughout the night and by dawn had cleared the Tebaga defile forcing the battered Germans to abandon Gabes and fall back on the Wadi Akarit. Here they were once again smashed by Montgomery and pursued to the Enfidaville position.

Alexander now transferred 7th Armoured Division, 4th Indian Division and 201 Guards Brigade to the First Army front where the ground was more suitable for armour. By the last week in April the whole of the Axis forces were penned in the northeast corner of Tunisia and had lost command both of the sea and air. They were thus in no position either to remain where they were or to withdraw. On 6 May Alexander attacked with the British Ninth Corps and the United States II Corps. The Axis defences collapsed in a few hours and von Arnim was forced to surrender on the following day with about a quarter of a million men. The war in Africa was over: it only remained to secure Sicily to ensure complete command of the Mediterranean.

Two vital Allied Conferences between Churchill and Roosevelt in early 1943 virtually decided the form of operations for that year and the first half of 1944. At Casablanca in January, whilst operations in North Africa were still in progress, it was agreed to invade Sicily and thus finally consolidate Allied sea and air supremacy in the Mediterranean. In May at Washington, 'Overlord', the Anglo-American plan for the invasion of France was finally made, to use Churchill's words, 'the keystone of Anglo-United States Cooperation' for 1944 – in other words, given priority over all other Allied operations. Furthermore, it was agreed to withdraw in November four American and three British divisions from the Mediterranean to the United Kingdom for the invasion of France. Eisenhower however was given permission after the conquest of Sicily to go on to the mainland with the forces he then had if Italy collapsed.

Owing to the absence of commanders on opera-

tions and the fact that the planners were separated in London, Algiers, and Cairo, it was not until May that the plan for 'Husky' took its final form of a landing by the 7th US Army under Patton and the 8th Army under Montgomery in the south-east corner of the island in order to ensure the speedy capture of the major airfields. Opposing them were one Italian Corps at the west end of the island and one at the east, backed by XIV Panzer Corps under Hube and consisting of 15th Panzer Grenadier Division and the Hermann Göring Panzer Division. The actual invading force commanded by Eisenhower assisted by Admiral Ramsay, with Alexander commanding the Land Forces, Cunningham the Allied Navies and Tedder the Allied Air Forces, constituted the largest combined operation of the war. Over 2,000 landing craft were used. The actual landing on 10 July, carried out under conditions of air and sea dominance, was a complete success despite the fact that, owing to inexperienced pilots, the airborne landings were less effective than had been hoped. By 16 July, the Allies held 15 airfields and were firmly ashore. Thereafter, owing to lack of complete accord between the Allied commanders, the intricate nature of the country and the skilful handling of the German rearguard in the difficult country around Etna, operations proceeded more slowly than had been expected. Finally the Germans succeeded in withdrawing in their own time with most of their equipment across the Straits of Messina.

Meanwhile secret negotiations had been going on with the Italians with a view to their changing sides. Mussolini fell on 25 July. Eisenhower, therefore, with the aim of capturing Naples and securing the Foggia airfields for use by the strategic air forces ordered Mark Clark, commanding 5th Army, to plan for a landing at Salerno ('Avalanche') and Montgomery, after the completion of the conquest of Sicily, to cross the Messina Straits. This Montgomery did with little opposition on 3 September and pushed north. On 9 September the Italian capitulation was announced on the radio. First Airborne Division sailed into Taranto unopposed to be followed by the 78th Division: both then advanced northwards. Unfortunately at Salerno the Germans had taken over the defences from the Italians even as the invading force was approaching the shore. The British 10th Corps got ashore reasonably well and Commandos and Rangers seized the defiles leading into the Plain of Naples. On the right however the landing of the US 6th Corps was confused. The Germans soon found the gap between the British and the Americans in the Sele valley. They had all the advantages of observation and at times the situation was critical. The British lost Battipaglia and the Americans were pushed back to within three miles of the sea. Mark Clark at one time considered evacuation but was reassured by the Royal Navy whose ships' guns brought the German tanks to a halt. On 16 September, however, the approach of the 8th Army caused the Germans to pull out. Seventh Armoured Division now burst into the Naples Plain. Eighth Army was then switched to east of the Apennines and on 27 September secured the Foggia airfields. Naples fell on 1 October. The autumn rains and the need to reorganise the administrative backing now necessitated a temporary pause.

In November a decision was reached at the Teheran Conference between Stalin, Roosevelt and Churchill which profoundly affected the future of the whole Italian campaign. Stalin agreed with the Americans that simultaneously with the landings in Northern France in 1944 divisions should be taken from the Italian front to land in the south of France and develop an offensive up the Rhone valley. This suited Stalin: it would keep the British and Americans away from the Balkans and Eastern Europe. This decision ultimately hamstrung the Italian campaign as will be seen.

For the moment however the Western Allies were agreed that the advance should be continued up the Italian peninsula with a view to tying down as many German divisions as possible away from the intended main effort in north France and also of securing the valuable prestige objective of Rome. Desirable though these aims were strategically, tactically most of the advantages were with the Germans. The country was ideally suited to defence and cut in half by the central mountain mass with few laterals. In ever deteriorating weather the German 10th Army under Vietinghoff slowly withdrew to the Gustav Line. This ran roughly along the Garigliano and Rapido rivers, by Monte Cassino, through the central mountains to the river Sangro. Three months work had gone into the preparation of the position: it was immensely strong. In the centre Monte Cassino with the world-famous monastery on its crest dominated Route 6 up the Liri Valley, the only suitable line of advance to Rome.

The fierce battles of January 1944 on the Garigliano at Cassino and Anzio had their origin in Churchill's meeting with Alexander and Eisenhower at Carthage on 25 December, Mark Clark was ordered to combine an attack on the Garigliano front using X British Corps, II United States Corps and the French Expeditionary Corps with a landing by VI Corps at Anzio 65 miles to the north in the hope of

General Alexander (later Field-Marshal the Earl Alexander of Tunis) and General Eisenhower (later President of the United States) conferring in Tunisia

The Italian Campaign

Cassino. The strategic Air Force has bombed the town and New Zealand troops are about to
launch the attack which captured the town and Castle Hill (right background)

forcing the enemy to divide his forces and then, apparently, break through on one front or the other.
For the Anzio landing there were only sufficient
assault craft to land 1st British Division, 3rd US
Division and 5th US battalions. Alexander's orders
for VI Corps prescribed an advance to the Alban
Hills: Headquarters V Army, which took a gloomy
view of the prospects of the landing, watered this
down to 'on the Alban Hills'.

On 17 January X Corps attacked across the
Garigliano near its mouth and met with such success
that Kesselring was compelled to send I Para Corps
from his strategic reserve in the Rome area to stabilise
the situation. Further north, US II Corps followed
with an attack at S. Angelo with 36 Division which

failed. The other division of this corps, however, 34th
Division, succeeded in vile weather in reaching
Caira in the foothills of the Cassino feature. Further
north the French Expeditionary Corps reached the
Colle Belvedere.

The landing at Anzio on 23 January secured complete surprise. By midnight both divisions were on
their D Day objectives. There were in fact for the
next 48 hours no more than the equivalent of two
battalions in the area. However, Lucas the corps
commander did nothing except consolidate his
bridgehead for nearly a week. When he did advance
on 30 January there were two German divisions
waiting for him with all the advantages of higher
ground. In the first week of February VI Corps only

Opposite above: British troops land in the docks at Salerno 11 September 1943
Below: Allied troops land at Anzio. On the right two DUKWS (amphibious vehicles) manned
by US troops move towards the shore

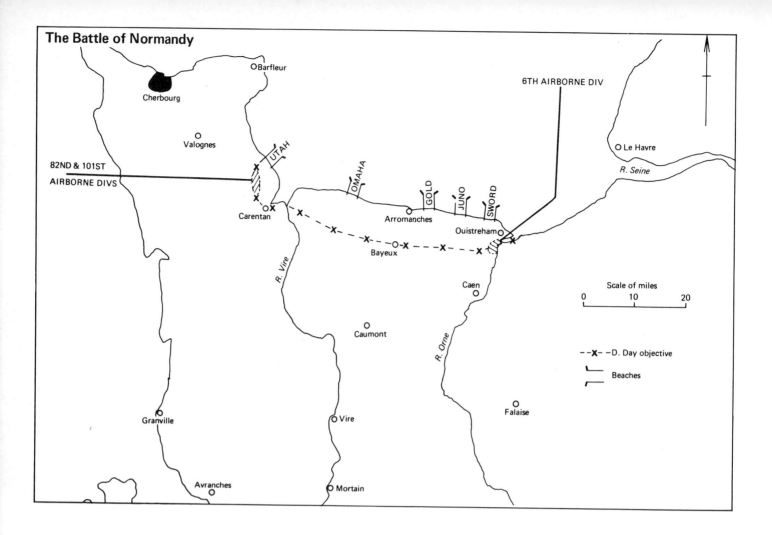

The Battle of Normandy

just succeeded in holding the very violent German attempts in great strength to drive them into the sea.

In February the 1st New Zealand Corps (2nd New Zealand, 4th Indian and 78th British Divisions) under Freyberg took over the Cassino front. Now followed the bombing of the Monastery and the epic attempts in this month and March to carry it by storm. With morale at a very high level on both sides and all the advantages of an almost impregnable defensive position with the Germans, the battle ended on 23 March in stalemate.

Alexander decided to suspend operations until the weather improved. Meanwhile he was fulfilling his strategic aim of forcing the Germans to retain in Italy the maximum number of divisions at the time of launching 'Overlord'. For the final battle of Cassino he chose to use 8th Army on the right and 5th Army on the left respectively on Routes 6 and 7 to destroy the right wing of the German 10th Army and drive its remains north of Rome. Giving the impression that he intended to land a force at Civita Vecchia and thus forcing Kesselring to retain reserves north

of Rome, he secretly achieved a concentration of 13 divisions against 5 between Cassino and the sea. The battle opened on 11 May: in the course of bitter fighting the French Expeditionary Corps in the Aurunchi Mountains broke out and threatened the German escape route down the Liri Valley. On 18 May Cassino fell to the Poles; on 23 May VI Corps, built up to 6 divisions, broke out. Within two days it had linked up with 5th Army coming up from the south and was within striking distance of Valmontone on Route 6, where Alexander intended it should cut off the retreating 10th Army. Mark Clark decided instead to change direction with VI Corps and thrust direct on Rome. In consequence a large number of Germans got away. However on 4 June American armoured cars entered Rome. Thus it came about that what Hannibal had failed to do, was achieved by Mark Clark – without elephants, a surprising oversight on his part. Twenty-six German divisions had been severely mauled, some of which had it not been for the efforts of 5th and 8th Armies might well have tipped the scale against us in Normandy.

268

The river Orne. Sappers are constructing a pontoon bridge. Beyond them can be seen the permanent bridge which glider borne troops landed on and captured by a brilliant surprise attack in the early hours of 'D' Day

Below: Sherman tanks massing for an attack on Caen, 8 July 1944

For 'Overlord', the invasion of France, Eisenhower, the Supreme Commander, had Tedder as his deputy, Ramsay commanding the Allied Navies, Montgomery commanding the Land Forces until Supreme Headquarters was established in France and Leigh-Mallory commanding the Allied Expeditionary Air Forces. Montgomery planned to land in Normandy with 1st United States Army on the right and 2nd British Army on the left between the Rivers Orne and Vire on a front of five divisions, dropping two United States Airborne Divisions to protect the right flank and 6th Airborne Division to protect the left east of the Orne and to have 18 divisions ashore by the end of the first week. Before landing, the Allied Air Forces had partially crippled the French railways system and destroyed 18 out of the 24 bridges over the Seine. The plan was disguised from the Germans by creating the impression that the invasion when it came would be in the Pas de Calais. The actual site selected for the landing came within the domain of Army Group 'B' commanded by Rommel who in his turn was responsible to von Rundstedt. The former wished

to place the armoured divisions well forward so that they could prevent any landing on the beaches: the latter favoured holding them back for a counterstroke in force once the main landing was clearly defined. Hitler ordered a compromise – the infantry forward and the armour back.

Under conditions of complete air dominance the actual landing caught the Germans off balance: Rommel was away. On Omaha Beach the Americans met with particularly heavy opposition: this was overcome. The British landings were well supported by the Royal Navy and the specialised tanks of 79th Armoured Division.

Montgomery's intention, once ashore, was to threaten to break out on the eastern flank at Caen and by these means to draw the German Panzer Divisions in this direction. Having done this, he proposed to break out on the west flank with the American armies. This was his original conception and, despite intrigue centring around Tedder, he never deviated from it. Meanwhile the Americans had struck fighting of a peculiarly difficult character

Overleaf: The 13th/18th Hussars going ashore in Normandy, 6 June 1944. A guiding flare is burning on the beach

British troops supported by Churchill tanks making an attack in Normandy

in the *bocage* country of the Cherbourg peninsula. In the latter half of June and throughout July, fighting of the fiercest character developed around Caen between the British and Canadians and the majority of the Panzer Divisions. As a result when Bradley's breakout started on 25 July at St Lo, near Caumont, 6 of the 8 Panzer divisions were in the Caen area opposite the British. Hitler now (6 August) issued orders which can only be described as insane – he ordered all the Panzer divisions under Eberbach to strike due west from Mortain to Avranches. As a result they were battered to death by the air forces and the artillery and penned into a pocket called the Falaise Pocket by the American, British and Canadian armies. A quarter of a million men, 1,500 tanks, 3,000 guns and 20,000 vehicles were destroyed. Montgomery now proposed that all the Allied administrative resources should be concentrated with all speed for a single thrust in overwhelming strength designed to seize the Ruhr and then move on to Berlin. Eisenhower, who took command of the land forces in addition to his duties as Supreme Commander (1 September), had other ideas.

In consequence from 1 September onwards the Allied armies advanced not so much on a broad front as on several uncoordinated fronts. Space does not permit discussion of the complex issues of the Broad versus Narrow Front controversy. It will suffice to say that for Montgomery's concept of concentration on a narrow front to have succeeded, the decision would have had to be taken at the end of August to enable the necessary administrative and planning arrangements to be made. When the British 11th Armoured Division captured Antwerp on 4 September pressure should have been applied to clear the approaches as well. Concentration then on a single Allied thrust in overwhelming strength before von Rundstedt and his staff had succeeded in restoring order in the German forces might at least have secured a crossing over the Rhine before the autumn rains came. As it was, it was not until 17 September that the Arnhem operation was launched. The plan was ambitious, too ambitious as it turned out. Two river crossings were to be seized by the American 101st and 82nd Airborne divisions, and a third, the vital crossing of the lower Rhine at Arnhem, was to be captured by the British 1st Airborne Division. XXX British Corps was then to advance and link the crossings up. The operation was hastily planned, the intelligence on which it was based was bad and the weather after the first day was unsuitable for airborne operations. Unfortunately shortage of aircraft necessitated a fly-in by 1st Airborne Division in three lifts. The dropping zones selected were virtually on the doorstep of the 9th and 10th SS Panzer Divisions and too far from the objectives: a parachute brigade should have been dropped on the polders close to Arnhem bridge. XXX Corps was expected to advance 60 miles over three major and two minor water obstacles on a single road off which tanks could not operate owing to the boggy nature of the ground. Nevertheless the epic struggle of the 1st Airborne Division especially at the Arnhem bridge reached a standard of courage equal to any displayed at any time in the Army's history.

By the first week in October the brutal truth had to be faced that the last chance of crossing the Rhine had gone for the time being. On the Eastern front the Russians after dramatic advances had obviously shot their bolt until frost conditions enabled mobile operations to be resumed. Meanwhile in Italy Alexander's Army Group had been brought to a standstill at the Gothic Line. In July after the fall of Rome at the height of his pursuit he had had to give up the four experienced American divisions and the French Mountain Corps for the landing in the south of France. This had gone in on 15 August too late to affect the operations in Normandy where the battle was already won. Nevertheless 8th Army's attack at the end of August on the Adriatic flank of the Gothic Line, followed by 5th Army's attack through the mountains towards Bologna came very near success. Had it not been for the damnable weather bogging down the armour they might well have got through into the Po valley. They now faced a winter of great physical hardship in the mountains.

On the Western front with the arrival of the autumn gales which smashed the Mulberry harbour in Normandy, Eisenhower faced an administrative crisis. Until the port of Antwerp could be opened there could be no further advance on any scale. Montgomery was therefore ordered to open the Scheldt as a first priority. The operations which followed were tedious, protracted and costly. They involved in addition to the Canadians, 49 and 52 Lowland Divisions, 79th Armoured Division, 104th United States Division, the Poles, the Czechs, the Royal Navy, the Royal Marines and the RAF, and they cost 30,000 casualties. They fell into three phases; the clearing of the Breskens Pocket, a bitter struggle between the Canadians and the 64th German Division, the conquest of the South Beveland Peninsula and the taking of the island of Walcheren by a fiercely contested amphibious attack. The weather was vile and the resistance of the Germans obstinate. Walcheren island was not captured until 4 November and the port of Antwerp itself was not open to receive shipping till 28 November.

The part played by the British Army in Bradley's abortive November offensive was confined to XXX Corps, which distinguished itself on the northern flank in the operations around Gielenkirchen.

Although Montgomery with the 9th American

s

Army and part of 1st American Army under his command personally played a conspicuous part in the Battle of the Ardennes in the second half of December, this was essentially an American battle decided in the end by the courage and endurance of the American soldier. At the time when the columns of the 5th and 6th Panzer Armies were approaching the Maas Montgomery diverted XXX Corps to the west bank between Liège and Namur but did not use it because to have done so would have raised administrative complications and because the Americans were fully capable of dealing with the situation themselves. When the American counter-offensive got under way in early January XXX Corps using 53rd Welsh Division, 51st Highland Division and 6th Airborne Division, put into battle alongside the Americans on the River Ourthe, had some of the toughest fighting of the campaign before they broke the back of the resistance in front of them. Concurrently with these operations, 52nd Lowland Division, 43rd Wessex Division and 7th Armoured Division took advantage of the hard frost conditions to wipe out the two German divisions in the Heinsberg Triangle west of the River Roer.

Eisenhower now issued orders for 'one more great campaign aggressively conducted on a broad front' designed to carry the armies to the Rhine and beyond. For 21st Army Group, which included 9th American Army, this involved the operations known by the code names of 'Veritable' and 'Grenade' – a 'pincer'

The bridge over the Rhine at Arnhem. On the evening of 17 September 1944 men of the 2nd Battalion the Parachute Regiment captured the far side of the bridge. Unsupported, they put up an epic resistance against unceasing German attacks, until on Thursday 21 September the survivors were finally over-run. German armoured vehicles which they had destroyed can be seen at the approaches to the bridge

Men of the Seaforth Highlanders advancing through the Reichswald. In close support are flame throwing Churchill tanks

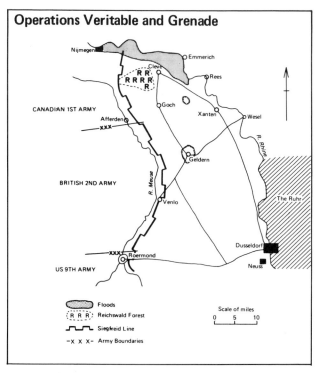

Operations Veritable and Grenade

operation by 1st Canadian Army striking south from the Nijmegen salient between the Rhine and the Meuse (operation Veritable) and a thrust by the 9th American Army due north from the Roer to meet the Canadian Army about the line Geldern-Xanten (operation Grenade). Originally these operations had been designed to take place almost simultaneously in conditions of hard frost in January but were delayed by the German attack in the Ardennes. By the first week in February a thaw had set in. 'Veritable' in consequence proved to be a test of courage and endurance as hard as any in the whole war. First Canadian Army, consisting of 13 divisions of which 9 were from the British Isles, duly attacked on 8 February and brought the whole weight of 1st Parachute Army on itself. The Germans then opened the stopcocks of the Roer dams and so flooded the battlefield on 9th Army front that they could not intervene until a fortnight later. The resistance of the German parachutists was obstinate to a degree – altogether it cost them 90,000 casualties. As a result when they were finally driven across the Rhine at Wesel they were in no condition to hold the Rhine barrier.

The crossing of the Rhine on the night of 23–24 March was Montgomery's final masterpiece, executed admittedly in a manner since outmoded, but a masterpiece nonetheless. Altogether it involved $1\frac{1}{4}$ million men. Ninth American Army on the right and 2nd British Army on the left on a front of about 40 miles between Duisburg and Doetinchem ten miles

east of Arnhem forced the crossing supported by the fire of 2,000 guns. Simultaneously 1st Commando Brigade assaulted Wesel after preliminary bombardment by the RAF. Next morning XVIII Airborne Corps including 6th Airborne Division were dropped a few miles east of the river within artillery range of the guns on the west bank to help the advance. By the evening of 28 March the bridgehead was 35 miles wide and 20 miles deep. Poised ready to advance into the North German Plain Montgomery had 20 divisions and 1,500 tanks all up to strength and with an administrative build-up behind them adequate to carry them all the way to Berlin. Model with Army Group 'B' faced inevitable encirclement in the Ruhr. To the south Bradley's and Devers' Army Groups were forging ahead against collapsing resistance.

To the astonishment of the British and incidentally of posterity Eisenhower now decided to make his main effort under Bradley, not towards Berlin but towards Dresden, to withdraw the 9th American Army from Montgomery's command and to reduce the role of his Army Group to protecting Bradley's northern flank and taking Hamburg and Bremen. Twenty-one Army Group accordingly advanced on a front of three Corps against sporadic resistance, except on the front of XXX Corps where the survivors of 1st Parachute Army fought on with something of their old form. Bremen fell on 27 April and Hamburg on 2 May. On the same day 11th Armoured Division and 5th Division reached Lübeck and 6th Airborne Division got to Wismar on the Baltic coast just before the Russians. At 18·30 hours on 4 May all German forces in Holland and North West Europe, over two million strong, surrendered to Montgomery on Lüneburg Heide with effect from 08·00 hours on Saturday 5 May. Fighting on the Italian Front had ceased three days previously.

The Second World War thus ended with the Army at a higher standard of efficiency than at any time in its history except perhaps in 1914. In the first years of this war the Germans of all ranks had proved themselves more highly professional than the British. Ironically the Germans created one of the main instruments of their own destruction. When the fighting ceased the technical skill of the British officers, warrant and non-commissioned officers was as good, and in some cases better, than that of the Germans. Of the higher commanders it can at least be said that they satisfied Montgomery and Alexander, which is

saying a lot.

Morally the Army was immensely strong. It could look back with pride on its long and often bitter march to ultimate triumph. It was bound together by many loyalties: the mutual loyalty of men who have shared the same risks and hardships together for a long time, the loyalty of the troops to their regimental officers who knew their jobs and shared their dangers, the loyalty of the services to the front line troops, the loyalty to the divisions whose very titles emphasised the vitality of the amalgam of national and provincial prejudices and traditions which constitute the psychological make-up of the British people. Above all they had a loyalty to Churchill, Montgomery and Alexander because they won their battles. But above all they knew that they fought in a noble cause – the destruction of the most evil tyranny Europe had ever known.

Royal Air Force Stirling bombers towing Horsa gliders over the Rhine

CHAPTER 31

The War in the Far East
1941–45

JAMES P. LAWFORD

Almost totally divorced from the war in the Mediterranean and western Europe, a mortal conflict with Japan was waged in the Far East, a conflict which the British government and people, mesmerised by the urgent and compelling dangers of Europe, were always to consider secondary, a conflict in which the requirements of the British forces were only met when all needs elsewhere had been satisfied, but a conflict which, despite a final Allied victory, was to see the end of European dominance in Asia and, ultimately, Africa. When on 15 February General Percival surrendered Singapore to the Japanese General Yamashita, the 'Tiger of Malaya', three centuries of European military supremacy lay buried in its ruins.

The fortifications on Singapore island faced seawards to protect the naval base from a seaborne assault – to have encased the seventy mile perimeter of the island in barbed wire and concrete would have been as expensive as futile. The defence of Singapore depended on British naval and air superiority. By 10 December both had vanished.

Nevertheless, a savage land campaign was fought in the vain hope that somehow the balance in the air might be tilted back, and disaster averted. At the start of the campaign Percival commanded some 88,000 men including volunteers and base personnel. The Japanese order of battle, as given in the official history, amounted to 125,000. In addition, the Japanese had the 56th Division in Japan at call for the invasion. Some gross distortions of the Japanese strength have been made and indeed numbers culled from ration strengths can be misleading. Is the storeman at an ordnance depot in khaki a soldier, but in plain clothes a civilian and not to be counted? If we compare strengths of fighting formations, the Japan-

ese had overwhelming strength in the air and on the sea; on land General Yamashita had the 5th, 18th and Imperial Guards Divisions, the 56th Division at call from Japan and an armoured group equivalent to a British armoured brigade. Percival had the 9th and 11th Indian and 8th Australian Divisions, and two Malay brigades for the defence of Singapore. Subsequently, two semi-trained Indian brigades and one British from the 18th East Anglian Division joined him. The rest of that division disembarked at Singapore in time for the last few days of fighting. The Japanese infantry strength at the outset was somewhat greater than Percival's and the Japanese armour which played a decisive role in the fighting could be opposed only by passive anti-tank weapons. A balanced force was opposed to one which lacked the weapons of the *blitzkrieg*, tanks and aircraft.

As is usual geography governed the strategy of both sides. Malaya is a peninsula shaped somewhat like an elongated pear about 450 miles long and lying approximately north and south. Down the centre runs a mountainous jungle-clad spine only passable in a few places. The best communications run down the west coast.

To defend Malaya successfully it was necessary to control its coastal waters. It had been planned to dominate these from the air. To this end a large number of airfields had been built all the way down the Peninsula. These had to be protected. As a result Percival had to stretch his forces from one end of Malaya to the other. His three divisions were separated by hundreds of miles, the 11th Division was stationed in northern Kedah, the 9th guarded the east coast, and the 8th Australian Division held Johore to guard against a Japanese landing in the Mersing area which would bypass his forward divi-

Opposite: Men of the West Yorkshire Regiment searching Meiktila for snipers March 1945

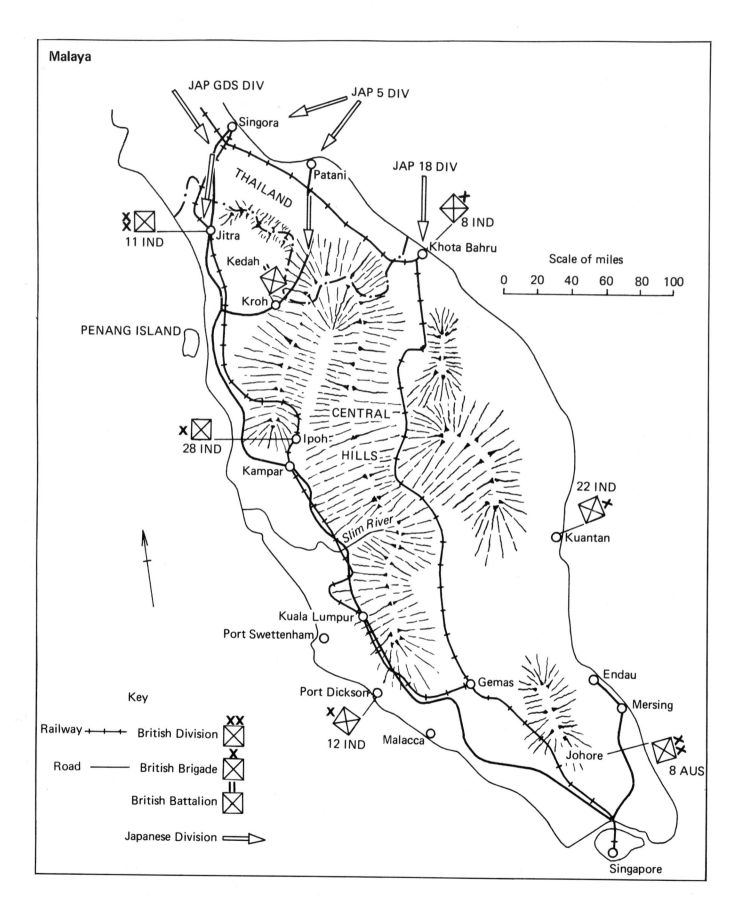

Malaya

JAP GDS DIV

JAP 5 DIV

JAP 18 DIV

Singora

Patani

THAILAND

Kedah

Jitra

Kroh

Khota Bahru

8 IND

Scale of miles

0 20 40 60 80 100

11 IND

PENANG ISLAND

28 IND

Ipoh

Kampar

CENTRAL

HILLS

22 IND

Slim River

Kuantan

Kuala Lumpur

Port Swettenham

Gemas

Endau

Port Dickson

Mersing

12 IND

Malacca

Johore

8 AUS

Singapore

Key

Railway ┼┼┼┼ British Division

Road ─── British Brigade

British Battalion

Japanese Division ⇒

278

sions. The 9th and 11th Divisions were grouped to form General Heath's 3rd Corps. They had only two brigades each; but 3rd Corps had the 28th Gurkha Brigade as a reserve and Percival kept the 12th Independent Brigade under his own hand. Singapore island itself was garrisoned by two Malay brigades and some fortress troops.

After dark on the night of 7 December 1941 troops from the Japanese 18th Division landed at Khota Bharu, and after a struggle penetrated the beach defences. At the same time the 5th Japanese Division came ashore at the Thai ports of Singora and Patani, while the Imperial Guards Division marched overland on Bangkok.

On learning of the landings, Admiral Tom Phillips steamed out of Singapore with the battleships *Prince of Wales* and *Repulse* to intercept the invading armadas. On 10 December he sank with his two great ships beneath a rain of bombs and airborne torpedos. In the air Japanese aircraft swarmed over the Peninsula shooting down the few obsolescent aircraft of the RAF, attacking airfields and destroying installations. By 10 December the Japanese ruled both the sky and the sea.

While this sombre drama unfolded Percival and Heath, commanding 3rd Corps, reacted energetically and with decision. Heath reinforced the 11th Division on the west coast with his corps reserve the 28th Brigade while Percival moved the 12th Brigade to cover the 11th Division's line of retreat threatened by a Japanese advance from Patani towards Kroh.

The first major clash occurred at Jitra in northwest Kedah between the Japanese 5th Division and the 11th Indian Division. The action opened disastrously. On 11 December at small cost a Japanese armoured column overran and destroyed two outpost battalions. Next day a Japanese attack bit deep into the defences. The penetration was by no means fatal. General Murray Lyon, the divisional commander, however, on hearing that a Japanese force had advanced on Kroh and was threatening his communications with Singapore, resolved on an immediate retreat. The Japanese followed up swiftly and inflicted crippling losses on his division. As it retreated the 12th Brigade came to its assistance. For the next fortnight, harried from the air and attacked at every opportunity from the ground, the division marched southwards. Then on 30 December at Kampar the tired weary men turned on their pursuers and fought them to a standstill. In this action the East Surreys and Leicesters, amalgamated to form a single weak battalion, won particular glory.

The Japanese author Tsuji at that time serving

The tunnel area on the Buthidaung-Maungdaw road. This area had been fought over during the 1942–3 Arakan campaign and was the main objective of Slim's offensive. It was captured in the operations that followed the rout of Tanahashi force, but only after a desperate struggle as the shattered jungle mutely testifies

with the 5th Japanese Division records in his book: 'The full strength of the Army Division and the air groups co-operated for an attack on the front line, but up to the evening of 31 December ... the position was beginning to look grave'.

However, Kampar was outflanked from the sea and the endless retreat was resumed. Then on 2 January at the Slim river came complete disaster. A Japanese armoured attack broke through the rearguard and the tanks, driving straight down the road spitting fire like iron-clad salamanders, sliced clean through the 28th and 12th Brigades. They lost all their transport and equipment and dissolved into small groups of men trying to find their way back through the jungle.

Now the Japanese advance assumed an irresistible momentum. In Johore the 8th Australian Division scored some initial success, then the Japanese juggernaut rolled inexorably onwards crushing all resistance. As disaster followed disaster Percival's shattered army withdrew to Singapore. Here on 31 January the gallant survivors of the Argyll and Sutherland Highlanders, having seen all others across, were played over the Causeway to the island by their two surviving pipers.

On the island, Percival fatally decided to man the whole of its seventy mile perimeter, stretching a weak

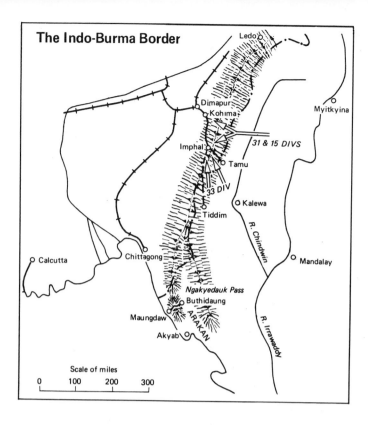

The Indo-Burma Border

Kohima immediately after its recapture, looking towards the District Commissioner's bungalow

cordon right round the coast. After dark on 8 February the 5th and 18th Japanese Divisions stormed ashore on the sector held by 22nd Australian Brigade. The Australians fought with great gallantry and inflicted considerable loss, but the Japanese surged between their scattered isolated positions. Attacked from all sides and suffering severely, the Australians gave ground. Next day Percival with his troops stretched on a vast circle could only muster the weary remnant of the 12th Brigade for a counter attack. The Japanese were firmly ashore, and the following night the Imperial Guards Division broke through by the Causeway. The tired beaten troops on the island had lost confidence in their commanders and their commanders in each other. The unblooded 18th East Anglian Division, just landed in Singapore after the long voyage from England, was plunged into the maelstrom. As the Japanese tanks bore down on Singapore city the outcome became certain. What was remarkable was not that the Japanese landed successfully, but that Percival's weary battle-drunk soldiers never wholly lost their cohesion, that on 14 February when, with the island water supply lost, Percival saw no alternative to surrender, a line still held round Singapore and not a single Japanese soldier had managed to penetrate into the city.

In Malaya Japanese troops with complete naval, air and armoured superiority achieved a magnificent

success. But the British humiliation should not obscure the many valiant deeds of men and units, nor the fact that, when the final surrender came, men who had fought right down the Peninsula without respite or hope still faced their foe with weapons in their hands. Undoubtedly there was shame, but there was also much courage no less because unsung.

Meanwhile the Japanese advanced on Burma. They trapped the 17th Division east of the Sittang river and the fate of Rangoon was sealed. By the end of May 1942 all British forces had withdrawn to India, and the monsoon had put an end to campaigning.

Early in 1943 Wavell attacked in the Arakan. The ill-fated 14th Indian Division, however, was cut to pieces by a Japanese counter-attack and nothing was achieved, before the monsoon again ended the fighting. In central Burma Wingate led a special brigade supplied entirely from the air through jungle trails into the heart of Burma. In this foray, known as the first Chindit expedition, Wingate lost a third of his men before returning to India. He had, however, demonstrated how men might live and move in trackless jungle and rely confidently on the air for their supplies.

By the autumn of 1943 the relative Japanese and British positions had scarcely altered, but a new Imperial army, the 14th, had been created and

General (now Field-Marshal the Viscount) Slim appointed to command it.

Slim now initiated a slow methodical advance supported by tanks in the Arakan. On 3 February 1944 the Japanese hit back. A strong force under Colonel Tanahashi skirted the landward side of the British troops and seized the Ngakyedauk pass where the main British supply route crossed the steep, densely forested hills of the Mayu range. Slim put his two forward divisions, the 5th and 7th, on air supply and struck back at Tanahashi with the 26th Indian and 36th British Divisions. Between, as Slim himself termed it, the anvil of the forward troops and the hammer of the reserves Tanahashi and his men despite a most desperate resistance were utterly crushed.

Before the monsoon the British secured a jumping-off place in the Arakan for the next campaign and the Japanese were forced on to the defensive.

Meanwhile a major Japanese offensive had opened against Imphal in Manipur state. Here the 4th Corps with the 17th, 20th and 23rd Divisions held the Imphal plateau deep in the mountainous jungle-clad region of the central front. The Japanese 15th Army attacked frontally with the 33rd Division while the 15th and 31st Divisions encircled the plateau and cut it off from India. The 15th Division then attacked the plateau from the rear and the 31st Division lunged on towards the base area at Dimapur. At Kohima the 31st Division encountered a scratch garrison built up round the Royal West Kent Regiment and the Assam Rifles. The garrison put up a heroic defence and checked for a time the Japanese advance.

Slim reacted quickly and with decision. He flew two brigades of the 5th Division to Imphal and arranged an airlift to carry all its supplies to the surrounded 4th Corps. Behind Kohima he massed the 7th Indian and 2nd British Divisions. It was the same stratagem of the hammer and the anvil. For the next two months a titanic struggle raged. On the Imphal plateau in a series of bloody desperate combats the 4th Corps foiled all Japanese efforts to seize the vital Imphal and Palel airstrips. At Kohima the 2nd and 7th Divisions remorselessly pressed back the Japanese 31st Division. The monsoon broke. Jungle trails became quaking bogs which men or mules could scarcely traverse. Starved of supplies, outnumbered and outfought, the 31st Japanese Division collapsed. Striking rapidly towards each other the British forces at Imphal and Kohima linked up, destroying the Japanese 15th Division between them. On the plateau the 4th Corps now attacked, and the 33rd Japanese Division was swept helplessly back-

The breakout from Imphal. Gurkha troops are seen on a newly captured hill. Shell fire has destroyed nearly all the jungle and drifting monsoon rain clouds shroud the scene

wards. The Japanese invasion had foundered.

Disregarding the appalling monsoon conditions, Slim pursued the fleeing Japanese without mercy. The shattered Japanese 15th Army fell back towards Mandalay.

While this violent battle was in progress Stilwell had led a Sino-American force into northern Burma and, with the help of Wingate's second Chindit expedition and after a very protracted siege, had succeeded on 3 August in taking Myitkyina.

As the Japanese retreated trying desperately to reform and reinforce their shattered formations, 1944 slipped into 1945. In the Arakan the advance recommenced. The 15th Corps under General Christison closed in on Sakurai's 28th Army, captured Akyab island and plunged southwards outflanking the retreating Japanese from the sea. At Kangaw the 3rd Commando Brigade defended a beach-head hill through a long night and at dawn counted 300 Japanese corpses littering the hillside in front of them. But it was around Mandalay that the fate of Burma was to be decided and it was here that Slim achieved his masterpiece.

THE BATTLE OF MANDALAY – MEIKTILA

At this time General Kimura the Japanese Commander-in-Chief in Burma had under him three armies. In the north the 33rd Army under General Honda consisting of the 18th and 56th Divisions and one regiment from the 49th Division faced Stilwell and his Chinese; here the Japanese aim was to hold Lashio and prevent Stilwell reopening the Burma-China road. In the centre General Katamura had taken over the beaten 15th Army, still composed of the 15th, 31st and 33rd Divisions but with the 53rd added to it; to him fell the task of holding Mandalay.

In the south 28th Army under General Sakurai (54th and 55th Divisions and some *ad hoc* formations) was to guard the southern approaches from Yenaung-yaung to the Arakan coast. Kimura made the 49th Division and the 16th Regiment of the 2nd Division his personal reserve. (The rest of the 2nd Division was withdrawn to Indo-China). In addition units of the 14th Tank Regiment were distributed to the armies.

While the Americans and Chinese in the north kept Honda's 33rd Army pinned down, and Christison's 15th Corps occupied Sakurai's 28th, Slim planned to complete the destruction of Katamura's 15th Army in the plains round Mandalay. In boxing terms he proposed a heavy left lead to the head to draw up the Japanese guard, followed by a lightning and knock-out right hook to the stomach. General Stopford's 33rd Corps (19th and 20th Indian Divisions, 2nd British, 254th Tank Brigade and 268th Infantry Brigade) was to be the heavy left lead and to approach Mandalay from the north and west. General Messervy's 4th Corps (7th and 17th Indian Divisions, 254th Tank Brigade, 28th East African Brigade and the Lushai Brigade) had the job of dealing the knock-out right hook. It was to move secretly down the Myitha Valley to Gangaw and sneak up to the Irrawaddy river. From there it was to deliver a lightning blow into the main Japanese administra-

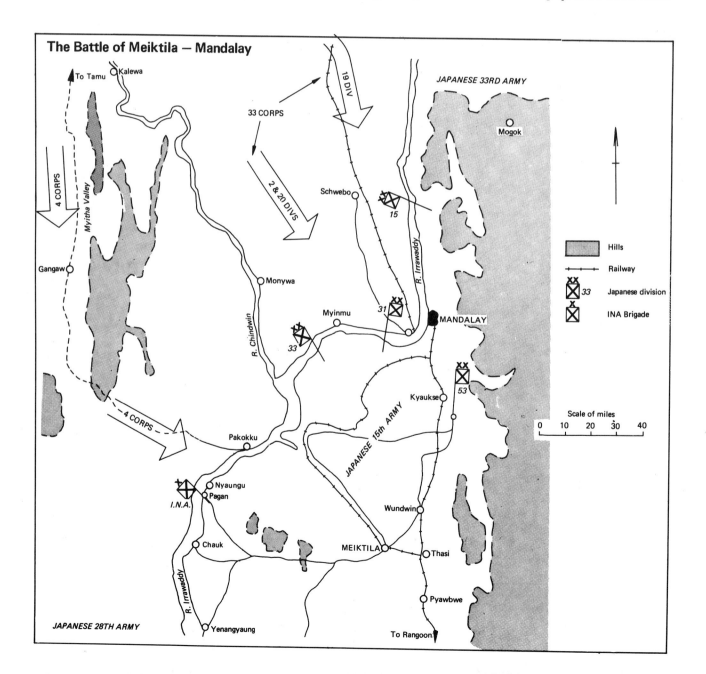

tive base south of Mandalay, seize Meiktila and cut off Honda's Northern Army and Katamura's Central Army from Rangoon.

The main tactical features of this enormous battle-front were the Irrawaddy river varying in width near Mandalay from 1,500–2,000 yards, and the open tankable country of the Irrawaddy basin. In addition it was distinguished by a complete lack of all-weather roads.

Katamura's plan with the 15th Army was to delay the advance of the 14th Army up to the Irrawaddy and to fight his main action on the far bank in the hope that he might catch the 14th Army divided by that great obstacle.

January, 1945, Phase I – The build-up on the Irrawaddy

During January the 33rd Corps converged on to the Irrawaddy against stubborn Japanese rear-guards. In the north the 19th Division, by a magnificent march across difficult jungle country, reached Shwebo on 9 January. On the night of 15 January two of its brigades slipped across the river east of Shwebo unobserved. When he discovered their presence Katamura took strong action. He ordered the 15th Division responsible for that portion of the river and his own army reserve, the 53rd Division, to drive in the bridge-head. His other two divisions, pursued by the 2nd and 20th Divisions, were still west of the river and retiring to take up their allotted positions on the east bank west and south-west of Mandalay. For three weeks the Japanese were to dash themselves to pieces in fruitless attacks on the bridge-head. But while the 19th Division received these attacks with a granite-hard front, the 20th and 2nd Divisions rolled on towards the Irrawaddy. Their threat forced Katamura to draw in his 53rd Division back to reserve. To the south, unsuspected by the Japanese and screened by the Lushai and East African brigades, the 4th Corps traversed the Myitha Valley, grabbed Gangaw, and closed in towards Pakokku.

February 1945, Phase II – The main crossing of the Irrawaddy

The crossing of this mighty obstacle, in places wider than the straits separating Singapore from the mainland of Malaya, was one of the supreme logistical feats of the war. In Slim's own words he asked his men to cross 'on a couple of bamboos and a boot-lace'. The lack of boats and rafts forced him to pass his divisions across the river either one by one or far apart.

On the dark windy night of the 12 February the Border Regiment spearheaded the 20th Division across the Irrawaddy at Myinmu. When dawn came

The Arakan. The beach-head on the *chaung* (creek) at Kangaw

the leading brigade was all across. The initial Japanese resistance was slight. By the 15th the bridge-head was firmly established in the face of Japanese assaults which steadily grew in intensity. From the 19th to the 25th the Japanese 215th Regiment from the 33rd Division and the reserve 16th Regiment supported by tanks strove desperately to drive the British into the river. The RAF joined the fray and on one occasion aircraft knocked out 15 of the few tanks still remaining to the Japanese. The defence held firm but it was not until 5 March that the divisional artillery passed over the river and the 20th Division was concentrated for a break-out.

On 14 February, shortly after the 20th Division had begun to cross, the 7th Division of the 4th Corps, after some initial mishaps, succeeded in establishing themselves across the river at Pagan and Nyangu well to the south. The Japanese did little. Katamura still believed that the 4th Corps was far to the north. He considered that the landings were a diversionary attack towards the Yenanyaung oilfields and were aimed at inducing him to disperse the forces guarding Mandalay. Between 18 and 21 February the 17th Division and 255th Tank Brigade crossed over. The right hand was coiled for the knock-out punch. To persuade the Japanese still to keep their 'guard up', Slim now ordered General Nicholson's 2nd Division over the Irrawaddy.

On the moonlit night of 24 February the Cameron Highlanders and Worcesters ferried themselves over the river some ten miles down-stream of Mandalay. They encountered heavy automatic fire and the Worcesters were forced to withdraw. The Camerons

283

under cover of smoke, however, gallantly pressed on and effected a lodgement. Thereafter the division crossed without much difficulty. Katamura's resources had become exhausted. By 5 March the 2nd Division was across the river and ready to pounce.

Meanwhile, some 40–50 miles to the south General Cowan's 17th Divisions with the 255th Tank Brigade were racing for Meiktila. As they went, surprised and dismayed administrative troops surrendered their dumps and scampered off into the fields. But at Meiktila a hastily assembled force of 3,500 Japanese supported by numerous guns prepared themselves for a fight to the death. The town, the approaches restricted by lakes, lent itself to defence. Failure to capture Meiktila quickly could wreck Slim's plan. On 2 March Cowan opened the attack. The 63rd Brigade assaulted from the west, 48th Brigade from the north, 255th Tank Brigade with two lorried infantry battalions seized the airfield and attacked from the east. In ferocious hand-to-hand fighting Cowan's forces penetrated deep into the town, but the Japanese, fighting with an almost inhuman disregard for life or normal human values, showed no signs of wavering. The savage combat was resumed next day and by 6·00 p.m. resistance virtually ceased. The Japanese garrison had died to a man. The punch had landed but the battle was by no means over.

Phase III, March 1945 – The Dogfight

Now Slim had to face a bitter shock. Confronted by Japanese successes on the Chinese mainland Chiang Kai-shek demanded the return of his divisions in the north and air transport to fly them out. Slim managed to retain his air lift without which his forces would have been paralysed. But the defection of the Chinese increased the number of foes he had to face.

To the Japanese Commander-in-Chief, Kimura, an accurate picture of the battle was at last taking shape. Beneath the remorseless pressure of the 33rd Corps Katamura's 15th Army was beginning to crumble. The attempt to hold the Irrawaddy line had failed. The stranglehold of the 4th Corps on Meiktila was throttling his armies. He realised that unless he recaptured Meiktila they were doomed. He directed Honda to fall upon that town with a reconstituted 33rd Army consisting of the 18th and 53rd Divisions from the northern and central fronts and the 49th Division from Army reserve. The 15th Army was to cover this operation from the north, while Sakurai's 28th Army was to drive in the 7th Division's bridgehead at Nyaungu. The greater part of the Japanese army in Burma was now engaged.

With his usual clear judgement, Slim foresaw the crisis; he brought forward his only reserve, the 5th Division, to Monywa and flew its airborne brigade to Meiktila. The 14th Army's overstrained logistical machine seemed about to seize up, but Slim's administrative staff granted him one more miracle.

Now the storm broke over Meiktila. Cowan with the 17th Division had been patrolling aggressively outwards while the Japanese ring tightened steadily. Then, unwilling to wait longer, the Japanese on 12 March, although all their forces were not yet fully assembled, launched an all-out assault. It failed.

Attack then followed attack. On 15 March the

Crossing the Irrawaddy River on a 'shoe-string'. Oil drums have been fitted to the carrier to give it buoyancy and it is crossing under its own power

Airborne Brigade of 5th Division flew in while the airstrip was under Japanese artillery fire. As the Japanese 18th and 49th Divisions joined in, the combat reached a tremendous climax. A bitter struggle raged around the airfield. Japanese tanks broke on to the runway but were repelled. To the west a mixed force, equivalent to about two regiments, from Sakurai's 28th Army drove up both sides of the Irrawaddy towards the 7th Division's bridge-head. The 7th Division, with the timely reinforcement of two brigades from the 5th Division dealt summarily with them. At the same time the 7th Division thrust fiercely to reopen communications with Meiktila. In Meiktila itself the Japanese attacks began to lose momentum in the face of appalling casualties. By 29 March Honda's 33rd Army had been fought to a standstill.

During this time Katamura's 15th Army in the north had met with final disaster. Towards the end of February General Rees with his 19th Division broke out of his bridge-head, sweeping the battered Japanese 15th Division before him.

The Japanese took refuge in Mandalay, with the 19th Division in hot pursuit. By 11 March Mandalay hill had been stormed and its garrison slaughtered to a man. Now the 19th Division driving through Mandalay was confronted with the moat and enormous crenellated ramparts of Fort Dufferin, dominating the centre of the city. Wellington had faced similar problems and Rees tackled them much as Wellington might have done. He erected parallels and positioned breaching batteries of medium guns within 500 yards of the fortifications. Aircraft bombed them from the air, but failed to break down the enormously thick walls. On 16 March Rees attempted a storm, complete with 'forlorn hopes', but his men were beaten back.

He renewed the bombardment. Breaches appeared in the massive walls. Consultations were held to decide whether they were practicable. On the 20th just before the next assault was due to go in the Japanese garrison pulled out. They tried to escape in small groups through the town; few succeeded. The Japanese 15th Division was no more.

While Rees was busy at Mandalay the 20th and 2nd Divisions smashed out of their bridge-head scattering the remnants of the Japanese 31st and 33rd Divisions before them. By the 16 March they approached the railway south of Mandalay on a broad front and on the 30th the Japanese base at Kyaukse fell. Nothing now remained of Katamura's 15th Army but dispersed bands of fugitives seeking shelter in the Shan hills to the east.

April–May 1945 – The Coup de Grâce

Now Honda's 33rd Army stood at bay, his right resting on Thasi and his left on Pyawbwe. Here the 5th and 17th Divisions exacted a stern retribution for their ordeal at Meiktila. Yet with all hope gone the Imperial Japanese Army still fought on to a finish. Thasi was eventually captured by a brigade from the 19th Division, while at Pyawbwe the 48th Brigade of the 17th Division annihilated what remained of the Japanese 49th Division; in its ruins were 2,000 dead; 31 guns and 8 tanks were taken.

Thus the battle ended with six Japanese divisions irretrievably routed. Save for the 56th Division in the north and the depleted 54th and 55th Divisions of Sakurai's 28th Army, Kimura's Burma Army had been dispersed. Slim rapidly organised an advance on Rangoon. On 3 May the 26th Division from Christison's 15th Corps took that city from the sea. But the Japanese were gone. Kimura and his broken legions were east of the Sittang river.

Early in September 1945 landings were made in Malaya, but by then Japan had surrendered unconditionally. The Indian Army spent a vexatious year accepting the surrender of the Japanese armies in South East Asia and trying to impose some order on that troubled region. By the end of 1946 all Indian units had returned to India. Then, with the partition of that sub-continent, the Army that Stringer Lawrence and Clive had started nearly two centuries ago was dissolved. But its last battle was not unworthy of its forebears, the victors of Plassey and Assaye; and its traditions it bequeathed to the new born states of India and Pakistan.

General Slim with U Aung Gyaw, one time Commissioner of Meiktila

CHAPTER 32

After the War: 1945-68

ANTHONY H. FARRAR-HOCKLEY

As Europe began to revive after the years of military occupation and destruction and as the political echoes of the second atomic explosion spread outwards from Asia, Great Britain observed victory in a day of rare emotional celebration, when relief and joy were mixed. Then, almost overnight, the nation reverted to the attitudes and appetites of peace.

A remarkable feature of this reversion was the change in the national attitude to the armed forces, particularly to the Army. Guardians of the island's supply lines, the Royal Navy continued to enjoy some of its traditional popularity. The Royal Air Force were cherished as defenders of the homeland against the enemy's bombers. While acknowledging the Army's merit in war, the public saw now, with the onset of peace, swarms of soldiers embodied to no apparent purpose. The Army occupied citizens' houses, their shops and offices. Army trucks seemed to have plenty of petrol when the private motorist had almost none. Private and common land was enclosed by government for Army training. A popular topic of conversation turned on the question: when is the Army going to send all its men home back to work?

The demobilisation scheme had been executed immediately after the armistice with Germany; Mr Churchill had been determined to avoid the muddles and disorders of 1918-9. As the older men left the colours, however, and donned the homely suits of civilian clothing presented to them by the government at the dispersal centres, the National Service Act drew in a high proportion of replacements. On 1 July 1945, the British Army, still at war, stood at 2,931,000 men, but after two years, on 1 August 1947, stood at little more than ¾ of a million. A Labour government had succeeded the war coalition and it was not at all anxious to maintain such a huge peace-time army; but it had inherited too many commitments to permit a return to pre-war strength.

In Europe, the United Kingdom was obliged to provide its quota of occupation troops in Germany and Austria. In Venezia Giulia, British soldiers became involved in keeping the peace between Italians and Jugoslavs. In Greece, the British garrison assisted the government in their persistent grumbling struggle against the communist guerrillas. All these commitments were seen in Whitehall as part of the legacy of war, matters that would be solved by long-term political agreement amongst the allies.

Quite apart from European responsibilities, however, Britain had others, wide ranging, as a colonial and protecting power. Long determined on complete independence, the national political parties of India found to their surprise after the war that it was to be offered to them by the British Government, whose concern was a peaceful transfer of power and partition between a predominantly Hindu state of India and the majority of Muslims in Pakistan. Loyal through many wars to the Raj, the Indian Army was at once riven by religious differences. Only its British units might be wholly relied on when Hindu or Muslim zealots set upon the other's people. It was, however, a relatively short task. Independence Day came and the Union Jack dropped for the last time. A battalion of British Light Infantry marched away to close the history of the Army in India.

While this was taking place, two divisions, the 1st Infantry and the 6th Airborne, had been drawn to

287

Malaya. Men of the 13th/18th Hussars in a Malayan incident. The burning lorry has just been towed off the road and efforts are being made to put the fire out

Palestine to maintain order. The occupants of the Jewish National Home there were determined to establish an independent Zionist state. The British Government was uncomfortably aware that, while the Jews *in situ* and the many more seeking entry from Europe had both a political claim and a cause for sympathy, the claims of the Arabs were equally strong. The Jewish settlers had a military organisation in being, the Haganah, which had once been used by the British authorities in its pre-war struggle to suppress Arab terrorism. Now the Haganah, reorganised and rearmed, many of its number trained as soldiers in war with the British Army, began to exert pressure by acts of sabotage and gross disobedience. It stopped short of murder; but there was no such restraint amongst two groups of national extremists: the Stern Gang and the Irgun Zvai L'eumi. In the glorious mild climate of the Levant, amidst the familiar Biblical names – Beersheba, Gaza, Bethlehem, Nazareth, Jerusalem – the British soldiers began a deadly game of hide-and-seek with an enemy concealed by a Jewish populace rarely openly hostile, never remotely cooperative.

This same commitment of peace-keeping was common to those British soldiers serving in the Far East. Here, too, there was an occupation force – in Japan. The major task was not the enforcement of armistice terms, however, but in dealing with the consequences of Japanese conquest and occupation. In Indo-China, Burma, Malaya, Singapore, Borneo and the Dutch East Indies, Asians had seen an Asian power, Japan, overthrow the European colonial authority by conquest. Though these same Europeans had returned to overpower and dismember the Japanese empire, and though the local peoples had fought openly or covertly with the allies, in almost every territory there was a determination to assert or demand political independence.

It was only a few months after Japan had acknowledged defeat when the British troops in the Dutch East Indies found themselves engaged in operations against guerrillas. The British had arrived to round up the Japanese armies in Java and Sumatra. Cooperating with the Dutch, newly returned to reestablish government, the British became increasingly occupied in fighting to preserve what was, in effect, Dutch rule against local nationalists. The soldiers concerned were badly placed. They had no quarrel with the Sumatrans and Javanese. The majority of men were young soldiers, conscripted since 1945, with few experienced veterans to direct and lead them. Fortunately, just as these difficulties became acute they were withdrawn and the quarrel was left to those concerned, the Dutch and the native peoples.

As the force returned to Malaya, there were signs that similar trouble was shortly to occur in the Malay States. Though somewhat divided racially and politically, the Malay, Indian and Chinese peoples in the Peninsula were agreed in one aim: they wished for independence. The majority were confident that they would win it by open, democratic demands on the British Government. Underground, a group of communists, predominantly Chinese, decided to use terrorism to overthrow both the colonial rulers and their local competitors for power.

The principal weapon of the Communists was murder. A number of European planters, businessmen and officials were attacked – particularly those in remote areas. But, more effective, there were widespread attacks on local officials: police officers in the security and criminal branches; local government officers. Besides, individuals known to cooperate with the authorities or those who refused shelter, food or money to terrorists were murdered mercilessly. The police were too few to cope once terrorism began as a deliberate policy and thus British armed forces were drawn in. Of these, the British Army was overwhelmingly the largest element.

The campaign of terrorism was begun by the Malayan Communist Party in June 1948. It was difficult for the Army and police to counter it: townspeople and villagers did not want to become involved; they feared that operations would destroy their livelihood; some feared more the threats of the terrorists. After several early arrests of his men in the towns, Chin Peng, the terrorist leader, had ordered his forces, 2,600 strong, into jungle bases; and thus the soldiers had to find these without betraying their discovery and then to destroy their enemy. Malaya is generally tree-covered, mostly with primary jungle, otherwise with plantations or rice padi. There are several steep mountain ranges and there are mangrove swamps. Without intelligence, a thousand battalions might range the country and never stumble upon a single group. At the outset, there were only ten British units and, since there were no helicopters, all movement was by truck along the limited roads or on the rivers and, for all tactical purposes, on foot.

At the outset, operations were hampered by lack of a common policy. In the state and federal capitals, officials struggling to restore Malayan agriculture, industry and trade believed the acts of terrorism in the rural areas to be a minor vexation which the army and police should deal with. The police force, hard pressed and losing some of its number every week, killed or wounded, resented the attitude of many army units who tended to feel that they had been called in to act because the police had failed. In these conditions, terrorist successes multiplied. By 1950 it was clear that, unless emergency measures were taken, Chin Peng might succeed. A soldier, General Sir Harold Briggs, was appointed Director of Operations with full powers to direct all naval, military, air and police operations under the High Commissioner, Sir Henry Gurney. At once, General Briggs set up a joint headquarters in Kuala Lumpur, the capital, in which all elements of security forces and those concerned from civil government were represented. He reminded everyone engaged in combating terrorism that there were two requirements to satisfy if operations were to be successful: a cooperative populace and good intelligence.

The combination of police, military and government officers was continued down to local sectors, where battalion or company commanders joined the district officers and police superintendents. The latter two had the task of persuading villagers in the kampongs to pass information of terrorist movements at once and to deny food or shelter to Chin Peng's men. For protection, village Home Guards were trained and armed, though sometimes it was necessary to move whole villages to safe areas.

The soldiers – British, Gurkha, Australian and New Zealand – depended on this information for their jungle searching. Often these tips were valueless; rarely was there a quick result. A typical example was an operation in Selangor State where three battalions laid ambushes, patrolled and watched daily for two months. On the last day, when hope of success was at an end, four terrorists walked into an ambush to be killed or captured.

Operating in small parties in the jungle was demanding enough without the delicate and dangerous hunt for terrorists. Men rarely saw the sun for

T

Malaya. Men of the Seaforth Highlanders on patrol in the jungle searching for Communist insurgents

days but lived in the long green twilight beneath the canopy of tree tops. Their paths were hindered by such impedimenta as belukar, the tall, tough ferns of south-east Asia. Leeches were everywhere; malaria, dengue and leptospyrosis threatened high fevers.

By 1952 the British Army had over 24,000 men in Malaya. Amongst the units there were few who had fought in Burma with Slim; and in any case, new techniques were required. As each reinforcement party arrived in the country, it was sent to a jungle warfare training centre to learn how to live; how to track, cordon, ambush; how to communicate; how to receive supplies.

After the early successes, Chin Peng's force recruited steadily until he had 10,000 men under arms spread throughout Malaya in regiments and companies. Most of these were Chinese. Gradually, the various counter-measures began to take effect and, as successes diminished, so did recruiting to the Communist cause. Surrenders by those disenchanted with the harsh discipline of the communist camps and the increasing difficulty in obtaining food became more frequent. Yet at the end of 1951, terrorist murders were still a daily occurrence and, if checked, there was no sign that Chin Peng was beaten.

Just at this time, the direction of operations received a severe setback. Sir Henry Gurney, the High Commissioner, was murdered. General Briggs, who had stayed on under immense pressure of work well beyond his contract, left to go home, where he died a few months later. An anxious British Government selected one man to replace both High Commissioner and Director of Operations: General Sir Gerald Templer.

A man of restless energy, shrewd and imaginative, General Templer was fortunately a big enough man in character to accept the successful policies of his predecessors. He enlarged their scope and pressed fearlessly their execution. A few weeks after his appointment, in March 1952, a young British assistant district officer and a small escort of police went out to repair a water pipe blown up by terrorists. They were ambushed and killed. Shortly afterwards, General Templer went to the local town, Tanjong Malim, and called together 300 leading citizens. He pointed out that guerrilla activity was rife all around them: the railway was under attack, the roads frequently ambushed, the toll of murders growing. He was well aware that Chin Peng's men were getting food from the town and these same terrorists had now killed a further twelve men who were attempting to reconnect the town's water.

'This is going to stop,' he said. 'It does not amuse me to punish innocent people but many of you are not innocent. You have information which you are too cowardly to give.'

Severe collective penalties were imposed. Citizens were confined to their houses for 22 hours a day; rations were reduced by half.

Harsher measures still were taken with the village of Jenderam, whose inhabitants continued to offer succour to several communist groups after many warnings. One day at dawn, the village was cordoned and every man, woman and child was removed to a detention centre; the houses were razed; the crops and plantations destroyed.

Such events were rare, for the majority of villagers and townspeople, even the Chinese element, were not at heart supporters of Chin Peng. Moreover, the firm promise of independence when the emergency was over and an immediate improvement in local government resources encouraged full cooperation with the security forces. The Briggs Plan had forced Chin Peng to break up his regiments into platoon detachments. The soldiers now had to hunt these down.

Cooperation by the populace, desertions and captures from the camps gave an increasing flow of intelligence to the security forces. This intelligence became so refined that it became possible to strike selectively

Sarawak, Borneo. A patrol leaves a helicopter which has landed on a hill. The landing has been prepared by a patrol already operating in the area

at the main source of influence in Chin Peng's organ-isation: the 'government' and political bureaux.

By the end of 1954, the Communist self-styled Malay Races Liberation Army was on the defensive and General Sir Geoffrey Bourne – General Templer's successor as Director of Operations – began the important task of winning the confidence of the many Chinese community leaders who sat still on the political fence. His success in this field and the cumulative results of the combined security organisa-tion brought operations to a close in 1960. After twelve years Chin Peng's command had shrunk to 500, many of them aging men and women, who sought refuge in the remote area of the Thai-Malay border.

Twelve years of operations in Malaya had exacted much from the British Army in numbers of men and cost of material. Yet it had provided an operational task which had sharpened the skills and capabilities of the many officers and men who had been there and had forced the pace of weapons and equipment development. But for National Service, the supply of men would have become acute. For there were many other demands on the Army; in the Suez Canal zone of Egypt and intermittently elsewhere in the Middle East. In 1950, as the Briggs Plan began to operate, the British Government agreed to contribute to the United Nations force in the Korean War and it im-mediately became necessary to institute special short-service engagements to enlist volunteers to fight in that theatre. The 27th Infantry Brigade hastened from Hong Kong to take part in the critical defence of the Pusan perimeter and the 29th soon came from England to join them. A British administrative base was established for their support in Korea and Japan. In May 1951 a British Commonwealth Division was formed, contingents from Australia and New Zealand combining as successfully in operations with their British friends as they had done in Malaya. The Canadian Army maintained a strong element in the division and South African and Australian airmen flew with the United Nations air command.

When the Korean War came to an end in 1953, the government made haste to redeploy the British forces there and to release those men who had enlisted solely for the campaign. Plans were made to end National Service completely in the middle or late 1950s and the long term structure of the regular British Army was calculated. Mr Churchill's last Conservative administration was now in power. It might consider with satisfaction the end of war expenditure in Korea and the progressive reduction of support costs in the Malayan operations, but there were new require-

ments for troops on the horizon. Shortly after Winston Churchill retired, giving way to Anthony Eden as Prime Minister, the island of Cyprus became overnight the stage of a terrorist campaign.

The terrorists were commanded by a Greek general, Grivas, of Cypriot origin, who had given his services to the cause of Greek nationalism. A majority of Cypriots considered themselves tied to Greece by blood and culture and demanded independence. Their spokesman was the orthodox primate, Arch-bishop Makarios, himself secretly a director of EOKA, the terrorist organisation.

The organisational lessons of the Malayan conflict were quickly put to use. A Directorate of Operations was established; military, police and civil govern-ment combined to prosecute operations. But one essential difference denied success: the populace could not be brought to cooperate en masse against EOKA.

The Turkish minority helped where it could but terrorism was not encountered in the predominantly Turkish areas. Probably many of the Greek Cypriot villagers wanted only to be left alone to pursue their struggle for livelihood from their small holdings, but as time passed they became more amenable to EOKA than to the government. EOKA had the power to murder those who cooperated with government. Government lacked the ability to protect them. In the towns there was widespread support for union with Greece, particularly amongst young people. The pattern of murders amongst loyal Greek Cypriot police and government officers was similar to that in Malaya and, due to popular acquiescence, effective.

At the outset, there were few troops in Cyprus; it had been a pleasant leave centre while operations had persisted in Palestine and in the canal zone. It was more importantly a NATO air base and the site of the British military headquarters in the Middle East. Now the Commando Brigade were committed to counter-terrorism and soon, in January 1956, part of 16th Parachute Brigade arrived. Though standing by to operate elsewhere in the Middle East, the para-chutists were soon patrolling the pine forests and olive groves, or keeping order in the towns and cities with the many other British units arriving by air and troopship.

Due to popular reaction, intelligence was poor. But gradually, professional expertise combined with luck began to pay dividends. One after another of the terrorist groups was killed or captured. Grivas had the narrowest shave of his life when he was sighted unexpectedly by a patrol of parachutists as he sunned himself on a mountain slope, wearing only a vest and underpants. He sped away before the hunters closed.

In June 1956 Colonel Nasser, president of the United Arab Republic, abrogated the agreement solemnly made with the other governments owning with Egypt the Suez Canal. In November the commando and parachute brigades returned to Port Said with the French in a whirlwind operation by parachute, helicopter and seaborne assault which captured the canal as far as Kantara before the United Nations intervened. Perhaps an act of political misjudgement by the United Kingdom, the initial landings against very strong Egyptian forces were a success.

Meantime, the operations in Cyprus drew in more and more of the British Army. Supplies of arms and a steady flow of recruits enabled Grivas to maintain control of the populace by terrorism, though there were relatively few attacks directly against the security forces. Government had to decide whether to end National Service as promised and did so in 1957. It made good its shortage of infantry by converting temporarily a number of artillery regiments for counter-guerrilla operations in Cyprus and reducing its commitments in Malaya, where Malay battalions and police field force units were assuming a greater share in active operations.

If the Malayan and Korean campaigns had drawn most attention during the early part of the 1950s, the British Army had had much to do elsewhere. In Kenya the Mau Mau gangs, recruited from the Kikuyu tribe, had taken to the dense rain forests from which they made sorties to attack Europeans and Africans. The Kikuyu were land hungry. Their discontent was used to further the aspirations of urban Africans for political independence. Over eight years, 1952–60, British battalions, batteries and engineer squadrons, supported by small but intensely-worked communications and administrative teams, broke the movement in alliance with a devoted police and civil government organisation, many of them Africans or Asian settlers. Only when this had been done was the cause of Kenyan independence advanced.

In Aden, the tribes in the protectorate continued to make intermittent raids on one another and against government agencies. Their activities were aided by a free supply of arms and ammunition from Egypt, much of it passed by the British Government to the Egyptians as part of the original terms in closing military bases in the Nile delta and canal zone. In Muscat and Oman, the Sultan asked for and received a small force of Cameronians and Special Air Service to suppress his rebellious relatives. In the Persian Gulf, the Trucial Oman Scouts, under British Army

Sarawak, Borneo. Placing sandbags round a gun position in preparation for firing a 105mm howitzer

officers, combined with British Army and air detachments to protect the Buraimi oasis from Saudi depredations. But the two biggest operations in this area in this period were in Jordan and Kuwait.

In 1958 the discontented elements amongst the displaced Palestinian Arabs and others, politically ambitious, were encouraged by Egypt to attempt a coup in Amman. Already to the north the royal family and cabinet in Iraq had been murdered in a brutal fashion. Now the King of Jordan, Hussein, asked the British Government on 15 July 1958, to assist him. Positioned in Cyprus, 16th Parachute Brigade was roused early one morning and told to hasten to Amman. A force of Hasting and Beverley aircraft, Royal Air Force Transport Command, flew off piecemeal as individual aircraft were loaded, the brigade commander and his brigade major being the first to land at about eight o'clock at Amman airport. A number of aircraft were turned back due to difficulties in flying over Israel but sufficient troops had landed by 10·00 a.m. to dissuade the rebels from taking action. The Bedouin units and people remained loyal to the King. Royal Air Force Hunters landed to reinforce the Jordanian Air Force. The 1st Cameronians joined the parachutists by sailing up from Aden and landing at Aquaba. The political atmosphere grew cooler.

Towards the end of the year the British forces left Amman, the parachute brigade returning to its United Kingdom base, save for one battalion left in Cyprus. In that island peace was brought about at this time by a settlement involving cession of bases to Britain and the establishment of a national government in Nicosia with safeguards for the Turkish minority. The popular demand for union with Greece diminished and was at length dropped by Archbishop Makarios after he had taken office as president of the new republic.

Garrison life in Cyprus was not unpleasant for the British units, quartered from 1959 onwards in the ceded bases areas. The local hills provided good training ground. The pleasant climate was enjoyed by soldiers' families, many of whom were now able to join their husbands and fathers abroad for the first time since 1939. The battalion of the Parachute Regiment, the 1st, left behind after the withdrawal from Jordan, was replaced by the 2nd.

It was this battalion which was stood to suddenly in July 1961 to be ordered to Kuwait.

Kuwait, the sheikdom at the head of the Persian Gulf, had for some time been uneasy at the pressure of claims by Iraq on its oil-rich territory. All at once, threatening movements by the Iraq Army gave weight to the rising political pressure and the ruler of Kuwait asked for British assistance.

Fortuitously a commando carrier of the Royal Navy was close by and Royal Marines were quickly brought to close helicopter range for a landing. A brigade was brought from East Africa, support troops from Aden, and the parachute battalion from Cyprus was reinforced by a battery and other supporting troops from 16th Parachute Brigade in the United Kingdom.

It was high summer. The troops, obliged to live out in their positions in the desert, had a trying time. The 11th Hussars and 3rd Dragoon Guards with tanks and scout cars found these suffocatingly hot in this zone of intense heat and humidity. Bare metal on vehicles of any sort seared the naked skin if touched during the day.

Relief came when contingents from other Arab countries arrived to join the small Kuwaiti Army. Progressively, British forces were withdrawn to their original bases or to Bahrain, further to the south in the Persian Gulf.

Now came a lull for the British Army. The Malayan operations had ended. The Cyprus issue was settled. British administered territories in East and West Africa had come peacefully to independence. The occasional requirements for troops in the West Indies or Central and South America were not onerous. The training cycles in the United Kingdom and Germany were not interrupted by demands for troops for distant operations.

Possibly this condition of wholesome peace might have persisted but for the ambitions of a Brunei Malay named Azahari. Brunei is a tiny sultanate, a British protectorate on the north-west coast of the huge island of Borneo. It is sandwiched between the former colonies of British North Borneo (now Sabah) and Sarawak. These two larger territories had been persuaded by the United Kingdom to join Malaya in a new state, Malaysia; from which, after some hesitation, Brunei remained aloof.

Azahari had it in mind to overthrow the autocratic sultan, and had for some months in 1962 organised a personal military force secretly in and around Brunei town. The secrecy was somewhat open; the police knew well that drilling was going on and that green cloth had been bought for uniforms. But they were playing a waiting game and, perhaps because Azahari was a notorious playboy, wondering whether he could be a serious contender for power.

In December 1962 Azahari suddenly and unexpectedly gave the order to take over the miniature state's government. He was personally safe from consequences, being in Manila at the time enjoying night club life away from the stricter restrictions of his own Muslim community.

An urgent radio message was sent from Brunei to Singapore, headquarters of the British Far East Command. In short time, the Royal Air Force brought a battalion of Gurkhas to Brunei and a skilful pilot landed a Beverley full of Queen's Own Highlanders at the oil town of Seria to the south. The Azahari coup collapsed, and the rebel force fled. With a temporary commander in Brunei, Brigadier Jack Glennie, the ad hoc British relief force helped the police follow up the scattered rebels.

Indonesia now intervened. President Soekarno had been claiming portions of the former British Bornean territories for some time both in London and Kuala Lumpur. He chose early in 1963 to declare openly his support for the Azahari and expanded from this position to one in which, his claims to territory being rejected, he declared that he would 'confront' the new state of Malaysia. It was a conveniently vague term. It did not commit Indonesia openly to war but permitted Soekarno's forces to operate against Malaysia as opportunity offered.

The problems of offensive action were immense, even for a state with so many soldiers as Indonesia, supported by modern ships and aircraft supplied earlier by the Soviet Union. Malaya was separated by a stretch of open sea from the main Indonesian ports. In Borneo there was a common land frontier but it lay amongst rugged mountains, densely forested. On either side of the frontier ranges there were no roads; transport depended on rivers.

Defence of Malaysian Borneo and Brunei was equally difficult; more so when the initiative lies, as it did, with Indonesia. The frontier runs for 1,000 miles. Manifestly, it cannot be manned throughout this length. The lack of roads made quick response to any area threatened a slow one; and though helicopters and light aircraft with short landing capabilities were introduced, these were insufficient to meet the expanse of territory. Besides, sudden storms and frequent low clouds on the mountains restricted flying.

As the Indonesian forces began slowly to encroach on Sabah and Sarawak by small but painful raids, the combat structure, so well understood from the Malayan operations, was established. Major-General W. C. Walker, a Gurkha officer of long experience in jungle operations, took command, siting his headquarters in Brunei town. Sector commands were established in Kuching, capital of Sarawak, Brunei, and Tawau, a port at the northern extremity of the frontier in Sabah. It was a slow business. Initially one Royal Marine Commando, a squadron of 8th Hussars in scout cars and a light artillery battery garrisoned Sarawak. By 1965, there were seven battalions in the Kuching sector alone besides many other troops. But the British Government were understandably anxious not to be committed to a long and expensive campaign unless it was absolutely necessary. They had other and continuing tasks for troops in the Far East – the garrisons in Hong Kong, a reserve for SEATO, and the security of Singapore and Malaya, the last two being subjected occasionally to Indonesian raids.

Attacks at Tawau, into northern, central and western Sarawak, sporadic, often inefficiently conducted, and a massive build-up of Indonesian forces in Borneo forced the United Kingdom reluctantly to reinforce Borneo.

The jungle trail was trodden once again by British and Commonwealth soldiers. It was not quite a repetition of hunting terrorists, but the jungle made the same exhausting demands on physique and morale. A platoon might set off for eight days after being dropped off in some distant helicopter landing zone hacked out of the jungle by the engineers. During its patrol it might be hundreds of miles from any settlement. The jungle floor, still and twilit even at noon, is a lonely place.

The strength of the security forces lay in their experience in jungle operations, an experience retained and enhanced by the jungle warfare courses which had continued unabated since 1945. The populace, apart from a fractional element of communists, supported the security forces and were well used to dealing with the British Army, whose guerrilla operations many had supported in the Second World War. These relations were enhanced by friendly contacts

which offered medical treatment, even helicopter evacuations to peoples often ten days' march or paddle from the nearest doctor.

Intelligence flowed in. General Walker spent three years travelling up and down Borneo amongst troops, with the police, with civil government, writing his reports to Singapore to say what was the least he could do with in this huge, empty but hidden land. In 1965 he was succeeded by Major-General George Lea, also a veteran of the Malayan operations. By this date a completely joint Directorate of Operations was functioning on Labuan island. General Lea's task was to maintain the tempo of operations as cheaply as possible but with sufficient enterprise to persuade Indonesia that its policy of aggression was hopeless. But it was not to be Soekarno who reached that decision. The Indonesian president was deposed that year, the failure and futile expense of fighting Malaysia and the British being one of the charges levelled against him by his opponents.

Slowly, due to doubts and uncertainties concerning the communist groups remaining in the border areas, the British withdrew. The company base camps with their little shelters of sandbags, bamboo and atap were deserted. The perpetual damp soon eroded the structures; the eager jungle quickly grew over camp and air strip, boat stage and loading bay. Only the new roads and airfields remain. The Kazaks and Kenyas, the land and sea Dyaks and the many other Borneans of the interior have returned to their old ways. The coastal Malays and Chinese have settled to their daily round without the distraction of patrol boats or helicopters.

A new generation of soldiers learned the jungle ways in Borneo. As they did so, the closure of British military influence in Africa and Aden was in process.

The new independent governments in Tanganyika, Uganda, Kenya and Malawi did not, very naturally, wish to retain British garrisons. One by one these were wound up, though when this was almost done there was a critical week when mutinies occurred in almost all the East African republican armies and British infantry and gunners were obliged to restore order. Forty-five Commando Royal Marines made a spectacular helicopter landing at dawn to overpower the mutineers at Dar-es-Salaam.

In Aden the clamour of two opposing groups, FLOSY, the Front for the Liberation of South Yemen, and the National Liberation Front drowned the minority who wished for a federation of sheikhdoms and the colony of Aden city and port. Up country, the tribes were persuaded to rise at numerous points and the only motor road to Dhala was cut and mined. In April 1964 operations began to teach these dissidents that they were not immune from counter-attack. Major-General John Cubbon, commander of the Middle East Land Forces, sent a force up to Thumair, clearing the road. In May, 45 Commando pushed deeper and 3rd Battalion, The Parachute Regiment, supported by a light battery and a troop of engineers from the parachute brigade, advanced up the Bakri ridge into the base of the dissidents. The 4th Royal Tank Regiment closed from the south, the 1st Royal Anglian seized a mountain stronghold and the 1st King's Own Scottish Border Regiment moved in to maintain what had been won. It was the culmination of numerous operations to maintain the security of the Dhala road. The exacting, often dangerous campaign continued for two years, battalions and armoured regiments, batteries and engineer squadrons succeeding one another.

The area of decision was Aden colony, however. Having failed in its efforts to bring about an orderly transfer of power by popular election, the British Government at last agreed to give power to the self-elected 'liberation' forces. While negotiations continued, British troops and Royal Marine Commandos held the ring at some cost. Preserving order amongst the narrow streets of the colony townships was the worst operation of its kind that the Army had ever undertaken. Aware of the withdrawal of the British, there was scarcely any support from the populace and waning cooperation by the police. A company of 1st Battalion, The Royal Northumberland Fusi-

liers, was ambushed in the Crater district of the colony just prior to finishing its tour of duty. No Arab came to succour the wounded or stay their murder as they lay helpless under the terrorists' weapons. In the winter of 1967 the last British units withdrew. The republican government took power, to be deposed after a short rule by the Aden Army.

The years 1945–68 reflect for the British Army a period of resettlement after the war and then, with the withdrawal of United Kingdom authority east and west, of a series of operations to maintain law and order before and sometimes after transfer of power. All these are now past. What remains are the international commitments such as were honoured in Korea and Borneo. There are still a few overseas garrisons – Gibraltar, the Cyprus bases, Malta, soon to be evacuated, and Hong Kong. Nowadays much of the overseas service a British soldier sees apart from Germany is by training in the Libyan desert, or the remoter parts of Australia, Canada or Malaya. Yet the Army is still a force of long-service volunteers backed by a small band of 'week-end' soldiers in the Army Volunteer Reserve.

It is an army of persistent tradition despite the current passion for change at all costs. Its men are the direct descendants of the New Model Army and, more than they realise, correspond in their professionalism to the Army that went up to Mons and almost died at Ypres. Its strength lies in recruitment of men looking for a challenging task. While it continues to find these men, its history will long remain unfinished.

Western Aden Protectorate. A scout car of the Queen's Royal Irish Hussars pauses as it escorts a convoy through a wadi (dry river bed)

POSTSCRIPT

PETER YOUNG

We have outlined and illustrated the story of the British Army from its beginnings, through the Redcoat Age and the great wars of the first half of our century into the Nuclear Age. It is a story of triumph and disaster, of victories under Marlborough and Wellington, Roberts and Kitchener, Slim and Montgomery, but also of defeats, sometimes under gallant blockheads like Braddock, occasionally under hopeless incompetents like Elphinstone. It is a story, too, of neglect in peacetime and over-optimistic political direction in the early stages of practically every conflict. Often, as in 1940, the British Army had nothing to sustain it but its traditions and its discipline.

In these days of the 'deterrent' there are those, a handful of commissioned officers among them, who believe that 'tradition' has no value, that there is nothing to be learned from anything that took place before 1945. *Sancta simplicitas*. One wonders how these gentry explain away the events of June 1967 in the Sinai Desert, a World War II campaign with somewhat improved 'ironmongery'. Israel has shown the world that even in the Nuclear Age conventional warfare is still a possibility. The need to prepare for guerrilla warfare is still more obvious. It follows that any army that means business must still have well-read, experienced commanders at the top; young battalion commanders; officers who will lead from in front; NCOs prepared to take charge when they are on their own and a hundred other ancient virtues that have seen the British soldier through the crises of the last 400 years.

We may hope that the politicians will remember that an army requires reserves and administrative backing, as well as the means to expand in times of crisis – if the *History of the British Army* shows nothing else it shows that this is not exactly likely.

It is fashionable nowadays to talk of the need for the 'professional officer' as if such a being had never been heard of before the end of the Second World War. Much emphasis is rightly laid on the professional training of promising officers. It is as well at any period when it is fashionable to be clever and scientific to reflect sometimes on the primitive virtues. The next time the British soldier finds himself on campaign the words of Harry Lumsden, who raised the Guides Cavalry may still be found appropriate ... 'to be alert and ready; to rise equal to the occasion, be the case small or great; to be not easily taken aback in a sudden emergency; to be a genial comrade' – not a bad sort of C.O. to be with under fire ...

APPENDIX

The Army of 1661

Units	Companies or Troops	Commanders
His Majestie's Own Life Guard		Captain General
His Highness Royall the Duke of York's Life Guard		Captain: Sir Charles Berkeley
His Grace the Duke of Albemarle's Life Guard		Captain: Sir Philip Howard
The Royal Regiment of Horse (Blues)	7	Colonel: the Earl of Oxford
The King's Regiment of Guards at Dunkirk*	12	Colonel: Lord Wentworth
His Majestie's Own Regiment of Foot*	12	Colonel: John Russell
The Duke of Albemarle's Regiment of Foot	10	Colonel: the Duke of Albemarle
The Tangier Regiment of Foot		Colonel: the Earl of Peterborough
Sir Robert Harley's Regiment at Dunkirk	14	Colonel: Sir Robert Harley

* These two were incorporated and became the Grenadier Guards.

Garrisons 1661

Besides the Cinque Ports, which were not 'in charge with the Commissary-Gen. of the Musters', there were:

Garrison	Companies	Governor
Tower of London	3	Sir John Robinson
Cowes Castle	1*	Captain Humphrey Turney‡
Portland	1	Captain Robert Weld
Scilly Island, Tresco, and St. Marie's Isle	3	Sir Francis Godolphin
Pendennis Castle	3	Captain Richard Arundell‡
Jersey Island	2	Earl of St Albans‡
Guernsey Island	1	Sir Hugh Pollard‡
St. Mawes Castle	1	Sir Richard Vivian‡
Portsmouth	6	The Duke of York‡
Plymouth Fort and Island	2	Earl of Bath‡
Upnor Castle	1	Captain Thomas Writtle
Gravesend Block House (On Essex side)	1†	Captain William Lennard‡
Landguard Point Fort	1	Earl of Warwick, K.B.
Hull and the Blockhouses	6	Lord Belasyse‡
Scarborough Castle	1	Colonel Sir Jordan Crosland‡
Tynmouth Castle	2	Colonel Edward Villiers‡
Berwick-Upon-Tweed and Holy Island	6	Lord Widdrington‡
Carlisle	3	Lord Musgrave‡
Windsor	3	Lord Mordaunt‡
Chepstow Castle	1	Lord Herbert‡
Hurst Castle§	–	Major Edward Strange

* By ancient usage this garrison consisted of 50 men recruited locally and three gunners.
† A corporal, 30 soldiers, 1 gunner and two matrosses.
‡ All these were ardent Royalists and most of them had seen a great deal of fighting during the Civil Wars.
§ Master gunner, 11 gunners and a porter.

A comparison of the titles of the infantry regiments in the Army List of 1815 with those of the Army List 1908

1815	1908
1st or the Royal Scots	Royal Scots, Lothian Regiment
2nd or the Queen's Royal	Queen's Royal West Surrey
3rd East Kent or the Buffs	The Buffs (East Kent) Regiment
4th or the King's Own	King's Own (Royal Lancaster) Regiment
5th or the Northumberland Regiment of Foot	The Northumberland Fusiliers
6th or the 1st Warwickshire Regiment of Foot	The Royal Warwickshire Regiment
7th Regiment of Foot or Royal Fuzileers	The Royal Fusiliers (City of London) Regiment
8th or the King's Regiment	The King's Liverpool Regiment
9th or The East Norfolk Regiment	The Norfolk Regiment
10th or the North Lincolnshire Regiment	The Lincolnshire Regiment
11th or the North Devonshire Regiment	The Devonshire Regiment
12th or the East Suffolk Regiment	The Suffolk Regiment
13th or the 1st Somersetshire Regiment	The Prince Albert's Somersetshire Light Infantry
14th or the Buckinghamshire Regiment	The Prince of Wales's Own West Yorkshire Regiment
15th or the Yorkshire (E. Riding) Regiment	The East Yorkshire Regiment
16th or the Bedfordshire Regiment	The Bedfordshire Regiment
17th or the Leicestershire Regiment	The Leicestershire Regiment
18th or the Royal Irish Regiment	The Royal Irish Regiment
19th or the 1st Yorkshire (N. Riding) Regiment	Alexandra, Princess of Wales's Own Yorkshire Regiment
20th or the East Devonshire Regiment	The Lancashire Fusiliers
21st or Royal North British Fuzileers	The Royal Scots Fusiliers
22nd or the Cheshire Regiment	The Cheshire Regiment
23rd or Royal Welsh Fuzileers	The Royal Welsh Fusiliers
24th or the Warwickshire Regiment	The South Wales Borderers
25th or King's Own Borderers Regiment	The King's Own Scottish Borderers
26th or Cameronian Regiment	The Cameronians, Scottish Rifles
27th or Inniskilling Regiment	The Royal Inniskilling Fusiliers
28th or the North Gloucestershire Regiment	The Gloucestershire Regiment
29th or the Worcestershire Regiment	The Worcestershire Regiment
30th or the Cambridgeshire Regiment	The East Lancashire Regiment
31st or the Huntingdonshire Regiment	The East Surrey Regiment
32nd or the Cornwall Regiment	The Duke of Cornwall's Light Infantry
33rd or the 1st Yorkshire (W. Riding) Regiment	The Duke of Wellington's (W. Riding) Regiment
34th or the Cumberland Regiment	The Border Regiment
35th or the Sussex Regiment	The Royal Sussex Regiment
36th or the Herefordshire Regiment	The Worcestershire Regiment
37th or the North Hampshire Regiment	The Hampshire Regiment
38th or the 1st Staffordshire Regiment	The South Staffordshire Regiment
39th or the Dorsetshire Regiment	The Dorsetshire Regiment
40th or 2nd Somersetshire Regiment	The Prince of Wales's Volunteers (South Lancashire) Regiment
41st Regiment of Foot	The Welsh Regiment
42nd or the Royal Highland Regiment	The Black Watch (Royal Highlanders)
43rd or the Monmouthshire Regiment	The Oxfordshire and Buckinghamshire Light Infantry
44th or the East Essex Regiment	The Essex Regiment
45th or the Nottinghamshire Regiment	The Sherwood Foresters (Nottinghamshire & Derbyshire) Regiment
46th or the South Devonshire Regiment	The Duke of Cornwall's Light Infantry
47th or the Lancashire Regiment	The Loyal North Lancashire Regiment
48th or the Northamptonshire Regiment	The Northamptonshire Regiment
49th or the Hertfordshire Regiment	Princess Charlotte of Wales's (Royal Berkshire) Regiment
50th or the West Kent Regiment	The Queen's Own (Royal West Kent)

1815	1908
51st or the 2nd Yorkshire (W. Riding) Regiment (Light Infantry)	The King's Own (Yorkshire Light Infantry)
52nd or the Oxfordshire Regiment (Light Infantry)	The Oxfordshire and Buckingham Light Infantry
53rd or the Shropshire Regiment	The King's (Shropshire Light Infantry)
54th or the West Norfolk Regiment	The Dorsetshire Regiment
55th or the Westmorland Regiment	The Border Regiment
56th or the West Essex Regiment	The Essex Regiment
57th or the West Middlesex Regiment	The Duke of Cambridge's Own (Middlesex) Regiment
58th or the Rutlandshire Regiment	The Northamptonshire Regiment
59th or the 2nd Nottinghamshire Regiment	The East Lancashire Regiment
60th or Royal American Regiment	The King's Own Rifle Corps
61st or the South Gloucestershire Regiment	The Gloucestershire Regiment
62nd or the Wiltshire Regiment	The Duke of Edinburgh's (Wiltshire) Regiment
63rd or the West Suffolk Regiment	The Manchester Regiment
64th or the 2nd Staffordshire Regiment	The Prince of Wales's (North Staffordshire) Regiment
65th or the 2nd Yorkshire (N. Riding) Regiment	The York and Lancaster Regiment
66th or the Berkshire Regiment	Princess Charlotte of Wales's (Royal Berkshire) Regiment
67th or the South Hampshire Regiment	The Hampshire Regiment
68th or the Durham Regiment (Light Infantry)	The Durham Light Infantry
69th or the South Lincolnshire Regiment	The Welsh Regiment
70th or Glasgow Lowland Regiment	The East Surrey Regiment
71st Highland Regiment (Light Infantry)	The Highland Light Infantry
72nd Highland Regiment	Seaforth Highlanders, Ross-shire Buffs
73rd Highland Regiment	The Black Watch (Royal Highlanders)
74th Highland Regiment	The Highland Light Infantry
75th Highland Regiment	The Gordon Highlanders
76th Regiment	The Duke of Wellington's West Riding Regiment
77th or the East Middlesex Regiment	The Duke of Cambridge's Own Middlesex Regiment
78th or Highland Regiment (or the Ross-shire Buffs)	Seaforth Highlanders Ross-shire Buffs (Duke of Albany's Own)
79th Regiment of Cameron Highlanders	The Queen's Own Cameron Highlanders
80th Regiment or Staffordshire Volunteers	The South Staffordshire Regiment
81st Regiment	The Loyal North Lancashire Regiment
82nd Regiment or Prince of Wales's Volunteers	The Prince of Wales's Volunteers (South Lancashire)
83rd Regiment	The Royal Irish Rifles
84th York and Lancaster Regiment	The York and Lancaster Regiment
85th Regiment or Bucks Volunteers	The King's (Shropshire Light Infantry)
86th or the Royal County Down Regiment	The Royal Irish Rifles
87th or Prince of Wales's Own Irish Regiment	Princess Victoria's (Royal Irish Fusiliers)
88th Regiment or Connaught Rangers	The Connaught Rangers
89th Regiment	Princess Victoria's (Royal Irish Fusiliers)
90th Regiment or Perthshire Volunteers	The Cameronians (Scottish Rifles)
91st Regiment	Princess Louise's (Argyll and Sutherland Highlanders)
92nd Regiment	The Gordon Highlanders
93rd Regiment	Princess Louise's (Argyll and Sutherland Highlanders)
94th Regiment	The Connaught Rangers
95th Regiment	The Rifle Brigade, The Prince Consort's Own
96th Regiment	The Manchester Regiment
97th or Queen's Own Regiment	The Queen's (Own Royal West Kent Regiment)
98th Regiment	The Prince of Wales's North Staffordshire Regiment
99th or Duke of Edinburgh's (Lanarkshire) Regiment	Duke of Edinburgh's (Wiltshire) Regiment
100th or His Royal Highness the Prince Regent's County of Dublin Regiment	The Prince of Wales's Leinster Regiment (Royal Canadians)
101st or the Duke of York's Irish Regiment	The Royal Munster Fusiliers
102nd Regiment } 103rd Regiment }	The Royal Dublin Fusiliers
104th Regiment	The Royal Munster Fusiliers

Note: As a result of the Cardwell reforms, the old regiments of Foot were linked in pairs to form the first and second battalions of the new regiments. The first time therefore, that a regimental title is given under the heading *1908* it refers to the first battalion, the second time to the second battalion. As an example the 29th Foot became the First Battalion, The Worcestershire Regiment, while the 36th Foot became The Second Battalion, The Worcestershire Regiment.

The Growth of the Army during the
American Revolution from 1775–80

Great Britain, whose population at this time was about 11 million, put forward tremendous efforts in the long struggle of the American Revolution. Between September 1775 and September 1780 no fewer than 76,885 men were raised for the British Establishment. Nor were Loyalist American troops altogether wanting. In December 1780 there were 8,201 Provincial Rank and File in America. In April 1775 Britain had but 27,063 men under arms. By September 1780, including Provincials, Militia, and Germans, she had 147,152 men under arms. Their distribution was:

South Britain	63,616*
North America	33,466
West Indies and on passage	11,153
Canada	7,471
North Britain (i.e. Scotland)	7,102
Gibraltar	5,786
Embarked for service	3,637
Convention Army	3,617†
Additional companies raising for the infantry	3,438
Jersey	2,182
Minorca	2,132
Guernsey	2,099
East Indies (excluding East India Company troops)	1,245
Africa	208

* Including 5,860 Cavalry and 36,973 Militia.

† The troops who had surrendered at Saratoga were not lawfully prisoners of war and were still included in the returns.

ACKNOWLEDGEMENTS

All colour illustrations are reproduced by courtesy of the National Army Museum, with the exception of the engraving at top of page 58 which is reproduced by courtesy of the Parker Gallery, and the engraving on page 109 which is reproduced by courtesy of the India Office Library.

The editors and publishers wish to thank the following for the valuable assistance they gave in the preparation of the book: H. R. Leighton Esq. of the Photographic Library of the National Army Museum who was tireless in his quest for illustrations; T. A. Heathcoat Esq., Curator of the Art Department, and B. Mollo Esq., Curator of the Manuscript Department of the National Army Museum; J. E. Goulding Esq. of the Imperial War Museum; Miss Pauline Harrold of the India Office Library; Hutchinson Ltd for permission to use material from *Victorian Military Campaigns*, (1967) by Brian Bond in his chapter on 'Colonial Wars and Punitive Expeditions'; and to Lt-Col J. A. Macnabb, T.D., for permission to quote the letter written by Lt J. C. Macnabb to his mother (pages 164–5).

Thanks are also due to the following for permission to reproduce the black and white photographs in this book: Reproduced by gracious permission of Her Majesty the Queen are the photographs on pages 49 and 133 (top); His Grace the Duke of Marlborough for the photographs on pages 30 and 38–9; Brigadier Peter Young for the photograph on page 279; the Parker Gallery for the photograph on page 204; The City of York Art Gallery for the photograph on page 13; The National Portrait Gallery, London, for the photographs on pages 8, 14, 27 and 172; *The Illustrated London News* for the photographs on pages 188 and 189 (bottom); The India Office Library for the photographs on pages 75–6, 78, 138, 144 and 166–8; The Library of the Royal Military Academy for the photographs on pages 63, 116 and 126; the National Army Museum for the photographs on pages 10, 12, 15–24, 28, 31–5, 42–8, 50, 56, 61–2, 65–72, 79–108, 114–5, 117–24, 129–31, 133 (bottom), 134–7, 140–1, 149–65, 169–70, 175–87, 189 (top), 191–4, 201–3, 209 and 243–6; and the Imperial War Museum for the photographs on pages 206–7, 210–41, 247–77 and 280–95.

The diagrams on pages 20, 21 and 22 were drawn by P. Vaughan Williams, who also drew the maps and battle plans, some in collaboration with Oxford Illustrators Ltd. Part of the information for the maps of Burma and Malaya on pages 278, 280 and 282, was taken from the official history, *The War Against Japan* by permission of Her Majesty's Stationery Office.

The sketch on page 174 was drawn by Lt-Col Frank Wilson.

INDEX